DIGITAL COMPUTER BASICS

Prepared by

BUREAU OF NAVAL PERSONNEL

DOVER PUBLICATIONS, INC.
NEW YORK

Published in Canada by General Publishing Company, Ltd., 30 Lesmill Road, Don Mills, Toronto, Ontario.

Published in the United Kingdom by Constable and Company, Ltd., 10 Orange Street, London WC 2.

This Dover edition, first published in 1969, is an unabridged and unaltered republication of the work originally published in 1968 by the Bureau of Naval Personnel as Navy Training Course NAVPERS 10088.

International Standard Book Number: 0-486-22480-5
Library of Congress Catalog Card Number: 77-88026

Manufactured in the United States of America
Dover Publications, Inc.
180 Varick Street
New York, N.Y. 10014

PREFACE

This training course is intended for use by U. S. Navy and Naval Reserve personnel whose duties require an elementary and general knowledge of the fundamental concepts of electronic computers and data processing, and as an introductory course for those aspiring to the Data Systems Technician rating.

The coverage of the five basic sections of a computer are treated in sufficient detail to equip the reader with a knowledge of the circuits and functions peculiar to each section and to show how these sections are related. Programming techniques are treated in three chapters. Part I presents a definition of terms, the procedure for stating the problem, and the development of flowcharts. Part II builds on the previous chapter and concludes by showing how the problem is converted into actual computer (machine) language. Part III describes the conversion of a mnemonic language to machine language as accomplished through the use of compilers. Other subjects treated include: Number Systems, Boolean Algebra, Analog-Digital and Digital-Analog Conversions, and Diagnostic Maintenance Routines.

As one of the Navy Training Courses, this book was prepared by the Training Publications Division of the Naval Personnel Program Support Activity, Washington, D. C., for the Bureau of Naval Personnel.

THE UNITED STATES NAVY

GUARDIAN OF OUR COUNTRY

The United States Navy is responsible for maintaining control of the sea and is a ready force on watch at home and overseas, capable of strong action to preserve the peace or of instant offensive action to win in war.

It is upon the maintenance of this control that our country's glorious future depends; the United States Navy exists to make it so.

WE SERVE WITH HONOR

Tradition, valor, and victory are the Navy's heritage from the past. To these may be added dedication, discipline, and vigilance as the watchwords of the present and the future.

At home or on distant stations we serve with pride, confident in the respect of our country, our shipmates, and our families.

Our responsibilities sober us; our adversities strengthen us.

Service to God and Country is our special privilege. We serve with honor.

THE FUTURE OF THE NAVY

The Navy will always employ new weapons, new techniques, and greater power to protect and defend the United States on the sea, under the sea, and in the air.

Now and in the future, control of the sea gives the United States her greatest advantage for the maintenance of peace and for victory in war.

Mobility, surprise, dispersal, and offensive power are the keynotes of the new Navy. The roots of the Navy lie in a strong belief in the future, in continued dedication to our tasks, and in reflection on our heritage from the past.

Never have our opportunities and our responsibilities been greater.

For sale by the Superintendent of Documents, U.S. Government Printing Office
Washington, D.C., 20402 - Price $1.75

CONTENTS

CREDITS

Illustrations indicated below are included in this edition of Digital Computer Basics through the courtesy of the designated companies. Permission to use these materials is gratefully acknowledged.

Source (illustrations)	Figure Nos.
Control Data Corporation	1-3
International Business Machines	7-2
	7-4
	7-5
	7-6
	7-8
	7-9
	7-10
	7-11

Chapter 1

INTRODUCTION TO DATA PROCESSING

The technological advances made in data processing systems in the past decade are astonishing. The reasons for these advances are twofold. With each system development there arises new applications of the system, and with each new system application, an insight to further developments is realized. Consequently, the sophistication of the system and the boundless applications of data processing systems, mutually contribute to the development of new and improved systems.

Originally, machines are designed and built to meet specific needs. A newly engineered machine usually increases productivity or quality, and decreases production time. It may simplify the process although this is not a requirement.

The data processing concept is not new. In fact it was perceived more than a century ago. Recent advances in data processing systems have been, and are being motivated by the need for faster and more efficient ways of processing large quantities of data. Considering the rate of population increases, the rising ability of manufacturers to produce more materials for our comfort and use, the complexities of our military operations, and our continued advance toward greater ideals, it is easy to see that data processing systems will become more and more involved in all phases of our civilization.

For example, modern communications, radar, and missile equipments depend almost entirely on the ability of data processing equipments to perform calculations and provide updated and accurate control information. So dependent are these equipments on data processing systems (particularly the computer) that they are rendered completely useless if the controlling data processing system fails. Nevertheless, because of the high reliability of the controlling systems, and too, because of the ability of the systems to provide instant and accurate control of all operations simultaneously, it is expected that electronic systems such as these will become automated to an even greater extent in future years.

SCOPE OF THIS COURSE

Digital Computer Basics, NavPers 10088, is intended for use as a basic reference for all Navy personnel whose duties require them to have a knowledge of the fundamentals of electronic data processing. It presents a coverage of the basic concepts of computers and automatic data processing. Emphasis is placed on logic functions and the theory of operation of representative data processing circuits and components. Detailed treatments of specific equipments will not be considered in this text.

A knowledge of basic mathematics and basic electricity and electronics (equivalent to that derived by completing correspondence courses based on Basic Electricity, NavPers 10086; Basic Electronics, NavPers 10087; and Mathematics, Vol. 1, NavPers 10069-C), is necessary before the student can expect to comprehend the material presented in this course.

This course begins (a little bit later in this chapter) by presenting some background information and introductory concepts of data processing systems. Following the introductory chapter (in chapters 2 and 3), a treatment of number systems and Boolean Algebra is presented so that an understanding of computer logic and symbology can be attained prior to any consideration of the actual internal operation of computer circuits.

The treatment of the Control Unit (Ch. 4), the Arithmetic Unit (Ch. 5), the Memory and Storage Unit (Ch. 6), and the Input/Output Unit (Ch. 7) presents basic operations of these computer sections and their interrelationships, and some of the circuits commonly used in each of these sections. A thorough knowledge of the contents of these chapters is essential to an understanding of the programming concepts presented in chapters 8, 9, and 10.

The principles of programming are presented in three parts. Part I treats basic concepts. Part II establishes the characteristics and assumes a repertoire of instructions for a hypothetical computer. It explains how the computer interprets the instructions and operates using machine language. Part III explains the purpose and uses of compilers.

Because digital computers are used in many applications to solve problems concerning analog data, it is necessary to convert the analog input to digital data. A consideration of the basic principles of analog-to-digital conversions is presented in chapter 11.

The text concludes by showing how diagnostic maintenance routines (maintenance programs) are used to isolate malfunctions in a data processing system.

PROCESSING OPERATIONS

Data processing (fig. 1-1) is the process of collecting data (from an input source), manipulating them according to a set of rules (within the computing device), and providing a useful output at the output device. (For the purpose of this discussion, it can be assumed that the input/output device is a teletypewriter.) Any system which performs this set of operations is a data processing system. A more elaborate system can be constructed by first, adding more input/output devices, and second, by adding one or more additional digital computers.

There are many such data processing systems in present use in the Navy. Navy supply personnel use a data processing system to maintain proper inventories in the supply system. A data processing system is used to compute pay at Navy Finance Centers. Maintaining

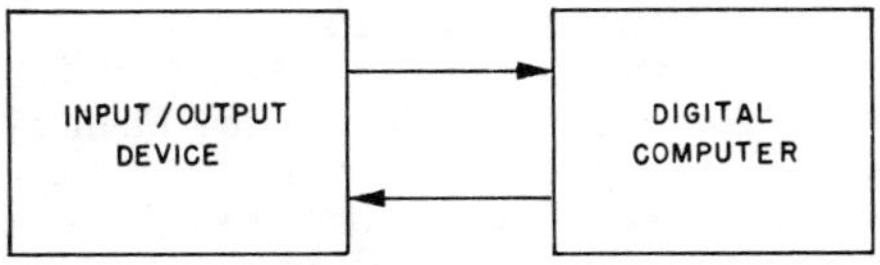

164.1
Figure 1-1.—Basic Data Processing System.

the air plot in CIC is a data processing operation. The little black book one uses to keep track of expenses is part of a data processing system.

In data processing, data are converted into information. This statement may seem odd at first because in ordinary usage, the two words "data" and "information" mean the same thing. With reference to data processing, however, the words "data" and "information" do not have the same meaning. "Data" means the mass of facts about a single subject, and "information" means the desired content of the data.

To illustrate the difference between information and data, consider the following example. The list of all parts in a storeroom (listed by stock number, number on hand, and allowance of each item) is an example of a mass of data. The list of items that should be requisitioned to fill the storeroom to the allowance level is an example of information. The process of extracting the information (items to be ordered) from the data (items on hand and allowance) is data processing. The procedures and equipments that will accomplish the desired operations constitute a data processing system.

All data processing, regardless of the facilities actually used, require three fundamental operations:

1. Collection of data
2. Manipulation of data
3. Production of useful output

COLLECTION OF DATA

The first part of any data processing operation is the collection of new data. Before any processing can be done, data must be "captured." Since data seldom occurs in a form that a system can use directly, the collection of data usually involves three steps: (1) acquisition; (2) conversion; and (3) verification.

Acquisition

Data may exist in a variety of initial forms. It may be in the form of the number of like items in a bin, a blip on a radar indicator (PPI-scope), or the time clock punches on a time card.

To find the quantity on hand of a particular item, the storekeeper counts these items. To establish an air contact the radarman watches a spot of light on a scope. To total the number of hours a man worked in a week the timekeeper notes when the man punched in and out each day of the week. All of the operations involve the acquisition of data.

Conversion

The acquired data may not always be in a form usable by the computer device. Therefore the data must be converted to a form suitable for processing by the computer. In the first analogy, the storekeeper writes the item stock number and the item count number, thereby converting a mental item count to a permanent record. This record is his usuable form of data. The radarman notes the range and bearing of a contact blip, and records it. In this analogy, the range and bearing notation is his usuable form of data. To obtain his usuable data, the timekeeper notes the time of arrival and departure of the worker for each day of the week, adds the number of hours worked and thereby ascertains the number of hours for which the man should be paid. All of these conversion operations involve changing of the initial data to a more usable form which, as one can see, is dependent on the particular application and situation.

Verification

In the collection of data, the acquisition and conversion steps serve no purpose if an error has been introduced. Therefore it is necessary to make certain that the acquired data is valid. In the case of the storekeeper, he may count the items in the bin twice to make certain his count is correct; the radarman may check his initial contact within a few seconds, and then double check the range and bearing; and the timekeeper may cross check his computations to ensure their accuracy. Similarly, these conceptual procedures, which are intended to eliminate the possibility of introducing erroneous data into the data processing system, are part of verification.

MANIPULATION OF DATA

The manipulation portion of a data processing system includes all operations which use collected data to provide output information. All manipulations may be grouped into two operations: (1) rearrangement, and (2) processing.

Rearrangement

Since data seldom appears in a usable arrangement it must be classified and arranged so that it will fit into the system with the least possible amount of "friction." Any operation which changes the sequence of data, or inserts or extracts data without performing any computation, is considered to be rearrangement. Most rearrangement operations fall into one of two categories: (1) classification, or (2) sequencing. Classification is the process of grouping data items which are alike. Sequencing is the process of placing data items into some desired sequence.

Processing

The processing operation consists of those operations which directly involve the extraction of information from a mass of data. More specifically, operations which actually produce a desired output by means of arithmetic computations within the computing device are considered to be processing operations. In electronic data processing systems, which are our prime consideration in this text, these operations are accomplished by an electronic computer.

PRODUCTION OF USEFUL OUTPUT

The third part of any data processing operation is the output. Everything that happens in the system is aimed at providing the output. In any system there are usually several distinct outputs. Some of the outputs of the inventory maintenance system discussed earlier are: (1) requisitions to replenish stock; (2) an accurate list of the actual contents of the storeroom; and (3) activity information (turnover rate) about each item. Other systems may have more sophisticated outputs such as map displays or paychecks. The output is the reason for the existence of the data processing system.

In summary, all data processing systems have three operations: (1) data collection; (2) manipulation of the data; and (3) output. The overall function of any data processing system is to collect masses of data and provide useful information from the data. Data collection usually involves data acquisition, data conversion, and verification. Manipulation involves rearrangement and processing. Output is the actual provision of the information that is desired from the system.

We have examined what a data processing system accomplishes. In this text we will examine the equipments which make up data processing systems and their relationships. When beginning the study of a new system, an initial effort to determine the devices which collect data, those which manipulate the data, and those which provide the output is time well spent. No matter how complex the system is, these general concepts are applicable.

CONCEPTS OF THE HUMAN PROCESSOR

The oldest and still most common data processor is man. In fact, man is still the most efficient data processor if size, mass, and power consumption are used as the criteria. The input to the human data processor is mostly through the eyes and ears. His memory (brain) stores data to be processed and the instructions for processing the data. His brain also functions as the arithmetic and logic element and as the control element. The output can be verbal, written, a physical action or a decision not to act.

Taken in perspective, the human being is the most versatile data processor. He has the ability to interpret his instructions in such a way that they will cover situations that were not explicit in the original form of the instructions. This, by the way, is not an ability inherent in the electronic data processor.

Human Auxiliary Equipment

Although man is a versatile data processor, he has some rather serious shortcomings. His memory capacity is rather limited (on a given subject). He is also unreliable. When called upon to remember large quantities of data, he has an annoying tendency to forget details. His calculating ability is quite limited. The average person, using only his mind, is unable to perform a series of simple calculations. Unaided, man is rather slow in performing the simplest data processing operation.

In addition, man is unreliable when performing repetitious operations. Most data processing operations are repetitious, i.e., the same basic operation is performed many times using different pieces of data. Man's ability to think tends to interfere with his performance of these boring operations. Thus, although man is a remarkable data processor, he needs some auxiliary equipment if he is to be part of an efficient data processing system.

Records

The first aid to data processing developed by man was the keeping of records. The term "record" is meant in the broadest possible sense. Recording is the process of storing data in a medium in such a way that it may be retrieved for use at a later time. Numbers, letters, and symbols were all developed for the recording of data. Once a piece of data is recorded it can be dropped from one's mind so that the memory can be used for other operations. He can recover the recorded data at any time merely by referring to the record.

Any data recording medium can be classified as being one of two main types: (1) temporary storage, or (2) long term storage. Scratch paper and the chalkboard are examples of temporary storage; ledgers and files are examples of long term storage. The technique of recording data has greatly increased man's capacity as a data processor.

Calculating Devices

After recording, the next aid to data processing was the development of calculating devices to relieve man of some of the tedious chores of arithmetic. The abacus, slide rule, and desk calculator are all calculating aids. In addition, each of these devices incorporates a form of data storage, i.e., the results of any operation are available in the device for use in the next calculation.

To illustrate the use of some of these data processing aids, let's examine a part of the process of computing a worker's pay. Assume that some processing has already been done and a clerk has a list of the hours each worker actually worked on each day of the pay period. The clerk has plenty of scratch paper and a desk calculator to use as aids in data processing.

First, the clerk clears the calculator to eliminate any data remaining from a previous operation. He then reads the time from the list (a record), enters it into the keyboard of the calculator (a storage medium), and presses the add button. The calculator adds the number in the keyboard to the previous sum (zero, stored in the gears of the calculator) and retains the new sum in the gear arrangement (a storage medium). The clerk repeats the operation until he has entered all of the time periods into the calculator. At that time, the calculator will be indicating the total number of hours the worker actually worked during the pay period. The clerk records this for future reference and then transfers the worker's wage scale from the list to the keyboard and presses the multiply key. The desk calculator performs the calculation and indicates a number which represents the worker's gross pay. The clerk enters this into a record for use in later computation. The clerk then repeats the whole operation for the next worker. The storage media (paper), keyboard, gears in the calculator, etc., relieve the clerk of the chores of having to remember a mass of data. The desk calculator relieves him of all of the routine arithmetic. The clerk's actions have been reduced to transferring data from one medium to another at the right time and pressing the right button on the desk calculator at the right time. The clerk's mental abilities are therefore freed to accomplish more important operations. The clerk's memory is now used for three functions: (1) very short term storing during the transfer of data from one source to another; (2) storage of the plan for processing the data; and (3) deciding what to do at any given time to implement the data processing plan.

DATA PROCESSING PLANNING

Examining the specific operations performed by the pay clerk, it is seen that he executes a set of steps which are a part of a larger, already developed payroll plan. His particular actions in the plan may be described as the "Develop and Store Gross Pay" process, and may be expressed in steps as follows:

Step 1. Get time sheets

Step 2. Pick up top sheet

Step 3. Press "clear" button on calculator

Step 4. Read number from sheet and enter into keyboard

Step 5. Press "add" button

Step 6. Any more time on this sheet?
- a. Yes: go back to step 4
- b. No: go to step 7

Step 7. Read total hours from calculator and write it on paper

Step 8. Read wage scale from list and enter into keyboard

Step 9. Press "multiply" key

Step 10. Read gross pay from calculator and write it on paper

Step 11. File time sheet just used

Step 12. Any more time sheets to be processed?
- a. Yes: go back to Step 2
- b. No: go to Step 13

Step 13. Stop. Request more work.

In data processing terminology, this list of instructions is referred to as a type of "program". The program is a major part of any computing process. However, the operation is rarely this simple and the problem is usually laid out in generalized logical steps. These generalized steps are arranged to form a "flow chart" as shown in figure 1-2. The details of flow charting and programming are treated in later chapters.

MACHINE DATA PROCESSING

Before data can be processed by machine it must be in a form that can be stored, transferred, and manipulated by mechanical and electrical methods. The forms taken by data are the basic determining factors in the actual design of data processing machinery. The actual representation method used in a particular situation is usually determined by the desired rate of handling the data. The data handling rate may vary from a few pieces of data per second to many million pieces of data per second in the same system.

Data Representation Methods

Any data representation method has three main aspects: (1) the storage medium; (2) the writing method; and (3) the reading method. The storage medium is the physical material in which data is actually held. The writing method is that technique whereby data is impressed into the storage medium. Usually the three aspects are so closely connected that it is difficult to separate them.

Storage Medium

A variety of storage media have appeared throughout history. Stone, clay, and wood were used many thousands of years ago as data recording media. Paper, cardboard, and plastic have come into common use in the last hundred years. The latter group has the advantages of easier writing and portability over the former, but the materials aren't quite as rugged.

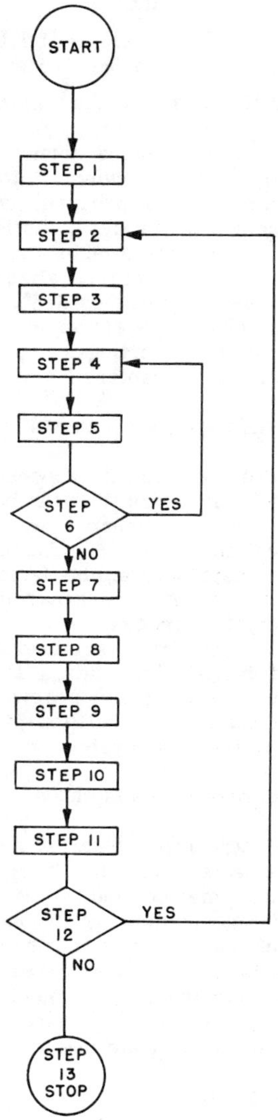

164.2

Figure 1-2.—Basic Flow Chart.

Since the advent of machine data processing, several new media have come into use, such as magnetic materials and transistors.

Writing Operation

The writing operation has two components: (1) the actual writing instrument; and (2) the element controlling the operation of the instrument. The physical configuration of the writing instrument is determined by the physical characteristics of the storage medium, while the physical configuration of the control element is determined by the manner in which the data is to be impressed on the medium. Instruments for writing include brushes, pencils, type, and electrical currents. The control element may be the training of a human being, but in electronic data processing it may be the hardware of a machine.

Reading Operation

The reading operation also has two components: (1) the detection of data in the storage media; and (2) the translation of detected data. Data detection schemes vary from recognition of complex symbols to the detection of the presence or absence of a single quantity. The subject of translation will be discussed in more detail at a later time.

MACHINE DATA REPRESENTATION METHODS

The basic method of representing machine processable data is quite different from the method used to represent data that is to be processed by human beings. An alert person is capable of recognizing small differences in data that may indicate great differences in exactly what is being represented. For example, such a person has no difficulty recognizing the difference between the letters "B" and "P", although the physical difference is very small. A machine could be constructed that is just as discerning, but it would probably be large, complex, and unreliable. Thus, most data representation systems that are to be used in machine data processing require only the recognition of the difference between the presence and absence of a piece of data, and complex pieces of data are encoded into groups of these yes/no pieces of data. This system is called binary information representation.

Electrical devices can be adapted to this two-condition system. Many devices, such as relays and switches are naturally two-condition devices. Vacuum tube and transistor circuits can be designed to operate between two conditions with a high degree of reliability. Magnetic materials may be magnetized or unmagnetized. In data processing devices, these two states are referred to as: one and zero, yes and no, or on and off. The basic unit of data representation is the presence or absence of one of the particular conditions.

Most information storage media used in machine data processing can be grouped into three basic categories:

1. Mechanical
2. Electrical
3. Magnetic

This classification is based on the manner in which the data are actually stored and not on the manner in which reading and writing take place. In the mechanical category, the data are retained in the physical configuration of the medium. In the electrical category, the data are retained in the electrical status of a device. In the magnetic category, the data are retained in the magnetic condition of a material. All three categories of storage may occur in close proximity within the same data processing system.

Mechanical Storage

The most common example of mechanical storage is holes punched into paper or cardboard. Small rectangular cards or long strips of paper (called paper tape) form the medium. The data are written into the medium by punching holes through the medium at certain points. Reading is accomplished by detecting the presence or absence of holes at certain points by mechanical, electrical, or photoelectric means. Punched hole systems are very commonly used as input/output media for electrical data processing systems.

Another common mechanical storage media is the electrical data switch. Information is written into the switch manually. Reading is accomplished by sensing whether the switch is an open or closed path for electrical current. Switches are commonly used as instruction inputs to a data processing system.

Electrical Storage

Electrical storage is one of the methods used when very fast access to data is required. The most common form of electrical storage is the flip-flop. A flip-flop is an electronic circuit with two stable states. Once established in one of its stable states, it will remain in that state until some external action causes it to change to the other state. Flip-flops are commonly used for temporary storage in data processing systems.

Magnetic Storage

Magnetic storage occurs in two main forms: (1) surface storage and (2) internal storage. In both forms, the data are stored in the magnetic state of a high-retentivity magnetic material. Once established in a certain state the material will remain in that state until it is affected by some external influence.

Surface storage is a very common data storage medium. It occurs in two basic configurations: (1) long thin strips of nonmagnetic material with a coating of a magnetic material, called magnetic tape; and (2) metal cylinders with a coating of magnetic material, called a magnetic drum. Magnetic tape is commonly used as large capacity, slow access auxiliary data storage. The magnetic drum is used as a medium capacity, fast access data storage device.

Internal (magnetic core) storage has the fastest access time of any of the magnetic data storage media. Magnetic core storage is usually used as the high speed operating storage medium of a data processing system. In this medium the data are stored in the direction of magnetization of tiny doughnut-shaped cores made of a magnetic material.

Data Organization and Processing

In a data processing system, the data are stored, transferred, and manipulated so as to form a useful output. The basic data representation form is the binary digit, but representations using these binary digits must be organized into a system intelligible to the computer if any useful work is to be accomplished. Imagine the work that would be required to keep track of the meanings of a billion binary digits of data if this information is without organization or if the organization system fails. Data bits are organized into characters, words, records, and files. Each of these terms represents a level of organization in a data processing system.

Bits (binary digits) are the basic units of characters and are organized into characters. A character is a unique symbol in a data representation system. Numbers, letters, and punctuation marks are familiar examples of data symbols. In data processing a single character may be formed by any number of bits of data depending on the character represented. (If a character in a system consists of N bits, then 2^N different characters may be represented.)

In most data processing systems the basic data unit is the word. For fixed word length computers, characters are formed into groups of a fixed size called words. Transfers and manipulations (internal to the computer and between input and output devices) usually take place using words of data. Each word is a fixed number of characters, each of which consists of a fixed number of bits.

The "record" is the next data representation level above the word level. A record is a group of words, all concerning the same subject. Each word in the record therefore conveys some particular data about the subject of the record.

A file is a group of records all about the same general subject. The file is usually the top organization level in a data processing system. The following example illustrates the uses of bits, words, characters, records, and files as they are used in a representative data processing system. Consider a storekeeper updating his master inventory using a data processing system.

The primary group of data in this data processing system would be called the master file. The master file contains all of the information necessary for maintaining inventory control of the storeroom and is an organization of a large number of records, with one record present for each item carried in the storeroom. Each record would contain a means of identifying that particular record. This identification item is called the key for that record. The key for a record in this system would be the stock number of the item concerned. The file would probably be arranged in an orderly sequence, proceeding from the lowest stock number to the highest stock number.

All records in the file would be organized in the same format, i.e., within each record a given relative position would contain the same information about the subject of the record, in all records of the file. Each record in this system would contain eight words of data as shown in Table 1-1.

Table 1-1. —Organization of a Record

Word No.	Data Classification
1	Stock number (key)
2	Quantity on hand
3	Quantity allowed
4	Reorder level
5	Cost per item
6	Bin location in the storeroom
7	Substitute stock number
8	Usage code

If the storeroom contained items with 50,000 different stock numbers, the master file would contain 50,000 of these eight-word records.

Each of the eight words in a record could consist of 12 characters, each character being one of the digits of the decimal system (0-9). Therefore, each record would contain 8 times 12 or 96 characters. Since the basic data representative of any data processing system is the binary code, each character would consist of four bits (4 bits will provide 16 possible combinations, only 10 of which are needed to provide representation of the 10 decimal digits.) Therefore, each word would be 4 times 12 or 48 bits. Each record would be 4 times 96 or 384 bits of data. If the master file contained 50,000 records, it would contain 400,000 words, composed of 4,800,000 bits of data. This file would probably be stored on about 2,000 feet of magnetic tape—about one reel.

In summary, the data are organized into a series of levels for processing. These levels are (1) bits, or one-zero representation; (2) character - groups of bits, representing one of the unique symbols of the system; (3) word - group of characters, forming the basic transfer and manipulation unit of the system; (4) record - groups of words, all representing data about the same specific subject; and (5) file - groups of records all representing data about the same general subject. The meaning of these terms and how they are used to control operations within the data processing system is one of the major considerations of this text.

COMPUTERS

The computer is the heart of the data processing system. A computer is a device which will perform sequences of reasonable operations with data, mainly arithmetical and logical operations. A representative electronic digital computer presently in use by some naval activities is the Control Data 1604-A Computer (fig 1-3).

Figure 1-3. —Representative Digital Computer (Control Data 1604-A Computer).

HISTORY OF COMPUTERS

In order to appreciate the high speed and accuracy of computers today, it is desirable to have some knowledge of earlier computers and their originators. The first calculator was built by Pascal in 1642. This machine could add and subtract, and was successfully applied to tax collection in France. In 1671, Leibniz built a machine which could add, subtract, multiply, and divide. Leibniz also recognized the advantages of the binary (or two digit) number system over the decimal (or 10 digit) number system which will be pointed out in chapter 2 of this course.

In 1842, Babbage started a machine called a "Difference Engine." This machine would have been able to construct tables of any function that could be described by the first five differences. Work on this machine ceased, however, when Babbage conceived the idea of an "Analytic Engine" which could tabulate any function. In 1910, his son completed building the latter machine and used it to calculate π to 20 decimal places. Babbage also suggested the use of punched cards (now used as input and output media for computers) and the possibility of a machine that could alter its operations according to the results of its calculations. Present electronic computers resemble his analytic engine in many respects.

Between 1937 and 1944, Aiken built the first general purpose automatic digital computer, called the "Mark I." It is electromechanical, using relays as one of the major calculating devices.

Between 1939 and 1945, Eckert and Mauchly built the "Eniac," also a digital computer. It consisted of 18,000 electron tubes, weighed 30 tons, and dissipated 150 kilowatts. The time required for an add operation was only 0.21 μsec compared to 300 μsec for the Mark I.

In 1951 Eckert and Mauchly built the first "Univac" for the United States Census Bureau.

The "Edvac," completed in 1952, was the first computer to use internally stored instructions (program).

CAPABILITIES

The two major characteristics of computers which make them so useful in military and commercial applications are SPEED and ACCURACY. The speed of computers is seen when we consider that problems which require days, weeks, or years to solve by man, with his slow pencil and paper tools, can be solved in seconds or minutes by a computer. This is conceivable when we consider that a single arithmetic operation can be solved and stored by a computer in a few microseconds whereas a mathematician needs a few seconds to do the same operation and record (or store) it on paper. Thus, the computer can solve the problems and produce an output record of its results, thousands or even millions of times faster than man.

The second characteristic of the computer is ACCURACY. Once a computer is provided with the correct instructions, the planned operations can be repeated millions of times without a single error. Computers make errors only when there is a breakdown in the computing system, or when there is human error in the prepared instructions. Once the breakdown or error is detected and corrected, the computer again operates at high speeds and without error.

Computers are used in many fields of research. In engineering, they are used in design. In business, they are used in bookkeeping and inventory; in government for the census; and by the military, in logistics and battle strategy problems. Any problem which can be reduced to and solved by a sequence of arithmetic steps can be done rapidly by a computer.

DIGITAL COMPUTERS

Computers are classified into two general types; digital and analog, although a variation of these types called a "hybrid computer" has both digital and analog characteristics. The hybrid computer is not treated in this text.

The digital computer, as implied in the name, produces its output by responding to changes in fixed increments, such as 0 to 1, or 1 to 2. The digital change may be accomplished in a gear train; by changing a voltage from one level to another; by the "on" or "off" condition of a switch; by the energized or deenergized condition of a relay; or by the presence or absence of electrical pulses.

Examples of digital devices are adding machines, cash registers, the abacus, thought processes in human calculations, and the odometer used in conjunction with an automobile speedometer.

In this text we shall concern ourselves with electronic digital computers. Here too, the input data must be in discreet increments (digital form). Three factors determine the rate at which the output data is available. These are: memory access time; instruction execution time; and the complexity of the problem.

Electronic digital computers can be made accurate to any desirable degree. They are usually more expensive than analog computers but are also usually more versatile. A digital computer can be given a sequence of instructions in which it can execute later steps using the results of the earlier steps. It can also alter the sequence of instructions according to the results of previous steps.

ANALOG COMPUTERS

The analog computer accepts continuously varying inputs, and supplies an instantaneous continuously varying output. Analog computers use physical changes as input data and indicate the significance which such changes have on the device or unit as a whole. The input/output data may be either electrical, mechanical, or a combination of both. Conditions such as temperature, pressure, and angular position, must be represented by electromechanical analogies. From this, note that an analog computer is, by nature, limited in its application to problems related to specific devices.

The accuracy of the analog computer is limited by the precision of its components, i.e., potentiometers, resistors, etc. Thus, accuracies greater than approximately .001% are not economically feasible.

BASIC COMPUTER BLOCK DIAGRAM

The basic sections of a digital computer are shown in figure 1-4. The three center blocks (arithmetic and logic, internal data storage, and control units) comprise what is generally referred to as the "central data processor."

Control Unit

The control section is comparable to a telephone exchange. It directs the operations of the computer under the direct influence of

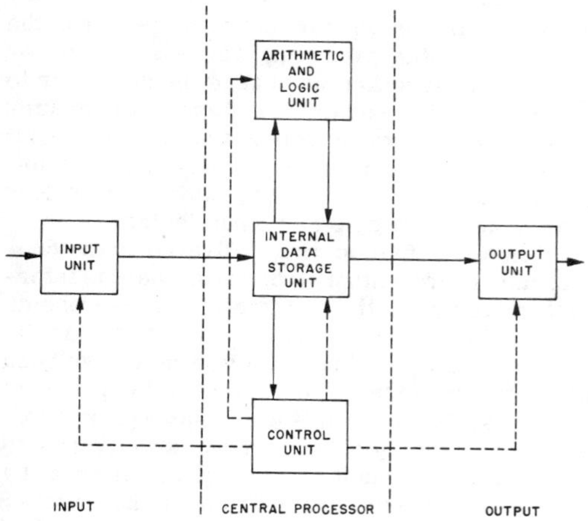

12.136

Figure 1-4—Representative Digital Computer Block Diagram.

a sequence of instructions called the "program." The instructions are comparable to the phone numbers dialed into a telephone exchange and cause certain switches and control lines to be energized.

The program may be stored in the internal circuits of the computer or it may be read instruction-by-instruction from external media. The internally stored program type of computer, generally referred to only as a "stored program" computer, is the most practical type to use when speed and fully automatic operation are desired.

In addition to the command which tells the computer what to do, the control unit also dictates how and when each specific operation is to be performed. It is also active in initiating circuits which locate any information stored in the computer and in moving this information to the point where the actual manipulation or modification is to be accomplished.

In the stored program computer, the control unit reads an instruction from the memory section (as instructed by the program). The information read into the control unit from memory is in the form of voltage levels that make up a "binary word," and represents a specific operation that is to be performed. The location of the data to be operated on is generally a part of the instruction, and energizes circuitry which causes the specified operation (add, subtract, compare, etc.) to be executed. Subsequently, the control unit reads the next instruction or jumps as directed, (explained later) to find the next instruction to execute.

The four major types of instructions are: (1) transfer; (2) arithmetic; (3) logic; and (4) control. Transfer commands are those whose basic function is to transfer data from one location to another. One of the locations is an address in memory and the other is either a register or an input/output device. Arithmetic instructions are those which combine two pieces of data to form a single piece of data using one of the arithmetic operations. In some types of computers, one of the pieces of data is in a location specified by the address contained in an instruction, and the other is already in a register (usually the accumulator). The results are usually left in the accumulator.

Logic instructions make the digital computer into a system which is more than a high speed adding machine. By using logic instructions the programmer may instruct the system on various alternate sequences through the program. For example, through the use of logic instructions, a computer being used for maintenance inventory will have one sequence to follow if the number of a given item on hand is greater than the order amount and another sequence to follow if the number on hand is smaller than the order amount. The choice of which sequence to use will be made by the control unit under the influence of the logic instruction. Logic instructions provide the computer with the ability to make decisions based on the result of previously generated data.

Control instructions are those which are used to send commands to devices which are not under direct command of the control unit, such as input/output units. The address contained in the instruction does not specify a location in memory but is usually a code group specifying an action required of a particular piece of equipment.

In a single address compute, i.e., where each instruction refers to only one address or operand, the instructions are normally taken from the memory in sequential order. If one instruction comes from a certain location, say X, the next instruction is usually taken from location X + 1. However, the execution of a logic instruction may produce a result which dictates that the next instruction is to be taken from an address as specified in a portion of the logic instruction. For example, the logic instruction may cause certain operations in the computer to determine if the content of a given register in the arithmetic section is negative. If the answer is "yes", the location of the next instruction is that specified in an address section of the logic instruction. If the answer is "no", the next instruction would be taken from the next sequential location in the memory.

Every computer provides circuitry for a variety of logic instructions for choosing alternate instruction sequences if certain desirable or undesirable conditions exist. The ability to "branch" at key points is the special feature of the computer that makes it able to perform such diverse tasks as missile control, accounting, or tactical air plotting.

Arithmetic Unit

The arithmetic unit of the computer is the section in which arithmetic and logic operations are performed on the input or stored data. The arithmetic operations performed in this unit include adding, subtracting, multiplying, dividing, counting, shifting, complementing, and comparing.

All arithmetic operations can be reduced to any one of four arithmetic processes; addition, subtraction, multiplication, or division. In most computers, multiplication involves a series of additions; and division, a series of subtractions.

The arithmetic unit contains several registers; units which can store one "word" of computer data. This group of registers generally include D, X and Q registers (so named for identification purposes only), and a unit called an "accumulator" (A register). During an arithmetic process, the D, X and Q registers temporarily hold or store the numbers being used in the operation, called "operands". The accumulator stores the result of the operation. The control unit instructs the arithmetic unit to perform the specified arithmetic operation (as requested in the instruction); transfers the necessary information into the D, X and Q registers from memory (discussed later); and controls the storage of the results in the accumulator or in some specific location in memory.

The arithmetic unit also makes comparisons and produces "yes" or "no" or "go-no-go" outputs as a result. The computer may be programmed so that a "yes" or "go" result advances the computer units to perform the next step in the program, whereas a "no" or "no-go" instruction may cause the computer to jump several programmed steps. A computer may also be programmed so that a "no" result at a certain point in the program will cause the computer to stop and await instructions from a keyboard or other input device.

Generally information delivered to the control unit represents instructions, whereas information routed to the arithmetic unit represents data. Frequently it is necessary to modify an instruction. This instruction may have been used in one form in one step of the program but must be altered for a subsequent step. In such cases, the instruction is delivered to the arithmetic unit where it is altered by addition-to or subtraction-from another number in the accumulator. The resultant modified instruction is again stored in the memory unit for use later in the program.

Memory Unit

In most digital computers the storage or memory section is constructed of small magnetic cores, each capable of representing an "ON" ("1") or "OFF" ("0") condition. A system of these cores arranged in a matrix can store any computer word which is represented in binary form.

All computers must contain facilities to store computer words or instructions (which are intelligible to the computer) until these instructions or words are needed in the performance of the computer calculations. Before the stored program type computer can begin to operate on its input data, it is first necessary to store, in memory, a sequence of instructions and all figures, numbers, and any other data which are to be used in the calculations. The process by which these instructions and data are read into the computer is called "loading."

Actually the first step in loading instructions and data into a computer is to manually place enough instructions into memory by using the console or keyboard so that these instructions can be used to bring in more instructions as desired. In this manner a few instructions are used to "bootstrap" more instructions. Some computers make use of an auxiliary (wired) memory which permanently stores the "bootstrap program," thereby making manual loading unnecessary. This process is explained in more detail in subsequent chapters.

The memory (or storage) section of a computer is essentially an electronically operated file cabinet. It is actually a large number (generally between 1 and 40 thousand) of storage locations; each referred to as a storage address or register. Every computer word which is read into the computer during the loading process is stored or filed in a specific storage address and is almost instantly accessible.

Input/Output Unit

Input and output devices are similar in operation but perform opposite functions. It is through the use of these devices that the computer is able to communicate with the outside world.

Input data may be in any one of three forms: it may be fed in manually from a keyboard or console; from instruments or sensors; or from a source on which data has previously been stored in a form intelligible to the computer.

Computers can process hundreds of thousands of computer words per second. Thus, a study of the first method (manual input) reflects the incompatibility of human-operated keyboards or keypunches to supply data at a speed which matches the electronic speed of digital computers. A high average speed for keyboard operation is 2 or 3 characters per second, which when coded to form computer words may have more than 15 to 20 binary digits. The computer is capable of reading several thousand times this amount of information per second. It is clear, therefore, that manual inputs should be minimized to make more efficient use of computer time.

Instruments are used as input sensors, and are capable of supplying several thousand samples regarding pressure, temperature, speed, etc., per second. This is equivalent to 10 or 20 thousand bits or binary digits per second. Digital computers which use these devices must be equipped with analog-digital converters to convert physical change to specific increments.

Input data which has previously been recorded on punched cards, perforated tapes, magnetic tapes or magnetic drums or disks in a form understood by the program may also be entered into the computer; this being a much faster method than entering data manually from a keyboard. The most commonly used input devices in this catagory are magnetic tape readers or paper tape (perforated tape) readers.

Output information is also made available in three types: human information, such as codes or symbols presented on a cathode-ray screen which are used by the operator to answer questions or make decisions; information which operates a control device such as a lever, aileron, or actuator; or information which is stored in a machine language or human language, on tapes, or printed media.

Devices which store or read-out output information include magnetic tape, punched cards, punched paper tapes, cathode-ray oscilloscopes, electric typewriters, line-at-a-time printers, and surface-at-a-time printers.

One of the main features of computers is their ability to process large amounts of data quickly. In most cases, the processing speed far exceeds the ability of input devices to supply information. One common limitation of most input devices is that each involves some mechanical operation, that is, the movement of a tape drive or card feeder. Because a mechanical movement of some part of these devices cannot take place fast enough to match electronic speeds within the computer, these input devices limit the speed of operation of the associated computer particularly in cases where successive operations are dependent upon the reception of new data from the input medium.

Several methods of speeding up mechanical operations have been devised, all of which are designed to move a smaller mass a shorter distance and with greater driving force. Many of these designs have been directed toward increasing the drive speed of magentic tapes. Present day tape drives can pass up to 150 inches of tape per second over a tape reading head. Card readers (discussed in a later chapter) can read between 100 and 2000 cards per minute, depending on the particular reader.

Another method of entering data into a computer which has not previously been mentioned is to link two (or more) computers together and program them to communicate with each other. This is the fastest method of entering or extracting data.

Basic Computer Operations

With an understanding of the function of the various computer sections, let us now consider a basic computer instruction and how this instruction is executed. Let the instruction be as follows:

> "Add the contents of the A register to the contents of memory address location 123 and store the results in address 456 in memory."

We will assume that the computer used is the stored program type and that all instructions, data, numbers, and symbols have been previously loaded or stored in memory at known addresses. The stored input may have been read from a magnetic tape (similar to that used with commercial tape recorders), from paper tape (similar to that used with teletype), or from punched cards.

If the instruction to be executed is the first programmed operation, energizing the start button will cause the control unit to issue an order "Read instruction." The instruction will be read into a register in the control unit where it will remain throughout the execution cycle.

Note that the mathematical operation requested in the instruction is ADD. The instruction word thus contains a code which is interpreted by the control unit as ADD.

After reading the instruction, the control unit automatically energizes circuits which will (1) read-out the contents of memory address 123, (2) transfer this information to a register (say the X register) in the arithmetic unit, and (3) perform an add X to A operation. The ADD process is thus accomplished, being constantly monitored by the control unit to ensure that no further actions are initiated before the ADD operation is completed. The results of the ADD operation are stored in the accumulator from which, by control request, it is transferred to address 456 in memory. This ends the instruction. The control unit will read and execute the next instruction.

If the result is to be displayed at the output immediately or at a later time (as stipulated in the programmed instructions) the control unit upon receipt of the instruction will issue an order to read-out the contents of memory address 456. Because read-out (which sometimes involve printing by some electromechanical apparatus) is extremely slow as compared to computer speed, most computers use a secondary storage device called a buffer into which data is read directly from the primary (main) storage at computer speeds. When read-out is desired, the control unit enables the buffer storage to read-out all or any part of the buffer storage data. The buffer read-out is independent of the main computer operation, and in some computers only one instruction is required to start and stop the read-out process.

COMPONENTS USED IN COMPUTERS

Unlike the mechanical computers, such as adding machines and odometers which are based on the decimal (ten) digit system, modern electronic computers use components which will represent only 2 conditions. These conditions are sometimes referred to as the 1 (energized) or 0 (deenergized) states. Early computers used relays and electron tubes; now transistors and silicon or germanium diodes are used because of the higher speeds at which they can react, and too, because of their lower power consumption.

Electronic circuits used in computers are basically simple. To a large extent these circuits are of four types: the OR circuit which produces an output when one or more of its inputs are active, that is, in the one state; the AND circuit which yields an output only when all inputs are active; the flip-flop circuit which is a bistable multivibrator; and the inverter circuit which yields a high output with a low input or a low output with a high input.

The reader should familiarize himself with basic electronic circuits by studying Basic Electronics, NavPers 10087 (revised). Only those circuits which are peculiar to computers will be treated in this text.

Chapter 2

NUMBER SYSTEMS

Since the earliest times, numbering systems have played an important part in daily life. Looking back in history to the earliest civilizations, methods of counting or representing numbers graphically have always been used. The Egyptians, Romans, and Greeks had means of counting and using a series of numbers as the basis for their computations in planning vast cities and building great structures.

The main use for the number system in early times was to keep records and to measure quantities, not to perform mathematical computations. With the development of science, old numeration methods became more and more outdated. This lack of an adequate system of number notation greatly hampered the scientific development of the early civilizations. For example, try to divide the Roman numeral MDXLVIII by CCVI. Quite difficult, isn't it? It is easy to realize from this example that the services of an expert of that day were required to perform simple operations like multiplication and division. Today's children can perform these simple operations in their early school years due to a better system of representing and manipulating numbers. The concept of writing numbers, counting, and performing the four basic operations of addition, subtraction, multiplication, and division is taught to everyone as a part of his elementary education. The process begins with positive integers and expands to complex numbers and vectors.

One of the most important factors in the advancement of science was the invention of the decimal number system. The Marquis de Laplace, a great mathematician, once stated:

> "It is India that gave us the ingenious method of expressing all numbers by means of ten symbols, each symbol receiving a value of position as well as an absolute value; a profound and important idea which appears so simple to use now that we ignore its true merit."

The counting in units of tens is believed to have stemmed from the fact that man has ten fingers. However, the use of ten as the base of our number system is not of itself important; any standard radix (base) would serve as well.

Laplace realized the value of a numbering system. As a future computer technician you too must realize the value of numbering systems, for it is numbering systems that provide the basis for all computer operations.

The discovery of two basic concepts simplified the operations needed to manipulate numbers: (1) the principle of positional value, and (2) the discovery and use of the zero.

The principle of positional value consists of assigning a number a value that depends both on the symbol itself and on its position in the quantity represented. For example, the digit 3 has a different value in each of the three numbers 123, 132, and 305. In the first number, the digit 3 has its basic or absolute value (3); in the second, it has the value of 30; and in the last number, it has the value of 300, or 3 times 10 times 10. Sometimes a position in a number does not have a value between 1 and 9. If this position was simply left out there would be no means of differentiating between quantities such as 205 and 25. Thus, the zero (0) is used to represent the absence of a value in a certain position (no positional value). In the number 205, there are two hundreds, no tens, and five units. In the number ten (represented graphically as 10) the number 1 represents 1 times the radix or base of the number system. The zero (0) indicates that there are no units. With the use of these two concepts (the principle of position and the numeral zero), counting and representing quantities become quite easy.

Now consider a few basic definitions that pertain to number systems.

1. Unit. . .A single thing
2. Number. . .An arbitrary symbol representing an amount of units.
3. Number System. . .A method of indicating the amount of units counted.
   a. All modern number systems include the zero.
   b. The radix, or base, of a number system is the amount of characters or symbols it possesses, including the zero.
4. Quantity. . .A number of units (implies both a unit and a number).
5. Modulus. . .The total number of different numbers or stable conditions that a counting device can indicate. (For example, the odometer on most automobiles has a modulus of 100,000 since it indicates all numbers from 00,000 to 99,999. The modulus of the hour hand on most watches is 12, and that of the minute hand is 60.

POSITIONAL NOTATION

The standard shorthand form of writing numbers is known as positional notation. As mentioned before concerning this subject, the value of a particular digit depends not only on the digit value, but also on the position of the digit within the number. Consequently, the decimal number 9751.68 is the standard shorthand form of the quantity nine thousand seven hundred fifty-one and sixty-eight hundredths. What the shorthand form really states is best illustrated by an example as follows:

$$9751.68 = (9 \times 10^3) + (7 \times 10^2) + (5 \times 10^1) + (1 \times 10^0) + (6 \times 10^{-1}) + (8 \times 10^{-2}).$$

A quantity can be expressed in the positional notation (standard shorthand) form in any numbering system. The general form is:

$$Q = (d_n \times r^n) + \ldots . + (d_2 \times r^2) + (d_1 \times r^1) + (d_0 \times r^0) + (d_{-1} \times r^{-1}) + (d_{-2} \times r^{-2}) + \ldots . + (d_{-n} \times r^{-n})$$

where: Q is the quantity expressed in positional notation form; r is the base or radix of the number system raised to a power; and d_2, d_1, d_0, d_{-1}, d_{-2}, etc. . . . . . are the characters of the radix.

Note that the radix point in the general expression (known as the decimal point in the decimal system) is not required because the exponent goes negative. In the shorthand form the radix point is placed between the $d_0 \times r^0$ and $d_{-1} \times r^{-1}$ values.

THE RADIX

Every number system has a radix, or base. When the radix is ten, the decimal system is indicated; when r is eight, the octal system is indicated; and when r is two, the binary system is indicated. The division between integers and fractions is recognized by the position of the radix point. Additional characteristics of the radix are as follows:

1. The radix of a numbering system is equal to the sum of the different characters which are necessary to indicate all the various magnitudes a digit may represent. For example, the decimal system, with a radix ten, has ten digits of magnitudes, 0 through 9.

2. The value of the radix is always one unit greater than the largest basic character being used. This is because the radix is equal to the number of characters, whereas the characters themselves start from zero. Thus, the octal system (discussed later) has a radix of eight and uses digits 0 through 7.

3. The positional notation does not, in itself, indicate the radix. The symbol "312" could represent a number written in the quartic (base four), octal, or decimal system, or in any system having a radix of four or greater. Binary numbers are usually recognizable from their string of ones and zeros. To avoid confusion, numbers written in systems other than the decimal system should have the radix noted as a subscript, i.e.,

$$315.72_8$$

The radix subscript is always written as a decimal (base ten) number.

4. Any number can easily be multiplied or divided by the radix of its number system. In decimal notation, to multiply a number by ten, move the decimal (radix) point one digit to the right of its former position, as follows:

$$\begin{array}{r} 34.564 \\ \underline{\text{x ten}} \\ 345.64 \end{array}$$

The following statement brings out a fact often overlooked. The radix point could remain stationary and the digits moved as follows:

$$\begin{array}{r} 034.564 \\ \underline{\text{x ten}} \\ 345.640 \end{array}$$

This is reasonable when one considers that the radix is fixed and the number represented in that radix is changed.

To divide a number by ten, move the decimal (radix) point one digit to the left of its former position, or more the digits one digit space to the right relative to the radix point as follows:

$$\frac{34.564}{(\text{ten})} = 3.4564$$

In the same fashion, a binary number is multiplied by two when the binary (radix) point is moved to the right one position value or the number is shifted to the left as follows:

10101.01 x (two) = 101010.1

COUNTING

The rules for counting numbers written in a system of positional notation are the same for every radix. The octal system is used in the following example to illustrate these rules.

1. Starting from zero, add "one" to the least significant digit until all basic characters have been used:

0, 1, 2, 3, 4, 5, 6, 7, ...

2. Since seven is the largest character in this system, a larger number requires two digits. Start the series of two-digit numbers with zero as the least significant digit and a "1" to left of the zero:

. . . . 6, 7, 10, 11, 12, 13, 14, 15, 16, 17, . . .

3. Whenever any digit reaches its maximum value (seven, in this case), replace it with zero and add "1" to its next more significant digit:

. . . 16, 17, 20, 21, . . . 26, 27, 30, 31, . . . 66, 67, 70, 71

4. When two or more consecutive digits reach the maximum value, replace them with zeros and add "1" to the next more significant digit:

. . . 76, 77, 100, 101, . . . 176, 177, 200, . . . 776, 777, 1000

NOTE: The symbol "10" always represents the radix in its own system. This is true because the radix is one unit larger than the largest character, and by the rules of counting, this value is written as "10".

For example:

Binary "10" = two (the radix of the binary system)
Octal "10" = eight (the radix of the octal system)
Decimal "10" = ten (the radix of the decimal system)

Binary System

The simplest possible number system is based on powers of two and is known as the binary system. This system, keyed to the decimal and octal systems, is used in the majority of modern computers and in all digital devices. By applying the rules of counting, an example of binary and octal counting evolves as shown in Table 2-1.

By a convenient coincidence, the two binary conditions (1 and 0) can be easily represented by many electrical/electronic components if the 1 binary state is indicated when the component is conductive and the 0 state is indicated when the component is nonconductive. The reverse of this will work equally as well, i.e., the nonconducting state of a component can be used to represent a 1 binary condition and a conducting state the 0 condition. Both procedures are used in digital computer applications and frequently within a single computer. Numerous devices are used to provide representation of binary conditions. These include switches, transistors, relays, and diodes.

Table 2-1. —Counting

Decimal	Binary	Octal
0	0	0
1	1	1
2	10	2
3	11	3
4	100	4
5	101	5
6	110	6
7	111	7
8	1000	10
9	1001	11
10	1010	12
11	1011	13
12	1100	14

The quantity represented using binary characters (or the characters in any numbering system) cannot be determined without knowing the positional weighting value of each character (digit). The positional value of binary characters from 2^0 (1) to 2^9 (512_{10}, or 512 base ten) are illustrated in Table 2-2.

Consider the following hypothetical example. A number of flip-flops (multivibrators) arranged in a chain to form a "register" can be gated by incoming pulses to some or all of the flip-flops so that some are driven to produce a SET or 1 output while others receive no input pulse and produce a CLEAR or 0 output. (This principle is discussed in detail in a later chapter.) If it is assumed that there are ten flip-flops in the chain, a binary condition (number) represented could be 0000010101. The value of this number can be determined by simply summing the positional values as indicated by 1's in the table. By this procedure, the top number in the table yields:

$$(1 \times 2^4) + (1 \times 2^2) + (1 \times 2^0) = 21$$

Thus,

$0000010101_2 = 21_{10}$,

and it is now known that the flip-flop chain is storing the decimal equivalent of 21.

The values of the other binary numbers in Table 2-2 are determined in the same manner.

By convention, weighting values are always arranged in the same manner. The highest one is on the extreme left and the lowest one is on the extreme right. Thus, the position coefficient begins at 1 and increases from right to left.

The leftmost 1 in any binary number (fig. 2-1) is always referred to as the "most significant digit." This is often abbreviated MSD. It is the "most significant" because it is multiplied by the highest valued position coefficient. The "least significant digit," or LSD, is always on the extreme right. It may be a 1 or a 0, and, when a 1, it has the lowest weighting value (1).

The terms most significant digit and least significant digit have the same meaning in any numbering system. The MSD of the decimal number 43,096 is 4, while the LSD is 6. When 43,096 is multiplied, divided, subtracted, or added to another number, the 4, being in the 10,000 place, will produce the greatest change in the answer. Thus, it is the MSD. The 6, being in the units place, will produce the least change in the answer. It is the least significant digit. In most practical computation, an error in the LSD has little significant effect. An MSD error, however, can result in an incorrect answer of more consequence.

Binary Coded Decimal

Each of the binary numbers that is shown in table 2-3 is called a "binary-coded decimal digit" or "coded digit". One can see that without using any other binary numbers, it is possible to represent any desired quantity by means of these coded digits. For example, in order to represent 736, we simply write the coded digit for each decimal, then we place the digit in the same order as the decimals, thus: 011100110110.

Binary coded decimal digits need not be spaced because we know that each one is composed of four binary digits. For easier reading, however, a space usually will be placed between each coded digit, thus: 0111 0011 0110. Note that this number is not pure binary; it is, instead, a binary-coded decimal number.

Table 2-2.—Positional Weighting Value.

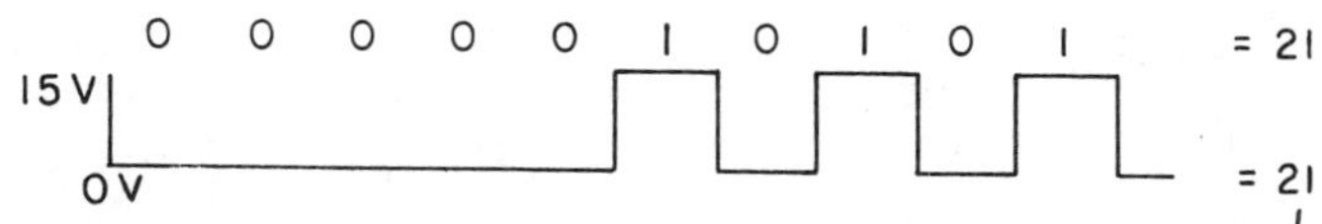

	2^9	2^8	2^7	2^6	2^5	2^4	2^3	2^2	2^1	2^0		
POSITION COEFFICIENT	512	256	128	64	32	16	8	4	2	1		
QUANTITIES IN BINARY	0	0	0	0	0	1	0	1	0	1	=	21
	0	0	0	0	0	0	0	0	0	0	=	0
	1	1	1	1	1	1	1	1	1	1	=	1023
	1	0	0	0	1	1	1	0	0	0	=	568
	0	0	0	0	0	0	0	1	0	1	=	5
	0	0	1	0	0	0	0	1	0	1	=	133
	0	0	0	0	0	0	0	0	0	1	=	1

164.64

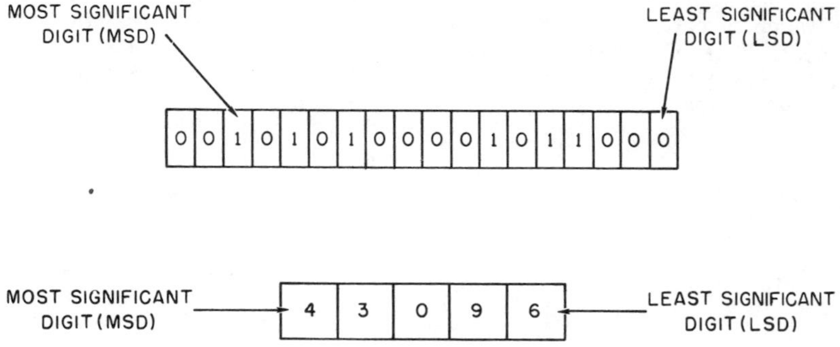

164.3

Figure 2-1.—Positional Value.

Table 2-3. —Binary-coded decimal digits.

Decimal Digit	Binary - Coded Decimal Digit			
0	0	0	0	0
1	0	0	0	1
2	0	0	1	0
3	0	0	1	1
4	0	1	0	0
5	0	1	0	1
6	0	1	1	0
7	0	1	1	1
8	1	0	0	0
9	1	0	0	1

Octal System

The octal system has eight distinct characters, hence its radix is eight. The octal system is quite useful as an accessory to the binary system, because eight is an integral power of two ($8_{10} = 2^3_{10}$). One octal digit is always equal to three binary and vice versa.

Octal to Binary			Binary to Octal		
2	2	5	010	010	101
010	010	101	2	2	5

Breaking a binary number into groups of three bits (BInary digiTs), starting from the radix point and working outwards to the left and right, the binary number may be written in a manner which is called BINARY CODED OCTAL (BCO). This makes the confusing string of 1's and 0's more understandable and facilitates the conversion of the binary number to an octal number. Such numbers would appear with the subscript $_{BCO}$; for example, 010010101_2 becomes $010\ 010\ 101_{BCO}$ and from there to 225_8. The binary number 010110.0111 becomes $010\ 110.011\ 100_{BCO}$ and 26.34_8.

Arithmetic operations in the octal system (or any numbering system) use the same basic procedures as does the decimal system. That is, carry and borrow quantities (in addition and subtraction) are treated identically; a multiplicand is multiplied by each digit of the multiplier, etc. However, the basic rules for the addition or subtraction of one digit to or from another digit, or the multiplication or division of one digit by another, are different for each number system. That is, two digits added in one system will give an answer; the same two digits, added in a different system may give a "different" answer. (The "different" answers are actually equivalent numbers.) The example below shows the results of an addition and a multiplication of the same digits in three systems.

(Note that 11_{10}, 13_8, and 14_7 are equivalent and that 30_{10}, 36_8 and 42_7 are equivalent.)

Each system requires its own addition and multiplication tables. These tables may be constructed by performing the required operation in the decimal system, and converting the answer to its equivalent. For example, the addition and multiplication tables for the octal system are shown in Tables 2-4 and 2-5, respectively.

The most important point to be remembered when performing arithmetic processes in any number system is to USE ONLY THE CHARACTERS (OR SYMBOLS) WHICH EXIST IN THAT SYSTEM.

Base 10 (decimal)	Base 8 (octal)	Base 7 (heptal)
$5_{10} + 6_{10} = 11_{10}$	$5_8 + 6_8 = 13_8$ $(1 \times 8^1 + 3 \times 8^0)$	$5_7 + 6_7 = 14_7$ $(1 \times 7^1) + (4 \times 7^0)$
$5_{10} \times 6_{10} = 30_{10}$	$5_8 \times 6_8 = 36_8$ $(3 \times 8^1 + 6 \times 8^0)$	$5_7 \times 6_7 = 42_7$ $(4 \times 7^1 + 2 \times 7^0)$

Table 2-4. —Octal Addition.

0	1	2	3	4	5	6	7
1	2	3	4	5	6	7	10
2	3	4	5	6	7	10	11
3	4	5	6	7	10	11	12
4	5	6	7	10	11	12	13
5	6	7	10	11	12	13	14
6	7	10	11	12	13	14	15
7	10	11	12	13	14	15	16

Table 2-5. —Octal Multiplication.

0	1	2	3	4	5	6	7
1	1	2	3	4	5	6	7
2	2	4	6	10	12	14	16
3	3	6	11	14	17	22	25
4	4	10	14	20	24	30	34
5	5	12	17	24	31	36	43
6	6	14	22	30	36	44	52
7	7	16	25	34	43	52	61

CONVERSION

If two numbers written in different numbering systems represent the same quantity, these numbers are equivalent (the represented quantities are equal although the numbers are not necessarily composed of the same characters). Any change which retains the equivalence of the original numbers results in a new set of equivalent numbers. Therefore, it is possible to convert numbers from one numbering system to another numbering system, that is, to change radices. Prior to discussing the mechanics of conversion the following point is stated.

To determine the decimal quantitative meaning of a number expressed in a system other than the decimal system, write the number in a power series summation, multiplying each digit of the number by its radix raised to the indicated positional power. The radix and the power must be expressed as a decimal number to obtain the decimal quantity.

Examples:

Problem: For what quantity does the binary number 10101.01 stand?

Solution:

$$\text{Quantity} = (1 \times 2^4) + (0 \times 2^3) + (1 \times 2^2) + (0 \times 2^1) + (1 \times 2^0) + (0 \times 2^{-1}) + (1 \times 2^{-2})$$
$$= (1 \times 16) + 0 + (1 \times 4) + 0 + (1 \times 1) + 0 + (1 \times 0.25) = 21.25_{10}$$

Problem: For what quantity does the octal number 25.2 stand?

Solution:

$$\text{Quantity} = (2 \times 8^1) + (5 \times 8^0) + (2 \times 8^{-1})$$
$$= (2 \times 8) + (5 \times 1) + (2 \times 0.125)$$
$$= 16 + 5 + 0.25$$
$$= 21.25_{10}$$

Note that the numbers 21.25_{10}, 25.2_8, and 10101.01_2 are equivalent.

BINARY - DECIMAL

One of the simplest, most direct, and most easily remembered methods of converting from binary to decimal and vice versa is the table method illustrated in Table 2-6.

NOTE: To find the decimal equivalent of a binary number (10101.01 in this case) by using the table method, insert the binary number in the table observing its binary positional value, and using the radix point as the reference. Then total the decimal values which have the binary character "1" below them. (A similar procedure was discussed earlier.)

Example:

Problem: Convert binary 101001.010 to its decimal equivalent.

Solution: Plugging the binary number into the table and summing

Table 2-6.—Binary - Decimal Conversion for Decimal Number 41.25

2_{10} raised to various powers	Continue as high as needed	2^5	2^4	2^3	2^2	2^1	2^0	2^{-1}	2^{-2}	Continue as low as needed
Equivalent expressed as a decimal		32	16	8	4	2	1	0.5	0.25	
Quantity expressed as a decimal		1 MSD	0	1	0	0	1	0	1 LSD	

Radix point

the decimal values result in:

$$\begin{array}{r} 32.00\ (2^5) \\ 8.00\ (2^3) \\ 1.00\ (2^0) \\ 0.25\ (2^{-2}) \\ \hline 41.25 \end{array}$$

Therefore, binary 101001.010 is equivalent to decimal 41.25. The procedure to find the binary equivalent of a decimal number is as follows:

1. Find the largest whole power of two that may be subtracted from the decimal number and place the binary character "1" underneath the decimal value of this whole power of two in the table.
2. Using the remainder, if any, from (1), again subtract the largest whole power of two possible. Place the binary character "1" underneath the decimal value of this whole power of two in the table.
3. Continue until the remainder is zero. Under every decimal value which does not have the binary character "1", place the binary character "0".
4. Rounding-off of fractions is necessary where exact conversions into binary are either not possible or necessary.

Example:

Problem: Convert decimal 41.25 to its binary equivalent.

Solution: Decimal 32 (2^5) is the largest whole power of two (Step (1)). A binary character "1" is placed beneath the decimal value 32 (2^5) in the table. The remainder (41.25 - 32) is 9.25. Decimal 8 (2^3) is the largest whole power of two which fits into 9.25. The remainder (9.25 - 8) is 1.25. A binary character "1" is therefore placed under the decimal 8 (2^3) in the table. The process continues until the remainder is zero or rounding-off is indicated. All squares not containing the binary character "1", are assigned the binary character "0".

Therefore, decimal 41.25 is equivalent to binary 101001.01.

BINARY - OCTAL

Since one octal digit is always equal to three binary digits ($8_{10} = 2_{10}^3$ as previously stated), conversion from binary to octal or octal to binary is quite simple. Binary to octal conversion is accomplished as follows:

1. Beginning at the binary point, mark off the binary number into groups of three digits

to the left and to the right of the binary point. Add the binary character "0" where needed to complete a group of three.

2. Replace each group of three binary characters with its octal equivalent which are:

$000 = 0_8$

$001 = 1_8$

$010 = 2_8$

$011 = 3_8$

$100 = 4_8$

$101 = 5_8$

$110 = 6_8$

$111 = 7_8$

Example:

Problem: Convert binary 101001.01 to its octal equivalent.

Solution:

Binary	101	001	.	010
Octal	5	1	.	2

Therefore, binary 101001.010 is equivalent to octal 51.2.

OCTAL - BINARY

Octal to binary conversion is simply the reverse of the above procedure. For each octal digit write the corresponding three binary digits.

Example:

Problem: Convert octal 51.2 to its binary equivalent.

Solution:

Octal	5	1	.	2
Binary	101	001	.	010

Therefore, octal 51.2 is equivalent to binary 101001.010.

DECIMAL - OCTAL

Rather than memorize rules and formulas, it is suggested (as a learning procedure) that conversion from octal to decimal or decimal to octal be accomplished by utilizing the binary system as an intermediary. The following examples point out how this is accomplished.

Example:

Problem: What is the decimal equivalent of octal 51.2?

Solution: From octal to binary by groups of three;

Octal	5	1	.	2
Binary	101	001	.	010

then from binary to decimal by powers of two table and summation;

Binary	1	0	1	0	0	1	0	1	0
Powers of two	2^5	2^4	2^3	2^2	2^1	2^0	2^{-1}	2^{-2}	2^{-3}
Decimal value	32		8			1		0.25	

summation of decimal values;
$32 + 8 + 1 + 0.25 = 41.25$

Therefore octal 51.2 is equivalent to decimal 41.25.

Problem: What is the octal equivalent of decimal 653.21?

Solution: From decimal to binary by whole powers of two and table;

Powers of two	2^9	2^8	2^7	2^6	2^5	2^4	2^3	2^2	2^1	2^0	2^{-1}	2^{-2}	2^{-3}	2^{-4}
Decimal value	512	256	128	64	32	16	8	4	2	1	0.5	0.25	0.125	0.0625
Binary	1	0	1	0	0	0	1	1	0	1	0	0	1	1

	653.21	
(-)	512.00	(Place a 1 under 512)
	141.21	Remainder
(-)	128.00	(Place a 1 under 128)
	13.21	Remainder
(-)	8.00	(Place a 1 under 8)
	5.21	Remainder
(-)	4.00	(Place a 1 under 4)
	1.21	Remainder
(-)	1.00	(Place a 1 under 1)
	0.210	Remainder
(-)	0.125	(Place a 1 under 0.125)
	0.0850	Remainder
(-)	0.0625	(Place a 1 under 0.0625)
	0.0225	Remainder

(The conversion will be stopped at this point for this example.) The binary equivalent of decimal 653.21 is therefore

1010001101.0011

which is now converted to octal by groups of three (starting at the radix point);

Binary	001	010	001	101	.	001	100
Octal	1	2	1	5	.	1	4

Therefore, the octal equivalent of decimal 653.21 is 1215.14. With practice, all of the above steps can be done mentally.

Another procedure used to convert a DECIMAL integral number to an OCTAL integral number is to divide the decimal number by 8, and the remainder equals the unit's position of the octal number. Divide the quotient (obtained from the first division) by 8 and this remainder equals the next (eight's) position of the octal number. Repeat the above process until the quotient zero is reached.

Example: Convert 149_{10} to an octal number.

$$\begin{array}{r} 18 \\ 8\overline{)149} \\ \underline{8} \\ 69 \\ \underline{64} \\ 5 \text{ remainder} \end{array} \qquad \begin{array}{r} 2 \\ 8\overline{)18} \\ \underline{16} \\ 2 \text{ remainder} \end{array} \qquad \begin{array}{r} 0 \\ 8\overline{)2} \\ \underline{0} \\ 2 \text{ remainder} \end{array}$$

(units digit in result) (8's digit in result) (64's digit in result)

The last remainder is the most significant digit in the octal number.

$$149_{10} = 225_8$$

To convert a DECIMAL fractional number to an OCTAL fractional number, multiply by 8 and develop the octal number as follows:

Example: Convert 0.149_{10} to an octal number.

1	Most significant digit in fractional result	0.149 × 8 = (1).192
1		0.192 × 8 = 1.536
4		0.536 × 8 = 4.288
2		0.288 × 8 = 2.304

Thus, $0.149_{10} = 0.1142_8$

The following conversion procedures, although not as simple as some previously treated methods, are representative of actual machine operation. It is expected that the reader will use the examples given in practice problems until the processes are understood.

The conversion of a decimal number to an octal number is best understood by re-examining the decimal number after polynomial expansion. Thus,

$$968_{10} = 9x10^2+6x10^1+8x10^0$$

FACTORING OUT 10^1 $= [9x10^1+6]10^1+(8x10^0)$

CONVERTING TO OCTAL $= [(11x12)+6]12+10$

$= [132+6]12+10$

$= (140x12)+10$

$= 1700+10$

$= 1710_8$

$$\therefore\ 968_{10} = 1710_8$$

The decimal to octal conversion of fractional numbers is likewise simplified by expansion. Consider the conversion of the decimal fraction .3983 to its octal fractional equivalent.

Expanding:

$$.3983 = 3x10^{-1}+9x10^{-2}+8x10^{-3}+3x10^{-4}$$

$$= 10^{-1}(3+9x10^{-1}+8x10^{-2}+3x10^{-3})$$

$$= 10^{-1}(3+10^{-1}[9+8x10^{-1}+3x10^{-2}])$$

$$= 10^{-1}(3+10^{-1}[9+10^{-1}\{8+3x10^{-1}\}])$$

Writing in octal:

$$12^{-1}\ (3 + 12^{-1}\ [11 + 12^{-1}\{10 + 3 \times 12^{-1}\}])$$

REARRANGING AND CONVERTING TO OCTAL $= \cfrac{\cfrac{\cfrac{10+3/12}{12} + 11}{12} + 3}{12}$

$= .3137337_8$

Showing the long division process,

.23146	.65075	.767227	.3137337
12)3.00000	12)10.23146	12)11.65075	12)3.7672270
2 4	7 4	10 6	3 6
40	63	105	16
36	62	74	12
20	114	110	47
12	106	106	36
60	66	27	112
50	62	24	106
100	4	35	42
		24	36
		110	47
		106	36
		2	110
			106
			2

Octal-Decimal

To convert an OCTAL integral number to a DECIMAL number multiply the highest order digit of the octal number by 8 and add the next lower order digit of the octal number to the product. Multiply this sum by 8 and add the next lower order digit to the result. When the lowest order digit has been added to the answer, the process ends.

Example: Convert 225_8 to a decimal number.

225
x8
16
+ 2
18
x8
144
+ 5
$149_{10} = 225_8$

To convert an OCTAL fractional number to a DECIMAL number, express the number in power of 8, add and divide as follows:

Example: Convert 0.1142_8 to a decimal number.

$$0.1142_8 = (1x8^{-1})+(1x8^{-2})+(4x8^{-3})+(2x8^{-4})$$

$$= 1/8 + 1/64 + 4/512 + 2/4096$$

$$= 610/4096$$

$$= 0.1489 \text{ or } 0.149$$

Consider another method, used here to convert the octal number, 1710_8 to its decimal equivalent. This method involves grouping the remainder from octal divisions as follows:

140	11	0
12)1710	12)140	12)11
12	12	0
51	20	(11)
50	12	
(10)	(8)	
OCTAL REMAINDER $10 = 8_{10}$	OCTAL REMAINDER $8 = 6_{10}$	OCTAL REMAINDER $11 = 9_{10}$

Group the remainders from the last division to the first to form the decimal number. Thus, $1710_8 = 968_{10}$.

A similar method can be used to convert a fractional octal number to its decimal fractional equivalent. To convert a fractional octal number to a decimal number multiply by 12_8 (10_{10}). The integer in the product is the 10^{-1} value of the decimal equivalent. Multiply the fractional value by $12_8(10_{10})$, using the integer in the product as a part of the decimal equivalent (this time the 10^{-2} value), and multiply the fractional value as before. Repeat this process until as many places as desired are obtained in the decimal equivalent.

Convert the octal fraction $.31373_8$ to its decimal equivalent.

.31373	.76716	.65014	.22170	.66260
12	12	12	12	12
62766	175634	152030	44360	154540
31373	76716	65014	22170	66260
3.76716	11.65014	10.22170	2.66260	10.37340
↘ 3	↘ 9	↘ 8	↘ 2	↘ 8

Thus, $.31373_8 = .39828_{10} = .3983_{10}$.

OPERATIONS

The following is a treatment of the four basic arithmetic operations; addition, subtraction, multiplication, and division.

ADDITION

Addition of binary numbers is performed exactly like addition of decimal numbers, that is, the arithmetic operations are identical. However, the following rules for deriving the sum and generating a carry when combining one binary character, A (the augend) with the second character, B (the addend) must be observed.

A	+	B	=	Sum	Carry
0	+	0	=	0	0
0	+	1	=	1	0
1	+	0	=	1	0
1	+	1	=	0	1

Carries are treated exactly like carries in the decimal system. An example will illustrate.

Example:

Decimal	Binary Equivalent	
26.1250	11010.0010	Augend
(+)55.0625	(+)110111.0001	Addend
1	11111	Carries
81.1875	1010001.0011	Sum

SUBTRACTION

Binary subtraction is identical to decimal subtraction. The following rules must be observed.

A	-	B	=	Difference	Borrow
0	-	0	=	0	0
0	-	1	=	1	1
1	-	0	=	1	0
1	-	1	=	0	0

The application of these rules is best illustrated by an example of the borrow method of subtraction.

Decimal

.1 borrow from this column

47.50 (5 circled) yields

(-)13.25

.05	borrow
.05	
47.40	Minuend
(-)13.25	subtrahend
34.25	difference

Binary Equivalent

.1 borrow from this column

101111.10 (1 circled) yields

(-)001101.01

.01	borrows
.01	
101111.00	minuend
(-)001101.01	subtrahend
100010.01	difference

MULTIPLICATION

Binary multiplication is identical to decimal multiplication. However, the multiplication table is simpler.

X	0	1
0	0	0
1	0	1

An example:

```
     Decimal                                      Binary Equivalent

                                                  1 0 1 1.0 1  multiplicand
       11.25                                 (x)      1 0.1 1  multiplier
(x)     2.75                                      -----------
       -----                                      1 0 1 1 0 1
        5625                                    1 0 1 1 0 1
        7875        Partial Products          0 0 0 0 0 0
       2250                                 1 0 1 1 0 1
     -------                                -----------------
     30.9375        Product                 1 1 1 1 0.1 1 1 1
```

DIVISION

Binary Division is identical to decimal division, as shown by the following example.

```
  Decimal                                        Binary Equivalent

               5.90<------(Quotient)                         101.111<--(Quotient)
(Divisor)--->5)29.50<------(Dividend)      (Divisor)--->101)11101.100<--(Dividend)
               25                                            101
               ---                                           ---
                4 5                                          100
                4 5                                          000
                ---                                          ----
                 00                                          1001
                 00                                           101
                 --                                          ----
                  0<------(remainder)                         1001
                                                               101
                                                              ----
                                                               1000
                                                                101
                                                               ----
                                                                110
                                                                101
                                                                ---
                                                                  1<--(remainder)
```

> NOTE: The binary division was stopped at the decimal equivalent of 5.875 plus a remainder. If further accuracy were required, the division process could have been carried on as far as necessary.

COMPLEMENT ARITHMETIC

A computer is usually designed to perform its arithmetic operations using either addition (only) or subtraction (only). Thus in a given computer all computations are performed by adding. In another machine all operations are performed by subtracting. This is possible since algebraically:

$$a + b = s \qquad \text{eq \# 1}$$

and $$a + (-b) = d \qquad \text{eq \# 2}$$

In equation (1), b is a positive quantity and a + b equals s (the sum). In equation (2), b is a negative quantity, and, when added, d represents the difference, or a - b. This procedure can be used in the computer only after a method is found for identifying and manipulating both positive and negative numbers; a process usually accomplished by using complement arithmetic.

DESCRIPTION

An arithmetical complement is defined as the difference between a number and the power of the base next in series. Thus in base ten:

2 is the complement of 8;
(10 - 8 = 2)

26 is the complement of 74;
(100 - 74 = 26)

744 is the complement of 256;
(1000 - 256 = 744)

Referring back to the definition, it is seen that complement arithmetic is not limited to base ten. Thus in base eight:

2 is the complement of 6;
(10 - 6 = 2)
4 is the complement of 74;
(100 - 74 = 4)
522 is the complement of 256;
(1000 - 256 = 522)

The relationship between any number and its complement in any base is then redefined by the following equation.

$$C = B^{D} - n \qquad \text{eq \# 3}$$

Where: n = any number
D = the number of digits in the number
C = the complement
B = the base of the system being used.

Observe that 2_{10} is the complement of 8_{10}, and at the same time 2_{10} is a number which has 8_{10} as a complement. Thus, developing a method of differentiating between 2 as a number and 2 as a complement of a number must also be accomplished before arithmetic operations can be performed using the complement method.

By modifying eq. #3 as follows:

$$C = B^{D+1} - n \qquad \text{eq \#4}$$

an interesting situation develops.

Considering the previously developed complements and using eq. #4 yields, in base ten;

92 is the complement of 8;
(100 - 8 = 92)
926 is the complement of 74;
(1000 - 74 = 926)
9744 is the complement of 256;
(10000 - 256 = 9744)

And in base eight;

72 is the complement of 6;
(100 - 6 = 72)
704 is the complement of 74;
(1000 - 74 = 704)
7522 is the complement of 256;
(10000 - 256 = 7522).

Observe here that the complement is preceded in each case by the highest digit in the base used. If all numbers which are not complements are preceded by 0; the identification of complemented numbers is solved. This removes the possible ambiguity which might develop in interpreting a positive 92_{10} and complement of 8_{10}. Before considering some of the finer aspects of this system as applied in the binary computer we shall work several problems using present developments and base ten arithmetic.

R's (RADIX) COMPLEMENT ARITHMETIC

It may now be stipulated without further proof that the complement of a number represents the negative value of that number. Thus, to perform a subtraction it is only necessary to complement the subtrahend and continue as in normal addition. If at any time a resultant is a negative number this will be indicated by the appearance of the complement form in the answer. Further, the complement of a complement is the original number.

Let a = 047 and a' = 953 (read the complement of a = 953) b = 023 and b' = 977

There are eight possible combinations of a and b which can occur, these are:

a ± (+b); a ± (-b); -a ± (+b); -a ± (-b)

Substituting the given values for a and b into each case we have the following:

1) a + (+b)

$$\begin{array}{r} 047\\ 023\\ \hline 070 \end{array}$$

2) a - (+b)

$$\begin{array}{rcr} 047 & & 047\\ -023 & = & +977\\ \hline 024 & & 1024 \end{array}$$

3) a + (-b)

$$\begin{array}{r} 047\\ 977\\ \hline 1024 \end{array}$$

4) a - (-b)

$$\begin{array}{rcr} 047 & & 047\\ -977 & = & +023\\ \hline & & 070 \end{array}$$

5) -a + (+b)

$$\begin{array}{rl} 953 & \\ 023 & \\ \hline 976 & = -24 \end{array}$$

6) -a - (+b)

$$\begin{array}{rcrl} 953 & & 953 & \\ -023 & = & +977 & \\ \hline & & 1930 & = -70 \end{array}$$

7) -a + (-b)

$$\begin{array}{r} 953\\ 977\\ \hline 1930 \end{array}$$

8) -a - (-b)

$$\begin{array}{rcrl} 953 & & 953 & \\ -977 & = & +023 & \\ \hline & & 976 & = -24 \end{array}$$

Consideration of the preceding examples brings to light an interesting phenomenon; that of overflow, as typified by the 1 in examples 2; 3; 6; and 7. Here the most significant digit (1) contributes nothing to the validity of the answer and is disregarded. This situation will be discussed at greater length later in this chapter.

All previously developed statements will apply to binary complement arithmetic. Thus the complement shall be indicated when the most significant digit is one, the highest permissible digit of the system, and a positive or uncomplemented number will be indicated if the most significant digit is zero. Further, the discussion is limited to the use of a finite number of digits, since this is the situation actually prevailing within the computer. For simplicity we will limit the binary number to fifteen places. Thus, looking at the binary equivalent of some numbers in the vicinity of zero:

5	000 000 000 000 101
4	000 000 000 000 100
3	000 000 000 000 011
2	000 000 000 000 010
1	000 000 000 000 001
0	000 000 000 000 000
-1	111 111 111 111 111
-2	111 111 111 111 110
-3	111 111 111 111 101
-4	111 111 111 111 100
-5	111 111 111 111 011

This representation is slightly awkward, but may be converted to the more conveniently handled octal form by grouping, giving:

5	00005
4	00004
3	00003
2	00002
1	00001
0	00000
-1	77777
-2	77776
-3	77775
-4	77774
-5	77773

Here each complement is developed by subtracting the absolute value of the number from 2^{15}.

Remembering that the only way to determine whether or not a number is positive or negative is by evaluating the most significant digit. We see that values from 00000 through 37777 (011 111 111 111 111) are positive and values from 40000 (100 000 000 000 000) through 77777 are negative (-40000 through -00001). However, since complementing a negative number gives a positive number, an undefined point exists, for complementing 40000 yields 40000, and the same number can not be both positive and negative. Thus our negative numbers are in fact limited to values from 40001 through 77777 (-37777 through -00001).

Now consider some sample problems.

1. (+5) + (-4) = 1

```
  00005
  77774
1 00001   Once again this overflow is dropped
```

2. (-6) + (-6) = -14

```
  77772
  77772
1 77764 = -14
```

3. (-12) - (-6) = -4

```
77766
00006
77774 = -4
```

4. (32000) + (32000) = 64000

```
32000
32000
64000 Complementing

100000 - 64000 = -14000
```

Note here that the addition has produced an overflow into the sign bit (highest order) position thereby indicating a negative result.

Once again it is reemphasized that the largest possible positive number the machine can contain as the result of a computation is 37777. This problem would have to be scaled (examined to determine if the result will produce an overflow) prior to entering it into the machine.

5. (-37775) + (-37774) = -77771

```
  40003
  40004
1 00007 = 7
```

Here again is an erroneous sum. The one is dropped and it appears that the sum is a positive seven. Once again the limitations of the machine have been exceeded since the largest negative number that it can properly define is 40001 (-37777). The solution is found in proper scaling of the factors.

The important facts about the R's complement arithmetic method to be reemphasized are:

a. The complement is indicated by the presence of the highest digit of the base being used in the most significant digit's position.

b. A positive number is indicated by the presence of a zero in the most significant digit's position.

c. The transition through zero is smooth, i.e., 00002; 00001; 00000; 77777; 77776.

d. A point of ambiguity exists at 40000 (in this case). This limits the magnitude of positive numbers to 37777 and negative numbers to -37777.

e. An erroneous result or an erroneous indication will be obtained if the sum of the factors exceed the limitations of the machine. The reader is encouraged to re-do the problems above in pure binary.

R's - 1 COMPLEMENT ARITHMETIC

Heretofore we have considered what is most commonly termed radix complement arithmetic. In this method the complement is formed by subtracting the number from a complete power of the base. Thus it is customarily abbreviated as R's complement. Another form of complement arithmetic, the R's -1 complement, is found to be uniquely convenient in binary arithmetic. (A comparison of the two systems is left until later in the discussion.) The R'-1 complement of a number may be obtained simply by subtracting one from the complement obtained by the previous method.

The following comparisons are made:

Number	R's Complement	R's - 1 Complement
5	00005	00005
4	00004	00004
3	00003	00003
2	00002	00002
1	00001	00001
+0	00000	00000
-0	undefined	77777
-1	77777	77776
-2	77776	77775
-3	77775	77774
-4	77774	77773
-5	77773	77772

The salient point here is the transition from positive numbers to negative numbers through zero. Note that when using R's - 1 complement arithmetic there exists a positive and a negative zero. Now however, if the largest positive number is permitted to be 37777, the complement of this is 40000. Thus the previous point of ambiguity no longer exists at 40000. Once again the absolute value of the largest possible number that the machine can contain is 37777.

Consider some problems using R's - 1 complement arithmetic.

1. (+5) - (+4) = 1

```
  00005
  77773
1 00000
└────→1
  00001
```

(Here an important difference in the two systems is demonstrated. In the R's complement system an overflow exceeding the limits of the machine had no significance and was dropped; the adder was said to be open ended. However, in R's - 1 complement arithmetic, as is seen from the example, the overflow is of significance and must be added to the least significant digit of what might be termed our partial sum. Thus, an R's - 1 complement adder is referred to as having end-around-carry.)

2. (-6) + (-6) = -14

```
  77771
  77771
1 77762
└────→1
  77763 = -14
```

3. (32000) + (32000) = 64000

```
  32000
  32000
  64000 = -13777
```

This is the same example that was used with the R's complement method. The capacity of the machine has been exceeded and overflow into the sign bit yields what appears to be a negative result.

4. (-37775) + (-37774) = -77771

```
  40002
  40003
1 00005
└────→1
  00006
```

Here is another example of exceeding the negative capacity of the machine. This also produces an erroneous answer.

5. (+5) - (+5) = 0

```
 00005
 77772
 77777 = -0
```

6. (+0) + (+0) = +0

```
 00000
 00000
 00000 = +0
```

7. (-0) + (-0) no equivalent in traditional arithmetic

```
  77777
  77777
1 77776
└────→1
  77777 = -0
```

8. (-0) + (+0) no equivalent in traditional arithmetic

```
 77777
 00000
 77777 = -0
```

Examples 5 through 8 demonstrate the conditions resulting in a zero answer. It should be observed that only in the addition of a positive zero and a positive zero is the sum a positive zero. All other manipulations result in a sum of negative zero. It is of importance for the student to realize that using either a positive or negative zero in a calculation will not affect the validity of the result. This may be readily demonstrated by working a few problems, and is left to the student for proof.

The salient facts about R's - 1 complement arithmetic to be remembered are:

a. The complement is indicated by the presence of the highest digit of the base being used in the most significant digit's position.

b. A zero in the most significant digit's position indicates a positive number.

c. The transition from positive numbers to negative numbers through zero is not smooth. Zero is represented by 00000 which is termed a positive zero, and by 77777 which is termed a negative zero.

d. Use of either value for zero does not invalidate the result.

e. An erroneous resultant is once again obtained if the sum of the factors exceed the limitations of the machine.

f. End-around-carry is a necessity when using R's-1 complement arithmetic. Overflow into bit position 2^{15} (which does not physically exist in the machine) is brought around and added to the least significant digit's position.

The time has now arrived when a few comments upon the relative merits of the two systems is in order.

The main advantage of the R's complement system is found in its smooth transition through zero. However, certain difficulties are encountered in designing the circuitry necessary for complementing. While these will not be elaborated on at this time, they generally limit the use of R's complement arithmetic to countertype applications. In countertype applications there is no interest in negative resultants; further, all complements will normally be entered by the operator or as a fixed function of the machine. The great simplicity in developing the complement in the R's - 1 system makes this the most frequently used in the arithmetic section of computers. To demonstrate this, consider the binary equivalent of 35452_8 and its complement in each system.

R's complement

```
011 101 100 101 010 = 35452
100 010 011 010 110 = 42326
```

R's - 1 complement

```
011 101 100 101 010 = 35452
100 010 011 010 101 = 42325
```

Here it is observed that each binary digit is reversed or complemented in the R's - 1 system, whereas the reversal in the R's complement system occurs only after the least significant digit, which is a one. Note that in forming the R's complement above that the first complemented digit occurs in the 2^2 bit position, and 2^1 is the first bit position containing a one.

For some applications the frequent occurrence of a negative zero in R's - 1 arithmetic may be objectionable. (We may even say the normal occurrence of a negative zero, since the only time a positive zero occurs is as the result of summing two positive zeros.)

Several methods have been developed to overcome this limitation. One of these is to detect for the occurrence of the negative zero and under its stimulus generate a false carry which will complement the negative zero. Thus:

```
     101  010  111  100  011  =  52743

     010  101  000  011  100  =  25034
     111  111  111  111  111  =  77777

false carry                1           1
 1   000  000  000  000  000  1    00000
 \                            |
Overflow                   Overflow
```

In this particular instance the further carry produced by summing with the false carry is disregarded. This method will not be explored any further at this time since a true appreciation of the system requires a more complete knowledge of mechanization techniques.

SUBTRACTIVE ADDERS

The other method for circumventing the production of negative zeros is through the use of a subtractive adder, i.e., an arithmetic unit which can only subtract. Just as it is possible to subtract using a unit capable only of addition so is it possible to add while limited to the process of subtraction. This is clearly demonstrated through the use of the following equation:

$$a + b = a - (-b)$$

There is only one new concept to consider when using a subtractive adder, and that is end-around-borrow. This is demonstrated by the next problem.

```
(00047) + (00023) = 00072

     1    00047
     |    77754
     |    00073
     |______ -1
          00072
```

This is a demonstration of end-around-borrow. Note that one is subtracted from the difference and added in the most significant digit's position of the minuend whenever the subtrahend is greater than the minuend. It is to be appreciated naturally that the actual circuitry using this technique does not step through the problem in precisely the manner indicated above. The important thing is that the above example can faithfully represent the action of the machine.

It now remains to consider the resultants obtained with problems which will produce a zero difference.

```
1. (00054)-(00054)=0     2. (-0) - (-0) = 0
       00054                  77777
       00054                  77777
       00000                  00000

3. 0 - (-0) = 0          4. (-0) - (+0) = -0
    1  00000                  77777
    |  77777                  00000
    |  00001                  77777
    |____-1
       00000
```

Here note that the only way a negative zero is obtained is by performing the operation indicated in step four. Thus to ensure the normal appearance of a positive zero it is only necessary to use a subtractive adder. All other previously developed rules as applied to R's - 1 arithmetic still apply.

As important reminders:

a. The absolute value of a number can not exceed 37777. . . . . 7.

b. Addition of two or more factors which exceed this limit will give either an erroneous answer or one that is interpreted erroneously.

c. All positive numbers will enter the machine preceded by a most significant digit of zero; all negative numbers will enter the machine in complement form.

d. Whereas, with the additive adder a subtract instruction caused the addend to be complemented it is shown that in the subtractive adder an add command will cause the subtrahend to be complemented.

e. Using R's - 1 arithmetic an end-around-borrow must be performed whenever the subtrahend is greater than the minuend.

f. The end-around-borrow is eliminated using R's complement arithmetic and a subtractive adder, however, the problem of mechanizing to form the complement is a limitation which precludes the use of this form.

Chapter 3

BOOLEAN ALGEBRA

Boolean algebra is a method of representing logical statements rather than numbers, which is the case in ordinary algebra. It can therefore be thought of as a shorthand method of expressing logical statements.

The name "Boolean algebra" is used to identify this system of logic representation in tribute to the English mathematician, George Simon Boole (1815-1864), who introduced the system in 1847. Actually, Boole developed the new system to simplify Aristotle's system of logic, which used, as a base, statements or expressions that were either true or false. Boole therefore based his "algebra" on a single-valued function with only two discrete possibilities. The advent of digital computers and their logic circuits found Boolean algebra a readily applicable tool. In digital computer logic circuits, certain physical conditions occur that follow the same logical rules of combination used to evaluate the truth or falsehood of logical statements.

This chapter treats the basic symbols, laws, axioms, and theorems of Boolean algebra in sufficient detail to enable you to analyze and solve (simplify) Boolean Equations. Equations with more than four variables will not be treated.

CONNECTIVES AND VARIABLES

Some commonly used connectives and variables peculiar to Boolean algebra are discussed below.

= The equal sign, just as in conventional mathematics, represents a relationship of equivalence between the expressions so connected.

· or x The dot or small x indicates the logical product, or conjunction of the terms so connected. The operation is also frequently indicated with no symbol used, i.e., $A \cdot B = A \times B = AB$. Most generally referred to as the AND operation, the terms so related are said to be "ANDed".

\+ The plus sign indicates the logical sum operation, a disjunction of the terms so connected. Usually called the OR operation and the terms so connected are said to be ORed.

$\overline{}$ The vinculum serves a dual purpose. It is at the same time a symbol of grouping and of operation. As a sign of operation it indicates that the term(s) so overlined are to be complemented. As a symbol of grouping it collects all terms to be complemented together. Terms so overlined are often said to be NEGATED, the process of taking the complement is then called NEGATION.

( ) [ ] { } These familiar signs of grouping are used in the customary fashion to indicate that all terms so contained are to be treated as a unit.

A, B, etc. Various letters are used to represent the variables under consideration, generally starting with A. Since the variables are capable of being in only one of two states the numerals 0 and 1 are the only numbers used in a Boolean expression.

LAWS

Three laws apply to the relationship of the variables in the Boolean. These are the Associative, Distributive, and Commutative laws.

ASSOCIATIVE

The associative law states that variables connected by like signs of operation may be grouped in any manner desired.

$$A + B + C = (A+B) + C = A + (B+C)$$

$$ABC = (AB)C = A \cdot (B \cdot C)$$

NOTE: $\underline{A + BC \neq (A+B)C}$

COMMUTATIVE

The commutative law states that terms connected by the same operation may be arranged in any sequence without changing the value of the expression.

$$A + B + C = B + C + A = C + B + A$$

$$ABC = CBA = CAB = BAC$$

DISTRIBUTIVE

The distributive law is best understood by considering the following examples.

$$A(B + C) = AB + AC$$

$$AB(C + D) = ABC + ABD$$

$$A + (BC) = (A + B)\ (A + C)$$

NOTE: The converse is also true; if a group of terms connected by like operators contain the same variable it may be removed from the terms and associated with them by the appropriate sign of operation.

$$AB + BC + BD = B\ (A+C+D)$$

$$(A + B)(A + C)(A + D) = A + BCD$$

AXIOMS AND THEOREMS

Because Boolean algebra is based on a function capable of being in either of two conditions (true or false) it is easy to realize that switches can be used as an analogy to express either a true or false condition. A switch is either closed (contacts made) or open (contacts not made). A closed switch represents a true statement and an open switch represents a false statement. Therefore, switches possess the same two-valued characteristics on which Boolean algebra is based.

AXIOMS

In Boolean logic two connectives express the relationship between two statements. These are referred to as the AND(·) or OR(+) operations. The opposite or denial of a statement is expressed by the negation, NOT (indicated by placing a vinculum over the statement). Using this logic, true is designated as 1 or in the case of a switch, as a closed circuit, and false is designated as 0 or as an open circuit.

Classes and the Venn Diagram

Consider how the concept of AND and OR are derived. To do this we shall refer to things about us as existing in groups or classes. Any group with one or more things in common may be referred to as a class, i.e., dogs, houses, etc.

The relationship between classes will give rise to other classes. If there is a class A and a class B it is possible to consider the class whose members are in either class A or class B, symbolically, A + B. Thus, A + B symbolizes a class whose members fall either in subclass A or subclass B. It is not necessary to know whether this is the only characteristic of the members of A + B or if some members are in fact in both A and B.

Just as consideration of the classes A and B gave rise to the class A + B, it is possible to see how it can give rise to yet another class; one whose members all belong to both A and B, symbolically, A · B. Once again it is not a matter of import to this discussion whether all members of A fall within B or vice versa, only that all members of AB are in both.

The Venn diagram (fig 3-1) is used to elaborate on and further clarify the class origins and relationships as just discussed.

Let the area within the rectangle represent the class of all classes or universe class. The universe class or any class under discussion is designated by 1. Then everything

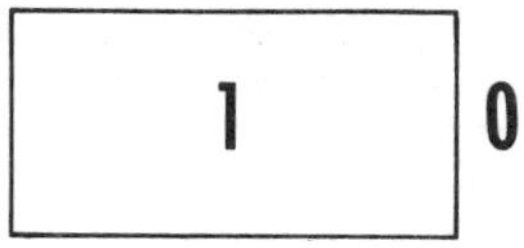

164.4

Figure 3-1.—Venn diagram for universe and null class.

which is not a member of the universe class must fall in the area without the rectangle, the null class, designated by 0. The following axioms now become apparent:

$0 + 0 = 0$	$0 \cdot 1 = 0$
$0 \cdot 0 = 0$	$1 + 1 = 1$
$0 + 1 = 1$	$1 \cdot 1 = 1$

The $0 + 1 = 1$ indicates that the discussion involves a new class with members in the universe class or with members in the null class. Since the null class has no members, the new class can therefore have only the members from the universe class. The statement (or class) $0 \cdot 1 = 0$ explores the possibility of a class whose members are in both the universe class and null class. This cannot be true as the classes are mutually exclusive. The class $1 + 1 = 1$ and $1 \cdot 1 = 1$ do exist as indicated by the result.

Selecting the class "A" in the universe class gives rise to the Venn diagram in figure 3-2. Note that by selecting the class "A", a class within the universe class whose members are not in A has also been defined, symbolically $\overline{A}$ (read A not or not A), and a certain relationship is seen to exist between the class A and the 0 (null) and 1 (universe) classes. Consequently, the following axioms are true:

$$A + \overline{A} = 1 \qquad A + 1 = 1 \qquad A + 0 = A$$

$$A \cdot \overline{A} = 0 \qquad A \cdot 1 = A \qquad A \cdot 0 = 0$$

164.5

Figure 3-2.—Selecting class A in the universe class.

Also,

$$A + A = A \text{ (not 2A)}$$

$$A \cdot A = A \text{ (not } A^2\text{)}$$

$$\text{and } \overline{\overline{A}} = A.$$

When classes A and B (which lie within the universe class) are considered, four distinct subclasses are defined. The derivation of these subclasses is discussed below using the Venn diagram in figure 3-3 and table 3-1. (The numbers 1 through 4 in the table and illustration are used for convenience in this discussion. These numbers are not usually shown in a Venn diagram.)

Note that when classes A and B are considered in the universe class in such a way that we may select either class A or B, the null class for these classes is $\overline{A}\overline{B}$. This area is defined in figure 3-3 as 4. All other areas (1, 2, and 3) represent the negation (complement) of this class because they contain A or B in some form. (The negation of $\overline{A}\overline{B}$ is indicated by the vinculum over this term in the second column of table 3-1.) Thus, for each class there exists the complement of that class. Because there are four subclasses of classes A and B (ways in which members of these classes can be represented) and because for each of these four subclasses there exists a complement, the eight subclasses of classes A and B are as shown in the left and rightmost columns in table 3-1. The reader is encouraged to identify these areas on the Venn diagram in figure 3-3.

OR Operation

Boolean algebra, because each of its variables can exists in either of two possible states, is readily described using switching circuits.

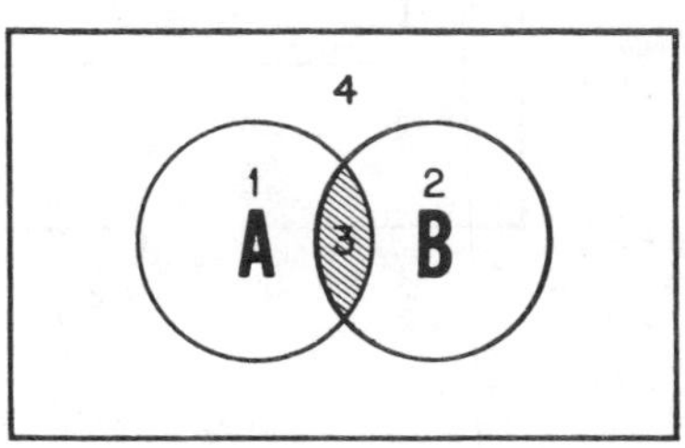

164.6

Figure 3-3.—Derivation of subclasses.

Table 3-1. —Derivation of Subclasses.

Subclass	area	Complement	Subclass not Defined	New Subclass
$\bar{A}\ \bar{B}$	4	$\overline{\bar{A}\ \bar{B}}$	1 + 2 + 3	A + B
$\bar{A}$ B	2	$\overline{\bar{A}\ B}$	1 + 3 + 4	$A + \bar{B}$
A $\bar{B}$	1	$\overline{A\ \bar{B}}$	2 + 3 + 4	$\bar{A} + B$
A B	3	$\overline{A\ B}$	1 + 2 + 4	$\bar{A} + \bar{B}$

Consider, for example the circuit shown in figure 3-4A. It is seen that "f" is high (i.e., equal to 1) when switch A or switch B is closed. Thus, the Boolean expression which describes this function is,

$$f = A + B.$$

The (+) is used to represent the OR operation. The shaded area in the Venn diagram in figure 3-4B represents the selection of class A or B. The logic diagram symbol for the OR operation is shown in figure 3-4C.

All possibilities of this circuit configuration, for an output of 1(f = 1) and an output of 0(f = 0), are best expressed in a table called a "truth table" (table 3-2). The table shows that when A = 0 and B = 0 (both switches open) the output equals 0 (low output); and that the output equals 1 (high output) for all other conditions of the switches, i.e., A = 0, B = 1; A = 1, B = 0; and A = 1, B = 1. Remember that the negation of a statement is

Table 3-2.—Truth table (OR operation).

A	B	f
0	0	0
0	1	1
1	0	1
1	1	1

12.134

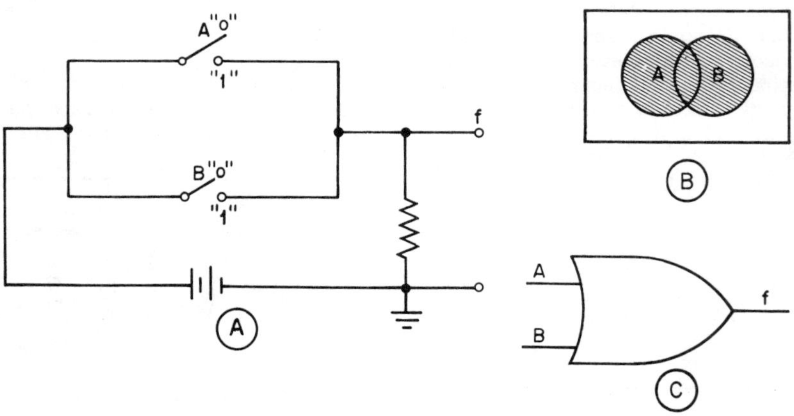

12.134

Figure 3-4.—OR operation.

expressed as NOT. Thus, the equation for the first entry in the table is:

$$\overline{A + B} = \overline{f}$$

read, not A or B equals not f.

In light of the previous discussion, it is to be understood that this circuit and truth table describe the condition for the class A or B.

AND Operation

Figure 3-5A shows a circuit in which both switch A and switch B must be closed at the same time before a 1 output is obtained at "f". This circuit (logical statement) is represented in Boolean algebra as:

$$A \cdot B = f.$$

The (·) represents the AND connective (operation). In conventional algebra this connective (used to indicate multiplication) is sometimes omitted. This is also true in Boolean algebra. The expression applicable to the above example then becomes:

$$AB = f$$

The shaded area in the Venn diagram of figure 3-5B represents the selection of the class A and B (AB). Figure 3-5C shows the AND symbol.

Just as was true for the OR operation, a number of switch conditions are possible for the AND operation as shown in figure 3-5. Truth table 3-3 shows all of the possible input combinations for this circuit. Note that "f" is zero for all conditions except when switches A and B are closed.

NOT Operation

In figure 3-6A, when A is 1 (as shown) a current flows in the circuit and the relay energizes, causing the contacts of the switch $\overline{A}$ (not A) to open. Thus, when A = 1, $\overline{A}$ equals 0. The output f(A) therefore equals $\overline{A}$, or f(A) = $\overline{A}$, the NOT operation. Note that if A = 0, $\overline{A}$ = 1.

Table 3-3.—Truth table (AND operation).

A	B	f
0	0	0
0	1	0
1	0	0
1	1	1

12.133

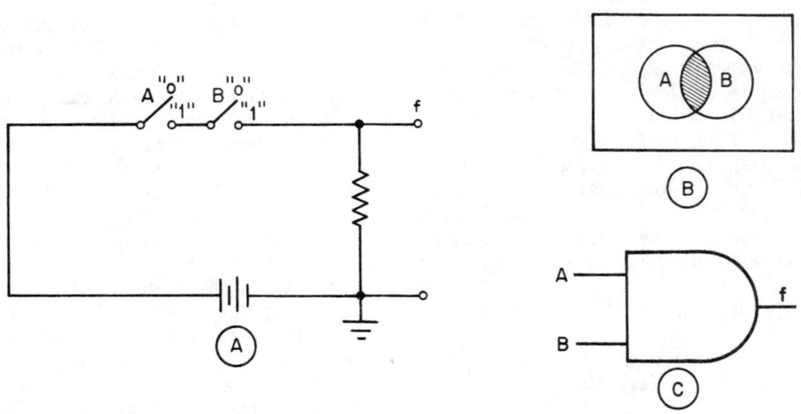

12.133

Figure 3-5.—AND operation.

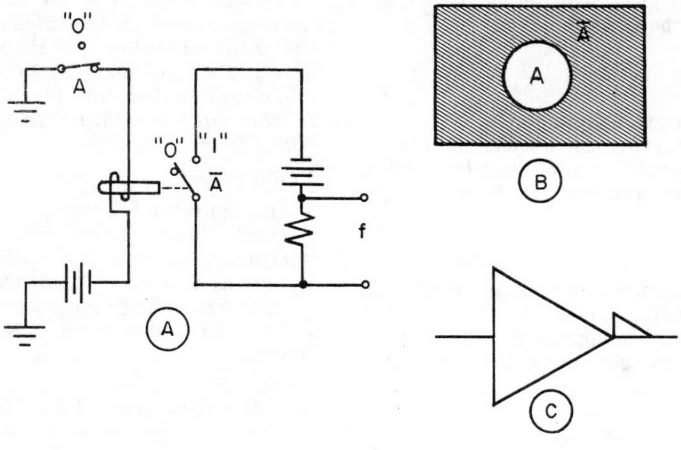

12.135

Figure 3-6.—NOT operation.

The Venn diagram of a NOT operation is shown in figure 3-6B. Table 3-4 is the truth table of this function, and figure 3-6C shows the NOT symbol.

KINDS OF LOGIC

If all signal lines on a logic diagram of a system or device are assumed to have the same state when active, and if both are electrical potentials, and if the more positive potential is consistently selected as the 1-state, the resultant system or device is said to have positive logic. If the less positive potential is consistently selected as the 1-state, the resultant system or device is said to have a negative logic. In either case, the system or device uses a "fixed" logic.

Consider the symbols shown at A and B in figure 3-7 and the truth table shown at C. In positive logic, the -3v level is the 0-state and the +2v level is the 1-state. Note that only the last combinations of input levels in

Table 3-4.—Truth table (NOT operation).

A	f(A) or $\bar{A}$
1	0
0	1

12.135

the table at C produce a high output, and the circuit performs the AND operation. The table at D shows the logic values substituted for the voltage levels represented in the table at C.

In negative logic, the -3v level is the 1-state (high) and the +2v level is the 0-state. With this logic, the circuit at B produces the -3v level output for all input combinations except the last, as shown in the table at C. This circuit performs the OR function. The table at E shows the substitution of the logic values for the voltage levels using negative logic. This is the truth table for the OR function and the circuit performs the OR operation.

A more recent method of assigning logic levels to binary logic elements uses "mixed" logic. The details of this method are delineated in the American Standard, Graphic Symbols for Logic Diagrams, Y32.14 of September 26, 1962. A brief description of this method is treated below.

Consider again the symbol shown in figure 3-7A and the truth table shown at C. The filled-in right triangle at the point where the signal line joins the symbol indicates that the 1-state (or activating signal) with respect to that particular logic symbol is the more positive potential. An open right triangle indicates that the 1-state for that particular logic symbol is the less positive potential. (Either of the

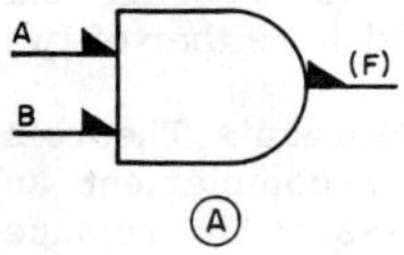

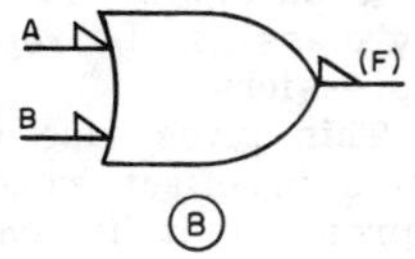

INPUTS A	INPUTS B	OUTPUT (F)
−3V	−3V	−3V
−3V	+2V	−3V
+2V	−3V	−3 V
+2V	+2V	+2V

(C)

INPUTS A	INPUTS B	OUTPUT (F)
0	0	0
0	1	0
1	0	0
1	1	1

(D)

INPUTS A	INPUTS B	OUTPUT (F)
1	1	1
1	0	1
0	1	1
0	0	0

(E)

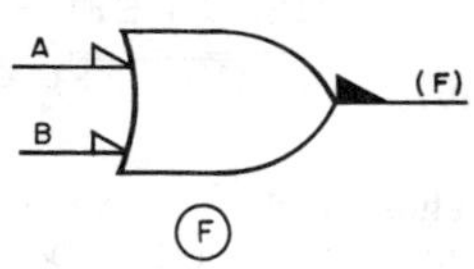

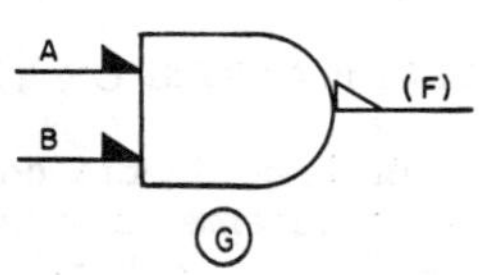

20.472

Figure 3-7.—Mixed logic.

two kinds of right triangles, open or filled, may be omitted provided the convention is suitably noted on the diagram.)

Again, the output (F) of each circuit is a function of two variables (A, B). The output and input levels may be either +2 volts or -3 volts.

The circuit at A produces the AND function only when the +2 volt level is taken as the activating level. The same circuit produces the OR function if the -3 volt level is the active level. Thus a method is available for using both positive and negative logic on the same diagram. Inverters are frequently used with mixed logic to ensure that the desired function is applied to a subsequent circuit at the selected activating level.

Recall now that with fixed logic (as heretofore considered) the basic symbols in figure 3-7A and B represent the AND and OR functions respectively. When mixed logic is used, a single circuit can perform either the AND operation or the OR operation. Thus, given a physical on-off device and a table of logic combinations, the logic function performed by the device is determined by the specified choices of the 1-state at its inputs and outputs.

It is also possible, using mixed logic, to have a circuit whose active output level is the opposite of the activating input level as shown in figure 3-7F and G. When both inputs to the circuit at F are low, the output is high. However, with fixed logic, the circuit can be thought of as combining the OR and NOT functions, and is sometimes referred to as the NOR circuit. Likewise, the circuit at G produces a low output at (F) when both inputs are high. This circuit combines the AND and NOT functions and is referred to as a NAND operation.

SIMPLIFICATION THEOREMS

The following is a treatment of several theorems which are used to simplify Boolean expressions. These theorems facilitate rapid usage of logic diagrams and should be memorized so that they can be easily recalled and used also as tools for simplification.

I $A + AB = A$

$= A(1 + B) = A$ From Dist. Law and Axiom

$A \cdot 1 = A$ From Dist. Law and Axiom

$A = A$ From Dist. Law and Axiom

or, $A + AB + AC + ABC = A$,
and $AB + ABC = AB$

II $A(A + B) = A$

$AA + AB = A$ Dist. Law

$A + AB = A$ Axiom

$A = A$ Th. I

III $A + \overline{A}B = A + B$

$A + AB + \overline{A}B = A + B$ Th. I

$A + B(A+\overline{A}) = A + B$ Dist. Law

$A + B = A + B$ Axiom

IV $AB + BC + \overline{A}C = AB + \overline{A}C$

$AB + BC(1) + \overline{A}C = AB + \overline{A}C$ Axiom

$AB + BC(A+\overline{A}) + \overline{A}C =$ Axiom

$AB + ABC + \overline{A}BC + \overline{A}C =$ Dist. Law

$AB(1 + C) + \overline{A}C(1 + B) =$

$AB(1) + \overline{A}C(1) =$

$AB + \overline{A}C$ Th. I

An equation of this form has a redundant middle term. The illustration below emphasizes the conditions necessary.

$$AB \quad + \quad BC \quad + \quad \overline{A}C$$

V $(A + B)(A + C) = A + BC$

$AA + AC + AB + BC = A + BC$ Dist. Law

$A + AC + AB + BC = A + BC$ Axiom

$A(1+C+B) + BC = A + BC$

$A + BC = A + BC$ Th. I

DUALITY AND DE MORGAN'S THEOREM

If the shaded area of the Venn diagram in figure 3-8 is the class AB (1 representing A and 2 representing B), then the unshaded area (including area 3) must describe the class $\overline{AB}$ (not AB). The class $\overline{AB}$ is described as follows:

$\overline{AB} = A\cdot\overline{B}$ (area 1) $+ \overline{A}B$ (area 2) $+ \overline{A}\,\overline{B}$ (area 3)

and $\overline{AB} = A\overline{B} + \overline{A}\,\overline{B} + \overline{A}B + \overline{A}\,\overline{B}$ (refer to axioms and laws)

$= \overline{A}(B + \overline{B}) + \overline{B}(A + \overline{A})$

$\therefore \quad \overline{AB} = \overline{A} + \overline{B}$

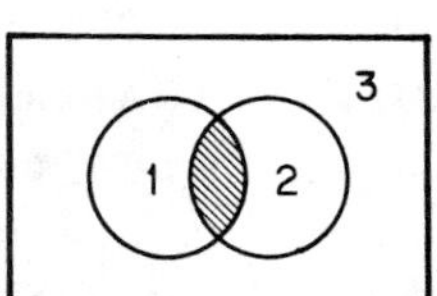

164.7
Figure 3-8.—Description of De Morgan's Theorem.

It should be noted from this theorem that any class can be represented by either of two expressions.

This gives rise to De Morgan's Theorem which in effect says that to complement an expression it is only necessary to replace all AND's with OR's, all OR's with AND's and to negate the variable. (ALL SIGNS OF GROUPING MUST BE OBSERVED.) Thus,

$$\overline{AB + CD} = (\overline{AB})(\overline{CD}) = (\overline{A} + \overline{B})(\overline{C} + \overline{D})$$

The following examples will further demonstrate the applications of this theorem.

1. $\overline{A + B + C} = \overline{A}\cdot\overline{B}\cdot\overline{C}$
2. $\overline{A(B + C)} = \overline{A} + (\overline{B}\,\overline{C})$
   CAUTION: $\overline{A}\,\overline{(B + C)} \neq (\overline{A} + \overline{B})\overline{C}$
3. $\overline{AB(CD + EF)} = \overline{A} + \overline{B} + (\overline{C} + \overline{D})(\overline{E} + \overline{F})$
4. $\overline{AB\,\overline{(CD + EF)}} = \overline{AB} + \overline{\overline{(CD + EF)}}$
   $= \overline{A} + \overline{B} + (CD + EF)$

Thus, either of two expressions may represent the same class. De Morgan's theorem is frequently used in the manner described above to simplify Boolean expressions.

APPLICATIONS OF THEOREMS

Boolean algebra comprises a set of axioms and theorems (discussed earlier) which are useful in describing logic equations such as those used in computer technology. Likewise, these laws and axioms are used to simplify logic equations so that logic circuits can be designed in their simplest and most economic form. For example, the equation below is a logic equation which describes the logic circuit in figure 3-9A in Boolean terms.

$$F = AC + AD + BC + BD$$

If Boolean algebra is used to simplify the logic equation,

$F = AC + AD + BC + BD$

$= A(C + D) + B(C + D)$ Dist. Law

$= (A + B)(C + D)$

then the logic circuit arrangement for the simplified expression is shown in figure 3-9B. Factors such as the loading and standardization

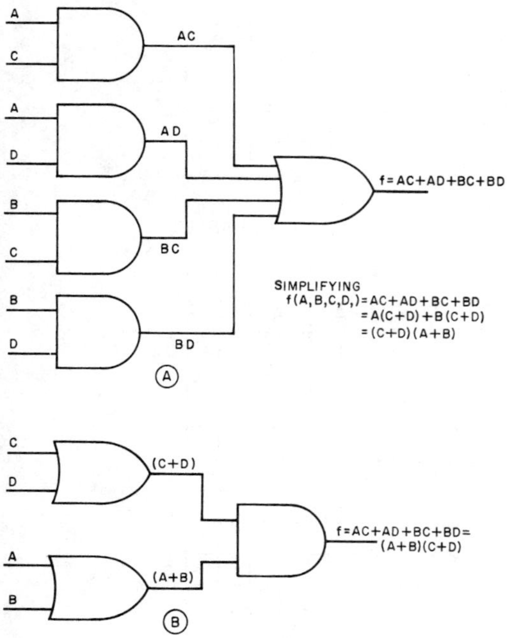

164.8

Figure 3-9.—Simplified logic circuitry resulting from simplifying logic equations.

of logic circuits may dictate the use of other than the simplest possible Boolean expression. In this discussion the only concern is with the equation simplification without regard to other design considerations.

Consider the following as a second example:

EXAMPLE: Simplify the logic equation,

$$f = ABC + AB\overline{D} + A\overline{C} + \overline{A}\overline{B}\overline{C}\overline{D} + \overline{A}C$$

SOLUTION: Rearrange terms and factor as follows:

$$f = ABC + A\overline{C} + \overline{A}\overline{B}\overline{C}\overline{D} + \overline{A}C + AB\overline{D}$$
$$= A(BC+\overline{C}) + \overline{A}(\overline{B}\overline{C}\overline{D}+C) + AB\overline{D}$$

Applying simplification theroem III to $(BC+\overline{C})$ and $(\overline{B}\overline{C}\overline{D}+C)$

Then:

$$f = A(B+\overline{C}) + \overline{A}(\overline{B}\overline{D}+C) + AB\overline{D}$$

Apply distributive law

Then:

$$f = AB + A\overline{C} + \overline{A}\overline{B}\overline{D} + \overline{A}C + AB\overline{D}$$
$$f = (AB+AB\overline{D}) + A\overline{C} + \overline{A}C + \overline{A}\overline{B}\overline{D}$$

Apply distributive law and axiom to $(AB + AB\overline{D})$ and rearrange terms. Then:

$$f = AB(1+\overline{D}) + A\overline{C} + \overline{A}C + \overline{A}\overline{B}\overline{D}$$
$$f = AB + A\overline{C} + \overline{A}C + \overline{A}\overline{B}\overline{D}$$

No further simplification is possible. Therefore:

$AB + A\overline{C} + \overline{A}C + \overline{A}\overline{B}\overline{D}$ is the simplest form of the logic equation

$$AB + AB\overline{D} + A\overline{C} + \overline{A}\overline{B}\overline{C}\overline{D} + \overline{A}C$$

The foregoing examples of simplification show the process to be rather difficult at first with no positive indication (for the beginner) that the simplest possible logic equation has been reached. Repeated use of these theorems is the only solution. Simplification theorems are of greatest value in the preliminary stages of simplification, or in the simplification of elementary functions.

VEITCH DIAGRAMS

A second approach to equation simplification is the Veitch diagram. These diagrams provide a very quick and easy way for finding the simplest logic equation needed to express a given function. Veitch diagrams for two, three, or four variables are readily constructed (fig. 3-10). Any number of variables may be plotted in a Veitch diagram, though the diagrams are difficult to use when more than four variables are involved. Generally, a function containing more than four variables will not be encountered.

Because each variable has two possible states (true and false), the number of squares needed is the number of possible states (two) raised to a power dictated by the number of variables. Thus, for four variables the Veitch diagram must contain 2^4 or 16 squares. Five variables require 2^5 or 32 squares. An eight variable Veitch diagram needs 2^8 or 256 squares - a rather unwieldy diagram. If it becomes necessary to simplify logic equations containing

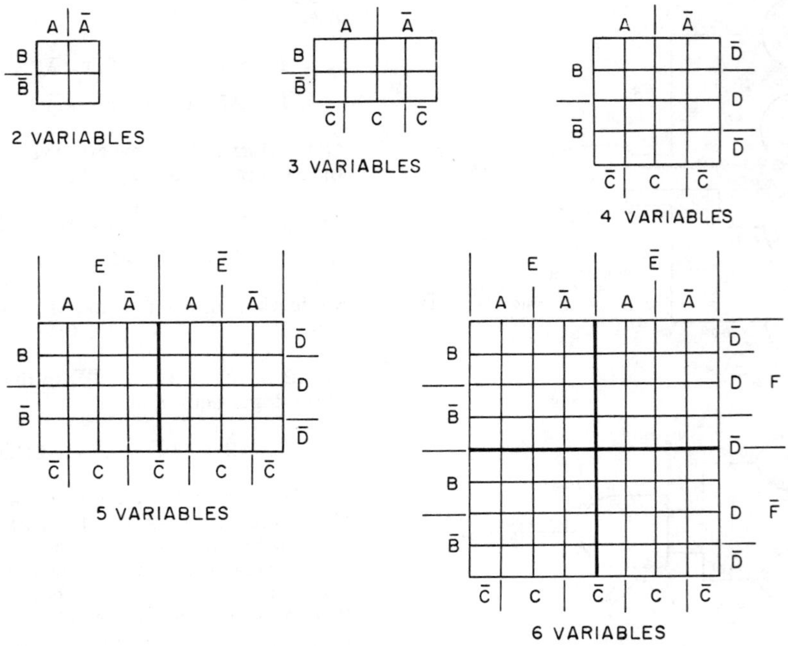

124.17

Figure 3-10.—Veitch diagrams.

more than six variables, other methods of simplification should be used.

An exploded view of a four variable Veitch diagram is shown in figure 3-11. Note the division of the diagram into labeled columns and rows. The entries into the diagram are placed in these columns and rows in accordance with the function values for a given Boolean expression.

Looking at the squares in the upper left corner of the main Veitch diagram in figure 3-11, and using the extensions, it is seen that it contains the variables $AB\overline{C}\overline{D}$; the next lower block contains $AB\overline{C}D$; the next lower block contains $A\overline{B}\overline{C}D$; and the block in the lower left corner contains the variables $A\overline{B}\overline{C}\overline{D}$. All of the squares in the diagram are similarly identified. Note that the term $A\overline{C}$ is contained in each of the four terms just discussed; and, by the Distributive Law, since the variables B and D appear in both asserted and complemented form they can be dropped. Thus, the left vertical column identifies the term $A\overline{C}$.

This is proven below by equation using the laws considered earlier.

$$A\overline{C} = A\overline{C}\ (1)$$
$$= A\overline{C}\ (B+\overline{B})$$
$$= AB\overline{C} + A\overline{B}\overline{C}$$
$$= AB\overline{C}\ (1) + A\overline{B}\overline{C}\ (1)$$
$$= AB\overline{C}\ (D+\overline{D}) + A\overline{B}\overline{C}\ (D+\overline{D})$$
$$= AB\overline{C}D + AB\overline{C}\overline{D} + A\overline{B}\overline{C}D + A\overline{B}\overline{C}\overline{D}$$

The final expression represents four of the maxterms of the term $A\overline{C}$. Also note that a two-variable term is represented by four squares. A study of the diagram will reveal that a term with one variable is represented by eight squares; a three-variable term by 2 squares, and a four-variable term by 1 square.

To illustrate the use of the Veitch diagram, the logic equation

$$f = ABC + AB\bar{D} + A\bar{C} + \bar{A}\bar{B}\bar{C}\bar{D} + \bar{A}C$$

will be used. (This is the same equation used in the earlier example to show some applications of the simplification theorems.) Because there are four variables, a four variable Veitch diagram is needed. A step-by-step process is as follows:

Step 1. Draw the appropriate Veitch diagram (Table 3-5).

Step 2. Plot the logic function on the Veitch diagram, term by term. This is accomplished by placing a "1" in each square representative of the term. (Use table 3-5 to identify the squares and table 3-6 to

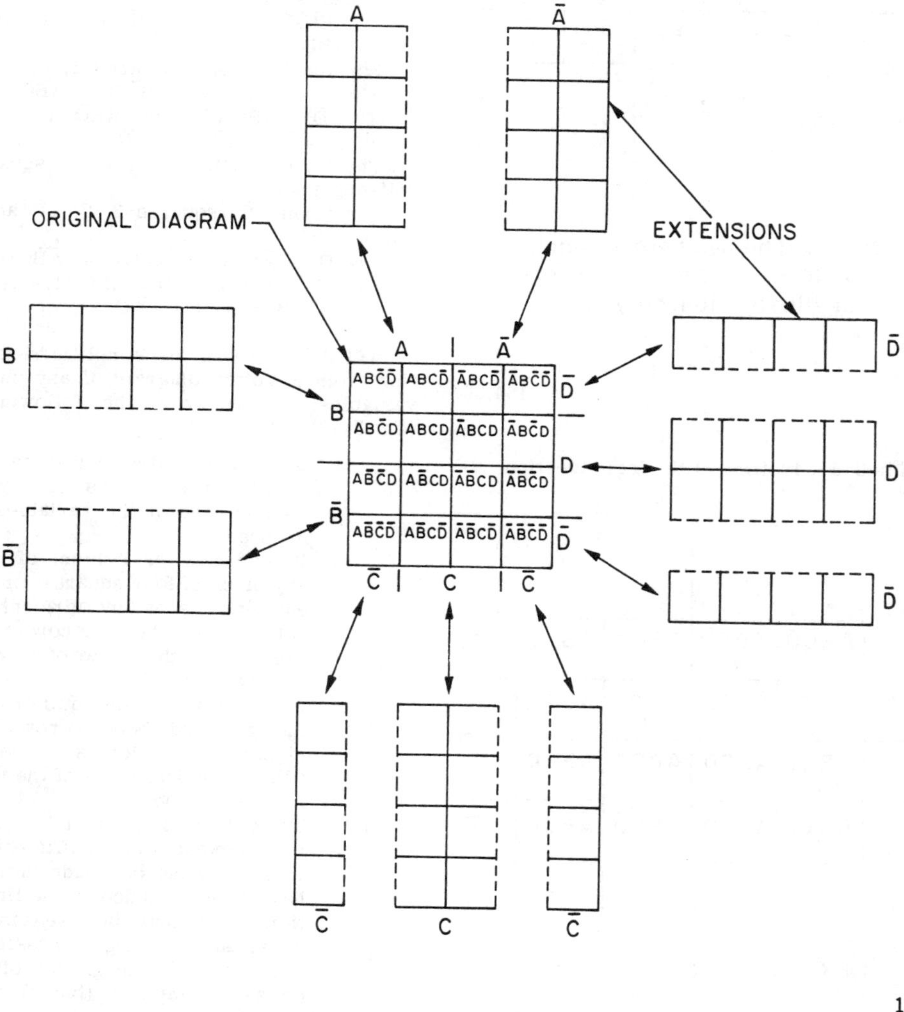

124.21

Figure 3-11.—Exploded Veitch diagram.

Table 3-5.—Identifying the squares of a Veitch diagram.

	A	A	$\bar{A}$	$\bar{A}$	
B	$AB\bar{C}\bar{D}$ 1	$ABC\bar{D}$ 2	$\bar{A}BC\bar{D}$ 3	$\bar{A}B\bar{C}\bar{D}$ 4	$\bar{D}$
B	$AB\bar{C}D$ 5	$ABCD$ 6	$\bar{A}BCD$ 7	$\bar{A}B\bar{C}D$ 8	D
$\bar{B}$	$A\bar{B}\bar{C}D$ 9	$A\bar{B}CD$ 10	$\bar{A}\bar{B}CD$ 11	$\bar{A}\bar{B}\bar{C}D$ 12	D
$\bar{B}$	$A\bar{B}\bar{C}\bar{D}$ 13	$A\bar{B}C\bar{D}$ 14	$\bar{A}\bar{B}C\bar{D}$ 15	$\bar{A}\bar{B}\bar{C}\bar{D}$ 16	$\bar{D}$
	$\bar{C}$	C	C	$\bar{C}$	

NOTE: The numbers in each square are for the purpose of illustration only.

164.66

Table 3-6.—Plotting of the logic function.

	A	A	$\bar{A}$	$\bar{A}$	
B	$AB\bar{C}\bar{D}$ 1	$ABC\bar{D}$ 1	$\bar{A}BC\bar{D}$ 1	$\bar{A}B\bar{C}\bar{D}$	$\bar{D}$
B	$AB\bar{C}D$ 1	$ABCD$ 1	$\bar{A}BCD$ 1	$\bar{A}B\bar{C}D$	D
$\bar{B}$	$A\bar{B}\bar{C}D$ 1	$A\bar{B}CD$	$\bar{A}\bar{B}CD$ 1	$\bar{A}\bar{B}\bar{C}D$	D
$\bar{B}$	$A\bar{B}\bar{C}\bar{D}$ 1	$A\bar{B}C\bar{D}$	$\bar{A}\bar{B}C\bar{D}$ 1	$\bar{A}\bar{B}\bar{C}\bar{D}$ 1	$\bar{D}$
	$\bar{C}$	C	C	$\bar{C}$	

164.67

understand the plotting of the terms on the diagram.)

$$f = ABC + AB\bar{D} + A\bar{C} + \bar{A}\bar{B}\bar{C}\bar{D} + \bar{A}C$$

The term ABC of the equation is identified in the Veitch diagram by squares 2 and 6. The derivation is as follows:

$ABC\bar{D} + ABCD = ABC\,(\bar{D} + D) = ABC\,(1) = ABC$

The term $AB\bar{D}$, identified by squares 1 and 2 as follows:

$AB\bar{C}\bar{D} + ABC\bar{D} = AB\bar{D}\,(\bar{C} + C) = AB\bar{D}\,(1) = AB\bar{D}$

For the term $A\bar{C}$, squares 1, 5, 9, and 13: $AB\bar{C}D + AB\bar{C}\bar{D} + A\bar{B}\bar{C}D + A\bar{B}\bar{C}\bar{D} = AB\bar{C}\,(D + \bar{D}) + A\bar{B}\bar{C}\,(D + \bar{D}) = AB\bar{C}\,(1) + A\bar{B}\bar{C}(1) = A\bar{C}\,(B + \bar{B}) = A\bar{C}\,(1) = A\bar{C}$

The term $\bar{A}\bar{B}\bar{C}\bar{D}$, identified by square 16 is self-explanatory.

The term $\bar{A}C$, squares 3, 7, 11, and 15 as follows:

$\bar{A}BC\bar{D} + \bar{A}BCD + \bar{A}\bar{B}CD + \bar{A}\bar{B}C\bar{D} = \bar{A}BC\,(\bar{D} + D) + \bar{A}\bar{B}C\,(D + \bar{D}) = \bar{A}BC\,(1) + \bar{A}\bar{B}C\,(1) = \bar{A}C\,(B + \bar{B}) = \bar{A}C\,(1) = \bar{A}C$

STEP 3. Obtain the simplified logic equation from a Veitch diagram of any number of variables by observing the following rules (fig. 3-12):

a. If 1's are located in adjacent squares or at opposite ends of any row or column, one of the variables may be dropped.
b. If any row or column of squares, any block of four squares, or the four end squares of any adjacent rows or columns, or the four corner squares are filled with 1's, two of the variables may be dropped.
c. If any two adjacent rows or columns, the top and bottom rows, or the right and left columns are completely filled with 1's, three of the variables may be dropped.
d. To reduce the original equation to its simplest form, sufficient simplification must be made until all 1's have been included in the final equation. 1's may be used more than once, and the largest possible combination of 1's in groups of 8, 4, 2, or as a single 1 (block) should be used.

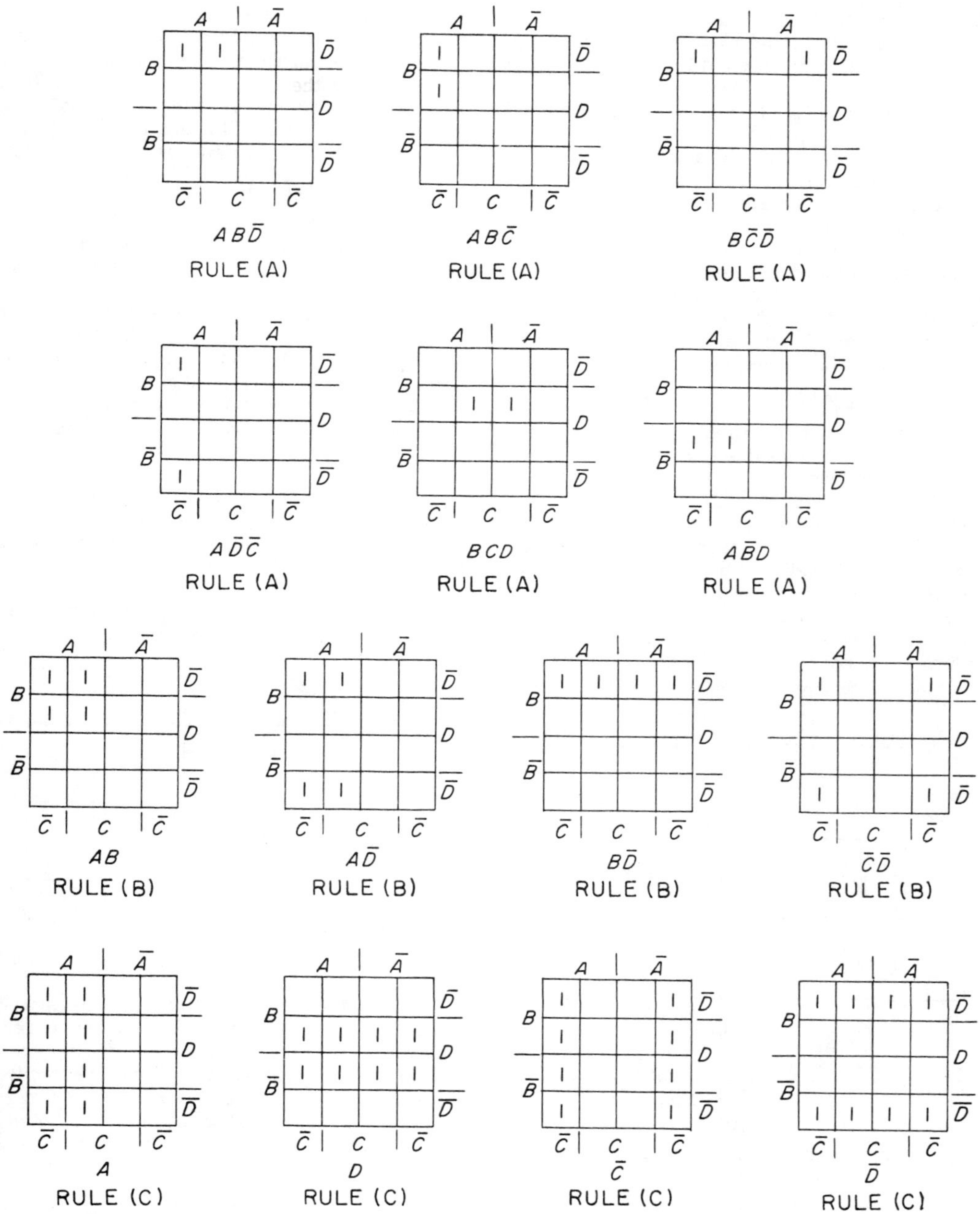

124.23

Figure 3-12.—Veitch combinations.

Continuing with the simplification:

Squares 1, 5, 9, and 13 are combined (Table 3-7) using rule (b) to yield $A\overline{C}$ (1's in B and $\overline{B}$ cancel).

Squares 3, 7, 11, and 15 are combined using rule (b) to yield $\overline{A}C$.

Squares 1, 2, 5, and 6 are combined using rule (b) to yield AB.

Squares 15 and 16 are combined using rule (a) to yield $\overline{A}\overline{B}\overline{D}$.

To keep track of the squares combined, draw loops around the combined squares. In doing this, the Veitch diagram takes on the appearance shown in Table 3-7.

All 1's have been used, therefore, a logic equation can now be written

$$f = AB + A\overline{C} + \overline{A}C + \overline{A}\overline{B}\overline{D}$$

which agrees with the simplified logic equation obtained by the use of the simplifying theorems.

A second simplification for the equation, $f = ABC + AB\overline{D} + A\overline{C} + \overline{A}\overline{B}\overline{C}\overline{D} + \overline{A}C$, the equation just discussed, is derived by grouping blocks 13 and 16. Although shown in the form of a table, the Veitch diagram in table 3-7 is to be considered as a cylinder in either direction. (This permits continuity of the variable, i.e., the rows containing $\overline{D}$ and $\overline{C}$ are contiguous though it is not readily possible to show this.) As such, the $\overline{D}$ blocks become adjacent when the bottom end of the table is folded back and up and the top is folded back and down until the ends meet. The $\overline{C}$ blocks become adjacent when the right end is folded back and to the left and the left end is folded back and to the right. Thus, blocks 13 and 16 are adjacent. The simplification of the equation is therefore,

$$f = AB + A\overline{C} + \overline{A}C + \overline{B}\overline{C}\overline{D}.$$

It is to be recognized from the above example that a single equation in Boolean can be represented in more than one simplified form.

A Veitch diagram provides a convenient means of finding the complement of a logic equation. This is done by plotting the original equation on a Veitch diagram, and then plotting ones on another Veitch diagram everywhere except where the original diagram has ones. An example will illustrate the procedure.

EXAMPLE:

If: f = ABC

What is $\overline{f}$?

A three variable Veitch should give the answer. The original equation is first plotted as shown in Table 3-8.

Table 3-7.—Deriving the result.

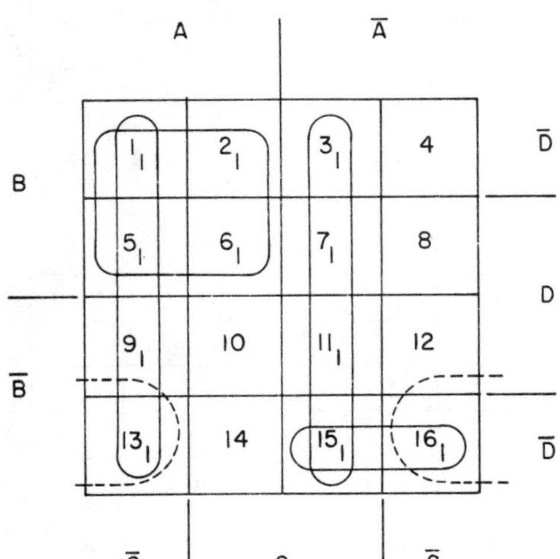

164.68

Table 3-8.—Three variable Veitch diagram showing statement true.

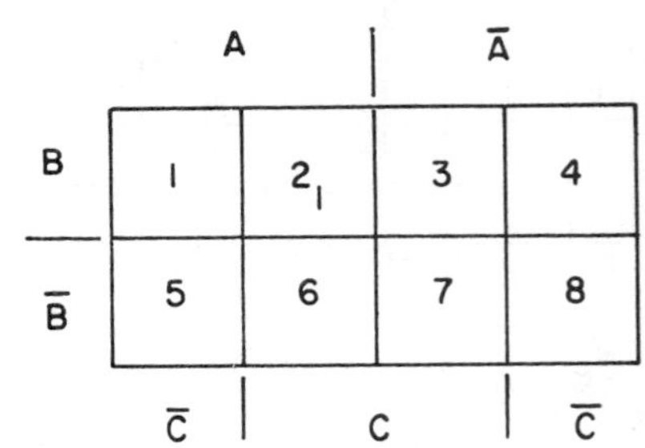

164.69

On another Veitch diagram, all squares which do not have a "one" in the original diagram, are assigned a "one" as (table 3-9).

Now the equation for $\overline{f}$ can be written. Squares 3, 4, 7, and 8 combine to form $\overline{A}$; squares 5, 6, 7, and 8 combine to form $\overline{B}$; and squares 1, 5, 4, and 8 combine to form $\overline{C}$. Therefore, the equation for $\overline{f}$ is,

$$\overline{f} = \overline{A} + \overline{B} + \overline{C}$$

which agrees with the result obtained by directly applying DeMorgan's theorem.

Table 3-9.—Three variable Veitch diagram showing statement complemented.

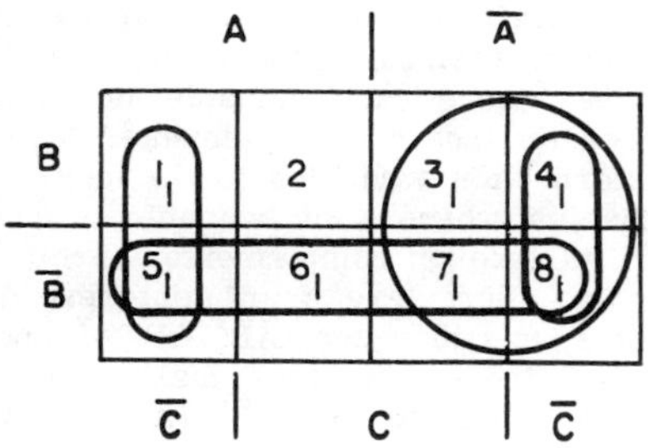

164.70

MECHANIZATION OF LOGIC EQUATIONS AND EQUATION SIMPLIFICATION

In the earlier discussion of logic Operations, switching circuits were used to illustrate the various operations. These switching circuits were actually the mechanization of the logic operations using conventional single-pole double-throw switches. Before using the actual logic symbols, the conventional switches are again used to mechanize an equation. The equation:

$$f = AB + A\bar{C} + \bar{A}C + \bar{A}\bar{B}\bar{D}$$

will be mechanized. (This is the equation used in the discussion on simplification.)

It will be recalled that the AND function used a series switching circuit and the OR function used a parallel switching circuit. Therefore, the mechanization of the above equation is as illustrated in figure 3-13. This diagram illustrates the AND and OR functions. The AND functions are each series connected switch grouping of the four possible parallel paths - the OR function. The above equation and mechanization is shown in figure 3-14 using the logic symbols for AND and OR gates. A logic equation can always be mechanized by a switching network. This involves the following four steps:

1. Construct a truth table.
2. Write the logic equation.
3. Simplify the equation, if possible.
4. Draw the required switching network.

The reader is encouraged to apply these four steps to several hypothetical problems.

MINTERMS AND MAXTERMS

In this discussion, consider the following equations:

eq (1) $f = AB + A\bar{B} + \bar{A}\bar{B}$
eq (2) $f = A + \bar{B}$

Equation (1) is the sum of three Boolean terms, each of which is the product of two variables

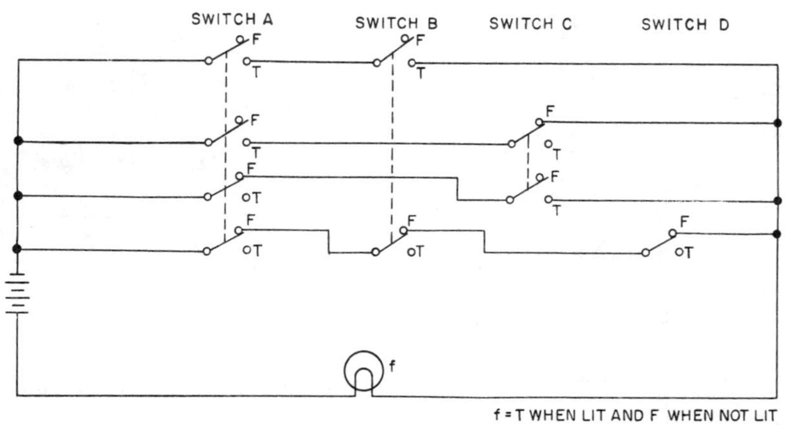

Figure 3-13.—Mechanization of a logic equation. 164.9

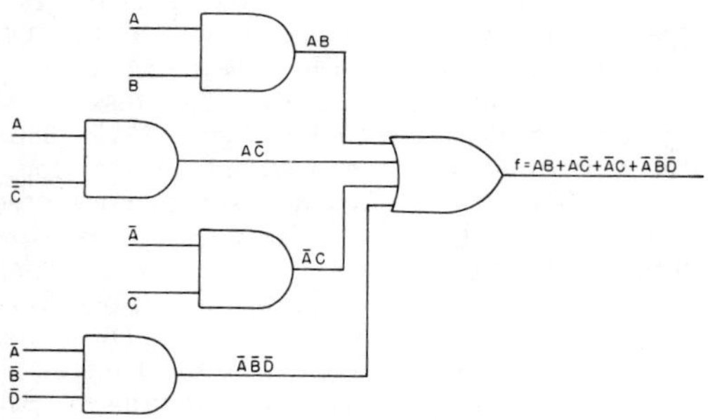

164.10

Figure 3-14.—Mechanization of a logic equation using logic symbols.

(A and B), each variable of which is represented in either its true or complemented form. Equation (2) represents the sum of the two variables A and B with B complemented. Equation (1) is a minterm expression of the two variables, and equation (2) is a maxterm expression of these variables. (The proof of the equality of the two equations is left to the reader.)

In general then, a minterm expression of n variables is defined as the product of these n variables where each variable is expressed in either its true or complemented form, and a maxterm of n variables is the sum of these n variables where each variable is added in either its true or complemented form. Consequently, there are four minterms of two variables, and they are ($\overline{A}\overline{B}$, $\overline{A}B$, $A\overline{B}$ and AB). Likewise, there are four maxterms of two variables. They are ($\overline{A} + \overline{B}$), ($\overline{A}$ + B), (A + $\overline{B}$), and (A + B).

There are eight minterms and eight maxterms of three variables as shown in table 3-10. As might be expected, there are 2^n minterms and 2^n maxterms where n variables are considered.

Observe that the minterm identified by an odd number in the upper left corner of each block in the left column relates to the next higher even number in the right column in accordance with De Morgan's Theorem. Using table 3-11, the unshaded area represents the minterm and the shaded area represents the maxterm.

Table 3-10.—Minterms and Maxterms of variables A, B, and C.

MINTERM		MAXTERM	
1	$\overline{A}\,\overline{B}\,\overline{C}$	16	$\overline{A}+\overline{B}+\overline{C}$
3	$\overline{A}\,\overline{B}\,C$	14	$\overline{A}+\overline{B}+C$
5	$\overline{A}\,B\,\overline{C}$	12	$\overline{A}+B+\overline{C}$
7	$A\,\overline{B}\,\overline{C}$	10	$A+\overline{B}+\overline{C}$
9	$\overline{A}\,B\,C$	8	$\overline{A}+B+C$
11	$A\,\overline{B}\,C$	6	$A+\overline{B}+C$
13	$A\,B\,\overline{C}$	4	$A+B+\overline{C}$
15	$A\,B\,C$	2	$A+B+C$

164.71

Table 3-11.—Representation of minterm and maxterm on a Veitch diagram.

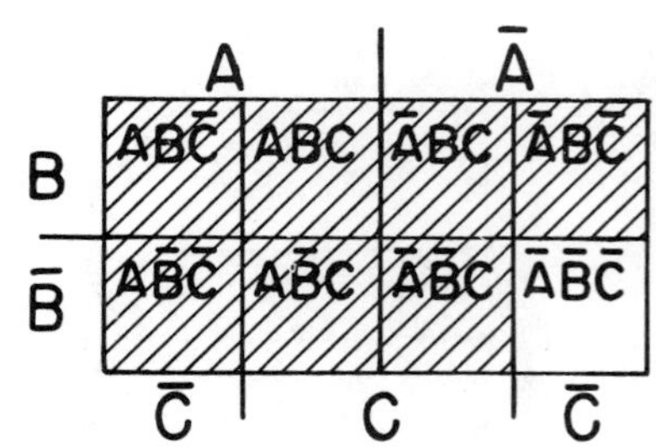

164.72

DEVELOPMENT OF AN ADDER USING THE VEITCH DIAGRAM

Consider the development of an adder circuit to further illustrate the use of Veitch diagrams. Table 3-12 is the truth table. The rules for addition are as follows:

$0 + 0 = 0$ (read 0 plus 0 = 0)

$0 + 1 = 1$

$1 + 0 = 1$

$1 + 1 = 0$ (with a carry generated)

$1+1+1= 1$ (with a carry generated)

The X and Y variables represent the digits that are being added and C is the carry input from a preceding stage. S is the sum at the output and C_o is the carry to the next stage. The Boolean equation for sum (S = 1) is:

$$S = \overline{X}\overline{Y}C + \overline{X}Y\overline{C} + X\overline{Y}\overline{C} + XYC$$

The Boolean equation for the output carry ($C_o = 1$) is:

$$C_o = \overline{X}YC + X\overline{Y}C + XY\overline{C} + XYC$$

Figure 3-15 is the Veitch diagram of the sum equation and figure 3-16 is the diagram of the output carry equation. By applying the principles already covered to the diagram in figure 3-16, it can be proven that the sum equation cannot be further simplified.

Table 3-12. —Truth table for an adder.

X	Y	C	S	C_o
0	0	0	0	0
0	0	1	1	0
0	1	0	1	0
0	1	1	0	1
1	0	0	1	0
1	0	1	0	1
1	1	0	0	1
1	1	1	1	1

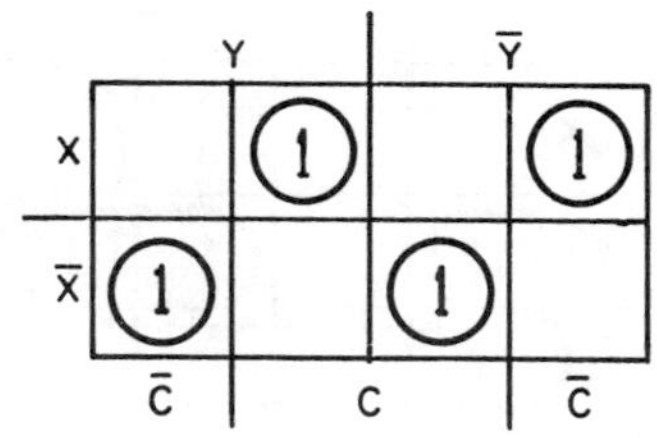

164.11

Figure 3-15.—Veitch diagram for S.

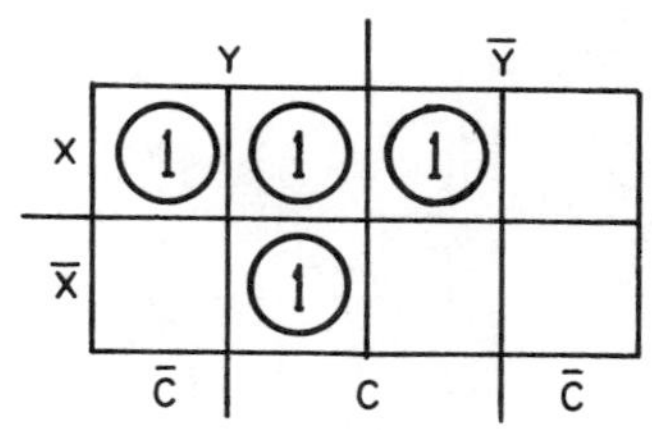

164.12

Figure 3-16.—Veitch diagram for C_o.

The combination of the two upper left checked boxes in figure 3-16 produces XY. The combination of the two center upper boxes produces XC and the combination of the two vertically arranged boxes just left of center produces YC. Thus, the carry equation is:

$$C_o = XY + XC + YC$$

Figure 3-17 shows the Veitch diagram for $\overline{C}_o$. It should be noted from table 3-12 that the equation for this function is:

$$\overline{C}_o = \overline{X}\overline{Y}\overline{C} + \overline{X}\overline{Y}C + \overline{X}Y\overline{C} + X\overline{Y}\overline{C}$$

NOTE: The reader is encouraged at this point to note again the cylindrical quality of Veitch diagram, i.e., the diagram can be thought of as a cylinder. As such, the box containing a 1 in the lower left corner of the Y sector (the lower block in the leftmost $\overline{C}$ column) is adjacent to or joins the two boxes containing 1's in the lower rightmost $\overline{C}$ column.

The logic circuit diagram for the simplified C_o equation is shown in figure 3-18. Each of

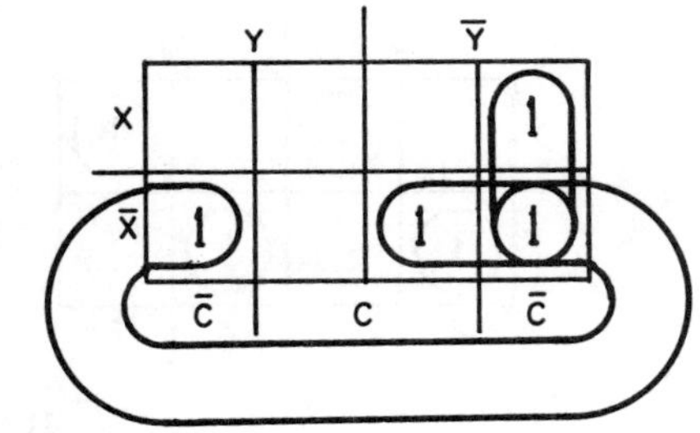

164.13

Figure 3-17.—Veitch diagram for $\overline{C}_O$.

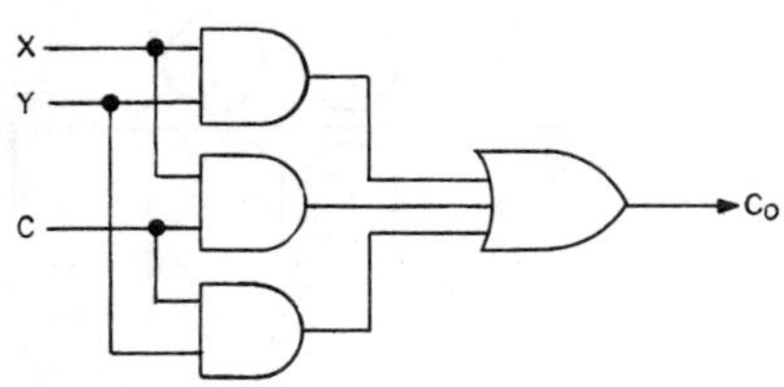

164.14

Figure 3-18.—Logic implementation of $\overline{C}_O$.

the three AND circuits handles a term of the equation. The OR circuit allows any combination of the three variables which generates a carry to produce an output at C_O.

The implementation of the $\overline{C}_O$ equation can be accomplished by simply inverting the C_O. Figure 3-19 shows the use of an inverter to obtain $\overline{C}_O$.

To complete the adder implementation (the S circuit portion) using a minimum of logic circuits, compare the S Veitch diagram of figure 3-15 with the Veitch diagram of figure 3-17. Note that the two diagrams contain the same terms except for the XYC function in

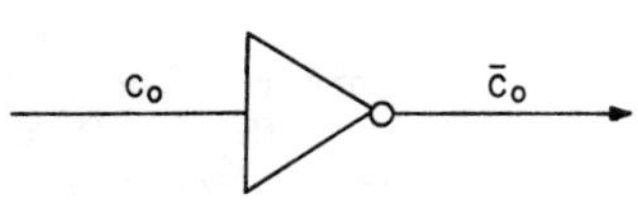

164.15

Figure 3-19.—Logic implementation of $\overline{C}_O$.

the S diagram and the $\overline{XYC}$ function in the $\overline{C}_O$ diagram. It is possible then to derive the S output by using the $\overline{C}_O$ function.

A sum (S) output is desired when any one or all three variables are 1. Note that the $\overline{C}_O$ output is 1 when any one of the variables is 1, and when none of the variables are 1. Consequently, $\overline{C}_O$ is 0 when all three variables are 1, a condition that is not desirable if the $\overline{C}_O$ output is to be used to implement the sum output. Therefore, to implement the S output by using the $\overline{C}_O$ output of the inverter (fig. 3-19), the $\overline{X}\ \overline{Y}\ \overline{C}$ function must be eliminated and the X Y C function must be added.

The X Y C function can be added by ANDing the variables and ORing the output with the $\overline{C}_O$ output as shown in figure 3-20. This action adds only the X Y C term to what already represents the $\overline{C}_O$ function. The output is the $\overline{C}_O$ function plus X Y C.

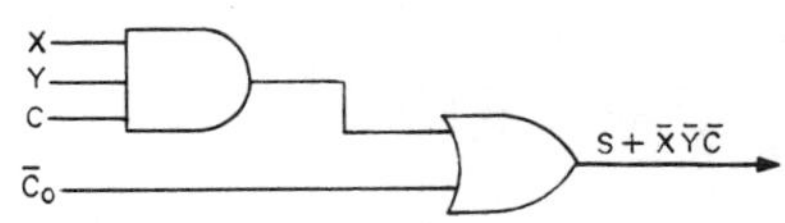

164.16

Figure 3-20.—Logic mechanization of the term $S + \overline{X}\ \overline{Y}\ \overline{C}$.

The function (f) representing the output is,

$$f = (X+Y+C) + \overline{XYC} + XYC = S + \overline{XYC}$$

To remove the $\overline{X}\ \overline{Y}\ \overline{C}$ term, the X+Y+C term is produced and ANDed with $S + \overline{XYC}$ as shown in figure 3-21. This illustration shows the complete adder as derived from the use of Veitch diagrams.

THE HARVARD CHART

One other technique of interest is the Harvard Chart. Its use is demonstrated in Table 3-13.

Simplify $f = AB\overline{C} + ABC + \overline{A}BC + \overline{A}B\overline{C} + A\overline{B}C$

1. Draw a line through all rows whose terms are not contained in the expression being simplified (Rows 1, 2, and 5).

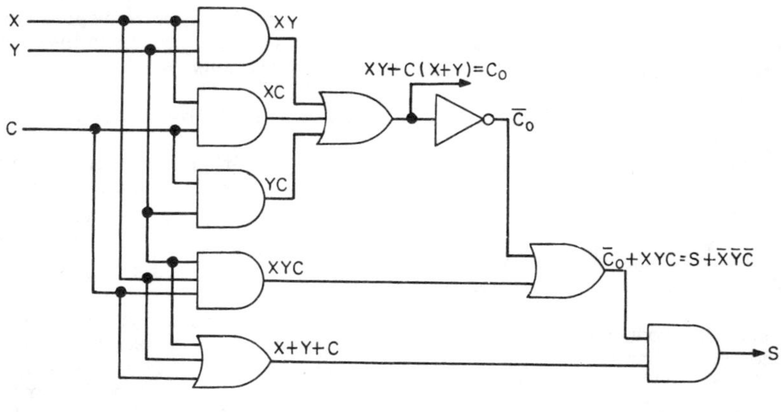

164.17

Figure 3-21.—Implementation of full adder.

Table 3-13. --Harvard Chart Columns

1	2	3	4	5	6	7	
A	B	C	AB	AC	BC	ABC	
~~$\bar{A}$~~	~~$\bar{B}$~~	~~$\bar{C}$~~	~~$\bar{A}\bar{B}$~~	~~$\bar{A}\bar{C}$~~	~~$\bar{B}\bar{C}$~~	~~$\bar{A}\bar{B}\bar{C}$~~	Row 1
~~$\bar{A}$~~	~~$\bar{B}$~~	~~C~~	~~$\bar{A}\bar{B}$~~	~~$\bar{A}C$~~	~~$\bar{B}C$~~	~~$\bar{A}\bar{B}C$~~	Row 2
~~$\bar{A}$~~	(B)	~~$\bar{C}$~~	~~$\bar{A}B$~~	~~$\bar{A}\bar{C}$~~	~~$B\bar{C}$~~	~~$\bar{A}B\bar{C}$~~	Row 3
~~$\bar{A}$~~	(B)	~~C~~	~~$\bar{A}B$~~	~~$\bar{A}C$~~	~~BC~~	~~$\bar{A}BC$~~	Row 4
~~A~~	~~$\bar{B}$~~	~~$\bar{C}$~~	~~$A\bar{B}$~~	~~$A\bar{C}$~~	~~$\bar{B}\bar{C}$~~	~~$A\bar{B}\bar{C}$~~	Row 5
~~A~~	~~$\bar{B}$~~	~~C~~	~~$A\bar{B}$~~	(AC)	~~$\bar{B}C$~~	~~$A\bar{B}C$~~	Row 6
~~A~~	(B)	~~$\bar{C}$~~	~~AB~~	~~$A\bar{C}$~~	~~$B\bar{C}$~~	~~$AB\bar{C}$~~	Row 7
~~A~~	(B)	~~C~~	~~AB~~	(AC)	~~BC~~	~~ABC~~	Row 8

2. Starting with the left column (column 1) cross out all terms which have been lined out in step 1. ($\bar{A}$ is lined out in rows 1 and 2 and A in row 5. Thus, all terms are lined out in the left column of this example.)

3. In column 2 only $\bar{B}$ is eliminated. Circle all B's for easy identification as a part of the final answer.

4. Going to the right, cross out all terms containing B in all rows with a circled B. (For example, in row 4 the terms $\bar{A}$B, BC, and $\bar{A}$BC are lined out.)

5. Continue with column C, etc.

6. In column AC the term AC is not crossed out, circle it.

7. Going to the right in the rows containing AC, cross out all other terms containing AC.

All terms in columns BC and ABC (columns 6 and 7) are now crossed out and the process ends. Only B and AC are left. The final answer is therefore; f = B + AC.

Proof of this solution by use of the simplification theorems or Veitch diagrams is left to the reader. While it is easier to use Veitch diagrams and simplification theorems with problems containing four variables or less, this is not the case when more variables are involved. Harvard charts are more suitable for solving problems with five or more variables.

BASIC ARITHMETIC OPERATIONS

As aforesaid, the relationship between logic and mathematics makes possible the use of logic circuits to perform arithmetic operations. For a simple illustration of this concept consider the arithmetic subtraction of two binary digits.

INHIBITOR CIRCUIT

There are three possible subtraction combinations of the two binary digits, 0 and 1. These are as follows:

M		S		
0	-	0	=	0
1	-	0	=	1
1	-	1	=	0

(The fourth, which is not possible without a borrow, is 0 - 1, which is not considered at this time.)

A circuit that will produce the correct result for each of the three possible subtractions is the "inhibitor" (fig. 3-22). The inhibitor symbol is shown in figure 3-22A. A truth table, showing the inputs and outputs from the circuit is shown in figure 3-22B.

The inhibitor circuit produces an output when there is a signal on M but not S. An inverter (small circle) connected in the S input path causes the S input to the AND-element to be inverted. (The interter output to the AND-element will be 1 when the S input is 0, and 0 when the S input is 1.) Thus the inhibitor output is 1 when (and only when) the voltage pulses at the input represents $M\overline{S}$. For all other input combinations the inhibitor output will be 0. The actions of this circuit thus satisfy the basic requirements of a binary subtractor. Although this is a relatively simple illustration of the relationship between mathematics and logic, it is representative of logic principles used to perform more complex arithmetic operations.

THE EXCLUSIVE-OR CIRCUIT

A conventional OR circuit (fig. 3-4C) with inputs A and B produces an output signal if:

(1) a signal exists at A; or
(2) a signal exists at B; or
(3) a signal exists at both A and B.

For certain applications a circuit is needed that will produce an output only for condition (1) or condition (2). This type circuit, called an exclusive-OR circuit will produce an output signal at F if a signal exists at A (but not at B) or at B (but not at A). The truth table for this function is shown in table 3-14. No signal is produced at the output if a signal exists at both inputs. In other words, an output is obtained only if the inputs are <u>different</u>. Symbols make this more obvious:

$$F = A\overline{B} + \overline{A}B$$

Before continuing, let us reexamine both of the terms at the right in the above equation. You can see that $A\overline{B}$ and $\overline{A}B$ (taken separately) are the symbols for an inhibitor. Therefore an exclusive-OR circuit is simply a set of two inhibitors connected by an OR, (fig. 3-23A).

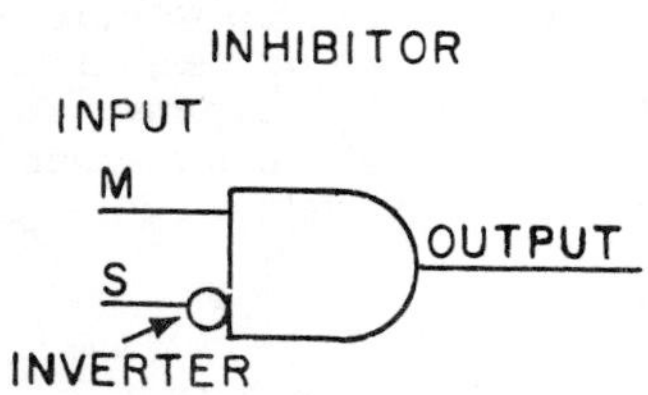

A SYMBOL

INPUT MINUEND (M) (A)	SUBTRAHEND (S) (B)	OUTPUT DIFFERENCE ($M\overline{S}$) ($A\overline{B}$)
0	0	0
1	0	1
1	1	0

B TRUTH TABLE

124.38.1

Figure 3-22.—Inhibitor.

Table 3-14. --Truth table for Exclusive--OR

INPUT		OUTPUT
A	B	F
1	1	0
1	0	1
0	1	1
0	0	0

The same circuit can be simplified to two inputs as shown in figure 3-23B. A third connection of this function is shown in figure 3-23C. Here both inputs feed simultaneously into an OR circuit and an AND circuit. The OR output is the "normal" input to an inhibitor circuit, while the AND output becomes the inhibiting input. Note that when the functions A+B and AB are both high i.e., equal to 1, the output at F is inhibited. Figure 3-23D shows the Exclusive-OR symbol.

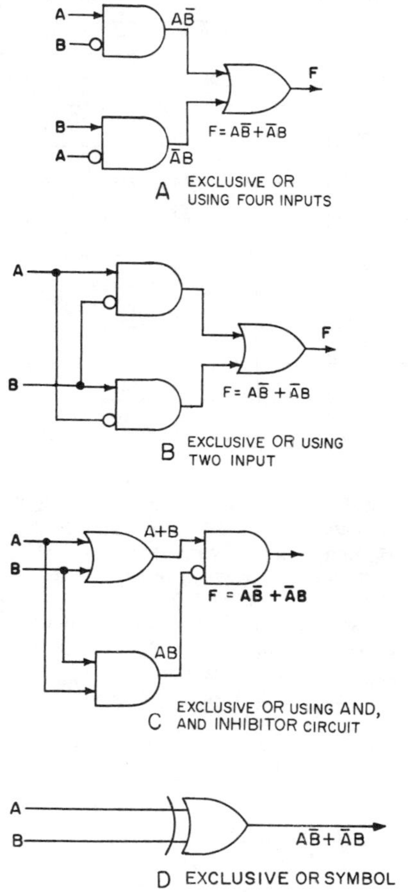

124.38.2
Figure 3-23.—Exclusive-OR circuit.

THE NOR OPERATION

The NOR operation (also called the "INCLUSIVE OR") is a combination of two of the three fundamental logical algebra operations, discussed earlier in this chapter. The NOT operation and the OR operation are used to form the NOR operation. The word NOR is a contraction of the two words NOT OR. The NOR equation (shown below) is written as a combination of OR and NOT operations. A NOR function is defined as follows:

1. The function is false when any one of the logical quantities is true.

2. The function is true when none of the logical quantities are true.

Expressed as a logical equation the NOR function is as follows:

$$f = \overline{A + B + C}$$

where f denotes a logical function (in this case the NOR function) and A, B, C denote true logical quantities. This equation states that f will be true only when A, B, and C are false simultaneously (none of the logical quantities are true). Further, f will be false when any one of the logical quantities (A, B, C) is true, or more than one of these logical quantities are true. The NOR operation is thus seen as an OR operation combined with a NOT operation. The truth table for the NOR function is as follows (Table 3-15).

Table 3-15. —Truth table for NOR function

$f = \overline{A + B + C}$			
Logical Quantities			Logical Function
A	B	C	f
0	0	0	1
0	0	1	0
0	1	0	0
0	1	1	0
1	0	0	0
1	0	1	0
1	1	0	0
1	1	1	0

A simple switching circuit (fig. 3-24) is used to represent the NOR operation. In this figure, A, B, and C are switches which, when closed are true and false when open, f is a lamp which is true when lit and false when not lit. The lamp will be lit (f is true) only when all the switches are open (A, B, and C are false). If any one or more than one of the switches are closed the lamp will not be lit.

The logic symbol used to represent the NOR operation is shown in figure 3-25.

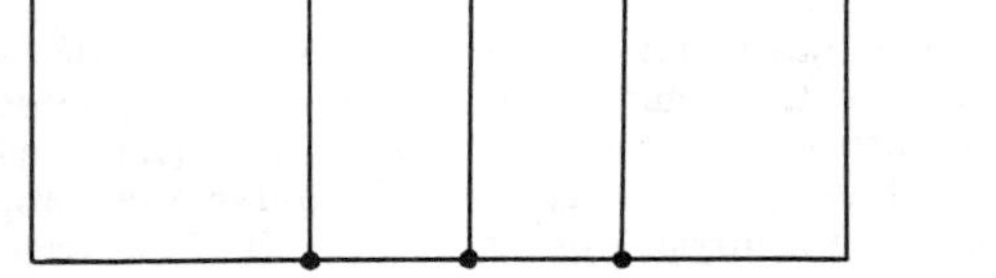

67.89.1

Figure 3-24.—Circuit representing the NOR function.

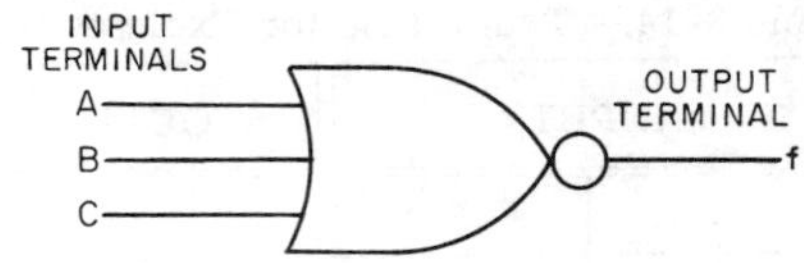

67.89.2

Figure 3-25.—Symbol for NOR operation.

THE NAND OPERATION

The NAND operation is also a combination of two of the three fundamental logical algebra operations. The NOT operation and the AND operation are used to form the NAND operation. The word NAND is a contraction of the two words NOT AND. The equation (shown below) is written as a combination of AND and NOT operations. A NAND function is defined as follows:

1. The function is true when any one of the logical quantities is false, or more than one of the logical quantities is false.

2. The function is false when all of the logical quantities are true.

Expressed as a logical equation the NAND function is as follows:

$$f = \overline{A\ B\ C}$$

where: f denotes a logical function (in this case the NAND function). A, B, C denote logical quantities.

This equation states that f will be true when any one of the logical quantities is false, or more than one of the logical quantities are false. The logical function, f, will be false when all of the logical quantities are true. The NAND operation is thus seen as an AND operation followed by a NOT operation. The truth table for the NAND function is shown in Table 3-16. The switching circuit in figure 3-26 may be used as an illustration of the NAND operation. A, B, and C are switches which when closed are true and false when open; f is a lamp which is true when lit and false when not lit. The lamp will be lit (f is true) when any one or more than one of the switches are open. The lamp will not be lit (f is false) only when all switches are closed (A, B, and C are true).

The logic symbol used to represent the NAND operation is shown in figure 3-27.

Table 3-16. —Truth table for NAND function

$f = \overline{A\ B\ C}$			
Logical Quantities			Logical Function
A	B	C	f
0	0	0	1
0	0	1	1
0	1	0	1
0	1	1	1
1	0	0	1
1	0	1	1
1	1	0	1
1	1	1	0

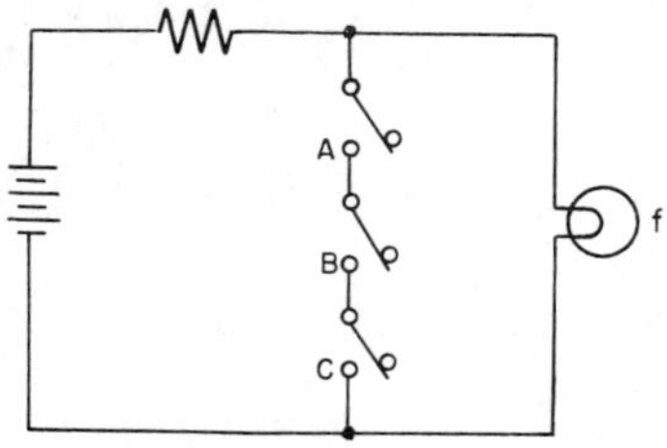

67.90
Figure 3-26.—Circuit representing the NAND function.

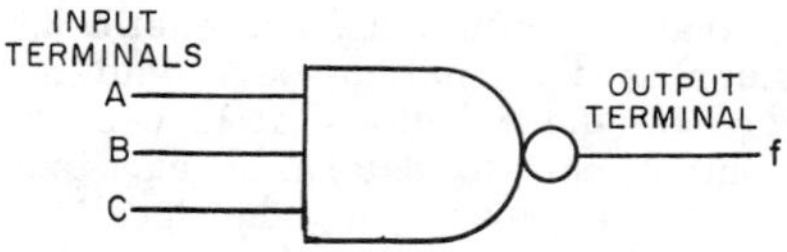

67.90
Figure 3-27.—Symbol for NAND operation.

Chapter 4

CONTROL UNIT

The control unit is the coordinator or director of all operations within the computer. Its actions include: directing the reading of information from memory; controlling the inputs and outputs of the computer; directing the operations within the arithmetic unit; and transferring information back into memory. To perform these actions, it is necessary for the control unit to determine each operation that is to be performed, the location of the data involved in the operation, and of course, where to place the results.

Actually, the control section must be able to tie together any circuit or group of circuits necessary to perform any operation capable of being performed by the computer. One might expect, and rightfully so, that a maze of components, wires, and circuits must be contained in the computer. However, this is minimized somewhat by design and by using a single circuit to perform many functions.

This chapter treats the control section by (1) considering the method of representing computer instructions; (2) discussing the functional operation of some circuits contained in the control section; and (3) discussing a few of the ways by which the control section coordinates the computer operations.

SPECIAL PURPOSE AND GENERAL PURPOSE COMPUTERS

There are two types of digital computers, special purpose and general purpose. Special purpose computers, as implied by the name, are wired to perform specific types of operations in a planned sequence. Changing the operation and the sequence by which they are performed necessitates changes in the wiring of the computer. Of course, this limits the usefulness of this type of computer to special applications where the solution of the problem is not modified by prevailing conditions.

General purpose computers, again as the name implies, are much more versatile since their circuits are designed to perform many different types of operations depending on the programmed instructions. The general purpose computer can be made to alter its sequence of operations based on conditions which occur while solving the problem. Thus, the programmed sequence can be changed or jumped to any step in the program on "condition," i.e., if certain conditions prevail. The sequence may also be altered "unconditionally," i.e., without regard to conditions.

This text discusses the operation of general purpose computers although many of the circuits and procedures are common to both types.

The general purpose computer performs its actions as determined by a list of instructions called a program which has been previously read into its storage or memory section in the form of computer words. For this reason, the general purpose computer is also referred to as a "stored-program" computer. Each computer instruction word is intelligible to the computer and is interpreted by the control unit and executed in sequence unless conditions derived during the calculations dictate otherwise.

INSTRUCTION WORD

It has been pointed out in an earlier chapter that computer circuits respond to "on-off" pulses. The presence of a pulse usually represents a 1 condition, whereas the absence of a pulse represents a zero condition. Each of the on-off pulses in an instruction word is referred to as a "bit."

Table 4-1 shows how 15 binary bits (represented in octal form) are used to represent a number.

Table 4-1. —Octal Representation of 010111101110011

OCTAL REPRESENTATION	2	7	5	6	3
BINARY REPRESENTATION	010	111	101	110	011

Significantly, the number represented in table 4-1 may not be interpreted by the control section as twenty-seven thousand five hundred and sixty-three, but rather as an instruction word. The two leftmost OCTAL digits may be a computer code for "READ-OUT." The remaining portion of the number (563) may be interpreted as an address in memory. Thus, the computer would interpret the group of characters represented in table 4-1 as an instruction word, meaning to read-out the contents of memory address 563.

Computer words also represent data, and in fact, it is often not possible (by visual inspection) to distinguish between data and instructions. It is therefore necessary to exercise care when organizing words in storage and to keep close track of the location of instructions and data stored in memory.

OPERATION CODE SECTION

Each instruction word contains at least two sections (table 4-2). The first section (65 in this case), consisting of one or more digits, indicates the function or operation code, i.e., ADD, SUBTRACT, etc. The second part can

Table 4-2. —Basic Instruction Word

	Operation Code		Address (or OPERAND)			
OCTAL REPRESENTATION	6	5	5	3	4	0
BINARY REPRESENTATION	110	101	101	011	100	000

be the operand, although it most frequently contains the address (or addresses) of the data (operand) involved. The operand portion of the instruction word may be the number to be used in a calculation; it may be the address in memory of the number to be used; it may indicate the number of operations to be performed, i.e., left shift the contents of a register x places, repeat the next instruction x times; or it may be the address into which data will be placed, or from which it will be moved.

The number of digits used to represent the operation code is sometimes determined by the number of different types of operations the computer can perform. If it is assumed that a given computer can only add, subtract, multiply, and divide, the particular operation code could be represented by the four possible combinations of two binary digits. Here, 00 could represent ADD; 01 could represent subtract; 10, multiply, and 11, divide. Thus, the address/operand section of the word will be preceded by one of these codes depending on the operation desired.

Generally, computers can perform many more than ④ operations as described above. In fact, some computers can perform more than 200 different types of operations. Where this is true, the operation code must contain a sufficient number of digits to represent any operation desired.

ADDRESS SECTION

The second part of the instruction word, namely the address section, generally represents the memory address (or addresses) of the data to be operated on (operand). It should be understood that in the storedprogram computer, the instruction word does not necessarily contain the operand but may be the address of the operand. The operand usually appears in the instruction word if it is small enough.

To further explain this point, assume that a certain computer has 32,000 memory cells, each of which can store a computer word (either an instruction word or an operand). Assume further that the operation code 134 means "ADD to the contents of the accumulator." During the load routine, instructions may be loaded into addresses 00000 to 20000. The remaining memory registers are filled with information words (data).

Now assume that memory address 00748 contains the instruction 13430155. This is interpreted by the computer as "ADD to the contents of the accumulator the contents of memory address 30155." In this case, 134 is the operation code and 30155 is the address of the operand.

Some computers operate with word lengths which vary from word to word and are called variable word length computers. Others use fixed word lengths wherein each word contains a fixed number of digits.

The use of either of the two types of words has certain advantages and the choice of one over the other is a design feature. The fixed word length computer does not always lend itself to an economic conservation of memory cells since words which are normally shorter than the fixed limit must be filled with the number of zeroes (spaces) necessary to complete the word, or additional instructions must be written to pack and unpack the data. Several short words could therefore waste a large number of memory spaces. On the other hand, fixed word lengths which are compatible with the number of bits that can be stored in a memory address facilitate orderly storage and simplify the instructions necessary to store-in or extract-from the memory section.

In the variable word length computer, one block of data may be stored in one, two, or more cells (depending on the length of the word). Thus, variable word-length computers make possible far more compact storage of information in memory by filling up all spaces (except for word separators). When this method is used, the stored information is not referenced by location alone, but by its position relative to other information in the program. Instruction words must therefore be made more complex in order to locate the correct information to be used in a given operation.

SINGLE AND MULTIPLE ADDRESS COMPUTERS

Although the number of instructions necessary to solve a given problem can be minimized by using the multiple address computer, instructions which reference a single address are much simpler. Generally a single-address computer is one in which each instruction word references a single address in memory. (A general usage of single-address instructions is explained earlier using Table 4-2.) This type of computer begins its operation at the first or some specified instruction in the program and continues by taking instruction words one at a time from memory in sequence unless interrupted by a stop or jump instruction.

For example, ADD THE CONTENTS OF ADDRESS A TO THE ACCUMULATOR, is a single-address instruction because only one memory address is referenced (address A). A variation of the single-address instruction is a "replace ADD" instruction, which may read "ADD THE CONTENTS OF ADDRESS A TO THE ACCUMULATOR AND REPLACE IN A. Again only one address is referenced.

Another variation of the single-address method where the word length of the registers permits, is to place two instruction words in a single memory address. This method is used in the Control Data 1604-A Computer (Chapter 1, fig. 1-3), which is widely used by the Navy. In this type machine, two instructions will be performed each time a word is read. This method is illustrated in Table 4-3.

Table 4-3. —Two-Instruction Words Using Single-Address Operation.

First instruction word		Second instruction word	
OPERATION	ADDRESS	OPERATION	ADDRESS

The left instruction is usually executed first, followed by the execution of the right instruction. Where this method can be used, it increases the operating speed of the computer by making fewer references to memory and also provides a far more efficient use of memory spaces.

A two-address computer word is shown in table 4-4. As the name implies, the word consists of a single operation code and the two addresses (A and B) which are included in the operations. An instruction for this type of machine may read ADD THE CONTENTS OF ADDRESS A TO THE CONTENTS OF ADDRESS B. Here, two addresses are referenced by a single instruction. The "replace ADD" instruction may also be used such as, ADD THE CONTENTS OF ADDRESS A TO THE CONTENTS OF ADDRESS B AND REPLACE IN A.

Table 4-4. —Two-Address Computer Word.

OPERATION CODE	ADDRESS A	ADDRESS B

The two-address instruction word is sometimes used as illustrated in table 4-5. Because the instruction specifies only one address involved in the computer operations, this word is sometimes called a one and one-half or one-plus-one address word to distinguish it from the conventional two-address word.

Table 4-5. —Variation of Two-Address Instruction Word

OPERATION CODE	ADDRESS A	ADDRESS OF NEXT INSTRUCTION

The three-address instruction word (table 4-6) generally contains the operation code, two addresses (A and B) and an address C for storing the results of the operation performed on the information from the A and B addresses.

Table 4-6. —Three-Address Instruction Word

OPERATION CODE	ADDRESS A	ADDRESS C	ADDRESS C (for storing the result of A modified by B)

The four-address word (table 4-7) contains the operation code, two data addresses (A and B), address C for storage, and the fourth address which is the address of the next instruction to be performed.

The number of addresses in each instruction word is a design feature. Words containing more than four addresses do not seem practicable at this time.

Table 4-7. —Four-Address Word.

OPERATION	ADDRESS A	ADDRESS B	ADDRESS C FOR STORAGE OF RESULTS	ADDRESS D NEXT INSTRUCTION

CONTROL CIRCUITS

To be able to understand the circuits used to perform control operations, it is first necessary to study and understand the functional operation of such circuits as OR, AND, NOR, NAND, counters, flip-flops, decoders, and inverters which are used extensively in the control unit as well as throughout the computer. Each of these circuits uses semiconductor or solid-state devices such as the silicon diode or transistor. The operation of solid-state components is treated in the training course, Basic Electronics, NavPers 10087-B.

The OR, AND, NOT (inverter), NOR, and NAND circuits are introduced in the discussion of Boolean Algebra in chapter 3 of this course and are not repeated here. An understanding of the material treated is important to an understanding of the circuits which follow.

SERIAL AND PARALLEL OPERATION

Computers may process information pulses in either serial or parallel form. In serial form the pulses occur as a timed series, one pulse at a time (fig. 4-1). In parallel operation, all pulses occur simultaneously and are transferred within the computer on separate transmission lines. Serial and parallel data are explained in detail in a later chapter.

The counter circuit shown in figure 4-2 can be used to perform several computer operations. For example, if we consider a series of toggle pulses at the input to the first flip-flop, say 4 pulses, the counter will advance to a state

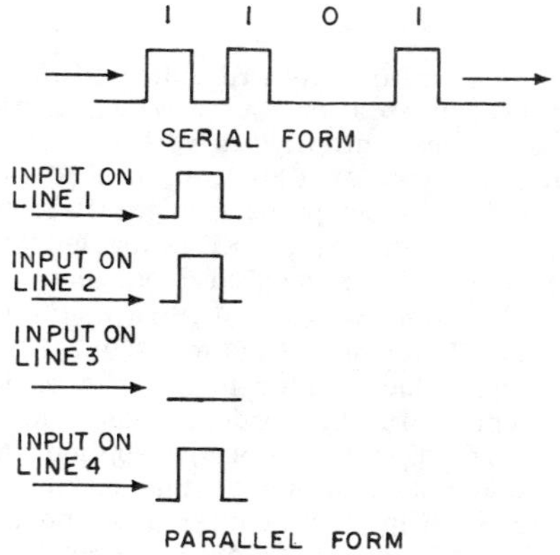

124.29

Figure 4-1.—Serial and parallel coded pulses.

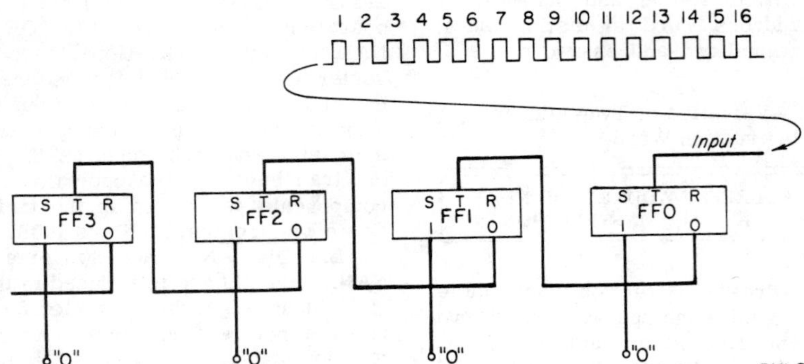

OUTPUT of FF3	OUTPUT of FF2	OUTPUT of FF 1	OUTPUT of FF0	PULSE COUNT
0	0	0	1	1
0	0	1	0	2
0	0	1	1	3
0	1	0	0	4
0	1	0	1	5
0	1	1	0	6
0	1	1	1	7
1	0	0	0	8
1	0	0	1	9
1	0	1	0	10
1	0	1	1	11
1	1	0	0	12
1	1	0	1	13
1	1	1	0	14
1	1	1	1	15
0	0	0	0	0

124.28

Figure 4-2.—Flip-flop counter.

where the set outputs will indicate 0100, which may represent a computer word. Assuming all FFs are initially in the 0 state, each input pulse toggles FF0, i.e., if FF0 is in the "0" state an input pulse changes it to the "1" state. Each subsequent FF is toggled when the preceeding FF is toggled from the 1 to the 0 state. (The operation of flip-flops is treated in Basic Electronics, NavPers 10087-B.)

Because the counter is a static device and will remain in the condition described above unless subsequent pulses are applied, the circuit remembers or stores this count. In this respect, a flip-flop counter may be used as a REGISTER, since it stores a computer word.

A second application of this circuit is seen when it is assumed that five additional pulses are applied to the counter input. The count now advances to 1001 (9) which is the sum of the two input pulse series. This process is called serial addition. This circuit arrangement thus acts as a basic accumulator.

PARALLEL ADDER

The circuit shown in figure 4-3 is used to illustrate the basic example of parallel addition. Note that 4 binary digits (bits) are received in parallel, (one at the set input of each flip-flop). This input is the "augend". The four toggle inputs accommodate the addend. If we assume that the number stored in the counter (the augend) is 0011 or 3, as shown in the first line below the set terminals) and the input pulses applied to the toggle inputs are 1010 (10), the counter will add these pulses. In

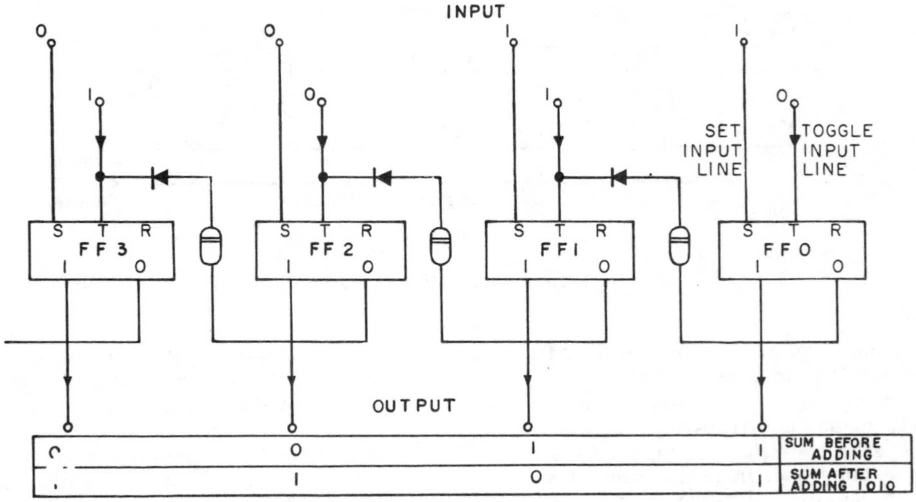

124.30

Figure 4-3. —Parallel adder.

the following explanation of the addition process it is assumed that the set position of the flip-flop, as well as a significant pulse, is represented by a 1 condition. Conversely, a reset output, as well as a no significant pulse input, represents 0.

A delay line is connected between successive flip-flops. The output of each flip-flop is used to provide a significant pulse to the delay circuit on its left only when the set output of that flip-flop changes from 1 to 0 and the reset output changes from 0 to 1.

A 1 input, whether at the toggle input or from the associated delay line, causes a flip-flop to change its state. Thus the flip-flop will change whenever it receives a 1 pulse from either of these sources.

Because the augend is 0011, the following changes will occur when the addend (1010) is received.

1. FF2 and FF0 receive no significant pulse from the toggle input and remain unchanged for the present.
2. FF3 and FF1 do receive 1-state toggle pulses and both change states. FF3 now reads 1 and FF1 now reads 0.
3. Of the four flip-flops only FF1 has changes from 1 to 0. Therefore, it is the only flip-flop to send a 1 pulse (carry) through its delay line to FF2.
4. This carry pulse changes FF2 from 0 to 1. The adder now reads 1101 (13), which is the correct sum of 0011 (3) and 1010 (10).

Note that the diodes prevent pulses from the toggle input (assumed to be positive-going in this case) from interfering with the adjoining flip-flops, while the delay lines prevent the pulses being fed to the adder and any carry pulses from appearing at any flip-flop input simultaneously. In a sense, then, the delay units are used to perform the carry operation.

RING COUNTER

Several flip-flops can be connected to form a ring counter (fig. 4-4); the name is derived from the fact that the output of the last flip-flop (FF3) is sometimes connected back to the input of the first (FF0). This is not a requirement, however, as other means can be provided to initiate the action in the first circuit at the proper time.

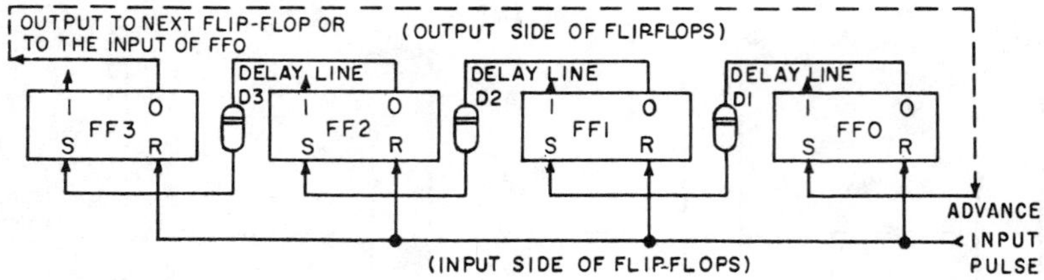

124.31

Figure 4-4. —Ring counter.

In many applications of this circuit, only one of the flip-flops is in the "on" (set) condition at a given time. An advance input pulse, which is applied to all flip-flops simultaneously, causes the "on" flip-flop to change its conducting state, and, in turn, transmit an input pulse to the next flip-flop to the left. The pulse output from the affected flip-flop is delayed until after the trailing edge of the advance input pulse has dropped to zero to prevent double-triggering. However, after the delay period, the input pulse to the flip-flop changes the conducting state in that circuit from "off" to "on".

The next advance pulse will cause the "on" condition to be established in the next flip-flop. This action continues until the "on" condition has advanced from FF0 to FF3. A subsequent advance pulse will cause the "on" condition to be transferred either to FF0 or to the next flip-flop in the ring.

The circuit in figure 4-5 is essentially a ring counter to which input paths are added for the purpose of reading-in (in parallel) the desired binary digits. As stated before, the four flip-flops make up a register. Because the action within the ring counter is to shift one digit one place (either left or right, but left in this case), an advance input pulse applied simultaneously to each flip-flop in the register will cause the bit previously stored in a stage to be shifted to the next higher order flip-flop. The bit previously stored in FF0 will be shifted to FF1; that previously stored in FF1 will be shifted to FF2; the

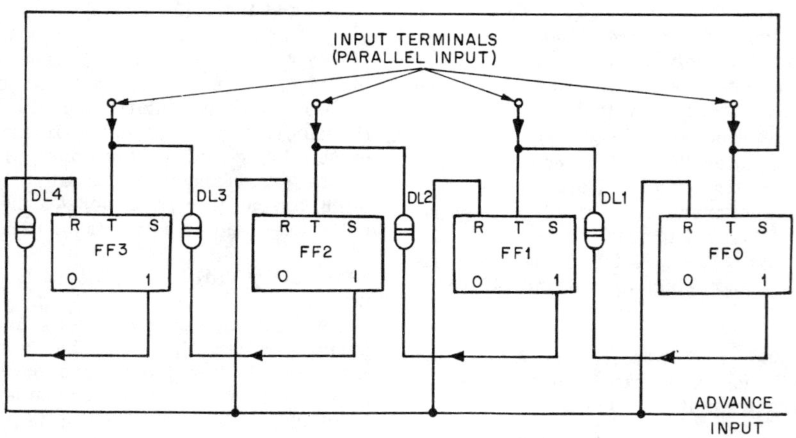

124.32

Figure 4-5. --Left shift register.

FF2 bit will move to FF3; and finally the bit previously in FF3 will be transferred to FF0. Thus, if 1011 has been stored before the arrival of the advance pulse, the advance pulse flips FF3, FF1, and FF0 from S to R. Slightly later a pulse from delay line 1 flips FF1 from R to S. Delay line 2 transmits a pulse that flips FF2 from R to S. Delay line 3 does not transmit a pulse, and FF3 remains in the reset condition. Delay line 4 transmits a pulse that flips FF0 from R to S. Thus, the 0111 condition is stored, This type register is called a "shift register." Left-shift registers are used extensively in computers to perform multiplication (as will be shown in the next chapter). Right-shift registers are used in the division process.

The ways in which flip-flops can be used to perform computer operations are too numerous to consider here. The reader must therefore study flip-flops and the application of these circuits as presented in this discussion until he is certain of their operation. Only with a thorough understanding will he be able to comprehend other applications of this circuit which are not so elaborately explained.

DELAY LINES

It has been stated that one of the basic functions of the control unit is to time all operations within the computer. Further, it was stated that the time to execute an operation depends on the type of operation to be performed. For example, a multiply operation generally requires more time than an add operation, a divide operation requires more time than a subtract, etc. To perform in this manner, the control unit must (1) contain circuits which will generate the basic timing pulses say in a stabilized multivibrator, crystal oscillator, or delay line oscillator, (2) provide pulses to start an operation at a certain time; and (3) contain circuits which will count the timing signals and produce a pulse which will terminate a particular operation after a specified time or after its completion.

The circuit in figure 4-6 (called an artificial transmission line, or delay line) is used to explain one of the basic timing principles. The action is explained in more detail later in this chapter.

If a voltage is applied to the input terminals of the line, a definite amount of time passes (dependent upon the number of LC sections) before the voltage appears at the output terminals. The LC sections thus give the line the ability to delay the output voltage.

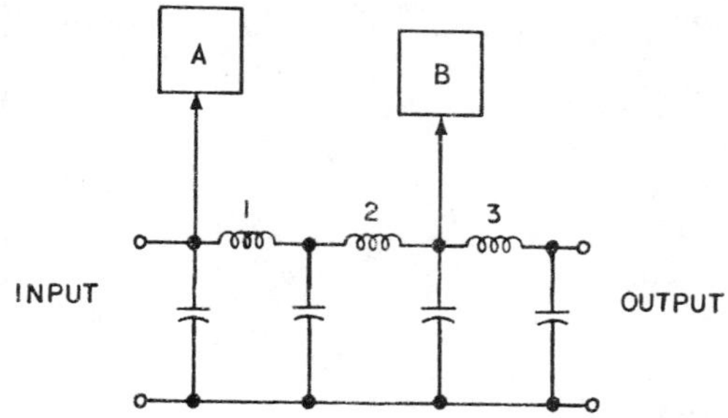

124.33

Figure 4-6. —Delay line.

Assume that a voltage must be applied to the circuit in block B one or two microseconds after it has been applied to block A. This condition can be satisfied merely by constructing the 1 and 2 sections of the line for the desired delay.

To avoid the bulkiness of an actual transmission line, an artificial line may be built of coils and capacitors. Such lines have approximately the same characteristics as actual lines but occupy a smaller space. This is the usual method of constructing delay lines.

Now suppose it is necessary to read into a register containing FF2, FF1 and FF0 (fig. 4-7) in parallel form and to read the information out (at 1.5 μs intervals) in serial form. One method of performing this operation is described below. Initially all flip-flops are cleared or reset by an input pulse on the reset line. The information to be stored (in the form of 1's and 0's) is fed over parallel lines to the appropriate flip-flops. A 1 input to any flip-flop will produce a 1 set output. In the following discussion the set output is taken to represent the 1 state of the flip-flop.

Assume that the multivibrator feeds a single pulse to delay line, D1, and to the AND circuit, A1. Because the set output of FF2 is in the 1 state, the coincidence of the inputs to the AND element (A1) causes this circuit to produce a 1 output during the period t_0. This pulse is read out at J_1.

The pulse applied to D1 at t_0 emerges from the delay line at t_1 and is applied simultane-

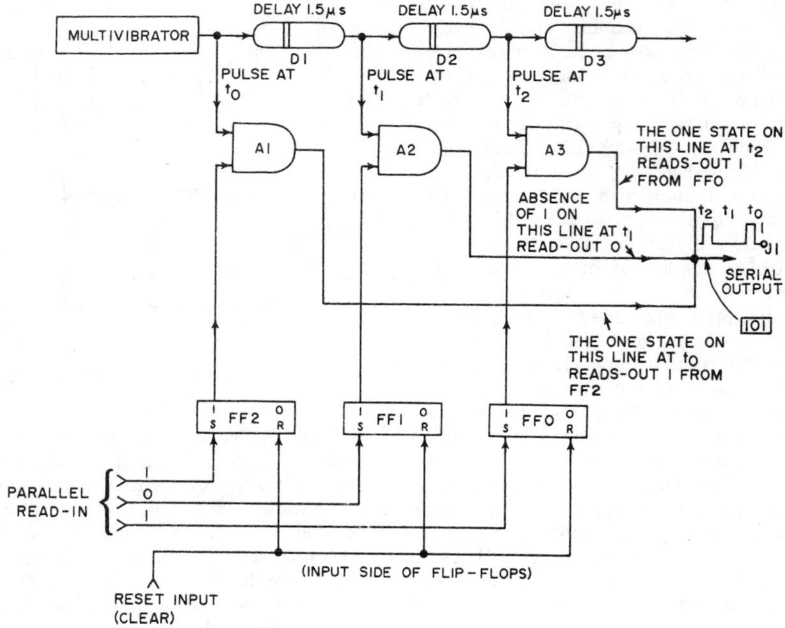

124.34

Figure 4-7. --One method of using delay lines for serial read-out.

ously to D2 and A2. The presence of this pulse at one input of A2 will not cause the AND element to produce an output (the set output of FF1 to A2 is 0) and the read-out at J_1 at time t_1 is 0. The pulse delivered from D2 at time t_2 is applied simultaneously to D3 and A3. Because the set output of FF0 is in the 1 state, the A3 AND circuit will produce an output at J_1 at time t_2. Thus, the serial read-out of the register is accomplished at the specified intervals, as 101.

TIMING CIRCUITS

Timing circuits in the computer ensure proper timing of events. Timing pulses enable some circuits and thereby permit certain operations to begin and certain other operations to be terminated. A few microseconds later the return of the enabling pulses to some new state signifies the expiration of time for the selected operations. Immediately after disabling one group of circuits, enabling timing pulses are applied to others and another set of operations is performed. This process of enabling some circuits and disabling others in sequence is repeated over and over again until the program has been completely executed.

CLOCK PHASES

A circuit arrangement called a "Master Clock" provides the main timing signals within a computer. A representative example of a master clock is contained in the Univac Digital Trainer (UDT) shown in figure 4-8. The control console is shown in figure 4-9. Some of the characteristics of this circuit are treated below.

The master clock system (fig 4-10) utilizes a four-phase output with a complete cycle time of 1.6 microseconds.

151.8

Figure 4-8. —Univac digital trainer and flexowriter.

The four clock phases are actually the master clock output pulses arranged in groups of fours. In the following discussion we will assume that the four phases are obtained from an arrangement of gates and multivibrators in such a way that only one phase is high in any given .4 microsecond period.

SEQUENCES

A "sequence" is a means of executing an instruction as a series of logical commands separated in time. The timing is achieved by a combination of the master clock output and a form of ring counter called a "timing chain." Although the specific function of a given sequence varies from one computer to another, a representative computer executes each instruction by determining the types of operations to be performed and then selects one or more of the sequences, although only one sequence is ever executed at any one time.

1. The A sequence reads the next instruction from memory, determines whether jump, stop, or abort conditions have been met and selects the next sequence.
2. The B sequence acquires the contents of the index register to allow for operand modification, if specified by the instruction.
3. The C sequence performs arithmetic and logical operations.
4. The D sequence acquires or disposes of the operand according to the requirements of the current instruction.

Assume that during the execution of the A sequence, it is necessary to clear a particular register and transfer data to that register from another. As a particular timing chain flip-flop is set, a command enable signal is sent to clear and load the receiving register. On a phase 4, the clear command will be fully enabled and the register will be cleared. On the next phase, phase 1, the loading gates are fully enabled and the register is loaded.

ENCODERS AND DECODERS

It has been stated that computers are designed to operate on data which is in the binary form, that is, either 1 or 0. In most computers, however, it is not practicable to enter numbers and other information into the computer in binary form, as this would require the programmer to spend too much time in the detailed effort of accurately representing large numbers of complicated alphabets and symbols.

Likewise it is not usually desirable to present the final computer output in binary form as this requires too much time in reading and interpreting. Thus it is necessary to perform conversion on both input and output information.

Computers are generally equipped with ENCODERS (units which change discrete inputs into a combination of coded outputs) and DECODERS which transform the internal binary data to its more conventional form at the computer output. Thus the programmer can use the familiar decimal system or the octal system to program the computer, depending on the encoder to convert the data to the binary form as required internally by the computer. Also the output of the internal circuits of the computer is changed by the decoder back into the familiar decimal form. The basic principle involved is illustrated in figure 4-11.

The simple decimal-to-binary encoder (fig. 4-12) receives any one of 10 decimal numbers

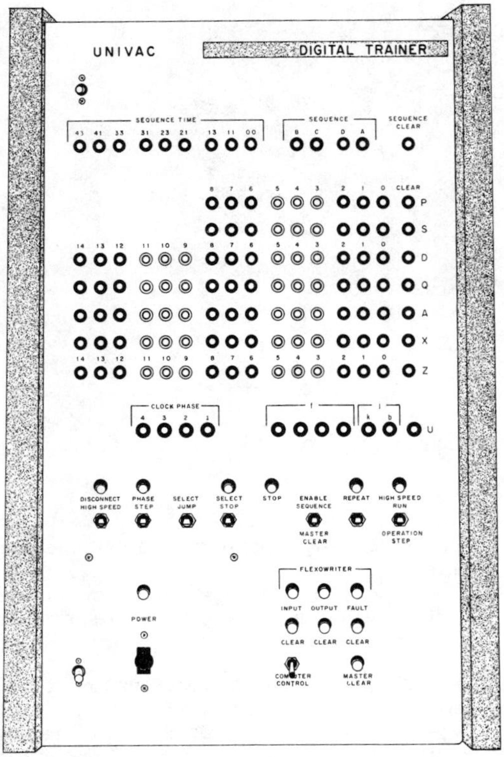

151.10

Figure 4-9. —Control console.

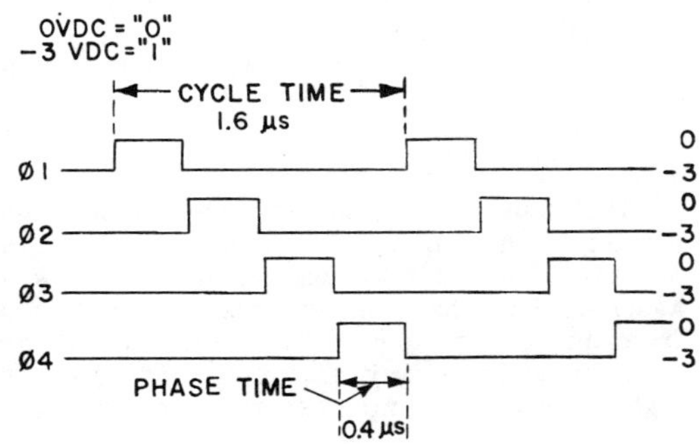

151.9

Figure 4-10. —Timing sequence for four-phase master clock.

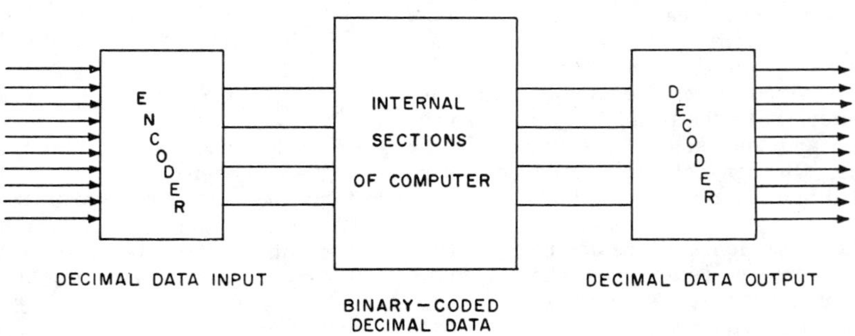

124.48

Figure 4-11. —Basic principle of encoding and decoding.

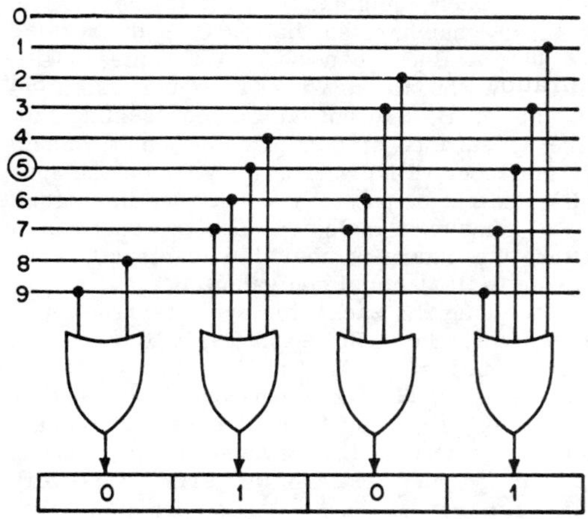

124.49
Figure 4-12. —Decimal-to-binary encoder.

at its input and produces a binary-coded decimal output. This action can be seen by a study of the circuit using OR logic. There are more complex types of encoders, as will be studied later.

The basic principle of binary-to-decimal decoding (fig. 4-13) uses flip-flops which provide the inputs to the AND element which in turn produces the decimal output. This type circuit produces an output only when the right combination of flip-flop outputs is applied to the inputs of the AND element. Appropriate use of either inverters or flip-flop output connections makes possible the decoding of any binary-coded decimal digit.

Although only binary-coded decimal conversions are illustrated here, similar procedures can be used to encode and decode numbers in all number systems.

A more advanced form of encoding and decoding uses a matrix to translate between number systems. A matrix is an array of circuit components such as wires, diodes, magnetic cores, and relays, which perform a specific function, such as converting from one numerical system to another. In mathematics, "matrix" means a set of terms which operate on one type of number to produce a second type; in other words, a number translator.

As discussed earlier, binary arithmetic uses only the two digits, 1 and 0. The manner in which these digits are arranged determines their numerical value. The advantage in using the binary system in digital computers is that

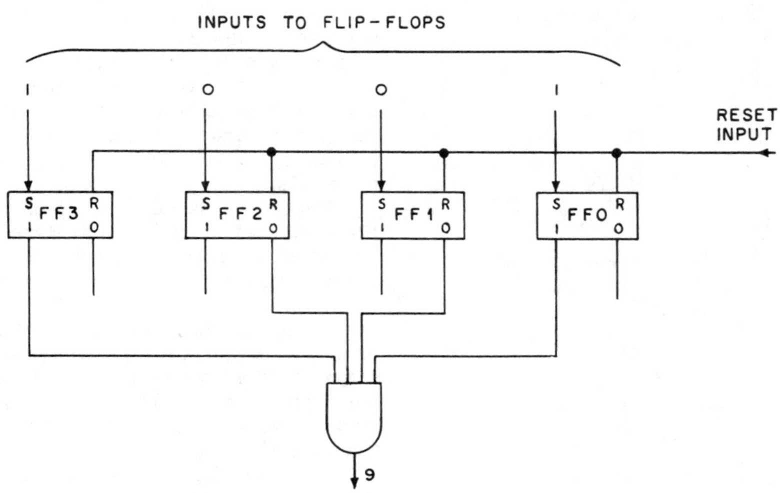

124.50

Figure 4-13. —Binary-to-decimal decoder.

the two digits (1 and 0) can be easily represented by the two possible stable states of certain electronic circuits and components.

The operation of a matrix is based upon certain principles which were first investigated by Mathematician James Sylvester in the mid-nineteenth century. You will recall that for any particular circuit heretofore discussed, a single output is produced if some specific combination of inputs exists. Further, there is a fixed number of possible input combinations (depending upon the number of inputs used) each one of which is called a "minterm". A circuit with two inputs, for example, has four minterms: $A\,B$, $\bar{A}\,B$, $A\,\bar{B}$, and $\bar{A}\,\bar{B}$. A three-input circuit has eight minterms: $A\,B\,C$, $A\,B\,\bar{C}$, $A\,\bar{B}\,C$, $\bar{A}\,B\,C$, $A\,\bar{B}\,\bar{C}$, $A\,\bar{B}\,\bar{C}$, $\bar{A}\,\bar{B}\,C$, and $\bar{A}\,B\,\bar{C}$. Thus it can be said that for "n" inputs, there are 2^n minterms. Consequently, for 2 inputs, there 2^2 or 4 minterms; for 3 inputs there are 2^3 or 8 minterms; and for 4 inputs there are 2^4 or 16 minterms, etc. Each minterm indicates one of the possible input combinations that can occur.

The logic matrix differs in one respect from other circuits discussed in this chapter in that a matrix with "n" inputs has 2^n outputs—one output for each minterm. It produces a signal at one specific output terminal for any one combination of inputs.

Consider the simplified illustration in figure 4-14. The matrix has three inputs, A, B, and C, each of which can be in either the 1 or 0

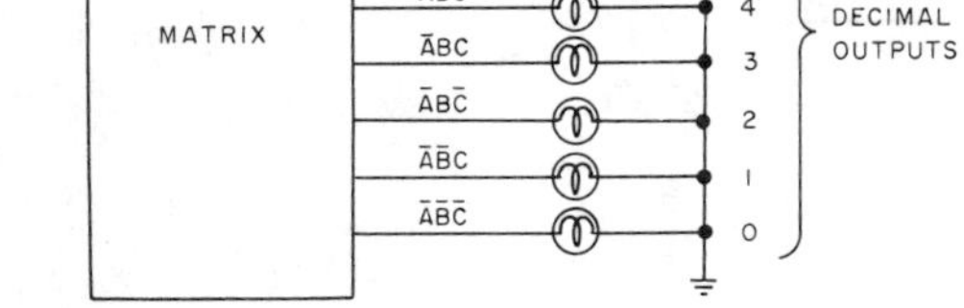

124.51
Figure 4-14. —Three-input matrix.

state. Each combination of digits represents a binary number, so that ABC is interpreted as 111, $\bar{A}\,\bar{B}\,\bar{C}$ means 000, $\bar{A}\,B\,\bar{C}$ means 010, etc. In the illustration, a signal exists at A and at B, but not at C, representing 110. The appearance of this combination of signals at the input will produce a signal on one specific matrix output. By connecting this output to a numbered indicating device, such as a lamp, the binary number 110 is directly converted to its decimal equivalent, 6.

In general, each minterm represents a specific number. For example, $\bar{A}\bar{B}\bar{C}$ = 000 = 0, $\bar{A}\bar{B}C$ = 001 = 1, $\bar{A}B\bar{C}$ = 010 = 2, . . . and so on to ABC = 111 = 7. In order to decode higher numbers, the number of inputs and outputs must be increased. Because a logic matrix has an output for each minterm, and every minterm represents a binary number, each output can be labeled with the appropriate decimal value.

Consider the circuit in figure 4-15, which is used to decode the binary coded decimal number 1001 (9). When the magnitude of the voltage at any one of the flip-flop outputs decreases below the bus voltage, one or more of the diodes conduct. Because the resistances are small and in parallel, most of the applied voltage is distributed across R_B. When, and only when, the flip-flops are in the condition shown, that is from left-to-right set, reset, reset, set, all diodes will be cut off and because of the high R load the voltage at the output rises in the positive direction. This rise in voltage indicates that a binary coded decimal 9 is stored in the flip-flops. Similarly, any binary number can be decoded by connecting the diodes to the proper flip-flop terminals.

A more versatile form of diode matrix is illustrated in figure 4-16. Here, diodes are connected to flip-flop terminals in a manner which will decode any one of 8 conditions representing 000 through 111. The diodes are normally conducting (low voltage or zero output) except when the associated flip-flop output is positive going. (This back-biases the diode.) Thus, a 0 is produced at the matrix output (rise in voltage from the zero level) when all flip-flops are in the reset condition. (Reset terminal is positive going.) A 1 output is produced when both FF2 and FF1 are reset and FF0 is set. A 5 is produced when FF2 and FF0 are set and FF1 is reset. In other words the set outputs of FF2 and FF0 and the

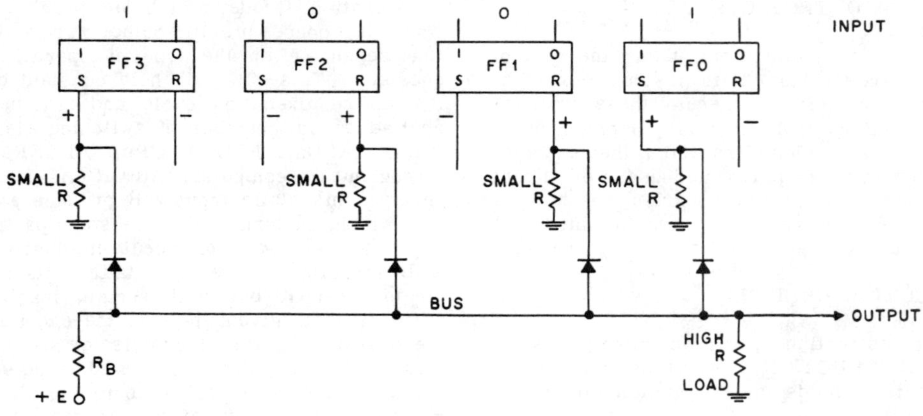

124.52

Figure 4-15. —Simple flip-flop decoder.

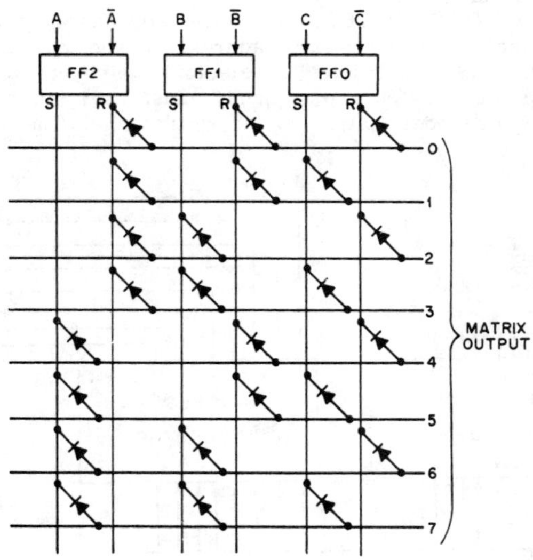

124.53

Figure 4-16. —Diode decoder matrix.

reset output of FF1 are positive going so that all diodes on the 5-level are cut off and the output voltage on that level is positive going. A study of the matrix for various combinations of flip-flop outputs reveal the conditions which exist when representing any decimal digit from 0 to 7. Higher order numbers can be decoded by increasing the number of flip-flops and connecting additional diodes to indicate higher counts.

CONTROL OPERATIONS

The two basic functions within the control sections are (1) to obtain instructions from memory, and (2) to execute these instructions. The control function performs these actions in two cycles—first fetch, then execute. The fetch cycle is performed under the direct influence of the stored program so that the instructions are read in a fashion which will lead to the correct solution of the problem.

INSTRUCTION REGISTER

Each instruction read from memory is fed to an INSTRUCTION REGISTER (fig. 4-17). This register holds the instruction throughout the execution cycle.

Operation Register

The instruction register is divided into two smaller registers; the OPERATION REGISTER, which receives and holds the operation code part of the word, and the ADDRESS REGISTER which receives the address of the operand. The operation code is fed to a decoder matrix or operation decoder which decodes the operation and produces a static output on a particular line depending on the type of operation requested. This output is held constant during the entire execution cycle and is generally applied to any number of switching elements (ORs, ANDs, FLIP-FLOPs, ADDERs, etc) throughout the computer. All OR circuits which receive this static input will produce an output, which, in turn, will cause some particular action as necessary to execute the instruction. AND circuits receive this static voltage as a single 1 input but will remain inactive to perform their given steps in the execution of the operation until a clock pulse or some other form of timing pulse is received at the second input. The decoder output is fed to all of the circuits in the computer as necessary to execute the particular operation.

Address Register

The address register, after receiving the address of the operand, enables an address selector, which, in turn, locates the operand and transfers it to an intermediate register (shown later). The intermediate register is

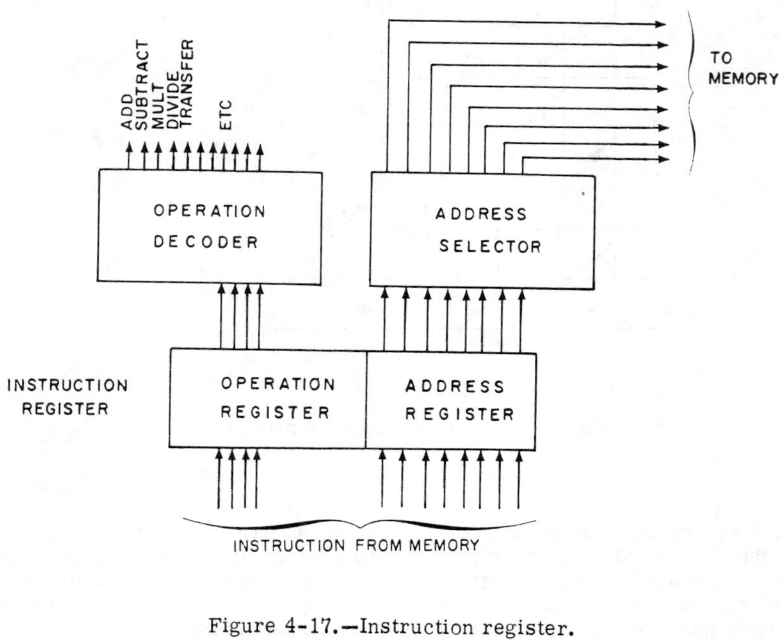

124.35

Figure 4-17.—Instruction register.

used as a form of buffer for reading information into or extracting information from the memory section.

In a stored-program computer, instructions are read and executed sequentially unless altered by conditions derived while executing an instruction, or, unless directed to jump or skip unconditionally. Normally, an instruction counter reads the instructions into the instruction register in the programmed sequence, starting at 0 and progressing in numerical order, 1, 2, 3, 4, etc. During the execution of each instruction, the instruction counter is advanced by 1. At the end of the execution cycle, switching circuits in the control unit initiate a command "READ NEXT INSTRUCTION"; whereupon the instruction cycle is again started by an enabling signal which is sent to the instruction counter causing the next sequential instruction to be read into the instruction register. Many other operations (not pointed out at this time) are accomplished in preparation for the next instruction.

WORD MODIFIERS

Each instruction which is used in the computation process is first read from memory into the instruction register (as described earlier). The instruction is subdivided into the operation register and the address register.

It is frequently necessary to alter or modify the address portion of the word in the control unit just prior to its use to obtain data from the main memory. In such cases, one or more address modifier sections are added to the instruction word to cause an automatic change in the address to be referenced in memory.

Indexing

An index register is a counter which is generally used (1) to change the numerical value of the address portion of a computer word to obtain an effective address, or (2) to monitor repeat instructions.

The first action (changing the numerical value of the address portion of a word to obtain an effective address) is accomplished by modifying the word address (the word in the address register) by the absolute value of a number stored in the index register. The index process does not alter the computer word or the number contained in the index register, thus making possible the use of the word as many times as necessary in its indexed or non-indexed form.

The need for indexing is explained using the following hypothetical example. Suppose it is necessary to read-in data to storage from a magnetic tape reader five times in the execution of a program and that ten instructions are required to cause the entire read-in to be executed. Without the use of indexing it is necessary to write a total of fifty instructions. If, however, the ten instructions for read-in of the tape are stored in memory (as instructions) and the index register is set five different times so that it contains the proper numbers to produce the desired addresses in memory into which the data must be read, only ten additional instructions will be necessary (five to initiate read-in at the proper time and one each time it is necessary to set the index register with the desired index number).

The index register is generally referred to as the "B-register group." The number of registers in the group vary depending on the computer. Each register is independent of the other and is separately used. The contents of any register in the group can be added to the contents of the address register.

When a B-register group is used, it is necessary to add a section to the computer word for the purpose of selecting and setting the desired B-register. This section is called the "b-designator" and may be 01 to designate the B1 register of the B-register group, 02 to designate the B2 register, etc. A single address word may be modified as illustrated in table 4-8.

Table 4-8. —Sample Instruction Word Using b-Designator

101	01	1011010
Operation Code	Index Register designator (b-designator)	Operand

If the B1 index register (designated by 01 in the instruction word in table 4-8) has been previously set so that it contains 0000101, the instruction in table 4-8 (when read from the main program) will produce an effective operand address of:

+1011010	Operand address in instruction word
+0000101	Contents of B1 index register
1011111	Effective address (represents address to which reference is made in memory).

The second use of indexing is illustrated using the following examples. Assume that it is desired to repeat a given operation x number of times. If the number (x) is loaded into the index register, the register will count backwards (toward zero) each time the instruction is executed until x counts have been performed.

If it is desired to alter the address portion of the instruction word by an amount n-1 for x number of instructions and before each of the instructions is executed, the action can be accomplished by setting the index register with the number by which the first instruction is to be modified and altering the index register contents as desired after each instruction to produce the desired effective address before the execution of the next instruction. After repeating this action x number of times, a programmed instruction causes an exit from this procedure.

A similar action, called a "loop function" is accomplished by repeating a given set of instructions (say a shift instruction) x number of times before exiting from the loop action. The exit may be caused by comparing the number of times the instruction is repeated with a number previously set in the index register (called the "criterion"), or by a programmed instruction.

Word Arithmetic

Word arithmetic, as defined here, refers to the process of removing a word from storage, altering the word by some arithmetic process in the arithmetic unit and returning the word to the same address in memory. The process may be repeated any number of times on the same word. Thus, modification of a word using arithmetic differs from modification by indexing since, in the latter process, the word is not changed in memory.

Designators

It has been shown that a computer word contains several sections. For convenience, these various sections are assigned a given letter, called a "designator." One instruction format in table 4-9 illustrates the use of word designators in a 24-bit word. A similar word is used in the Univac Digital Trainer, shown in figure 4-8.

Table 4-9. --Instruction Format Designator

f	j	k	b	y
101101	101	100	001	111001101

Designator		Specification	Interpretation
f	=	Operation Code designator	Type of operation to be performed
j	=	Branch condition designator	(1) jump or skip operation. (2) index (B) register specification. (3) repeat.
k	=	Operand interpretation designator	Read, store or replace instruction.
b	=	Address modification designator (index designator)	Register to be used for address modification.
y	=	Operand designator	Operand or address of operand.

CONDITIONAL AND UNCONDITIONAL TRANSFERS

If conditions are derived which necessitate a jump or conditional transfer to some step in the program other than the next sequential step, certain signals will be generated and fed to switching elements in the control unit to cause the necessary jump to be executed.

The unconditional transfer, as the term implies is accomplished without regard to prevailing conditions. It is initiated by an instruction which may state in effect, GO FROM PRESENT ADDRESS (say address 00030) to address 05275.

To illustrate the need for unconditional transfers, consider the following example. It is understood by this time that instructions and data are necessarily stored separately in memory. Normally then, a certain number of addresses (say the lower numbered addresses) are reserved for and contain instructions. We will assume that the data addresses begin at the next higher address immediately after the instructions, but that several of the highest numbered addresses are not used. Now if all instructions and data are loaded accordingly and it is later discovered that more instructions must be loaded in order to solve the original problem or to solve another phase of the problem we would logically decide to store the additional instructions in the vacant address rather than extract all data, load the additional instructions, and reload the data. In order to use these added instructions, we must instruct the computer control to jump to the address of the first added instruction "unconditionally."

SYNCHRONOUS CONTROL

There are many ways presently being used in control units to execute instructions. Every computer seems to have some unique control feature peculiar to that particular machine. There is no one so called "best method" since the control method cannot, in most cases, be decided without considering several other factors; such as storage access time, input-output devices, and the nature and time required to perform arithmetic operations.

The basic principles of synchronous and asynchronous methods of control are explained below.

Synchronous control is a mode of computer operation characterized by a fixed time period for the execution of each operation. Conversely, asynchronous control uses varying amounts of time to execute its operations, depending of course on the type of operation being performed. In the asynchronous control method the advance to the next command is signaled when the execution of the previous command has been completed.

The myriad operations performed in even the simplest control unit would be too great to explain in every detail. This is complicated by time considerations, i.e., showing all of the control signals which are fed throughout the computer during many small timed intervals. Thus, the control methods discussed below are hypothetical and are intended to show basically how the control unit orders and executes the major operations in the computer.

Consider the circuit in figure 4-18. A multivibrator receives trigger pulses from a crystal oscillator and provides input pulses to a delay line consisting of sections DO through D5. The number of sections is arbitrarily chosen. The time required for a pulse to traverse the line is slightly less than the period of the free-running multivibrator so that the output pulse at t5 will arrive at the multivibrator input at the time this circuit is about to produce its next pulse. This action synchronizes the multivibrator and keeps the multivibrator-delay line arrangement compatible.

Output pulses from the line, taken at t0, t1, t2, t3, t4, and t5 (clock pulses) are applied during their respective intervals to various switching elements throughout the computer. These circuits (ORs, ANDs, flip-flops, etc.) are too numerous to show in detail and are represented here by a single block from which a few of the outputs are shown on "command lines." The timed inputs, i.e., the pulses from the delay line at t0, t1, t2, etc., tell these circuits "when" to perform a given operation.

Now consider another aspect of control. As stated earlier, the instruction counter, or program address counter, as it is sometimes called, receives control pulses which are sent via the address selector to memory, thereby causing a particular instruction to be read from the memory into the instruction register. Each instruction word, as you recall, consists basically of the operation code and the address of the operand. In reading the instruction from memory, the operation code is fed to the operation register while the operand address is read to the address register.

Accordingly, the operation register feeds the operation code to the operation decoder, which, in turn, decodes the operation (as stated earlier) and supplies a static voltage output on a single decoder output line, the one selected, of course, being determined by the type of operation to be performed. This static voltage is fed to those switching circuits which are to perform some action in the execution of the instruction. In a sense, it is this static voltage which tells the computer circuits "what"

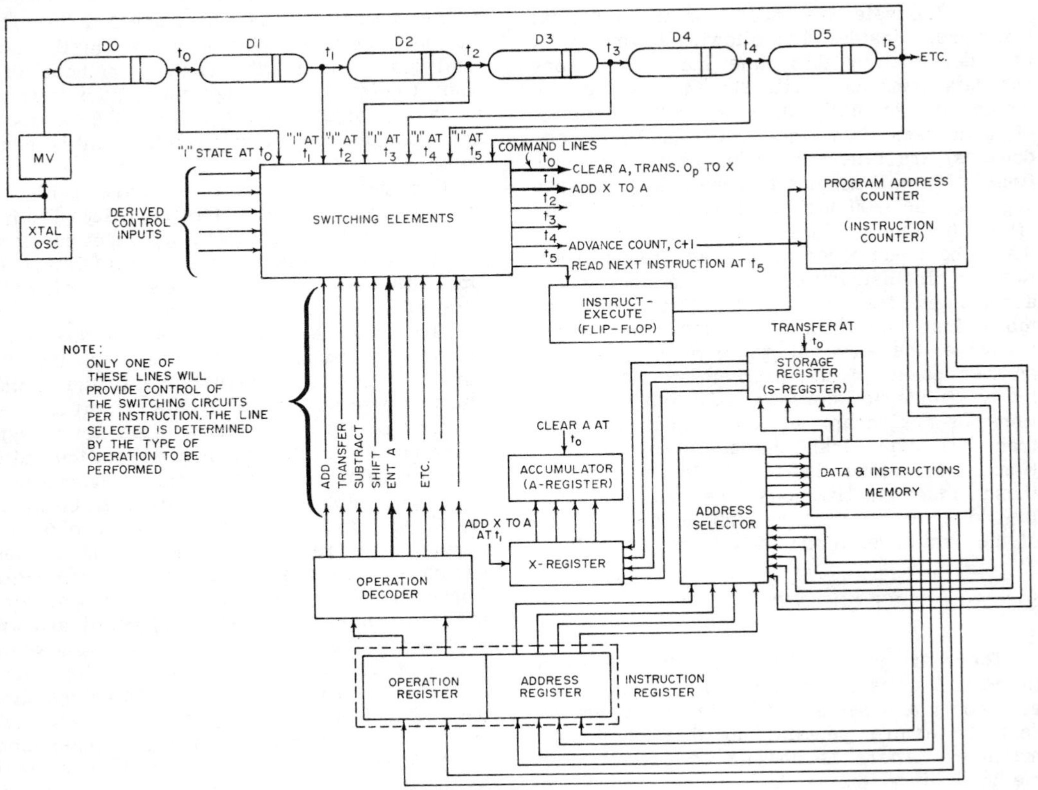

124.36

Figure 4-18. —Basic synchronous control operation.

to do. Knowing when to do each step, as dictated by the delay line inputs, and what to do, as dictated by the operation decoder output, the computer proceeds to execute the instruction.

The address register, immediately upon reception of its input, energizes the address selector circuits to cause the operand to be read into the S-register. The operand remains in this register until the instruction is executed or until it is transferred to some other register.

Now, consider the action in more detail. Given the following instruction "ENTER THE OPERAND IN THE A-REGISTER," we will follow the major steps in its execution.

The instruction is read into the instruction register from memory under the influence of the instruction counter. The operation decoder decodes the operation code and activates the "ENT A" line. This line, in turn, is fed to all of the switching circuits involved in the execution.

The address selector, by instruction from the address register, fetches the operand from the section of memory which contains data and stores it in the S-register.

The arrival of the t0 clock pulse to the switching circuits causes a command line to be enabled at t0, and the following part of the operation is executed: CLEAR THE A REGISTER (accumulator), and TRANSFER THE OPERAND TO THE "X" REGISTER.

The accumulator receives data by adding data to its contents. Thus, clearing the accumulator returns the register to 000. Adding a number to the accumulator after clearing is therefore no more than entering that number in the accumulator.

The arrival of the t1 clock pulse to the switching circuits causes the ADD X TO A command line to be enabled. This command adds the operand to the accumulator and the execution is completed.

Note that the execution of this instruction (in this example) does not require the use of the clock pulses from t2 and t3. A more complex instruction requiring a multiply or divide operation may use all clock pulse enable inputs.

Also note that during the execution cycle the instruction counter receives a signal as initiated during clock pulse period t4. This action normally causes the instruction counter to advance its count by 1 in preparation for reading out the next instruction from memory. The "ENT A" instruction is completed. At t5 the command to "READ NEXT INSTRUCTION" is initiated.

If a conditional transfer is initiated during the execution of an instruction, certain signals will be derived to cause the conditional jump. These signals are fed to the switching circuits as derived control inputs.

Because all operations are performed in synchronism with the clock pulses, this method of control is described as "synchronous control." Each operation requires a certain number of clock pulses, and consequently the time to complete any one of the various operations is an exact multiple of the clock pulse period.

ASYNCHRONOUS CONTROL

An example of asynchronous control is explained with the aid of figure 4-19. A one-shot multivibrator simultaneously feeds a pulse to AND circuit A1 and delay line D1. The pulse at A1 in coincidence with a 1 input from the inverter, causes a 1 output at A1 to initiate READ NEXT INSTRUCTION. The D1 output is delayed 0.5μs (in this example) to allow sufficient time for the instruction cycle (the time required to read an instruction into the instruction register from memory and perform all other operations in preparation for the new instruction).

Loops 1, 2, 3, etc., are designed respectively to perform a single type of operation, although miscellaneous control inputs to a loop may alter the loop, and thereby permit other very similar operations to be accomplished. Thus, a control unit of this type will contain almost as many loops as the total number of types of operations it can perform.

The pulse from the multivibrator, after delay in D1, is applied simultaneously to one of the inputs of the AND circuit at the input of each loop. The loop selected to execute an instruction will be determined by the operation decoder output. Each decoder output line is tied to a different AND element, or loop except where two or more similar operations are performed by the same loop; whereupon control of such similar operations will be directed from the decoder to the same loop.

Consider the execution of a three-address instruction as follows: ADD THE CONTENTS OF REGISTER S TO THE ACCUMULATOR: ADD THE CONTENTS OF REGISTER B TO THE ACCUMULATOR: STORE RESULTS IN REGISTER C.

Loop 1 is used to illustrate the timing sequence of operations progressing from steps A through F. The actual operation is hypothetical and is used here merely to show how certain parts of an instruction are executed at certain times.

Step A begins as soon as a 1 output is produced at A2. This part of the sequence causes the A register to be cleared, and the contents of the Z register (intermediate storage register) to be transferred to the S register.

After the D2 delay, enabling signals are produced (simultaneously) to cause step B (transfer S → A), step C (negate step B, if a miscellaneous input is received at the lower input terminal of A6) and step D (clear C). We will assume that the miscellaneous input to A6 is not received, and step B is executed. Transferring S → A (read S to A) is the equivalent of adding the contents of S to A as explained earlier.

After delay in D3, step E is executed and the contents of the B register are added to the accumulator (A).

Finally after delay D4, the contents of A which now represent the sum of operands stored in the S and B registers, are transferred to the C register (step F).

Now consider the instruction: ADD THE CONTENTS OF B TO THE ACCUMULATOR AND STORE IN C. Note the similarity of this instruction to the one just considered. If step B (S → A) is eliminated, loop 1 can again be used and only the contents of the B register

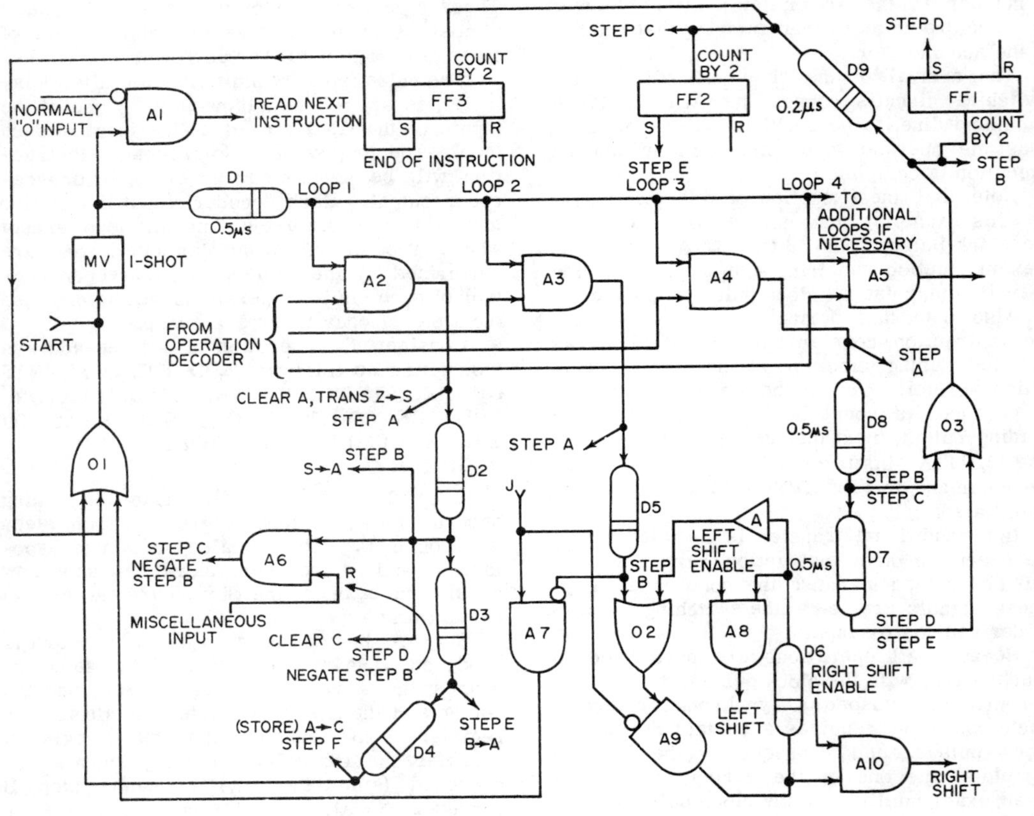

124. 37

Figure 4-19. —Asynchronous Control.

will be added to the accumulator. Thus, we assume here that the required miscellaneous input is received immediately after the delay in D2 and, step B is negated. With this understanding a further explanation of the execution of this instruction is not necessary.

Note that at the end of the D4 delay, the output from this line is also applied through OR circuit 01 to the multivibrator. The 01 input triggers the multivibrator, and causes an output pulse to be fed to A1. This action causes the next instruction to be read from memory.

A right or left shift operation can be accomplished using loop 2 to produce the required number of pulses to execute the desired shift count. Step A is not involved directly in the shift action, but is shown here as an enabling output to all other circuits involved in the execution of all other phases of this operation, even those which adjust other computer circuits for the up-coming shift.

At step B, OR circuit, 02, passes a pulse into a ring circuit consisting of 02, A9, D6, and the amplifier. The circuit of A9 has an inverter at its input so that if a 1 input pulse is not received at J, the pulse from D5 will continue through 02, A9, the delay line D6, the amplifier, and back to 02. OR circuit, 02, again permits the pulse to re-enter the ring. The amplifier compensates for losses in the pulse amplitude each time around the ring.

Shift outputs are taken from the line during each ring count and applied to one of the inputs of AND circuits A8 and A10 respectively. A left enable or right enable static voltage is applied as a miscellaneous input to either of the two AND elements depending on the type of shift desired.

When the shift has advanced through the desired count, a 1 input pulse is applied at J. This "1" input disables A9 (stopping the ring action) and produces an output from A7 through 01 to the multivibrator so that a multivibrator output will be generated and the next instruction will be read.

Because of the inverter at the right input of A7, the circuit is disabled only during the time when a pulse appears at the output of D5. An output pulse cannot be developed by A7 during this period, neither is such an output desired. However, after the trailing edge of the D5 output pulse, the inverter at A7 will again produce a 1 at the right terminal.

Loop 3 is designed to supply control pulses to various computer circuits at timed intervals. The particular operation performed is not important. Rather, the sequence and timing of control pulses as necessary to execute the operation is the significant consideration.

Here, the output pulse at step A causes the execution of the first part of the operation. After the delay in D8, a single pulse is passed through OR circuit, 03, to D9. Step B is executed before the D9 delay and is followed after the delay in D9 (0.2μs in this case) by the execution of step C. Count-by-2 circuits FF1 and FF2 are reset by the step B and step C enable pulses, and therefore do not produce the step D and step E enabling pulses at this time.

Note that the pulse from D8 is also fed into the D7 delay line. The delay in this line is long enough to permit steps B and C, totaling 0.2μs, to be executed before the D7 pulse evolves. When the D7 output is developed, OR circuit, 03, produces an output pulse which initiates step D by setting FF1. Step E will be executed after the D9 delay and the setting of FF2. Enabling pulses for steps B and C will be produced for each output pulse from 03.

In order to maintain the static operation decoder output, it is necessary to hold the instruction being executed in the instruction register throughout the execution cycle. The count-by-2 circuit (FF3) at the D9 output produces an "end of instruction" pulse only at its set terminal, thus it prevents the first pulse from D9 (after the execution of step C) from triggering the multivibrator and thereby prevents the start of an instruction cycle until after steps D and E have been executed.

Note that in this method of control the time required to execute an instruction varies, depending on the type of instruction.

Chapter 5

ARITHMETIC UNIT

As explained in Chapter 1, "Introduction to Digital Computers," the digital computer is composed of five basic sections: control, arithmetic, memory, input, and output. This chapter treats the arithmetic unit—its characteristics, operations, and contents.

RELATIONSHIP OF THE ARITHMETIC UNIT TO THE OTHER COMPUTER SECTIONS

The arithmetic unit of the computer performs all the necessary computations of the program in operation. Data that the arithmetic unit is to use in performing computations are obtained from the input section via the memory section (fig. 5-1). The data are usually stored in the memory section at the beginning of the program. The control section processes the program instructicn words, and then causes the data to be read into the arithmetic section from memory. Arithmetic operations to be performed are also determined in the control section, which sends these instructions to the arithmetic section. The results of the arithmetic operations are then either stored back into memory or sent to the output section, so that the processed data can be printed out.

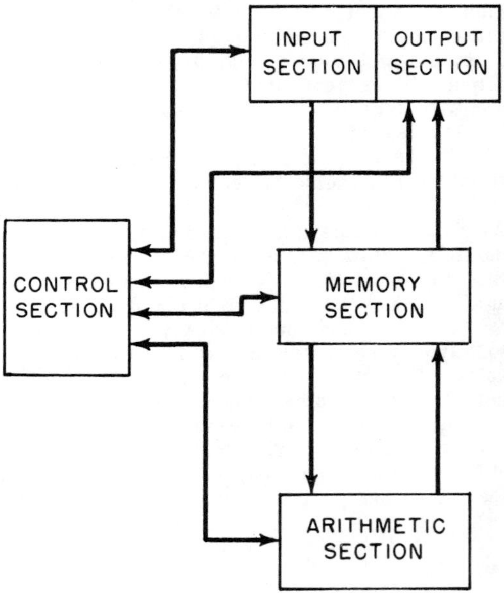

164.18

Figure 5-1.—Block diagram of a basic digital computer.

CHARACTERISTICS OF THE ARITHMETIC UNIT

The basic operations performed by the arithmetic section are addition, subtraction, multiplication, and division. The arithmetic section performs these operations either in parallel or serially; the method used depends on the manner in which data are transmitted to the arithmetic section from memory. In the parallel method (fig. 5-2), a separate input or lead is used for each binary bit of data; hence, all the bits of a word are entered into the arithmetic section at one time. In the serial method (fig. 5-2), the data bits are entered sequentially through only one input lead to the arithmetic section logic circuitry.

FUNCTION

When the instructions are received from the control section, the arithmetic section performs computations with data stored in memory. These data may represent payroll

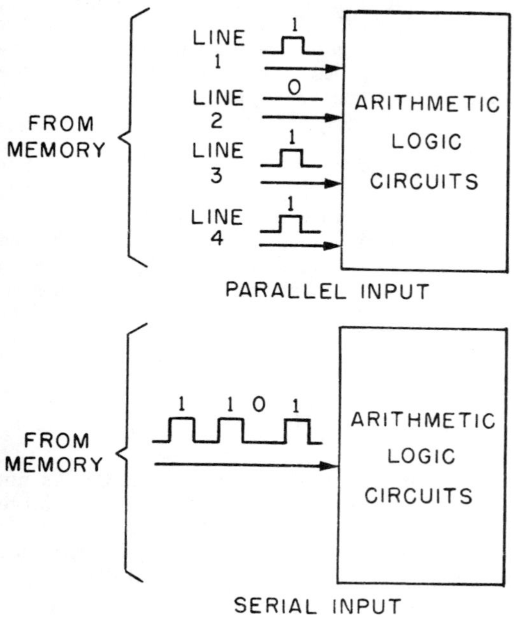

164.19
Figure 5-2.—Data transmission methods.

statistics for a large corporation, radar information to be calculated to find a ship's position, or many design variables from which the best combination is chosen. However, arithmetic operations are not used to solve mathematical problems only. Often arithmetic operations are used in "decision-making." Data can be compared with other data to decide whether the following operation in the program can continue. In addition, data can be shifted left or right. The arithmetic section uses the four basic arithmetic operations in error detecting and comparative counting, and making other simple yes-no decisions.

CAPABILITIES OF THE ARITHMETIC UNIT

Arithmetic operations in the arithmetic unit may be performed by the process of counting. Addition is often performed by counting, where the counts of one number are added to another number. For example, if 25 is added to 57, the 7 and 5 are added, and then the 5 and 2. A third number, the carry resulting from the sum of 7 and 5, is then added to the sum of 5 and 2. This may be shown as follows:

5	7	
+2	5	
7	(1)2	
+1 ←	←	Carry
8	2	

Subtraction is accomplished by complementing the subtrahend and adding the two numbers. For example, if 25 is subtracted from 57, the hundreds complement of the minuend, 57, and the carry of the highest order of addition is dropped, as shown in the following example:

	5	7	minuend
	+7	5	subtrahend
	(1)2	(1)2	complement
dropped	+1 ←	←	
carry--	(1)3	2	= 32

Multiplication is also accomplished by the process of addition. For example, to multiply 5 by 3, the arithmetic operation would consist of adding 5 three times, that is:

$$5 + 5 + 5 = 15$$

Division is accomplished by successive subtractions of the divisor from the dividend. Since, in most cases, subtraction is performed by complementing and then adding, addition processes are also used in division. For example, 15 divided by 5 is processed by using the complement of the divisor, 95, as follows:

1	5
+9	5
(1)0	(1)0
+1 ←	←
(1)1	0
+9	5
(2)0	5
+9	5
(2)9	(1)0
+1 ←	←
(3)0	0

The complemented divisor, 95, is successively added until the divisor equals 00. The numerical value of the largest order carry is then the quotient. In the previous example, the quotient is 3.

The arithmetic section performs decision-making operations by using the arithmetic operations just described. For example: a program is set up so that a certain value (in this case, the number 7) must be present in a data word before the program can progress to the next sequential step. If the number is not present, then the program will loop back to a previous step and repeat the operation. The arithmetic section, therefore, would compare the data word with the value of 7, possibly by using the subtraction operation. The test value of 7 would be subtracted from each number of the data word, the program will then proceed to the next sequential step. Since the presence of the number 7 in the word will result in a zero when the test number 7 is subtracted from it, comparison has been made, and the decision on whether to continue the program or loop back to a previous operation has been accomplished. The resultant zero produces a signal, which is sent to the control section to initiate the correct instruction. This may be shown as follows:

data word =	1	3	7	9	8
	- 7	7	7	7	7
	- 6	-4	0	2	1

Another capability of the arithmetic section is the shift left and shift right operations. Since digital computers use binary numbers instead of decimal numbers, the shift left and shift right operations can be used for binary multiplication and division. These operations are performed by the shift register, which is described later in this chapter. Often, these operations are used in rounding binary numbers. For example, by shifting a binary number one place to the right, the least significant digit is lost. If the same number is then shifted one place to the left, the least significant binary bit is zero. Thus, binary number 1011 in the register, when shifted right, results in 101. When the number is shifted left again, the number will be 1010. The shift right operation can be used for division. For example, when 110, the binary number for 6, is in the shift register and the contents are shifted right, the resultant number 011, the binary number for 3, will be obtained. A division by 2 has been performed. Consequently, if the shift left operation is performed, the number 110 in the register will be multiplied by 2, producing 1100, the binary equivalent of 12. The logic circuits are used to perform arithmetic operations are discussed in greater detail in the succeeding paragraphs.

UNITARY OPERATIONS

Unitary operations make use of the "unitary" code. The unitary code has only one digit, and the number of times that this digit is used in a number determines the quantity it represents. Thus:

1	=	1
11	=	2
111	=	3
1111	=	4, etc.

It can be seen, therefore, that this is not a very practical code for representing a large number such as 10,000. The unitary code is mentioned here only because it is required for the explanation of counters that follows.

COUNTERS

The unitary code is converted to a coded system of numerical notation when applied to the input of counters. For example, in figure 5-3 the unitary number 4 is converted by the decimal 4 (indicated by some readout device, like a lamp or odometer). When the unitary number 4 is applied to a binary counter, the number 4 is counted in pure binary (8, 4, 2, 1 code). There are many different types of counters', some of which are discussed below.

The capacity of a counter to count to a certain numerical value is known as the counter's "modulus." Thus, we speak of modulo-5 and modulo-10 counters in defining the maximum quantity that the counter in question is able to count to.

Let us examine the odometer, the mileage indicator in an automobile. Most commercial automobiles have odometers that have a decimal readout capacity of 99,999.9 miles. But, the modulus of this odometer is 100,000.0. Since 99,999.9 is the maximum readout, the recycling of the readout indicator to 00000.0 represents 100,000.0. Thus, the modulus of any counter is the fixed capacity of the counter plus one.

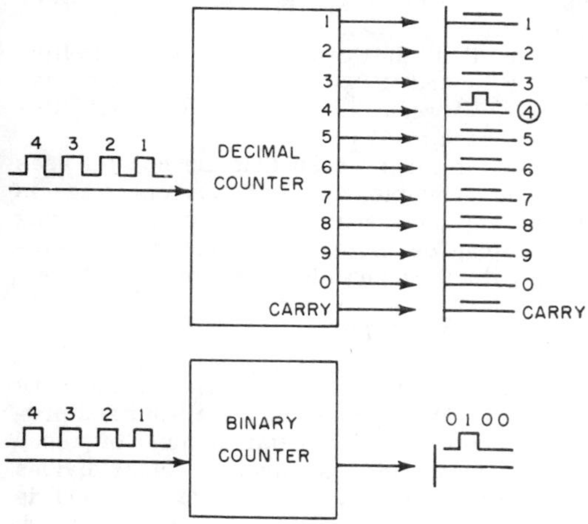

164.20
Figure 5-3.—Unitary code conversion to decimal or binary code.

Another example of a decimal readout counter is the mess deck counter. This hand counter is usually used in counting the number of men that pass through a cafeteria at a given period. The pressing of a button on the counter advances the counter by one. Its modulus would also be the fixed capacity of the counter plus one, the recycling of the counter.

The binary number system is used in all digital computers. Thus, the type of counter used most frequently in digital computers is the binary counter.

Binary Counters

A binary counter is merely a series of flip-flops. The number of flip-flops used determines the modulus of the counter. Figure 5-4 shows a four-stage binary counter. The input pulses (in unitary code) are applied to the flip-flop corresponding to the lowest order of binary number. Note that the C (clear) input from the 0-side of each flip-flop feeds the input of the next (higher order) flip-flop. The S (set) from the 1-side of each flip-flop provides the count readout. If a flip-flop is in the set position, the output from the 1-side of the circuit reads 1; if the circuit is in the clear position, the 1-side output reads 0. Every time the clear side changes from a 0 to 1 state

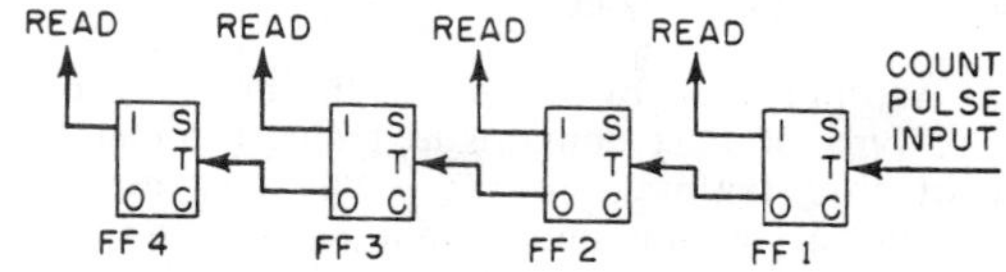

164.21
Figure 5-4.—Four-stage binary counter.

(1 to a 0 on the set side), a pulse is sent to the next higher order flip-flop input. An input to the counter, shown in figure 5-4, affects the flip-flops in the following manner:

Step 1. Assume that all four flip-flops are in the clear position. Each output reads 0 and the total counter output is 0000 (binary 0).

Step 2. A single pulse is introduced. FF_1 changes to its set position, producing a 1 at its output. However, the signal is not coupled to FF_2 because the flip-flop produces a pulse at its clear output only when changing from set to clear. The counter's output now reads 0001 (binary 1).

Step 3. Another pulse enters the counter's input. FF_1 changes from set to clear, producing a 0 at its set output. This time, a pulse is produced at the clear output (clear side changes from 0 to 1). The clear output pulse is coupled to FF_2, causing it to change from the clear to the set position. The FF_2 set output now reads 1. (Again, because each flip-flop couples a pulse only when going from the set to clear position, no pulse is produced from the FF_2 clear output, and the remaining flip-flops are not affected.) The counter's output now reads 0010 (binary 2).

Each successive input pulse to the counter affects the flip-flops in a similar manner. The third input pulse will change FF_1 to the set state, producing 0011 (binary 3). The fourth pulse will change FF_1 and FF_2 to the clear position and FF_3 to the set position, producing 0100 (binary 4). Continuing this analysis reveals that the circuit will count up to 15 pulses, indicating its tally in binary code.

Thus, the highest possible binary number in the counter's output is 1111 (binary 15). The modulus, therefore, is 15 + 1, or 16. Since FF_4 counts to 16 (24 in binary notation), the addition of another flip-flop will permit counting to 32.

Symbolized Ring Counter

Another type of counter is the ring counter. One type of ring counter is treated in chapter 4 of this training course. The ring counter is cyclic, having no beginning and no end. After it has reached its highest number, its next count is 0.

In the ring counter, only one element or stage is on at one time. Each input signal advances the ON or operating stage one step forward.

The ring counter shown in figure 5-5 uses flip-flops and AND circuits. Note that the input pulses never enter any flip-flop directly. Instead, they are applied to all of the AND circuits. An input pulse is used by each AND circuit to clear the flip-flop corresponding to that AND circuit (if the flip-flop is in the ON state), and to set the following flip-flop.

If we assume that the ON signal is currently in flip-flop FF_1, the operation would be as follows: When an input pulse is applied, AND circuit A_1 is the only one that produces an output signal because A_1 is the only AND circuit that has a set output signal at its second input. Note that this output signal branches and affects both FF_1 and FF_2. The output signal of AND circuit A_1 clears FF_1 to 0. This flip-flop is therefore no longer ON. The output signal from A_1 also sets FF_2 to its 1 position. FF_2 is now ON. AND circuit A_2 is now ready for the next input pulse from the input bus, since it already has a 1 at its lower terminal.

Note that the connections between flip-flops FF_2 and FF_3 are identical to the connections between FF_1 through the last flip-flop and back to FF_1.

Thus, it can be seen that the counter uses a cyclic principle, and that only one stage is ON at any one count. The modulus of a ring counter can be increased by adding more elements (flip-flops and AND circuits in this case).

FREQUENCY DIVISION

Binary counters are also used to count the number of input pulses to the circuit and produce an output after a certain number of pulses are received. In this way the counter divides the input frequency by some factor and is therefore referred to as a frequency divider. The function of a binary frequency divider or counter, is to divide, or scale down, the number of input pulses by some power of two. A single flip-flop, for example, divides by two. It produces one output pulse for every two input pulses.

The output pulses can be either in phase with or out-of-phase with the count pulses. The input and output (fig. 5-6), are positive. Flip-flop FF_1 can be made to produce a positive output so that a second flip-flop of the same type can, upon receiving the output of the first, again divide the input by 2. Thus, the output of a two-stage circuit produces only one pulse

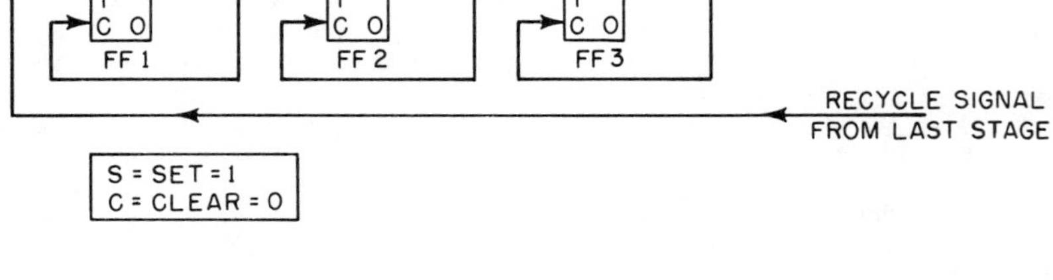

164.22

Figure 5-5.—Ring counter using flip-flops and AND circuits.

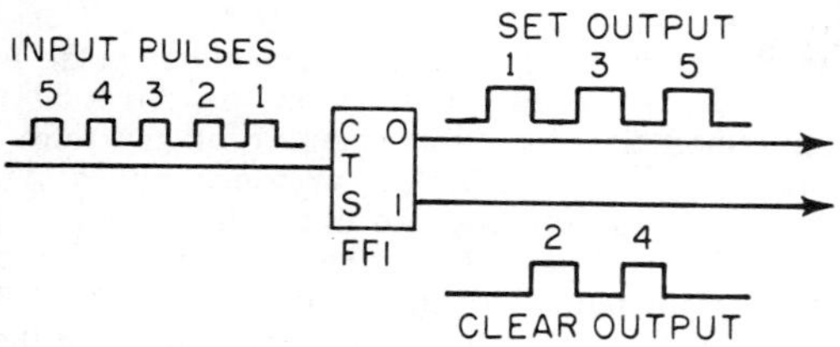

164.23
Figure 5-6.—Using a flip-flop as a scale-of-2 divider.

for every four pulses at the input, making it a divide-by-four circuit. Similarly, a third flip-flop will make it a scale-of-8 divider, producing one output pulse for every eight input pulses. Figure 5-7 shows a four-stage binary scaler and the pulse outputs of each stage. Note that each flip-flop produces only half as many pulses as the one before it, so that the final stage (FF_8) produces only one pulse for every 16 pulses introduced at the first stage. The circuit is therefore a scale-of-16 divider.

INFORMATION REPRESENTATION AND TRANSFER

Some methods used to represent instructions and transfer data in a computer are treated in chapter 4. Another method of manipulating data, called "shifting," is discussed below.

The advantage of parallel operation is that data is transferred more quickly than in serial operation. However, in serial operation, fewer circuits are required to perform the operation. The choice between the two methods is one of design. Although any storage device can be adapted to either method, some types are best suited to one method or the other.

Serial and parallel techniques are often used in the same computer during different operations. For example, a data word may be transferred to a shift register in parallel and then

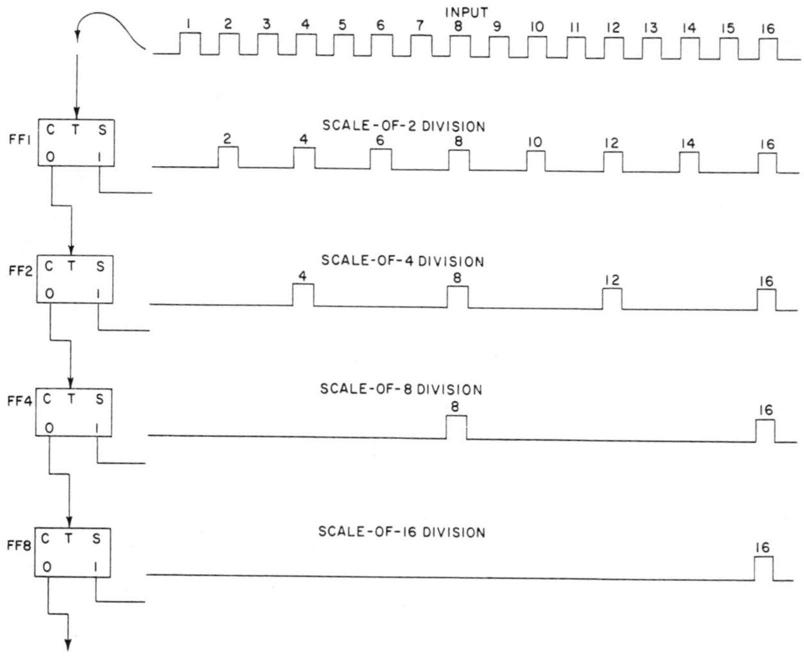

164.24

Figure 5-7.—Pulse train of a four-stage binary scaler.

read out of the register serially. The reverse is also true; a data word may be read into a register serially and read out in parallel. The following is an explanation of the operation of a shift register using serial and parallel techniques.

SHIFT REGISTERS

As explained in earlier sections, a register is a temporary storage device. Data are put into a register and can be read out of the register when needed for some operation. Shift registers can shift the data bits to the right or to the left, round off a number, or multiply or divide by 2, 4, 8, 16, etc. The shift left and shift right operations may use serial and parallel techniques. Figure 5-8 is a shift register which illustrates the concepts of right and left shifting using parallel techniques.

Right Shift

Assume that information is stored in the A-register (fig. 5-8). It is now desired to shift the information in the A-register (represented by the 1 state on the set sides of the flip-flops) to the right by one place. The clear pulse is applied to the clear sides of the X-register flip-flops to clear the register of any information present from a previous operation. Note that the clear pulse is applied in parallel to all the flip-flops in the X-register. If a shift right pulse is applied in parallel to AND circuits A2, A4, A6, and A8, the data from the set sides of the A-register flip-flops is transferred to the X-register, and, in the transfer process, is shifted one place to the right. This operation uses both a parallel and serial movement of data. All the information in the A-register is transferred to the X-register in parallel, while the shift motion is serial. For example, the output of the set side of FF_{A3} is ANDed with the shift right pulse at AND circuit A2. The output of this circuit is passed by OR circuit 02 to the input of the set side of FF_{X2}, thereby affecting transfer of a data bit from the first flip-flop in the A-register (FF_{A3}) to the second flip-flop in the X-register (FF_{X2}). Similarly, data from FF_{A2} is transferred to FF_{X1} and from FF_{A1} to FF_{X0}. The LSD (least significant digit) from FF_{A0} is lost during a right shift operation.

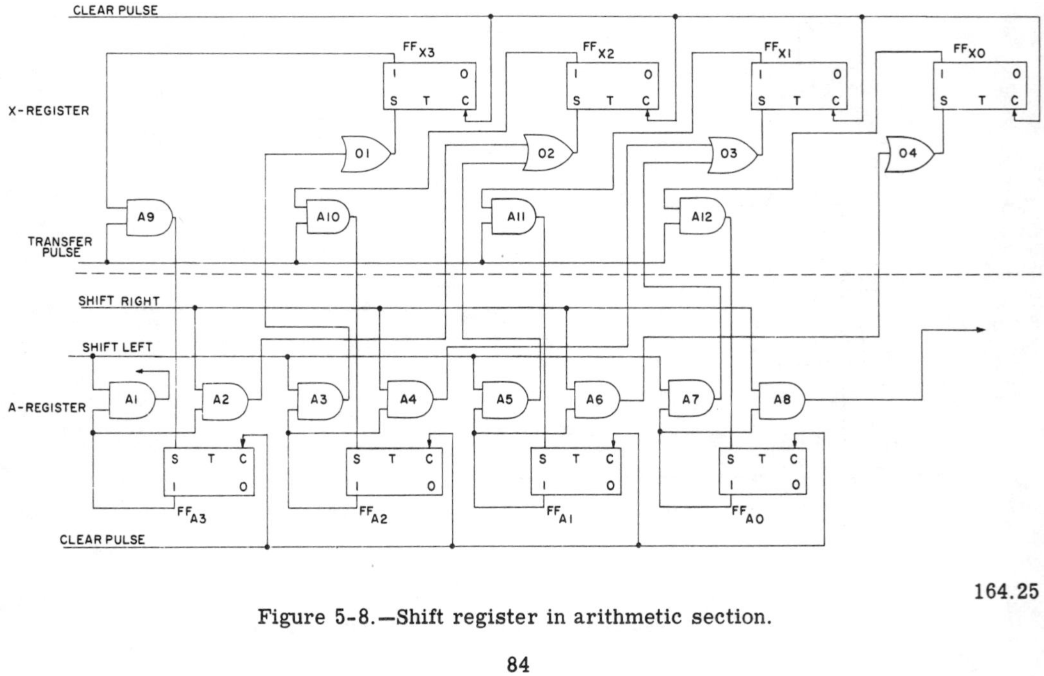

164.25

Figure 5-8.—Shift register in arithmetic section.

Next, the clear pulse is applied to the clear sides of the A-register flip-flops, thereby clearing these flip-flops of that data originally stored in the register. The transfer pulse is then used to transfer the shifted data, now in the X-register, to the corresponding flip-flops in the A-register by way of AND circuits A9, A10, A11, and A12. The transfer pulse is ANDed with the outputs of the set sides of the X-register flip-flops. The outputs of these AND circuits are applied to the corresponding set sides of the A-register flip-flops. Thus, data are now stored in FF_{A2}, FF_{A1}, and FF_{A0}, and a shift, one place to the right, has occurred. Note that FF_{A3} is not set during the transfer back to the A-register, since FF_{X3} remained in the cleared state during the original transfer from A to X.

Left Shift

The left shift operation is similar to the right shift operation, except that now AND circuits A1, A3, A5, and A7 are used for transferring and shifting. The X-register is cleared by the application of a clear pulse to the clear sides of the X-register flip-flops. Then, the shift left pulse is applied in parallel to A1, A3, A5, and A7. The outputs of the set sides of the A-register flip-flops are passed by the AND circuits (which simultaneously received a left shift pulse), and OR circuits (01 through 04) to the set sides of the X-register flip-flops. Thus, data is transferred and shifted from FF_{A0} to FF_{X1}, from FF_{A1} to FF_{X2}, and from FF_{A2} to FF_{X3}. Usually, during a left shift, the most significant digit is shifted to the least significant digit position i.e., FF_{A3} to FF_{A0}.

A clear pulse to the A-register flip-flops clears the register. The transfer pulse now enables the contents of the X-register to be transferred to the corresponding A-register flip-flops by way of A9, A10, A11, and A12, respectively. Note that the data are now stored in the A-register one place to the left of its original position.

LOGICAL DESIGN OF ARITHMETIC DEVICES

The following treatment of arithmetic devices presupposes that the reader is already familiar with previous discussions of arithmetic circuits and operations as treated in earlier chapters.

BINARY ADDITION

The addition operation is performed in the arithmetic section by the binary adder. The axioms of binary addition are:

X	Y	f_s	f_c
0	0	0	0
0	1	1	0
1	0	1	0
1	1	0	1

Where X and Y are variables, f_s represents the sum, and f_c represents the carry

HALF-ADDER

A half-adder (fig. 5-9) is a circuit which has two input points, identified here as X and Y, representing addend and augend, and two output points, S and C, representing sum and carry, respectively. This half-adder performs each of the axioms cited above. Each of the variables, X and Y, can assume a value of either 0 or 1. If the X and Y inputs are from flip-flops, these inputs and their complements are available. In

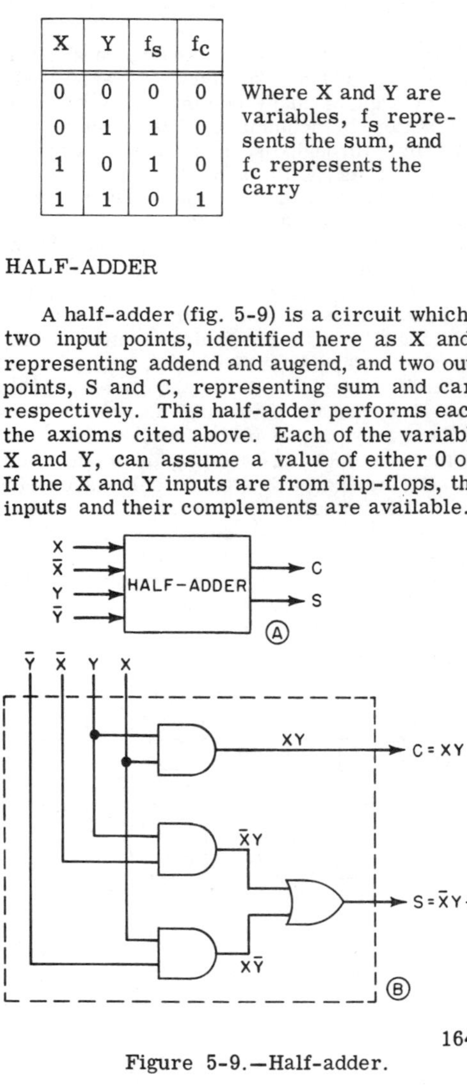

164.26

Figure 5-9.—Half-adder.

binary addition, the Boolean expression for the sum equal to 1 is:

$$S = X\overline{Y} + \overline{X}Y$$

The Boolean expression for the carry is:

$$C = X\ Y$$

FULL-ADDER

The full-adder circuit in figure 5-10 is designed to advance a carry (in serial addition) through as many columns as necessary. This action is accomplished by circulating a carry digit through the carry feedback circuit comprising A2, CR2, and D1, each time a 1 condition exists at the A2 output. The following example will illustrate this feature.

Consider the addition of 111 and 011 as shown. The serial columns are applied at times t^0, t^1 and t^2 respectively. OR circuit, G1, produces a 111 input to one terminal of inhibitor, I1, with one pulse applied during each time interval. AND circuit, A1, produces an inhibitory input to I1 during time intervals t^0 and t^1 so that the output of I1 is 100.

The carry digits (011) from A1 are also fed through CR1 (an isolating diode) to delay line, D1, where each digit is delayed one bit time. The output (110 corresponding to time intervals t^2, t^1, and t^0 reading from right to left) is applied to the lower input terminal of G2, causing the output of this circuit to be 110 during the time intervals shown.

Note that the input to G2 from I1 during the intervals t^2, t^1, and t^0 is also applied to one terminal of AND circuit A2, and that the first carry output (110) is applied to the other terminal. Thus, A2, produces a 100 output during intervals t^2, t^1, and t^0.

The 1 output of A2 during period t^2 causes the 1 input to I2 from G2 during the t^2 interval to be inhibited, and the output of I2 during this period is 0. The I2 output during intervals t^0 and t^1 appears uninhibited. Thus, the I2 output from t^2 to t^0 is 010.

The presence of a 1 in the A2 output indicates that a carry is yet to be added to one of the remaining columns before the true sum can be produced. The carry digit is fed through CR2 to D1 where it is delayed and shifted into the period t^3. The second output of D1 (shown as the second carry input to G2) is passed through G2 during the t^3 interval and combined with the serial train already at the output. This action produces the true sum (1010) of the binary inputs at G1. Note that a carry has been advanced from the first column to the fourth. In a similar manner, this circuit can advance the carry through any number of columns as required.

A parallel adder circuit which uses flip-flop as the basic element is treated in chapter 4 of this text. In the discussion of parallel addition it is shown that a carry digit is generated when any flip-flop changes from the set to the reset condition and that this carry is fed through a delay circuit to the next higher order. The delay circuit prevents the accumulation of the carry digit in the next higher

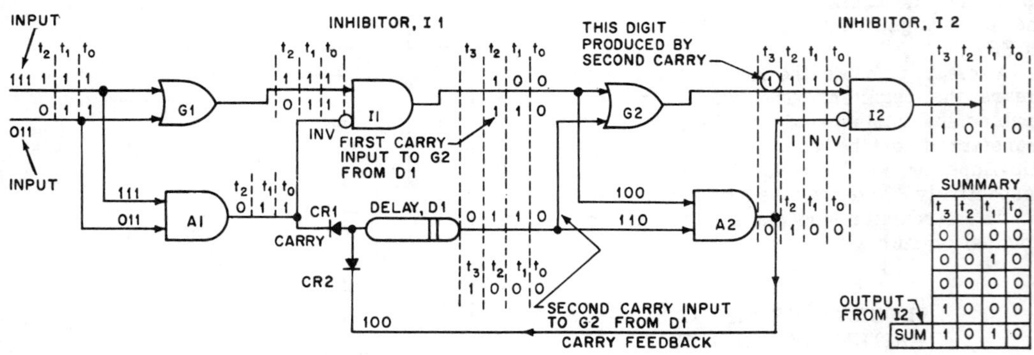

124.42

Figure 5-10.—Full-adder for accumulating multiple carry digits.

column until after the addition of the augend and addend in that column.

The axioms for the addition of two binary numbers treated earlier do not include all possibilities. When the addend and augend contain more than one column, a circuit designed to execute such additions must be able to accept and add a carry digit from a previous column. Table 5-1 shows all possibilities which may be encountered in the addition of such numbers where C represents a previous carry which is now to be added to the sum of the addend and augend in that column, C_n represents a new carry which is to be added to the next column, and S represents the sum.

Table 5-1. --f(A, B) Showing Previous Carry, New Carry, and Sum

A	B	C	S	C_n
0	0	0	0	0
0	0	1	1	0
0	1	0	1	0
0	1	1	0	1
1	0	0	1	0
1	0	1	0	1
1	1	0	0	1
1	1	1	1	1

From the truth table (table 5-1) it can be seen that the minterm equation (condition of the variables for which f = 1) for the sum (S) is:

$$S = \bar{A}\,\bar{B}\,C + \bar{A}\,B\,\bar{C} + A\,\bar{B}\,\bar{C} + A\,B\,C$$

and that the minterm equation for the new carry digit (C_n) is

$$C_n = \bar{A}\,B\,C + A\,\bar{B}\,C + A\,B\,\bar{C} + A\,B\,C$$

The truth table (and consequently the equations) indicates that the sum is 1 when only one input (either A, B, or C) is 1, or when all inputs (A, B, and C) are 1. The condition when A and B are 1 is not present in the sum equation since the sum output for this condition is 0. The C_n equation indicates that a new carry is generated whenever any two of the variables are 1, or when all variables (A, B, and C) are 1.

The C_n equation can be simplified as follows:

$$C_n = \bar{A}\,B\,C + A\,\bar{B}\,C + A\,B\,\bar{C} + A\,B\,C$$

Simplifying C_n

$$= \bar{A}\,B\,C + A\,\bar{B}\,C + A\,B\,(\bar{C} + C)$$

$$= \bar{A}\,B\,C + A\,\bar{B}\,C + A\,B\,(1)$$

$$= \bar{A}\,B\,C + A\,\bar{B}\,C + A\,B$$

$$= B\,C + A\,C + A\,B$$

The Veitch Diagram Simplification is constructed as shown in figure 5-11. Thus,

$$C_n = A\,B + A\,C + B\,C$$

AND and OR circuits can be combined as shown in the lower portion of figure 5-11 to produce a 1 condition at the sum output when any one of the conditions shown in the sum equation exists at the input. Likewise, the logic circuit arrangement in the upper portion of the figure produces a 1 carry output to the next higher order when any of the conditions contained in the carry equation exist at the input.

Remember that this circuit is designed to accommodate only two binary digits plus a carry digit contained in a single column. The addition of several columns of digits would require a similar circuit for each column (for parallel operation) or sufficient time between the application of binary inputs during serial operations to permit the carry function to be executed.

The equation can also be mechanized as shown in figure 5-12. This method is more commonly used in computers.

Looking at the sum equation again, consider the following simplification. (The symbol ⇒ is read "if".)

$$S = 1 \Rightarrow \bar{A}\,\bar{B}\,C + \bar{A}\,B\,\bar{C} + A\,\bar{B}\,\bar{C} + A\,B\,C$$

$$= C(A\,B + \bar{A}\,\bar{B}) + \bar{C}(A\,\bar{B} + \bar{A}\,B)$$

$$= C(\overline{A\,\bar{B} + \bar{A}\,B}) + \bar{C}(A\,\bar{B} + \bar{A}\,B)$$

Since, by DeMorgan's Theorem

$$\overline{A\,\bar{B} + \bar{A}\,B} = (A + \bar{B})\,(\bar{A} + B)$$

$$= A\,\bar{A} + A\,B + \bar{A}\,\bar{B} + B\,\bar{B}$$

$$= A\,B + \bar{A}\,\bar{B}$$

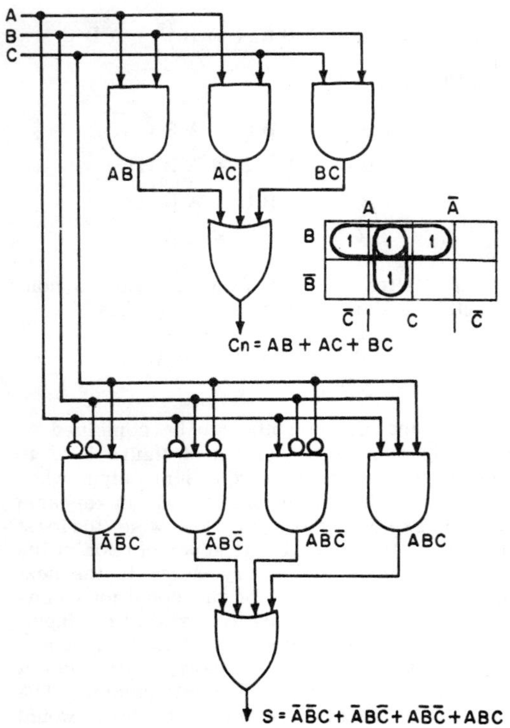

124.39

Figure 5-11.—Three-input adder.

To analyze the operation of this circuit, consider the output of the flip-flops FF_1 and FF_2 for a condition when A and B are Hi, and, when the carry input, C, is Lo. In this case, it is expected that the sum output of the stage X_2 (the stage under discussion) will be Lo and that the carry output will be Hi. These outputs can be verified by noting that the Hi output for A of FF1 and the Hi output for B at FF2 enable A1 to produce a Hi output. This Hi output passes through OR circuit, 02, and is applied as the carry input to the next higher stage (stage X_3, not shown). The A1 output is also applied through 01 to AND circuit, A4, as a partial enable for this circuit. Because the carry input from stage X_1 (the next lower order stage, not shown) is assumed to be Lo, A4 is not enabled and a Lo signal is produced as output. The low level C is inverted by I_2 to a high level which partially enables A5. However, the high level $AB + \overline{AB}$ signal at the 01 output is inverted by I1 to a Lo level and A5 is not enabled. As a result, both inputs to 03 are low, and the 03 output is Lo.

Now assume that the A, B, and C inputs to stage X_2 are Hi. The carry is produced in the same manner just described. Because C is also Hi in this case, A4 is enabled and the function $C(AB + \overline{AB})$ is Hi. Thus, the Hi output of A4 passes through 03 to represent a 1 condition sum for the stage X_2 output.

Consider a situation where A = Hi, B = Lo, and C = Hi. The outputs of A1 and A2 are Lo, resulting in a Lo output from 01 which disables A4. The Lo input to inverter, I1, is inverted and the resulting Hi output, representing an active complement of $A B + \bar{A}\bar{B}$ $(A\bar{B} + \bar{A}B)$ is applied as a partial enable to A3 and A5. Because C is Hi, the I2 output is Lo and A5 does not become fully enabled. However, the C input (Hi in this case) is applied directly to A3 so that with the Hi input from I1, A3 is enabled. In this condition, the function $C(A\bar{B} + \bar{A}B)$ is Hi. Thus, the 1 output of A3 passes through 02 as a 1 carry input to stage X_3.

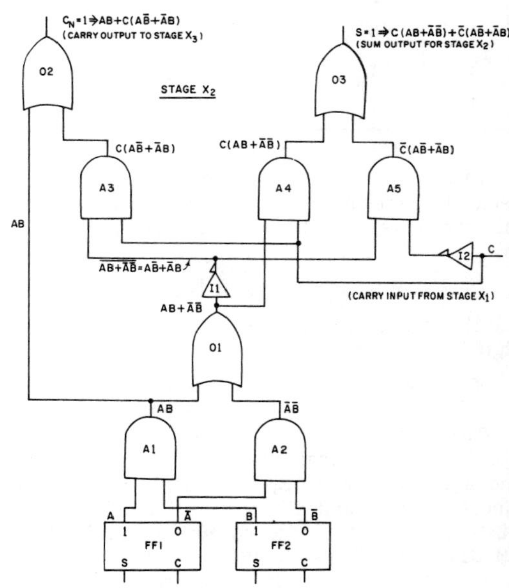

164.27

Figure 5-12.—Representative adder circuit mechanization.

Finally, consider a fourth example where the inputs are A = Lo, B = Hi, and C = Lo. Again, the input to I1 is Lo and the output is Hi. The Hi input to A5 along with the inverted carry input (inverted from Lo to Hi by I2) enables A5. The function $\bar{C}(A\bar{B} + \bar{A}B)$ is Hi. This Hi output passes through 03 to represent a 1 condition sum for the stage X_2 output. Note that A3 receives a Hi input from I1 but a Lo (non-inverted) carry input so that no carry is passed to the stage X_3.

The adder circuit shown in figure 5-13 is representative of adder circuits used in both the Univac Digital Trainer and CP-642A/USQ-20 computer, the latter is a component part of the Naval Tactical Data System (NTDS).

The circuit logic is identified in the truth table in Table 5-2. Note that when any input is Lo the output is Hi. Conversely, when all inputs are Hi the output is Lo.

To understand the operation of this circuit, first assume that the A and D inputs are Hi and

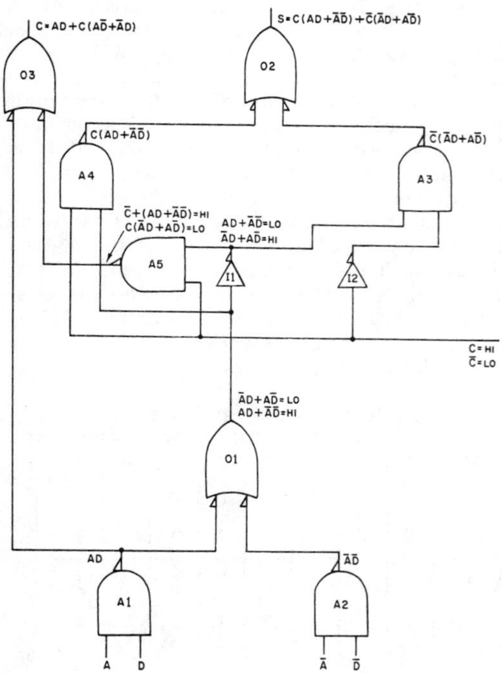

164.28

Figure 5-13.—Parallel adder using NOR logic.

Table 5-2. --Truth table for logic gates

A	D	C	LEVEL
Hi	Hi	Hi	Lo
Hi	Hi	Lo	Hi
Hi	Lo	Hi	Hi
Hi	Lo	Lo	Hi
Lo	Hi	Hi	Hi
Lo	Hi	Lo	Hi
Lo	Lo	Hi	Hi
Lo	Lo	Lo	Hi

the C input is Lo ($A D \bar{C}$). In this condition the A1 output is Lo. This Lo input causes the $A D + \bar{A}\bar{D}$ function at the 01 output to go Hi. The Hi 01 output serves as a partial enable to A4. However, the Lo carry input holds A4 in the disabled condition. The Hi 01 output is inverted by I1 so that the $A D + \bar{A}\bar{D}$ function at the I1 output is Lo to disable A5 and A3. Thus, neither A3, A4, nor A5 is enabled to produce a Lo output. Consequently, the 02 output remains Lo and the sum bit is 0. The Lo output of A1 and the Hi output of A5 (A5 not fully enabled) cause the 03 carry output to be Hi. Thus, a carry input is fed to the next higher order stage (not shown).

Now assume that the A, D, and C inputs are all Hi. The Hi carry output is generated in the same manner as just described. (The function $A D + \bar{A}\bar{D}$ is Lo at the I1 output so that A5 is disabled.) The Hi output of 01 (derived in the same manner as described in the previous example) is applied to A4 as a partial enable. The Hi carry input is also applied to A4. Thus, the A4 output goes Lo. This Lo output is an input to 02 and causes the 02 sum output to become Hi. Thus, for the assumed condition, both the carry and sum outputs are Hi (1).

Note the quality of the logic circuits as follows. Two functions are available at each output; the active function and its complement. The two outputs are at opposite levels, and obviously can not occur at the same time. Thus a decision is made when mechanizing the equation as to which function shall be shown in its active state. This is an important consideration in logic mechanization since either level from a given circuit can be used as the enable to another circuit.

The reader is encouraged to assume values of the A, D, and C variables not previously derived and determine the conditions throughout the adder which are active to produce the desired results.

SERIAL AND PARALLEL OPERATION

Adder circuits can be designed to accept input pulses in either serial or parallel form. In parallel operation, each bit of a binary number is carried on a separate transmission line. In serial operation the binary information is carried in the form of a series of timed pulses. The relative advantages and disadvantages of each form of data transmission are fairly obvious. Parallel operation is much faster because all bits are transmitted simultaneously, while serial transmission can pass only 1 bit at a time. On the other hand, serial transmission is much cheaper than parallel and requires less equipment. However, a true evaluation of the two methods is not quite so simple. For example, because the carry digit must be accumulated in the next higher order, the addition of N number of digits involved in an addition in a parallel machine is not necessarily accomplished N times as fast as can be done by a serial machine. Neither is it true that a parallel machine requires N times as much equipment. Thus, it would not be accurate to say that either of the two types of machines has a net advantage over the other, except where all features of the system are known and evaluated.

The choice of serial or parallel operation is also affected by the type of storage and the accessibility of stored data. The time required to read-up data from storage and to write information in storage are important considerations which add to the total time required to complete an arithmetic operation in both serial and parallel machines. This time is inherently available in serial machines because of the time between pulses in a train, but must be made available in parallel machines by introducing delay periods.

BINARY SUBTRACTER

A basic binary subtracter is a device that accepts the minuend and subtrahend digits at its input and produces a difference and borrow at its output. A truth table representing the conditions arising from the subtraction of 2 binary digits is shown in table 5-3. This function is that of an inhibitor, as discussed in chapter 3.

Table 5-3. —Truth table for subtracter

MINUEND (M)	0	1	0	1
SUBTRAHEND (S)	0	0	1	1
DIFFERENCE (D)	0	1	1	0
BORROW (B)	0	0	1	0

The Boolean equation for the conditions which produce a difference in table 5-3 is:

$$D = \overline{M}S + \overline{S}M$$

All other conditions produce a 0 difference. The borrow shown in the table exists when $B = \overline{M}S$.

As was true with addition of binary digits, more than 1 binary column is usually involved in the arithmetic process. Thus, table 5-3, although valid, is very limited. When more than one column of digits containing minuend and subtrahend is to be subtracted, each digit of the minuend is decreased by the amount of the subtrahend digit in that column, and if the minuend is reduced to a value less than 0 in the process the minuend digit of the next higher order must be reduced—the process by which the borrow is obtained. This is the method of subtraction most familiar to us, and, in fact, is a method in wide use in computer circuits.

Table 5-3 is also useful in a process called half-subtraction which does not take into account a borrow from a previous order.

Table 5-4. —Subtraction Table

M	0	1	0	1	0	1	0	1
S	0	0	1	1	0	0	1	1
B	0	0	0	0	1	1	1	1
D	0	1	1	0	1	0	0	1
B_N	0	0	1	0	1	0	1	1

Now consider a more complete subtraction table (table 5-4) which shows the minuend (M), subtrahend (S), borrow (B, which is advanced to that column from a lower order not shown), difference (D), and the borrow (B_N) which is the new borrow generated in the column in which the subtraction is taking place. From this table the difference equation can be derived by considering the conditions which produce a 1 as follows:

$$D = 1 \Rightarrow \overline{M}\,\overline{S}\,B + \overline{M}\,S\,\overline{B} + M\,\overline{S}\,\overline{B} + M\,S\,B$$
$$= \overline{B}(\overline{M}\,S + M\,\overline{S}) + B(M\,S + \overline{M}\,\overline{S})$$
$$\text{and} \quad \overline{M}\,S + M\,\overline{S} = \overline{M\,S + \overline{M}\,\overline{S}}$$
$$B_N = 1 \Rightarrow \overline{M}\,\overline{S}\,B + \overline{M}\,S\,\overline{B} + \overline{M}\,S\,B + M\,S\,B$$
$$= \overline{M}\,S + B(M\,S + \overline{M}\,\overline{S})$$

You will note that the binary subtracter logic circuit shown in figure 5-14 is similar to adder circuits already discussed. As might be expected, the analysis is basically the same. The only difference then is in the way the subtract operation is performed. Table 5-4 is the truth table.

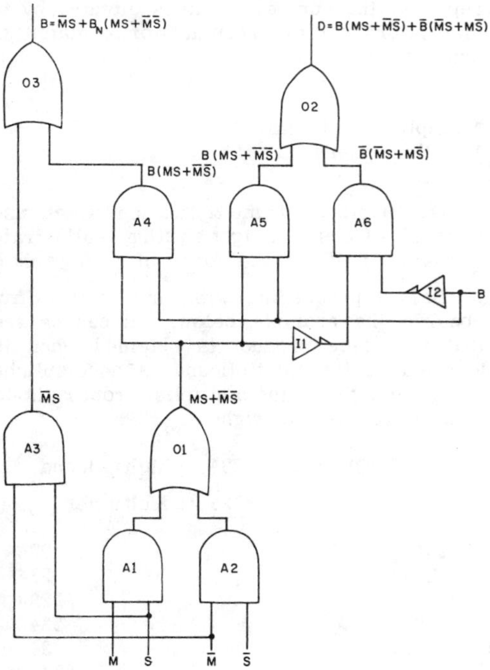

164.29

Figure 5-14.—Representative subtracter circuit mechanization.

Assume a condition where M, S, and B are all Hi. It is expected that the difference (D) and borrow (B_N) outputs will both be Hi. The action to produce these outputs is as follows.

With M and S Hi, the A1 output is Hi. The resulting Hi 01 output represents the true or Hi state of $M\,S + \overline{M}\,\overline{S}$. This output serves as a partial enable to A4 and A5. The Hi borrow input causes A4 and A5 to become fully enabled, to produce a Hi output at D via 02, representing the true state of the difference function $B(M\,S + \overline{M}\,\overline{S})$, and a Hi output at B_N via 03 representing the true or Hi state of the borrow function $B(M\,S + \overline{M}\,\overline{S})$. Thus, both the difference and borrow outputs are Hi.

Now consider the action when M is Lo, S is Hi, and B is Lo. By design, the output of AND circuit A3 goes Hi when M is Lo ($\overline{M}$) and S is Hi (S). Thus, the 03 output goes Hi to represent a borrow to the next higher order (B_N). The inputs ($\overline{M}$ S) do not enable A1 or A2 and the 01 output is low for the function $M\,S + \overline{M}\,\overline{S}$. This Lo output disables A4 and A5, but is inverted by I1. The Hi I1 output must therefore represent the absence of $M\,S + \overline{M}\,\overline{S}$ while simultaneously representing the presence of its complement which is $\overline{M}\,S + M\,\overline{S}$. This Hi input is a partial enable to A6. In a like manner, because B is Lo, the Hi I2 output must represent the complement of B, or $\overline{B}$. This Hi signal along with the Hi I1 output enables A6 and the resulting Hi output, representing the function $\overline{B}(\overline{M}\,S + M\,\overline{S})$, passes through 02 to represent a Hi difference output for the assumed inputs.

It is suggested that other underived conditions be examined so that a more thorough understanding of the subtracter action can be realized.

MULTIPLICATION

Like all other arithmetic operations, multiplication can be accomplished in computers in several ways. One of the most commonly used methods is multiplication by accumulation.

Serial Multiplication by Repeated Addition

The arithmetic unit contains several registers usually referred to as the X, Q, D, and A registers. These registers are capable of storing or holding a computer word of a length determined by design. In most cases, during

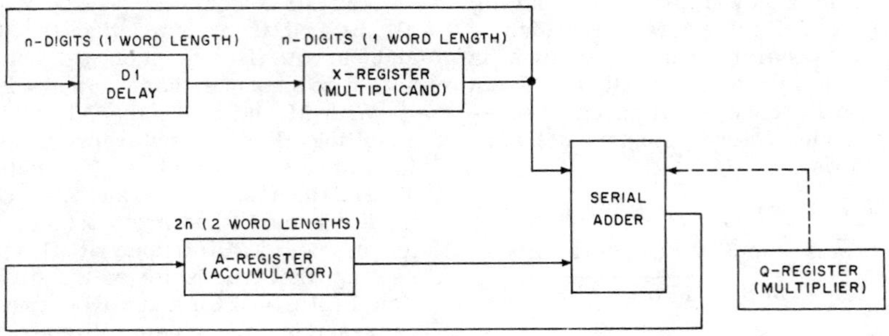

124.45

Figure 5-15.—A block diagram for serial multiplication by repeated addition.

multiplication, the Q-register (fig. 5-15), holds the multiplier; the X-register, the multiplicand; and the A-register (the accumulator) holds the sum or partial product. Because the product of two numbers, each containing n digits, can contain as many as 2n digits, the accumulator must be capable of holding twice as many digits as either the multiplier or the multiplicand.

The X-register reads its input (the multiplicand) into the serial adder in serial form at the same time that the accumulator input is being read through in serial form. Initially, the accumulator is cleared to 0.

The multiplier or Q-register is actually a counter which determines the number of times the particular multiplicand must be added to yield the correct product. If the multiplicand is to be multiplied by 3, the Q-register will initially be set to 3 and will count backwards 1 digit at a time, with the multiplicand and the accumulator contents being added in the proper order for each count.

Because the accumulator is initially set to 0000.... the first addition will produce the multiplicand in the accumulator. The second addition is delayed for 1 word length by D1 to compensate for the difference in word lengths of the accumulator and the X-register inputs. The delay assures that at the beginning of each count the least significant digit of the X-register and the least significant digit of the A-register will arrive in the serial adder simultaneously.

After the first addition, the contents of the Q-register are decreased by 1, and, after delay, the second addition begins by again adding the contents of the X-register to the accumulated sum. A second delay now takes place in D1, again to ensure that the lowest orders of the X- and A-registers will enter the serial adder on the third count at the same time. The process (diagrammed in the flow chart in figure 5-16), continues until the contents of the Q-register is reduced to 0 whereby the addition has been repeated the number of times dictated by the multiplier and the accumulator contains the product.

Multiplication Using Parallel Adders

One method of multiplication which uses parallel adders and right shifting is illustrated in figure 5-17 in the form of a flow chart.

Before proceeding with this method first observe the example below. It can be seen that the same product is obtained when the addition of the multiplicand is accomplished using the digits in the multiplier from right-to-left, or from left-to-right.

PROBLEM:	234	Multiplicand
	x123	Multiplier

```
234                 234
 234                234
 234                234
  234              234
  234              234
  234             234
28782           28782
```

Equivalent of left-to-right shift	Equivalent of right-to-left shift

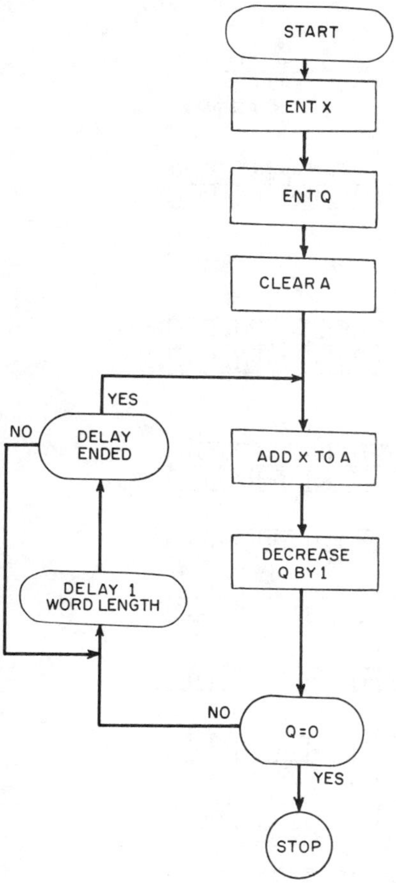

164.30

Figure 5-16.—Flow chart for serial multiplication by repeated addition.

Thus, multiplication can be (and is) performed by either left-shifting or right-shifting the multiplier.

The blocks in the flow chart in figure 5-17A represent the sequence of events necessary to arrive at a desired result, in this case, the product. In general, flow charts actually provide a logical presentation of a procedure. All of the steps involved in arriving at this procedure are accomplished under the direct influence of the control unit.

Assume that the multiplicand is 11111 (31), and that the multiplier is 101 (5) in the following example. The control sequences are as follows:

Transfer the multiplier (101) to the Q-register (fig. 5-17B).

Place the multiplicand in the X-register and clear the accumulator (A-register). Set the shift counter to equal the word length (9 bits in this case). The next command is to reduce the shift counter by 1 (this does not produce a shift in the AQ-register at this time). Now examine the lowest order bit in the Q-register. If this bit is a 1, i.e., if $Q_{00} = 1$, add X (multiplicand) to the A-register. This action places 11111 in the accumulatorⓐ. The next command is to shift the contents of the A- and Q-registers to the right 1 bit. In executing this function, the A and Q registers are joined together as a single 18 bit register and the least significant digit in the A-register is shifted into the higher order bit position in the Q-register ⓑ. This action drops the one bit in the lowest order of the Q-register and the 0 in the second order is now the least significant digit in the Q-register.

At this point we examine the shift counter (not shown), to determine if the count has been reduced to 0. If the answer is "no," as it will be in this case, since 8 counts remain, the command is issued to reduce the count by 1, and a subsequent command examines the Q-register to determine if the lowest order bit is a 1. In this case the answer will be "no" since the 0 bit has been shifted to the least significant bit position. Because the answer is "no," it is not necessary or required that the "add X to A command" be issued and this step is bypassed as indicated in the flow chart. The next command, therefore, shifts all bits in the A- and Q-registers to the right 1 bit position, and a 1 bit now appears as the least significant digit in the Q-register ⓒ. The following step again checks the shift counter to see if the multiplier count has been reduced to to 0. The answer is again "no" as there are 7 additional counts. Thus, the command to reduce the count by 1 is again issued. Upon checking the Q-register to see if the lowest order bit is 1, the answer will be "yes," and the command will be issued to add X (multiplicand) to A. This action adds the multiplicand to the previous accumulator sum as shown at ⓓ.

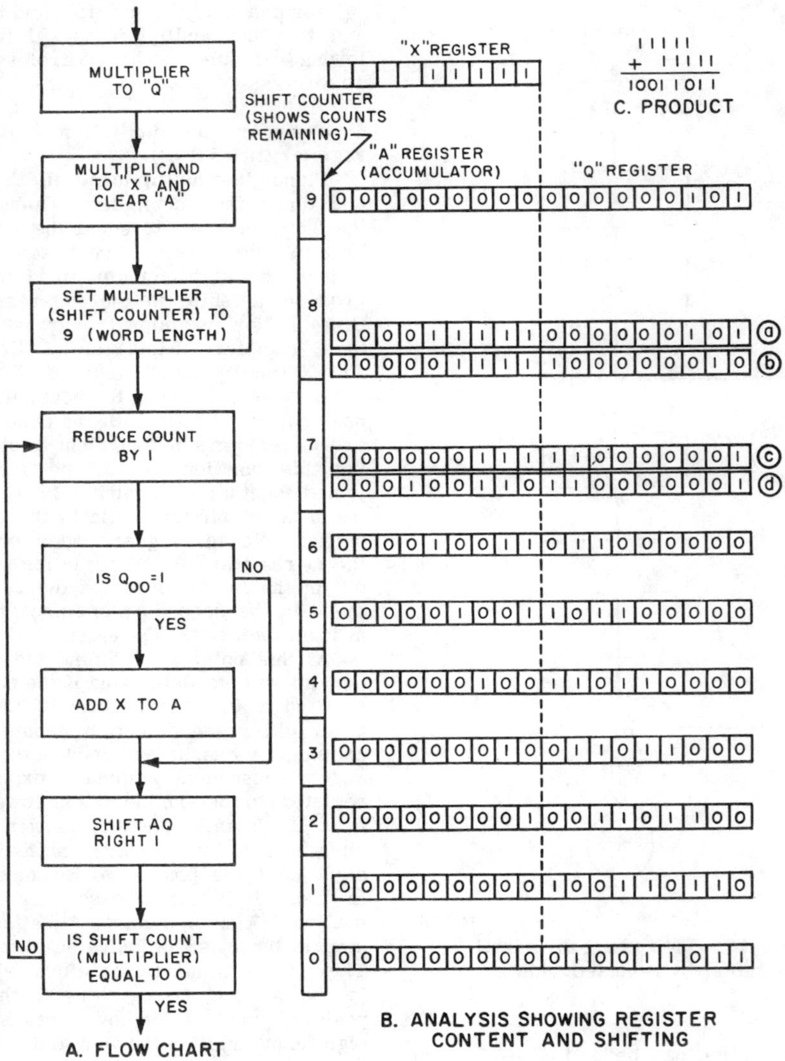

124.46

Figure 5-17.—Multiplication by addition and shifting.

A check of the shift counter reveals that the count has not been reduced to 0 and that 6 counts still remain. Because each of these counts produces a "no" answer when the Q-register is checked to determine if the lowest order bit is 1, the shift AQ right 1 command will be issued in sequential order as each bit is checked, until the shift counter shows the multiplier count to be reduced to 0. At this time the lowest order bit in the product will be in the lowest order position of the Q-register, followed at the left by each higher order bit, revealing the highest order bit in the product in the 8th bit position to the left. Thus, the contents of the Q-register is the true product.

Multiplication can also be accomplished by adding and shifting. Either left or right shifting may be used. One method of performing a left shift is illustrated in figure 5-18.

This method basically involves left shifting of the multiplier (0, 1, 2, or 3 positions in this case) and adding whenever a 1 bit is encountered in any one of the multiplier orders.

The number of switching elements used is determined by the number of digits to be multiplied. The multiplicand is applied on lines A through E, and remains as the static input throughout the multiplication process. The multiplier digits are applied as control inputs on lines W, X, Y, and Z.

If a 1 bit is present in the first order of the multiplier a shift is not required and the multiplier input lines (multiplication control lines) X and Z are placed in the 1 state. A careful study of the AND and OR elements will reveal that a nonshifted output is developed at the lower terminals I through M. This output represents a partial product which is fed to the adder circuits in the accumulator. Now, if the second order digit of the multiplier is a 1 bit, a shift of one place to the left is desired before addition and lines W and Z are in the 1 state. Thus, a left shift is produced (1 place to the left) in the upper part of the circuit and is passed through the lower section under the influence of the Z input. The output from terminals H through L is added in the accumulator to form a second partial product.

If the third place digit of the multiplier is a 1, the multiplication control lines X and Y are placed in the 1 state. This produces a third partial product output between terminals G and K which is fed to the adder circuits in the accumulator.

Similarly, the multiplication control lines W and Y are used to generate the fourth partial product output between terminals F and J if the fourth place digit of the multiplier is a 1. The output is added in the accumulator to produce the true product.

This particular circuit can also be used to execute multiple shifts in one operation if up to three of the lower order bits of a multiplier are all zero. This action circumvents the time

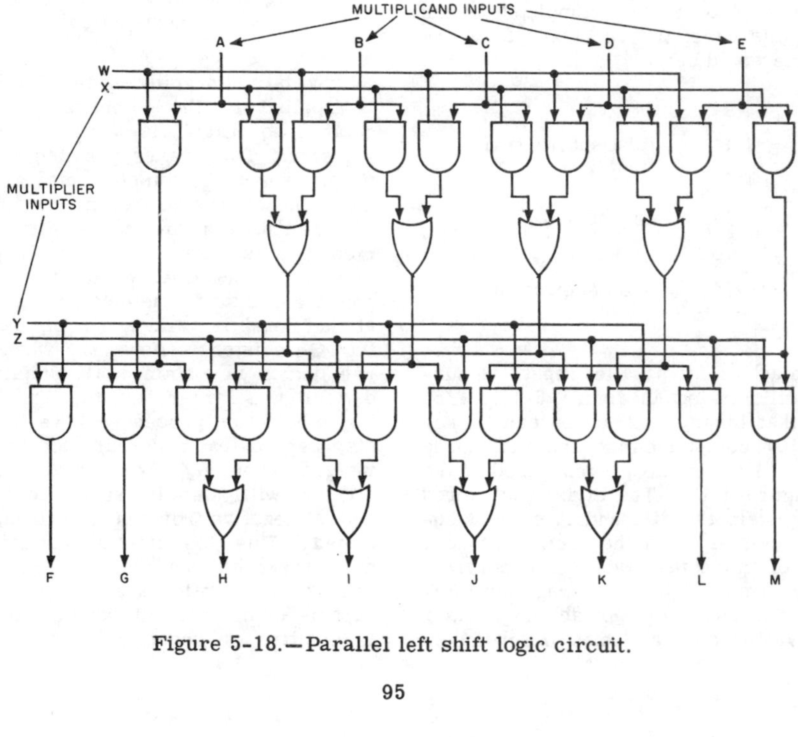

124.44

Figure 5-18.—Parallel left shift logic circuit.

consuming process of performing single shifts. The multiple shift can be used since the accumulator content will not be changed when the multiplier bit is zero.

A sensing circuit (not shown) is used to determine the number of zeros in the multiplier (up to three) counting from the least significant bit position. This sensing circuit must then enable the proper multiplier input lines as discussed in order to execute the desired shift.

DIVISION

Division can be accomplished by repetitive subtraction as illustrated in the following example using 36 (as the dividend) and 12 as the divisor. The dividend is reduced by the amount of the divisor for each subtraction.

12)36	36	
	12	first subtraction
	24	
	12	second subtraction
	12	
	12	third subtraction
	0	

The number of subtractions completed is the quotient, in this case, 3. In binary form the same example would be:

100100	=	44_8	
1100	=	14_8	first subtraction
11000	=	30_8	
1100	=	14_8	second subtraction
1100	=	14_8	
1100	=	14_8	third subtraction
0000	=	0	

A block diagram for parallel repetitive subtraction is illustrated in figure 5-19. You will recall that binary subtraction can be accomplished by complementing the subtrahend and adding. This is the process used in the circuit of figure 5-19. The divisor is stored in the X-register, the dividend is in the accumulator (A-register), and the quotient, that is the number of times the divisor is taken from the dividend is stored in the Q-register. Because it is necessary to subtract the divisor from the dividend several times, depending on their relative magnitudes, the X-register output is applied to the complementor and recirculated so that it is again stored in the X-register. This makes possible the read-in of the divisor to the complementor as many times as is necessary to reach the final quotient.

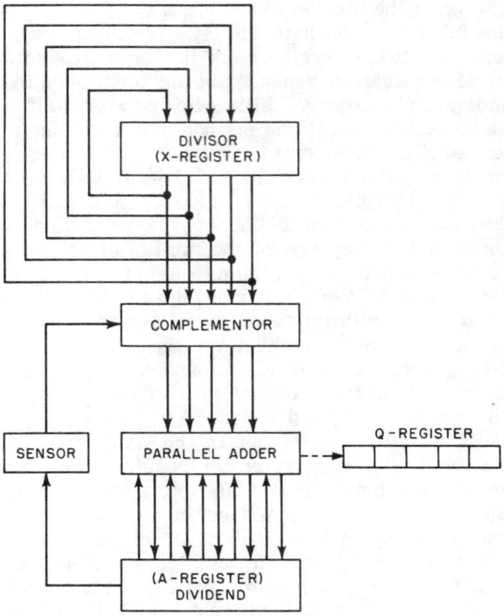

164.31

Figure 5-19.—Parallel repetitive subtraction.

When dividing by the repetitive subtraction method it is possible to obtain a positive remainder, a negative remainder, or 0. When a positive remainder is obtained, the subtraction at that level is valid and a bit is entered into the Q-register. However, when a negative remainder is obtained, it implies that the divisor was larger than the dividend and that the subtraction processes have been carried 1 step beyond that necessary to obtain the final integral quotient. When a 0 is obtained the divisor will also be subtracted from the 0 and a negative remainder will again be obtained. This, too, implies that the subtraction has proceeded one step too far. Thus, it is necessary to utilize a sensor circuit which is capable of determining whether the remainder is positive or negative. If the remainder is positive the sensor must allow the divisor input from X to be complemented and added. The sensor element must permit complementing each time the remainder is positive.

When a negative remainder is obtained (as a result of a 0 difference or a divisor which is larger than the dividend) the sensor must feed the correct voltage to the complementor to prevent complementing, so that the amount subtracted on the previous step will be added. Thus, the step beyond that necessary to obtain the integral quotient is nullified.

Although this is a rather simple procedure it is possible to reduce the number of steps (time) required, by using comparing and shifting. This is particularly helpful when the dividend is large and the divisor small.

The division process illustrated in the flow chart of figure 5-20 is similar to the adder circuits discussed earlier, except that subtraction is the arithmetic operation rather than addition. The AQ-register holds the dividend, and the X-register, the divisor. The shift counter contains the maximum number of shifts which may be required (one word length).

The contents of the AQ-register is shifted left one bit position after each subtraction and the quotient bit is entered in the least significant bit positions in Q. The highest order bit in the A-register is dropped. At the completion of the division process the quotient is contained in the Q-register.

Note the comparison to determine if A (the dividend) is greater than or equal to X (the divisor). If A > X then X is subtracted from A. This step is followed by setting Q_0 to 1, that is, setting the lowest bit in the Q-register to 1. If the A > X comparison results in a "no," a subtraction does not take place.

At the end of the subtraction process (as indicated when the shift counter reaches 0), a "yes" result is produced for the interrogation "is count = 0." Thus, the order "read next instruction" (RNI) is initiated.

Another method involves division by the familiar longhand method. In this method we make an inspection to determine the number of times the divisor can be subtracted from the

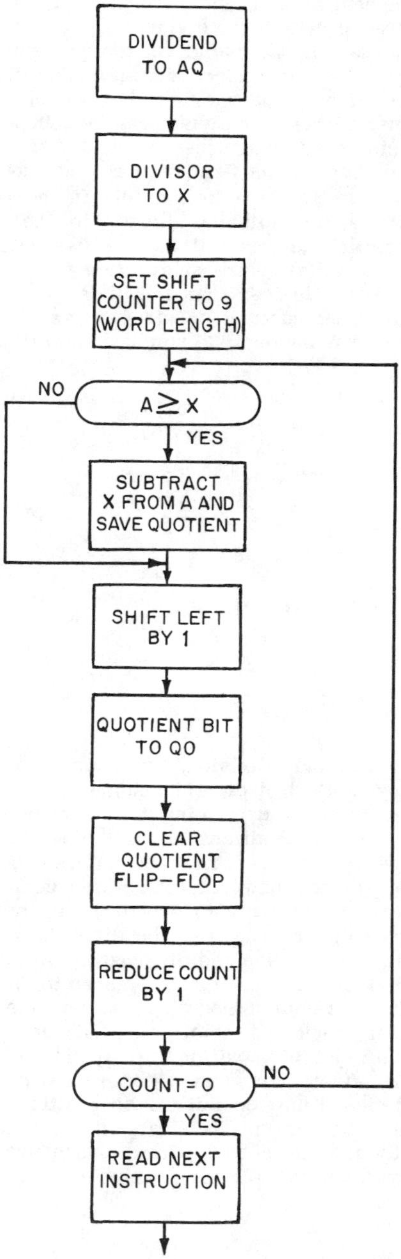

164.31

Figure 5-20.—Division flow chart.

highest order quantity which is greater than the divisor within the dividend and enter this number as the first digit in the quotient. We then get the remainder and shift the divisor one position to the right. Here we determine how many times the divisor can be subtracted from this portion of the dividend and enter this number as the first digit in the quotient.

After subtraction to obtain the remainder we again shift the divisor to the right one position and repeat the process until the remainder after the subtraction from the lowest position is less than the divisor. This yields the final quotient. This process is illustrated below using decimal numbers as follows:

```
     3117.5
15)46763.0
   45
    17
    15
     26
     15
     113
     105
       80
       75
        5
```

In binary division, (and common to the shifting method of division) some procedures must be used to determine the number of higher order bit positions of the dividend into which the divisor can first be entered to yield a 1 bit in the quotient. In some computers, an attempt is made to subtract the divisor from the higher orders of the dividend. If the result is positive the dividend is larger than the divisor, and a 1 bit is entered in the quotient. If the result is negative, the machine automatically negates this step and the divisor is shifted 1 bit position to the right. This action, in effect, halves the divisor, and because the dividend now contains 1 bit position more than the divisor, the subtraction is valid and the division proceeds. This procedure is illustrated in the following example.

(Check for position of first bit in quotient. When remainder is negative, i. e., not a real number, this step is nullified.)

```
                                  1011    (11)
                       1100(12) 10000100  (132)
                                1100
Not a real number ------------> -100
(nullified)
                                10000100
Result of a right                1100
shift --------------------------> 
                                 1001
                                 1100
Not a real number ------------>  -101
(nullified)                      10010
                                  1100
                                  1100
                                  1100
                                  0000
```

Unless the relative magnitudes of the dividend and divisor are restricted to values between two extremes, it is possible that the first subtraction at the higher order can produce a 1 bit and a remainder which is greater than the divisor. An example is shown below:

```
       1
011)111100
    011
    100
```

This inevitably will produce an erroneous result. The error can be prevented by restricting the minimum value of the divisor, the maximum value of the dividend, or both. In the above example the divisor could be restricted to 100, and/or the dividend to 101. In any case, the relative magnitude of the two should be such that the remainder will be less than the divisor after the subtraction of the divisor from the highest orders of the dividend.

In some computers (fractional computers or floating point) the quotient is always less than 1 and all significant digits appear to the right of the radix point. In these computers the above stated problem is solved, by ensuring that the divisor is always larger than the dividend.

Chapter 6

MEMORY AND STORAGE DEVICES

The memory section of the digital computer, also called the storage section, is one of the five basic sections of the computer. The other sections are the control and arithmetic sections (treated in Chapters 4 and 5, respectively) and the input and output sections (discussed in a later chapter). The memory section is used for (1) storing the data to be processed, and (2) for storing the program of instructions which are used to direct the processing of the data in a predetermined and organized fashion.

This chapter is a treatment of the devices used in the memory (storage) section of the computer or for mass storage of binary data. Specifically, these devices are the magnetic cores, magnetic drums, magnetic tapes, magnetic disks, electrostatic storage and thin film. The storage techniques and other related operations are shown. Special attention is given to the parts of the memory, and factors for determining the choice of memory form.

The student is encouraged to make use of the glossary to clarify words and terms that may aid in understanding the content of this chapter.

MEMORY PARTS, TERMINOLOGY, AND FORM

To explain the functional operations of the memory section of the computer, it is necessary to start with the parts of the memory. Some terms that are unique to the memory section will be defined. An explanation will be made of factors to be considered in selecting the memory form to be used.

PARTS OF THE MEMORY

The memory section (fig. 6-1) consists of five basic components: storage medium, memory address register, memory exchange register, storage selection circuits, and storage control.

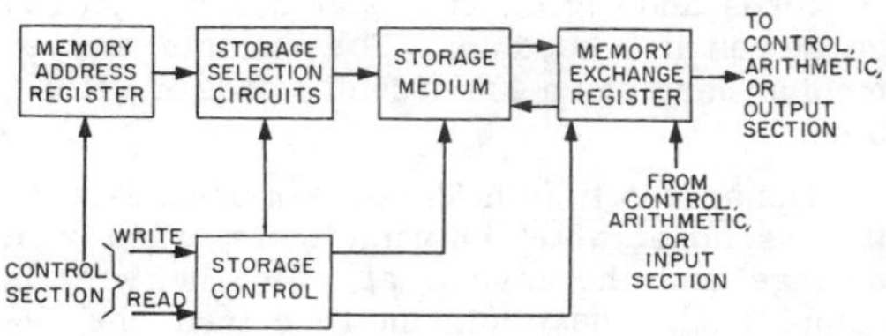

164.32

Figure 6-1.—Memory section.

At the start of a program, the data and instruction words are written into the storage medium and, when needed, are read out of the storage medium for use in the arithmetic section, control section, or input-output section.

The address of the word to be read or written is sent to the memory address register from the control section. If the word is to be written, the word itself is sent to the memory exchange register. The storage selection circuits decode the address and select the proper storage location in the storage medium. The control section also sends a write or read signal to the storage control to begin the selected process. When a write signal is received, the storage control gates the memory exchange register, the storage selection circuits, and the storage medium, thereby allowing the data in the memory exchange register to be transferred to the storage medium location selected by the storage selection circuits.

When a read signal is received the storage selection circuits (using address information received from the memory address register) select the storage medium location from which information is to be read out, and the information is transferred to the memory exchange register. The memory exchange register, in turn, sends the information to either the control section, arithmetic section, or output section depending upon the function code designator.

SPECIAL MEMORY TERMINOLOGY

In discussing the operation of the memory section, certain terminology is used which is peculiar to memory. These terms are defined briefly in the following paragraphs. More definitions are contained in the glossary.

Storage capacity is generally measured by the number of bits, or in terms of the number of words and digits, of a stated base that can be stored in a medium. For example, a given medium may store 4096 32-bit words or 131,072 bits.

The access time is the time interval between the instant at which information is called from storage and the instant at which delivery is completed. The minimum time from the beginning of one access to the beginning of the next is often important and is called the cycle time. The cycle time is generally longer than the access time.

A random access storage unit is one in which the time required to read or write a word is independent of the location. An example of a random access unit is the magnetic core storage unit (discussed later).

A sequential access storage unit is one in which the access time is dependent on the location of the desired word in the storage medium. Maximum, minimum, and average access times are often stated as well as the minimum time from the beginning of one access time to the beginning of the next. Magnetic tapes and card decks are examples of storage media which use sequential access.

Two types of sequential access are in use; the sequential cyclic (as used with drums or disks), and the sequential progressive (as used with magnetic tape or punched cards).

Periodic access refers to that type of access used for reading and recording on magnetic drums or disks. With these storage devices information is available under a reading or recording head only for a specified period of each revolution.

Speed measurements of a particular storage unit are least ambiguous when accompanied by a statement of the type of access used. Two classes of access are recognized; random and sequential.

FACTORS DETERMINING THE CHOICE OF MEMORY FORM

The choice of the storage medium to be used in a computer is dependent upon several factors. Among these are (1) the intended computer use or purpose, (2) physical size, (3) cost, (4) power consumption of the equipment, (5) access time, and (6) reliability. (Reliability is a measure of the ability of the computer to function without failure over a long period.)

The type of storage device determines the size and amount of data the computer can handle and also affects the timing of the control section. The speed of operation of the storage medium determines (to a great extent) the instruction execution time and thus the overall time required for the computer to execute a given program.

MAGNETIC DRUM MEMORY

The types of memory storage devices most frequently used in present day computer technology are magnetic drums, magnetic cores, thin film, magnetic disks and magnetic tapes. Magnetic cores and magnetic thin film are the only types presently being used for main computer memory.

MAGNETIC DRUM STORAGE TECHNIQUE

The magnetic drum storage device is a cylinder which rotates at constant velocity. Information is written on or read from the drum when its magnetic surface passes under magnetic heads which are similar to the magnetic heads found on commercial tape recorders.

Magnetic drums provide a relatively inexpensive method of storing large amounts of data. A magnetic drum (fig. 6-2) can be made by using either a hollow cylinder (thus the name "drum") or a solid cylinder. The cylinder may consist entirely of a magnetic alloy, or it may have such an alloy plated upon its surface. Many drums are made by spraying on a magnetite, such as iron oxide. The surface is then coated with a thin coat of lacquer, and buffed.

Representative drums have diameters ranging from 5 to 20 inches. The surface of the drum is divided into tracks or channels which encircle the drum. A number of read and write

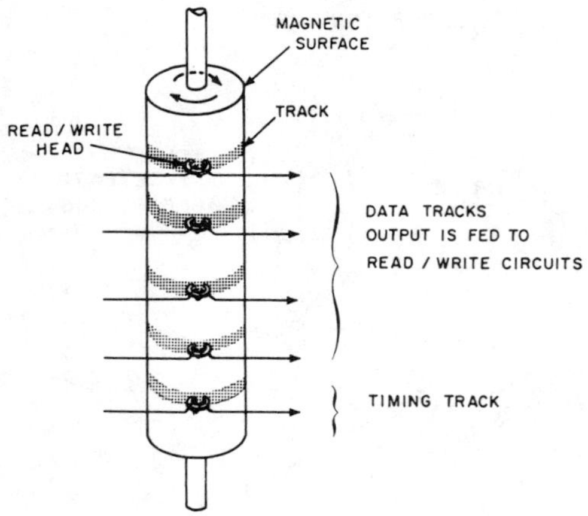

124.60
Figure 6-2.—Magnetic drum.

heads (at least one for each track) are used for recording and reading. The drum is rotated so that the heads are near but not touching the drum surface at all times.

As the drum rotates, the tracks are continuously passing under their respective head. Each track is subdivided into cells, each of which can store one binary bit. All of the cells that are positioned under the heads of a multitrack drum at the same time are called a "slot." With some drums, each head reads or writes one bit of a word. Thus, when a word is written into or read from a slot, each track contains one bit of that word. The number of heads used depends on the size of the word that the computer is designed to handle.

One of the tracks provides timing signals for the drum rotation. The timing track determines the location of each set of storage cells around the drum. Each timing signal denotes a unit of time of the drum rotation. For example, if the timing track is 80 inches long and timing signals are recorded at 120 pulses per inch, there are 9600 locations for bit storage on the track. If the drum has 32 tracks in addition to the timing track, the drum has the capacity to store a total of 307,200 bits.

Some drums use two or even three timing tracks. The timing tracks are used for synchronization purposes, and are sometimes called "control" or "clock" tracks. The timing pulses establish the time scale to which all circuits throughout the computer are synchronized.

When core memory is used all the data are stored in the cores in a static condition, and can be located at a given place at any instant. The data are easily read from that location in serial or parallel form to represent the same data that was stored in that location.

Dynamic storage refers to data stored on constantly rotating drums. Therefore, transfer of the data is complicated. Timing pulses are not used to synchronize the drum speed (which may vary slightly from time to time). Thus, some method must be used to ensure that data read into the drum memory in a given bit position, will be read from the memory with the same time reference. The probability of an incompatible time relationship between the drum speed and synchronizing (clock) pulses, makes it necessary to establish some means of compensating for variations in drum speeds.

In practice, the drum contains a control point and a number of sectors in a specific format. The control point is a magnetic mark that specifies a starting location on the drum. All data stored on the drum are referenced to this indexing point.

DRUM MEMORY CIRCUITS

A representative magnetic drum memory circuit is shown in figure 6-3. The functions of the storage control, memory buffer register, and memory address register are described in a preceding paragraph, titled "Parts of Memory." The read or write signal from the storage control circuit gates the read-write circuits, so that the data from the memory buffer register can be transferred to the magnetic drum heads. The location on the drum where data are to be recorded is supplied to the memory address register from the control section. This location data is fed from the memory address register to the storage (track) selection circuits. A control signal generated from the storage selection circuits is sent to the read-write circuits. This signal routes the data to the selected track area on the drum during a write order and routes the data from the selected location on the drum through the read-write circuits during a read order.

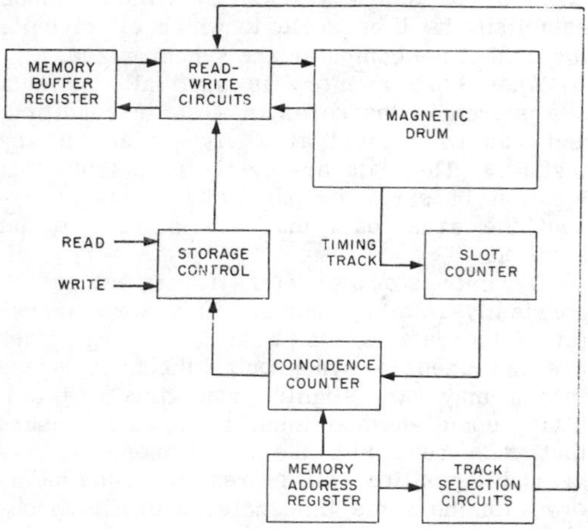

164.33
Figure 6-3.—Magnetic drum memory circuits.

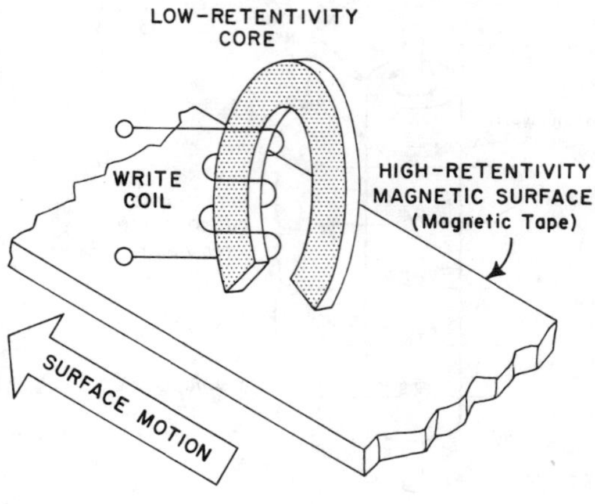

164.34
Figure 6-4—Surface magnetic wiring arrangement.

As the drum rotates, the timing track head sends signals to the slot counter which counts the slots passing under the read-write heads. Assuming that the duration of one complete drum rotation is 32 milliseconds and successive slots are 16 microseconds apart, the computer can process each word in approximately 64 microseconds. The slot count is compared with the address in the memory address register by the coincidence counter, where an interlace of four is achieved by having consecutive addresses refer to every fourth slot on the drum. As a result, consecutive addresses appear every 64 microseconds. When coincidence occurs, a pulse is sent to the storage control which, in turn, causes the reading or writing to take place in the selected track.

READ/WRITE HEADS

Surface magnetic writing is performed by means of a coil of wire (called the write coil) wrapped around a specially shaped core (Fig. 6-4). The core consists of low-retentivity magnetic material, such as Mumetal, and is provided with an air gap. The entire device is called a write head.

The application of a signal voltage across the write coil produces a flow of current; this creates a magnetomotive force that causes flux to pass through the series combination of core and air gap, and through that portion of the magnetic surface close to the air gap. Since the reluctance of the magnetic surface is very much less than that of the parallel air path, most of the magnetic flux passes through the magnetic surface. This resembles the manner in which current flows through a circuit containing two parallel resistors of unequal values. The magnetic surface is moved past the air gap at a constant speed, so that each element of the high-retentivity magnetic surface retains a portion of the magnetic flux that existed at the moment when that portion of the surface was near the air gap of the write head.

Characteristics of the Magnetic Head

The pole pieces, or end of the core that forms the air gap, are designed so that the lines of flux passing between their tips will lie parallel to the surface of the tape. In this manner, as shown in figure 6-5, the main magnetic field retained by the magnetic surface is parallel to the surface. This produces a strong retained field. The core may consist of solid metal, or it may be laminated in order to reduce eddy currents.

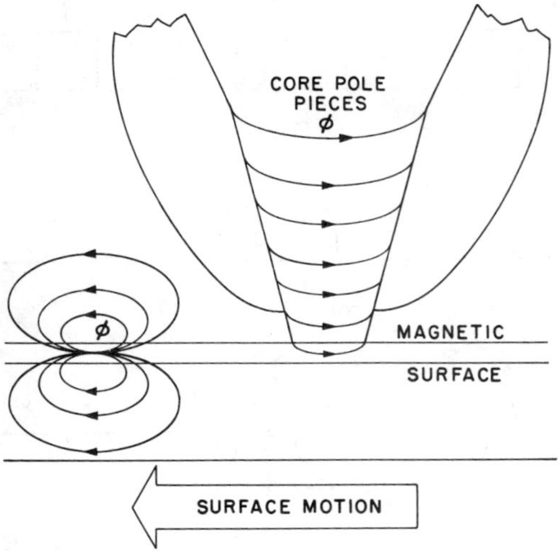

67.94

Figure 6-5.—Magnetizing a moving surface by the "longitudinal recording" method.

Magnetizing Techniques

The method of magnetizing the moving surface as shown in figures 6-4 and 6-5 is called "longitudinal recording." This term is applied to magnetic tapes, since the direction of flux is along the long axis of the tape.

In computer applications, the speed may be several hundred inches per second. Consequently, abrasive wear of the pole tips and the magnetic surface could become a problem if contact were permitted. Thus, in order to improve overall reliability, the pole tips of most computer magnetic heads are separated from the moving magnetic surface by a distance of a few thousandths of an inch. Although the increased path reluctance produced by this arrangement requires the use of greater driving currents, the absence of abrasive wear justifies its use.

During a reading operation, the magnetized magnetic surface moves past the air gap of a device that is very similar to the write head. In the course of the reading operation, some of the flux from the moving magnetic surface passes through the read core, which has a much lower reluctance than the surrounding air. As a result, voltages are induced across the coil mounted on this core. In some instances, both the write and the read coil are wrapped around the same core, and the device is then called a read-write head. When a read-write head is used, suitable external circuitry must be used so that the voltages induced in the read coil during a reading operation, and in the write coil during a writing operation, do not produce interference in the associated electronic driving and reproducing circuits. The waveform of the voltages induced in the read coil are similar to the waveforms of the signal originally used to magnetize the surface of the tape.

The space between the magnetic head pole tips is usually referred to as the gap width or the gap, and its dimensions are extremely important.

When pulses are to be written, the gap width determines the number of pulses that can be written on a given portion of the magnetic surface. Since each pulse magnetizes the entire portion of the surface across the air gap at a particular instant, the surface area on which each pulse is written is determined by gap width, gap length, pulse duration, and tape speed.

It is desirable from both a frequency-response and a pulse-writing point of view to use the smallest possible air gap. However, if the air gap width is too small, its reduced reluctance permits the loss of some flux that would otherwise have passed through the magnetic surface. Furthermore, the difficulties of manufacturing small, uniform gaps must be considered. In consideration of the foregoing criteria, the gap width is usually in the order of 0.001 inch.

A very important characteristic of a magnetic surface writing device is the number of pulses or bits of information (binary digits) that can be written upon a given length of magnetic surface. This is called the packing factor or bit density. When information is to be stored for future use, it is desirable to store as many bits as possible on a given length of surface. This decreases the amount of required storage space and also reduces the time required later to gain access to the information. Two main factors affect the maximum bit density: the previously discussed gap width of the read-write head, and the interaction of the magnetic fields of the storage surface.

Interaction of magnetic fields occurs between adjacent magnetized areas of the tape surface. If these areas, which possess the characteristics of tiny bar magnets, are too close together, their magnetic fields will combine. When the magnetic surface is read, only two pulses will be produced; one at the beginning of the series of combined flux pulse, and the other at the end of the series. This interaction is reduced when increased spacing is used between the magnetized areas. However, this increased spacing reduces the bit density. Spacing between magnetized areas can be made larger either by increasing the surface speed or by recording the data at a lower pulse-repetition frequency.

The actual areas of the magnetic surface that are separately and distinctly magnetized are sometimes called storage cells. A pulse is said to be "written in a storage cell." One storage cell is required to record each bit of any binary word written on a magnetic surface.

Besides writing, it is also necessary to be able to erase the data that are no longer needed. Two methods of surface erasing are commonly employed. The first method, DC erasing, magnetically saturates the surface, thereby masking all previously written data. The second method, AC erasing, actually returns the surface to a state of zero flux, or demagnetizes it.

Now consider some recording systems. Several types are used. In the simplest, a pulse indicates a binary 1, while no pulse (the absence of a pulse) indicates a binary 0.

POSITIVE-PULSE RETURN-TO-ZERO SYSTEM

In this system the waveforms of the binary word 101101 appear as in figure 6-6A or B. This method is abbreviated RZ.

The flux slope is positive at the leading edge of the pulse, zero at the top of the pulse, and negative on its trailing edge. During the reading process (fig 6-6C), a positive and a negative pulse are induced in the read head each time the flux pulse stored on the magnetic surface passes the air gap. This occurs because the induced voltage is proportional to the rate of change of the flux.

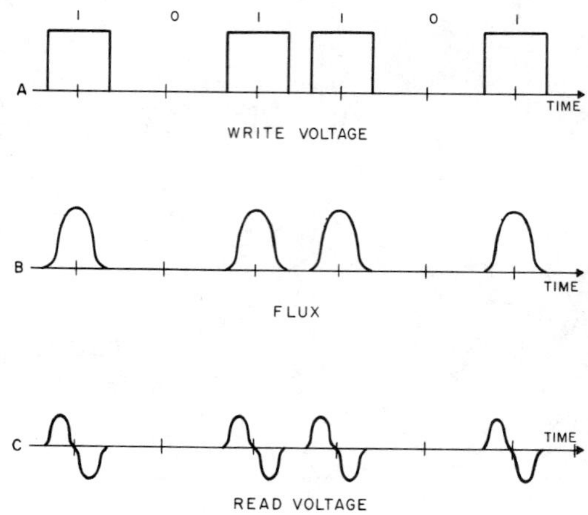

67.95

Figure 6-6.—Waveform of positive-pulse Return-To-Zero (RZ) system.

POSITIVE AND NEGATIVE PULSE RETURN-TO-ZERO METHOD

In this recording system, both positive and negative current pulses can be used to write a binary word. In this instance, a positive pulse can be used to represent a binary 1, and a negative pulse can be used to represent a 0 (fig. 6-7).

The output for binary 1 (fig. 6-8) will consist of a small positive pulse followed by a large negative pulse and then a small positive pulse. The opposite will occur for a binary 0 read pulse; that is, a negative pulse followed by a large positive pulse and then a small negative pulse. The larger pulse is generated when there is a maximum rate of change of flux. This occurs when the current changes from a maximum in one direction (either positive or negative) to a maximum in the other direction ($d\emptyset/dt = max$).

NON-RETURN-TO-ZERO SYSTEM

The NRZ system uses a slightly different principle. In an NRZ system, changing flux can be used to indicate a "1", while a constant flux is used to represent a "0". Thus, the magnetic flux is never returned to zero. This concept can be illustrated by writing

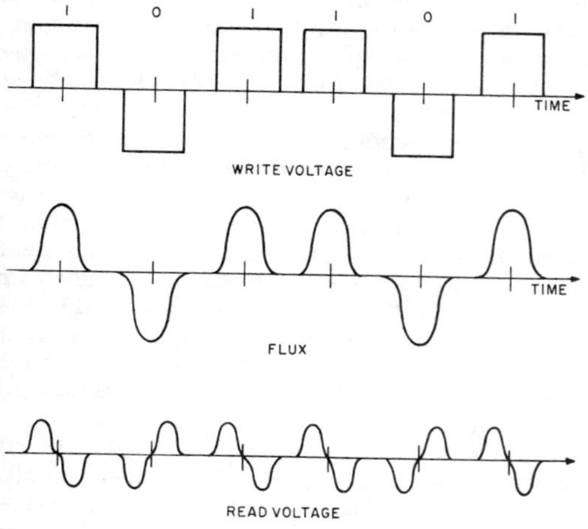

164.35
Figure 6-7.—Waveform of positive-and-negative-pulse Return-To-Zero system.

101101 in the NRZ system of recording as shown in figure 6-9.

SERIAL READ-OUT

To further clarify this point, consider the action for serial reading of the data represented in figure 6-10, using the AND circuit and the clock pulses (B_1). The operation of the AND circuit to produce the output ($F_1 = A_1B_1$) is understood. Because each bit of data using this method (return-to-zero-method) rises from the zero level to maximum voltage and remains at that level for a given period (long enough to permit the clock pulse to be ANDed with each bit of data in coincidence), and returns from the maximum level to zero, the time between clock pulses is necessarily long, and the overall time to read a single bit is long in relation to the actual AND operation. This in itself, is the read process.

The unique way in which the non-return-to-zero-method lends itself to faster reading is seen by studying the waveforms in figure 6-11 and their actions to produce the output ($F_2 = A_2B_2$) from the AND circuit. Note that the output produced in the 5μs read period for return-to-zero method is still 110111 (6 bits), whereas the non-return-to-zero output produced in the same period is 111100000011 (12 bits). Thus, serial data can be read in a shorter period using the non-return-to-zero method, since the clock pulses can be applied at a higher clock rate.

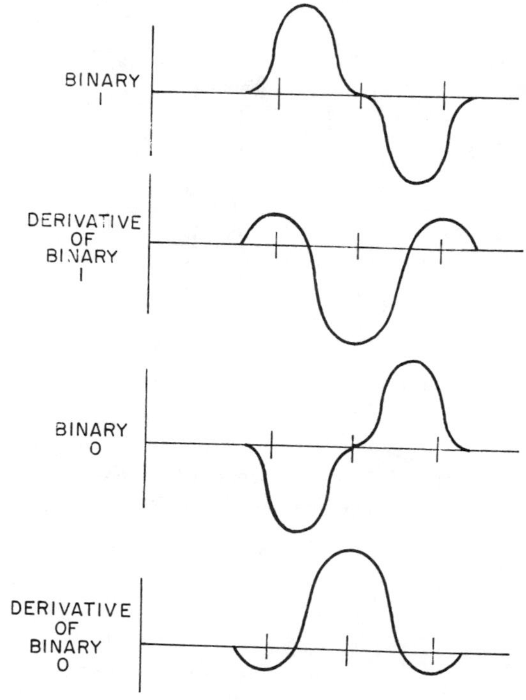

164.36
Figure 6-8.—Comparison of the waveforms of binary "1" and "0" and their derivatives.

MAGNETIC CORE MEMORY

The second type of storage device commonly used in digital computers is the magnetic core. Magnetic cores have certain advantages over magnetic drums, as will be pointed out in the following discussion.

CORE STORAGE TECHNIQUE

One of the most advanced methods to date for storing internal data in a computer is realized by using magnetic cores. Cores are generally constructed by either one of two

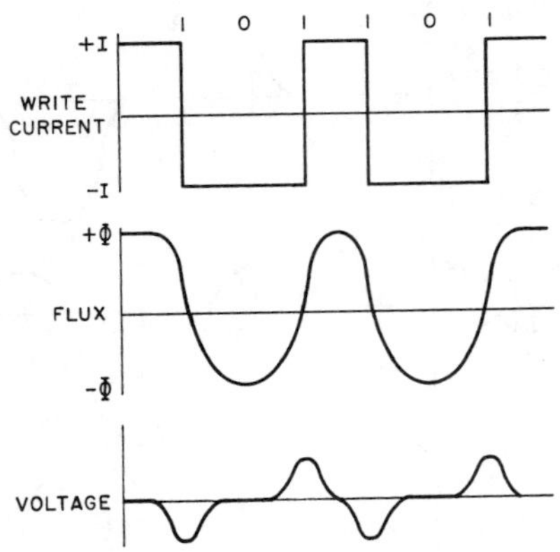

164.37

Figure 6-9.—Waveforms of the Non-Return-To-Zero (NRZ) system.

methods: the first type of core, called a tape-wound core, is fabricated by wrapping a tape of magnetic material around a non-magnetic toroidal form. A toroid is a term used to describe a doughnut-shaped solid object. The second type of core is called a ferrite core, and it is made by molding finely ground ferrite into a toroidal form. The ferrite used in this application is a ceramic iron oxide possessing magnetic properties. The ferrite particles are then heat fused or "sintered" by the application of heat and pressure. In both types, the rectangular B-H curves (shown later) of the cores indicate the characteristic which makes them ideally suited for use in digital applications.

In magnetic core memories, each data bit is stored in the magnetic field of a small, ring-shaped magnetic core (fig. 6-12). Magnetic cores generally have four wires running through them. Two wires are used for Read selection. (These same two wires are used

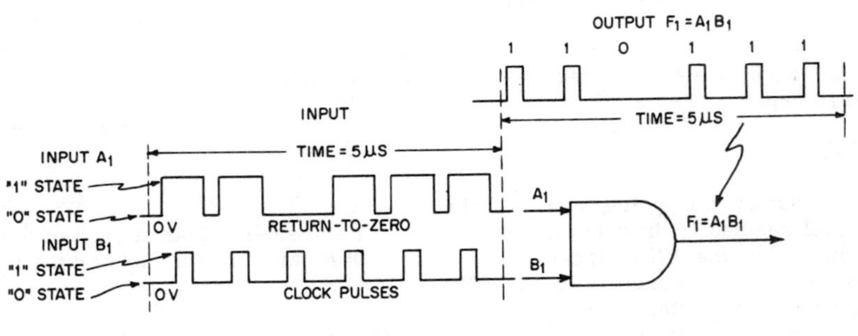

67.59

Figure 6-10.—Serial read-out (Return-To-Zero).

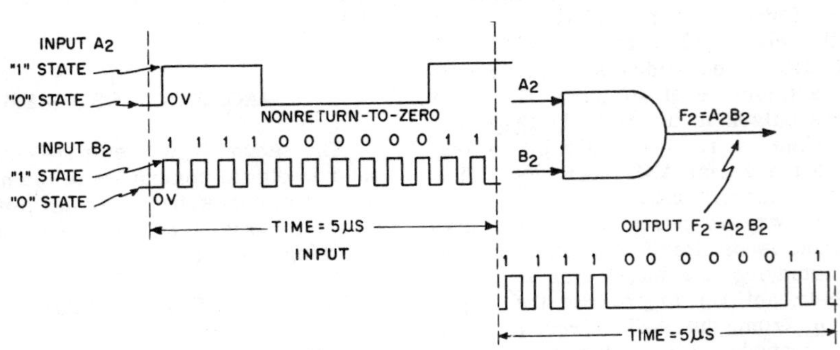

67.95

Figure 6-11.—Serial read-out (Non-Return-To-Zero).

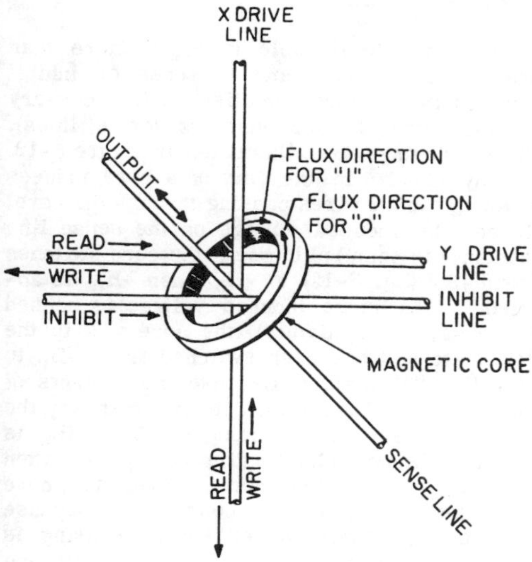

124.56
Figure 6-12.—Magnetic core showing "X," "Y," inhibit, and sense lines.

for write by reversing the direction of current flow.) An inhibit wire prevents writing a "1" when a "0" is to be written and the sense wire picks up the signal voltage generated by the shifting of a core from "1" to "0" in a read cycle.

Since a single core stores only one bit of a word, a large number of cores are required to handle all the bits in every word to be stored. These cores are arranged in "arrays," similar to the tracks and slots used in magnetic drum storage, in order to assign memory address locations and quickly write data and locate data for read-out purposes. The technique used most frequently for writing and reading data in magnetic core arrays is known as the coincident-current technique. This technique is explained in subsequent paragraphs.

In computer memory applications the ferrite core is magnetized by a flux field produced when a current flows in a wire (drive line) that is threaded through the core. It retains a large amount of this flux when the current is removed. Flux lines can be established clockwise or counterclockwise around the core depending upon the direction of the magnetizing current. A current in one direction establishes a magnetization in a core in a given direction. Reversing the direction of the current flow reverses the direction of the flux field and the core magnetization. These two unique states represent "0" and "1", respectively.

MAGNETIZATION PROCESS

The state of magnetism of a core is explained using the hysteresis loop shown in figure 6-13. The points defined on the loop illustrate the magnetic flux density in gauss (B) as a function of the field (induced by the current) in oersteds (H).

In this diagram it is assumed that all magnetism has been removed from the core. (This condition is assumed merely to show how a magnetizing force is established in the core and how the core magnetism enters into its hysteresis loop. Actually, this core and all magnetic material exist in nature in some state of magnetization as a result of the influences of the earth's magnetic field.) The 0 point in figure 6-13 represents a condition of 0 ampere-turns in oersteds (H) and 0 core magetization in gauss (B). If a current pulse is conducted through the drive line (fig. 6-12) with an intensity which produces a magnetomotive force of a magnitude $+H_m$ (fig. 6-13), the core magnetization will change (saturate) as shown along the magnetization curve defined

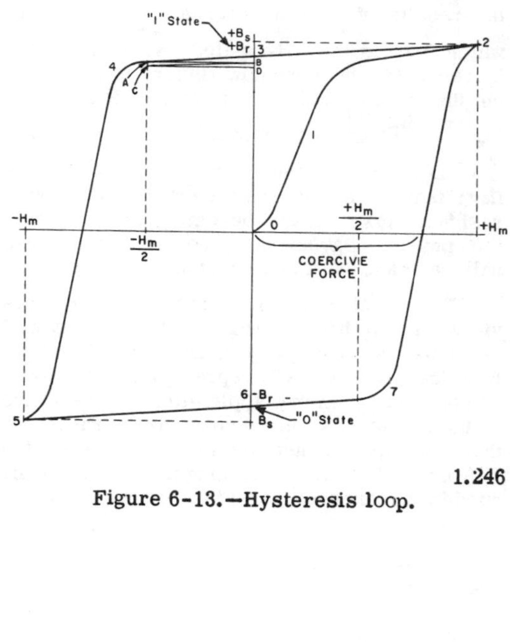

1.246
Figure 6-13.—Hysteresis loop.

by the numbers 0, 1, and 2. This action establishes a flux density in gauss (B) in the core of a magnitude indicated here as $+B_s$.

If the current is returned to 0, the core magnetism does not return to 0, but drops along the loop to a point $+B_r$ (3). This amount of magnetism (which is referred to as residual magnetism) is only slightly less than that produced when the driving current was present. Thus, the core stores almost the entire amount of the induced magnetism.

Another pulse of magnitude $+H_m$ would now merely shift the core to $+B_s$ again (from 3 to 2), and, after the pulse is removed, the core magnetism would return to $+B_r$ (2 to 3).

Now, if a current pulse of the same magnitude, but in the opposite direction, is conducted through the drive line so that a megnetomotive force of an intensity $-H_m$ is produced, the core flux shifts along the curve outlined by the numbers 3, 4, and 5. At 5 the core is again saturated, but because of the current reversal the magnetism is in a direction opposite to that first considered. Thus, the core saturates in the opposite direction when $-H_m$ is applied.

When the $-H_m$ magnetizing force is removed, the core magnetism drops along the loop from 5 to 6 (to $-B_r$), and will remain magnetized (stores its magnetism) at the $-B_r$ level (with negligible losses) for long periods of time.

The path of the curve from 3 to A shows the results of applying a force $-\frac{H_m}{2}$ to a core which was in the $+B_r$ state. When this force is removed, the core now returns to a point B, on the curve. Subsequent applications of the force $-\frac{H_m}{2}$ causes a similar transversal (B to C to D), with the important exception that the first transversal causes the major reduction of residual flux. After becoming familiar with the physical layout of a core memory, use will be made of this important characteristic.

The use of magnetic cores as storage devices should be obvious. If the $+B_r$ state of the core is arbitrarily called the "1" state, then the $-B_r$ state will represent the "0" state. In computer memory applications, several (up to 60 or more) of these cores are arranged so that each is magnetized to store either the "0" or "1" state. The magnetic state of the combined cores represents a computer word.

CORE WINDINGS

In order to be able to apply more than one drive current, and to sense or inhibit changes in the core condition, it is necessary to use several core windings (drive lines). These windings are illustrated in figure 6-12.

Any change in the flux of a core induces a voltage in all wires passing through the core. Hence, the induced voltage on the sense line (winding) is sampled to see if the core switches from $+B_r$ (fig. 6-13) to $-B_s$ when $-H_m$ is applied. If a large induced voltage is sensed (over say 50 millivolts), the core was in the "1" state and has been switched from $+B_r$ to $-B_s$ (the "0" state). Because the contents of the core are determined in this manner, the current pulse corresponding to MMF $-H_m$ is called a "Read Pulse." (The read pulse, when applied to a selected core, drives the core from the "1" to the "0" condition.) Because the core condition stored before sensing is destroyed during read-out, a memory utilizing this type of magnetic core storage element is referred to as a destructive-readout memory. If the data which was stored are to be used again, a restore (or rewrite) function is initiated to return the core to its original state.

MAGNETIZING CORES BY VECTOR SUMS OF CURRENTS

The use of windings to magnetize the core and to sense the signal resulting from the application of a read pulse is one method by which data can be read-out or written into the internal storage facilities of a computer. The use of straight current-carrying wires is an alternate method used when space is critical and small cores are used, because it is very difficult to wind coils on a very small toroidal form. It is desirable to use small cores in order to increase the storage capacity per given area and decrease the core switching time.

The magnetic intensity and the flux around a current-carrying wire form patterns of concentric circles around the conductor. Because the core and the wire are concentric, some of the flux created by the wire passes through the core, as shown in fig. 6-14.

If two current-carrying wires passing through a selected core are placed at right angles to each other, the effect is as though there was a single wire carrying the vector sum of the current. (See fig. 6-15.)

Switching the core involves the use of vector addition. The vector sum, or resultant, of the magnetic intensities of two current-carrying wires placed at right angle to each other is a third magnetic intensity located midway between the two original magnetic intensities. If each wire carries 0.707 of the current required to switch a core and if a core is oriented in the direction of the resultant magnetic intensity, the core will switch. If only one wire carries current, the core will not switch. This method is called the "coincident current" method of core switching.

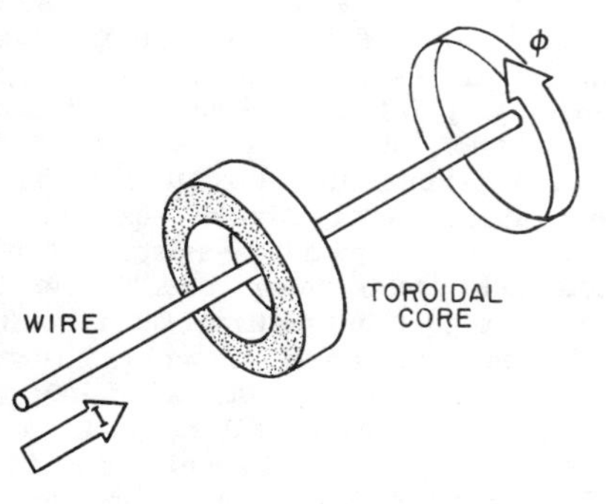

67.97

Figure 6-14.—Core magnetization using a single wire.

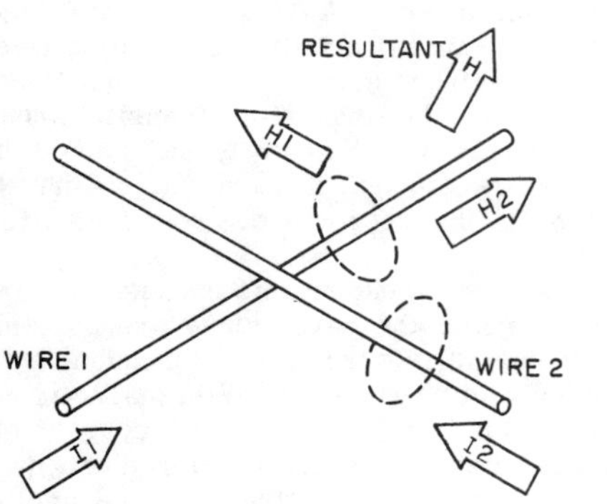

164.38

Figure 6-15.—Derivation of vector sum result.

COINCIDENT CURRENT IN CORE PLANE ARRAY

Coincident current core switching is used with an arrangement of wires and cores called a core plane array, similar to that shown in figure 6-16. This 4x4 array is made by crossing long lengths of insulated wires so that they form a squared-grid arrangement. A 4x4 array has 16 cores arranged in a square pattern of 4 cores on each side of the array.

Cores are placed at the junctions of the grid wires in such a manner that they encircle the resultant magnetic-intensity vector. These junctions can be thought of in terms of Cartesian coordinates; the horizontal locations assigned an "X" designator and the vertical a "Y" designator.

If a current equal to one-half of the current value required to switch a core (half-write current) is applied through both X3 and Y2 in the direction to produce a "1" condition, the only core that will be switched is the core located at the junction of the X3 and Y2 wires. The other cores along wires X3 and Y2 will not be switched, because the intensity of the magnetic flux produced by only one-half current is insufficient. These cores are said to be "half-selected." Core X3-Y2 is switched (if it is not already in the 1 state) because of the resultant magnetic intensity created by

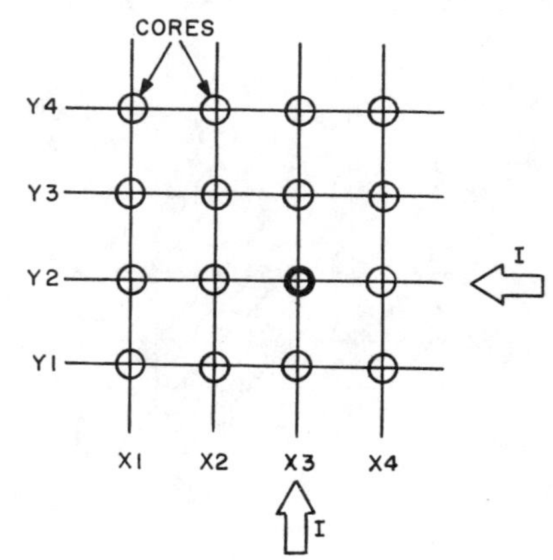

67.98.1

Figure 6-16.—Core plane array.

the combined one-half currents in a binary-"1" direction at the X3-Y2 junction. Any of the 16 cores in this core plane may be switched to store a "1" in a similar manner by the application of half-write currents through the associated X and Y wires.

The core at the junction of any two driving wires (one X and one Y) can be set to a "1" or "0" condition, depending on the direction of current flow through the driving wires.

To read the data ("1" or "0") which has been stored in a core, requires the use of sense winding. This winding passes through the center of each core, as shown in fig. 6-17.

Only one core in an array may be switched at a time. Therefore, when a read-current pulse is applied to wires X3 and Y2 (that is, opposite to the write currents), the magnetic flux of core X3-Y2 changes direction, (if the core is storing a "1") thereby inducing a voltage in the sense winding. Any core may be read in a similar manner by application of a read pulse to the associated X and Y winding of the core.

If a core has not been switched by half-write currents, as explained, it contains a "0". On application of the read pulse to the X and Y windings of that core, the direction of the magnetic intensity in the core does not switch. Therefore, a pulse is not induced in the sense winding.

Consider now that all of the cores on line Y2 (fig. 6-17) are storing a "1" and that the core at the junction of Y2 and X3 is being read. When read-currents (half-currents) are applied

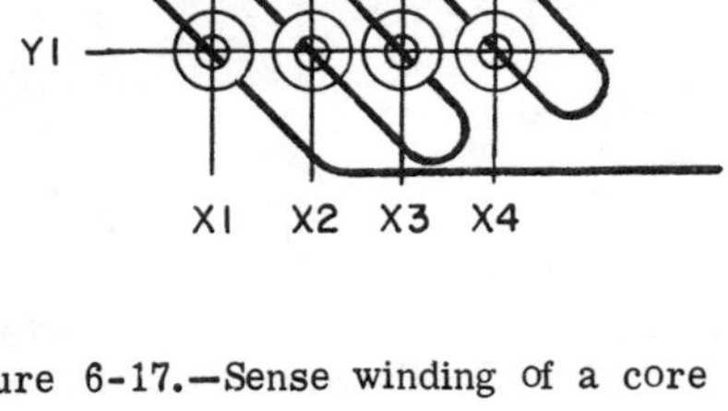

164.39
Figure 6-17.—Sense winding of a core array.

on lines X3 and Y2, all of the cores on line Y2 are disturbed. This disturbance causes low-amplitude (noise) inputs to be induced in the sense line along with the full-amplitude sense line input from the core at the X3-Y2 junction.

Two procedures are used to eliminate the effects of noise from adjacent cores during read-out. These involve the use of disturb and strobe pulses. The disturb pulse (equivalent to a half read) is a drive signal of an amplitude (coercive force) $-H_m/2$ which is applied to a core immediately after a "1" state is written in the core. The disturb pulse (fig. 6-13) drives the core magnetism from $+B_r$ (the state at which the magnetism is established in the core at the time the "1" is stored) to a point A on the hysteresis loop. When the $-H_m/2$ pulse is removed the core magnetism returns to point B. A subsequent half-read pulse drives the core to point C, and when removed permits the magnetism to be established at D. (Let this be equivalent to the induced noise from a half-selected core where a selected core is being read.) Note that the change in core magnetism from point B to point D is less than the amount of change when the first half-read pulse is applied. Consequently less noise will be induced in the sense winding from adjacent cores in figure 6-17 if a disturb pulse is applied on the line prior to reading the core at the Y2-X3 junction.

Noise pick-up during reading is further minimized by strobing. This technique involves the selection of the mid-amplitude portion of the amplified sense pulse. Selection is accomplished by ANDing the amplified sense pulse with an accurately timed pulse referred to as the "strobe pulse."

Because the magnetic intensity around a core storing a "1" is switched to a "0" direction on receipt of a read pulse, the datum stored in that core is destroyed (destructive read-out).

The ideal readout method is, of course, one in which the data stored are not erased, but remains stored for subsequent readout (nondestructive readout). With magnetic cores, however, if it is desired that a core which has been read should retain the stored data (a "1"), a subsequent write pulse must be applied to the core each time this "1" is sensed.

It may be desired to write each bit of a word into the internal storage of the computer, one bit per core array. Usually the number of core arrays used for this purpose is the same as the number of bits per word. The arrays are stacked on top of each other with the first bit stored in the top array, the second bit in the next to the top array, and so on.

To permit storing the bits of a word in the same relative core position of the stacked arrays, the same X and Y driver wires of each array are connected in series or parallel. Thus, when the coordinate wires of one core in an array are energized, every corresponding core in the other arrays also is energized.

This method of driving each X and Y winding of an array in series or parallel with every corresponding X and Y winding on the other arrays of the assembly introduces a problem. In storing a word, some "1"s and some binary "0"s are normally written in one vertically stacked column of cores. When the X and Y driving wires are energized to write a "1" in the selected cores, every core will switch and contain a binary 1. A method must therefore be incorporated to prevent or <u>inhibit</u> the writing of a "1" in those cores which must store a "0".

To prevent writing a "1" in the cores that are to contain "0"s the magnetic field that will switch these cores is canceled out. This is done by running an inhibit wire parallel to one of the driving wires (X or Y), as shown in figure 6-18.

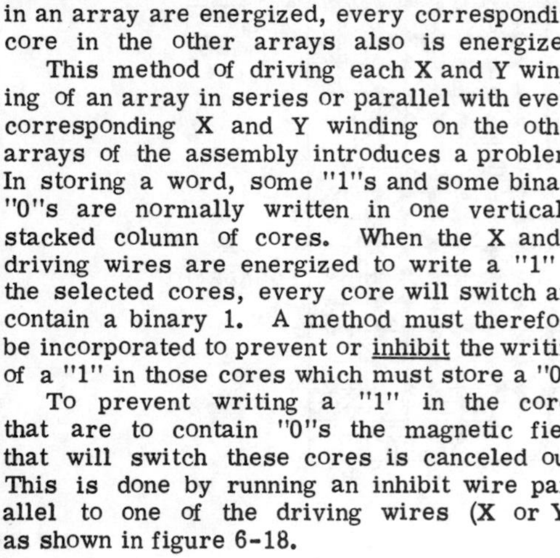

164.40
Figure 6-18.—Inhibit wire of a core array.

When, for example, current flows through a particular X driving wire, the same amount of current is made to flow in the opposite direction through the inhibit wire. Since the magnetic fields created by these parallel and closely spaced wires are equal and opposite to each other, the effective magnetic field is zero. Therefore, the flux of the Y driving wire (one-half write current) is insufficient to switch the core and the core is not switched, (retaining a "0") as desired.

REPRESENTATIVE CORE MATRIX

Figure 6-19 is a simplified diagram of a memory board which contains four memory matrices arranged in quadrants. The X and Y drive lines, the sense line and the inhibit line are shown for each quadrant.

Any one of the magnetic cores in the matrix can be selected (as discussed). A coincident half-amplitude current pulse is generated in a selected row and a selected column of a selected quadrant. The core at the intersection of the row and column receives a net full-amplitude current pulse and is therefore selected.

For example, assume core A in quandrant 3 is to be selected. Drive lines 13X and 15Y are each driven with half-amplitude current pulses. Core A, at the intersection of lines 13X and 15Y, receives a net full-amplitude current pulse. All other cores in the 13X and 15Y lines receive half-amplitude current pulses (cores B, C, D, and E, etc.), which is an insufficient current amplitude to switch or alter data stored in these cores. The cores which receive only half-amplitude current are half-selected. The remaining cores which are neither half-selected nor fully selected, are referred to as unselected cores (for example, core F). Core A is "selected".

A representative core matrix used in several Navy computers is shown in figure 6-20. The board is a 128 x 128 array arranged in 64 x 64 matrices and provides 16,384 one-bit storage addresses.

OTHER USES OF MAGNETIC CORES

Aside from receiving wide usage as the basic components of the memory section of computers, magnetic cores are used in other applications, such as ring counters, shifters, and circuits used for data transfer.

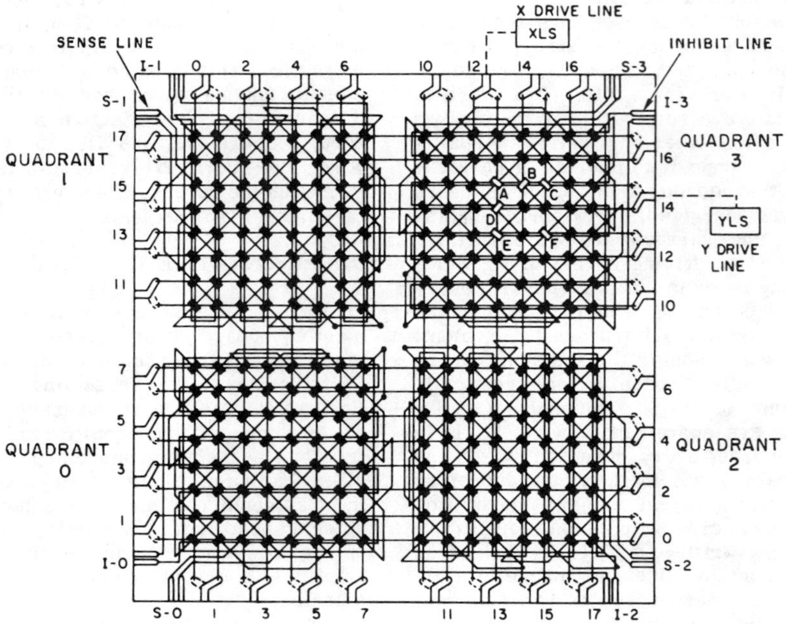

124.58

Figure 6-19.—A simplified magnetic core board, 16 by 16 array.

Core-to-Core Transfer

In the following discussion of a core-to-core transfer (fig. 6-21), actual core windings are represented, rather than single wires, in order to simplify the explanation. It is assumed that core A is already in the "1" state and that this 1 is to be transferred to core B which is in the "0" state.

An input pulse on the transfer winding (in the absence of a pulse on the write winding) clears core A to zero. The polarity of the voltage induced in the sense winding (by the shift in the condition of core A) is correct (plus toward the anode of CR1 and minus toward the cathode) to forward bias CR1 and a current flows in the write (or input) winding of core B. This action switches core B to the 1 state.

A subsequent write pulse input to core A will restore this core to the 1 condition, but will cause an induced voltage in the sense winding of the opposite polarity to that described above and CR1 will be reversed biased. The high back resistance of the diode prevents core B from switching back to the "0" state.

Core Symbology

Cores are sometimes represented in shifting (transfer) circuits and flip-flops as shown in diagrams (A) and (B) of figure 6-22. The core is represented by the circle. The 1's and 0's inside the circle in figure 6-22A signify the action which takes place within the core structure when a drive pulse appears on the associated input. For example, if a pulse is applied at the input line at A, a 1 condition will be established in the core. If a drive pulse is applied to the transfer (shift) line, the core is returned to the "0" state. Finally, the "0" at the output (sense) terminal indicates that a pulse appears in the output line when the core switches from 1 to 0.

124.58
Figure 6-20.—Representative core matrix (128 by 128 array).

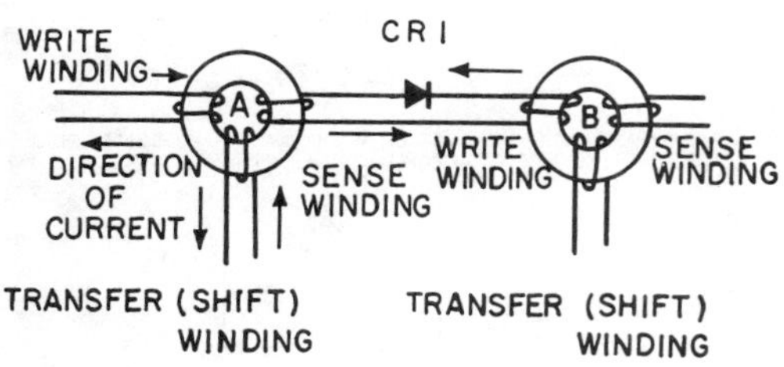

124.71
Figure 6-21.—Core-to-core transfer.

Magnetic cores are conveniently used as flip-flops (fig. 6-22B) if the 1 condition of the core (magnetized) is taken as the SET condition of the flip-flop and the "0" (demagnetized) condition is taken as the RESET condition. Cores used as flip-flops use the familiar SET, and RESET terminals and an OUTPUT terminal. An input pulse on the SET terminal places the core, (and the OUTPUT terminal) in SET or 1 condition. A RESET input clears the core to 0 and the output is zero.

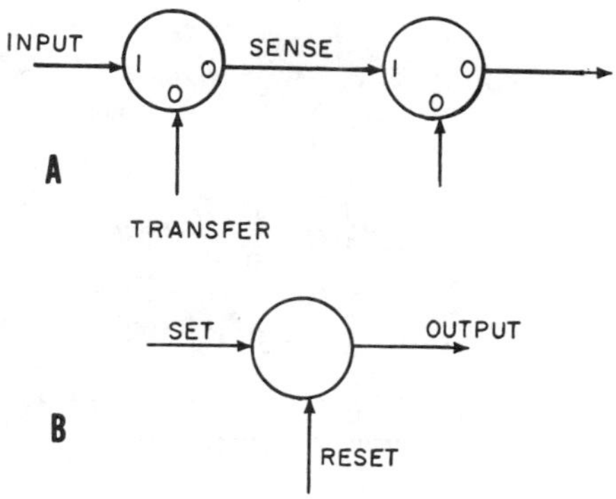

124.72
Figure 6-22.—Core symbology.

RING COUNTER

Because cores can be used as flip-flops, it follows that cores can also be formed into storage and shift registers and counters. A magnetic core ring counter is shown in figure 6-23.

If it is assumed that the shaded core (core A) is in the 1 state, lamp 4 will be "on." The first reset input will switch core A to zero extinguishing lamp 4, and produce an output which after delay in D1 is fed to core B. This core, in turn, switches to 1 and lamp 1 goes "on." The next reset input pulse will switch core B to zero and produce an input to D2 After delay in D2, an input is fed to core C causing this core to switch to the 1 state. The action continues to count 4 (the modulus of this particular counter) whereupon the count process is repeated.

THIN FILM

Thin film memory consists of a ferromagnetic material, permalloy, deposited (under controlled conditions in a vacuum chamber) on a substrate of thin glass. After all air has been removed from the chamber, a shutter arrangement is opened and vapors from molten permalloy pass through a mask and are deposited on the substrate. The pattern thus formed is determined by the shape of the mask. The thickness of each spot (magnetized area) is controlled by the amount of time the shutter is open.

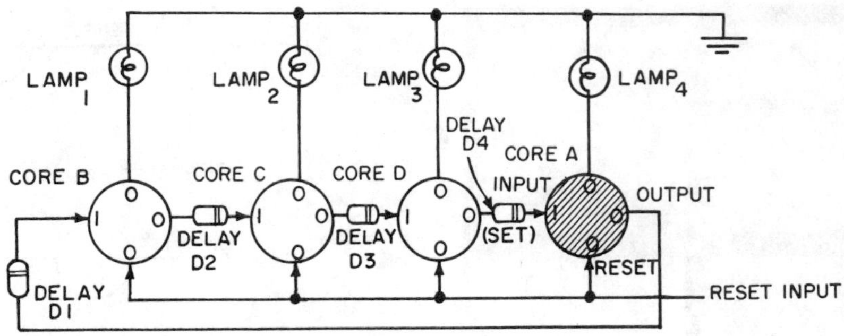

124.73

Figure 6-23.—Magnetic core ring counter.

A magnetic field is applied parallel to the surface of the substrate during deposition. The film spots thus become easier to magnetize in a direction parallel to that in which the magnetic field was applied during the deposition process. This direction is known as the preferred direction, likewise the axis of this magnetism is referred to as the preferred axis.

STORAGE

Thin film materials are well suited for storing binary data since they have a stable state of magnetization in each direction parallel to the preferred axis. The double-headed arrow in the circle shown in figure 6-24 is to be regarded as indicating the preferred axis. When the direction of magnetization is caused to rotate through 180 degrees (starting from the preferred axis), there is first a torque which tries to retain the magnetism along the preferred axis. If the magnetizing force is sufficiently strong the magnetism will be shifted to a point perpendicular to the preferred axis. Beyond this point, there is a forward torque which causes the magnetism to be aligned in the material exactly 180° from the preferred axis. The torque is caused by the field H_k which is produced during the deposition process. This field is called the anisotropic field. (The word "anisotropic" is used to describe the ability of the magnetic material to assume different positions in response to the action of external stimuli.)

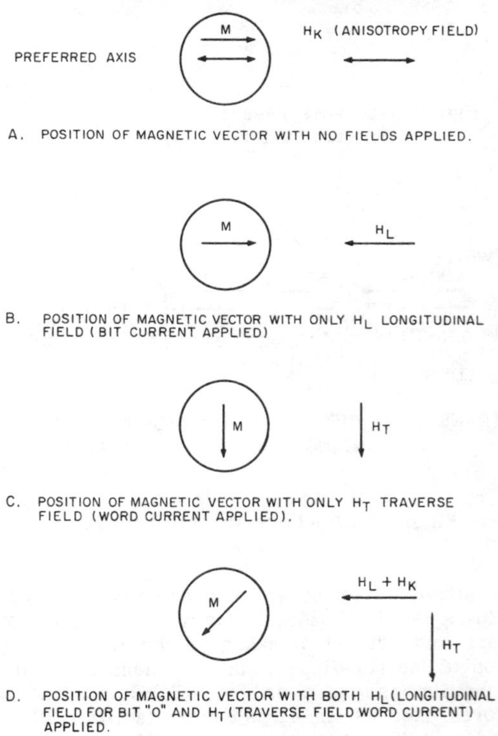

164.41

Figure 6-24.—Rotation of the magnetic vector on a film spot.

If the magnetic stimulus is removed after the anisotropic field is formed, this field (H_k) causes the magnetic vector to be aligned parallel to the preferred axis. If a coercive force, H_C, which is less than that required to switch the magnetization but produces a field parallel to the preferred axis is applied, no significant change results in the state of the magnetized material.

Applying only a tranverse field, H_T, (fig. 6-24C), i.e., a magnetic field perpendicular to the preferred axis, and which is stronger than H_K, causes the magnetic state of the spot to be rotated 90° as shown in figure 6-24C. If fields are applied so that the vector sum of $H_L + H_K$ are active forces on the spot, the position of the resultant magnetic vector will be as illustrated in figure 6-24D. If H_T is then removed from the spot, the direction of the magnetization becomes the same as that for H_L. When H_L is removed, the spot remains in the state until H_T is again applied. Thus, the direction of H_L determines the direction of the stable state of magnetization of the film spot.

SWITCHING

Because a concentric magnetic field is produced around a flow of current, it is possible to switch a film spot by passing current through drive lines that are placed in close proximity with the spot. The drive and sense lines (1 line array) is sometimes etched on Mylar sheets which are carefully aligned and attached to epoxy boards to give the required strength to the line array.

Figure 6-25A shows a film spot and the line array on one side of the spot. An identical set of these lines is placed on top of the film spot. The connectors for the line array are wired in a manner such that the sense and bit lines each produce one turn around the spot, and the word lines produce two turns. (Bit lines are effective in selecting a particular bit of a word. Word lines provide a partial enable for a word section of the memory.)

The arrow on the film in figure 6-25A shows the stable state magnetic vector with a "1" stored. If word current flows down the word lines, the magnetic vector rotates 90° as shown in figure 6-25B. If bias current is applied to the bit lines, the magnetic vector rotates toward the "0" stable state as shown in figure 6-25C. After the word current is removed, the vector completes the 180° rotation from the "1" state. Thus, a "0" is stored as shown in figure 6-25D.

If a "1" is to be stored in the spot (see figs. 6-25E and 6-25F), current applied to the bit lines is reversed. Thus, the magnetic field around the bit lines reverses and the magnetic vector is rotated toward the "1" state. If the word current and then the bit current are removed, the stable state of magnetization will represent a "1".

SENSING

The thin-film memory is a destructive readout memory, i.e., reading of a spot (location) clears the contents of that address. During

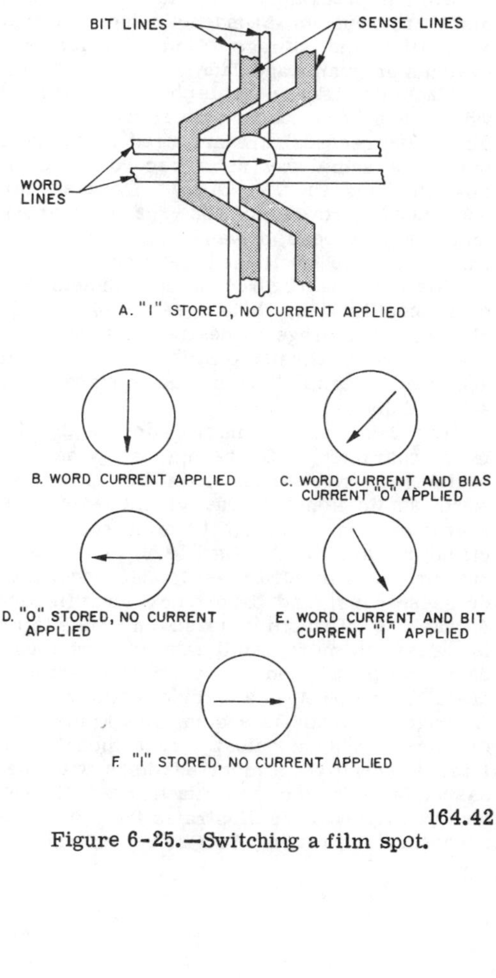

164.42

Figure 6-25.—Switching a film spot.

a readout, all of the addressed spots are switched toward the "0" state. The sharp change in the magnetic field around any spot causes a voltage to be induced in the sense lines. The magnitude of this voltage depends upon the change in the magnetic flux resulting from the switching process.

The output is read from the memory by ANDing a strobe pulse with the output from a sense amplifier (not shown) whenever a "1" is stored in the location being read. No output from the AND circuit indicates a "0" has been read.

MAGNETIC DISKS

Magnetic disks are a convenient medium for semipermanent storage of mass volumes of production programs. For many applications disks are superior to magnetic tape for rapid acquisition and storage of mass volumes of systems programs and data.

Magnetic disks resemble phonograph records which have been coated with iron-oxide. The disks (or records) are arranged in stacks in much the same way as a record stack in a modern "juke box." All of the disks are continuously revolving and spaced apart so that a record head, driven by an access mechanism, can be positioned between the disks.

The data are recorded at certain addresses on a specific disk. When readout of a particular bit of storage is desired, the recording head is automatically positioned and the data are read "serially" from the surface of the selected disk.

The basic unit of information on the disk is a character. By design each character contains a given number of bits (for fixed word applications). One or more of these characters in a group form a record. A circular data track (fig. 6-26), consists of one or more records, associated record addresses, gaps, and data track identification. A track of information as shown in this figure is defined in more detail later. A number of data tracks aligned on vertically arranged disks (fig. 6-27) form a cylinder of information. A magnetic disk file system may contain one or more banks (modules). Each module contains a specified number of disks with their associated cylinders and data tracks. The flow chart in figure 6-28 illustrates the procedures necessary to retrieve or store information.

TRACK FORMAT

One basic operation principle must be understood. The data are read or stored serially, character-by-charcter and bit-by-bit on a data track. All data tracks have the maximum storage capacity.

Index Points

Each data track (fig. 6-26) must contain a minimum number of control and addressing characters in a specific format. The index points are magnetic marks that indicate the beginning and end of a data track. They are used for timing purposes. In this case, the late index follows the early index by approximately 475μ sec.

Home Address One

Home address one (HA_1) is a prerecorded number. It is represented in the illustration shown as having four digits. This is the actual address of a data track, and is therefore referred to as the track number. HA_1 is the first group of characters to follow the late index.

Home Address Two

Home address two (HA_2) is written by the programmer and serves as a programmer's aid. It can be used for category and file numbers as identifiers. It can also be used as a file protect code. For example, it could be used to signal to a second user that this track is normally not to be used.

Record Address

The record address is also a programmer's aid. It can be used to identify individual records or for any other convenient purposes.

Gaps

Gaps are written between all address and record areas on a data track. They are used to distinguish specific data areas. Gaps usually contain check characters and internal synchronization information required for proper disk system operation.

Generally, one disk surface in a given module is used only for format tracks. A format track

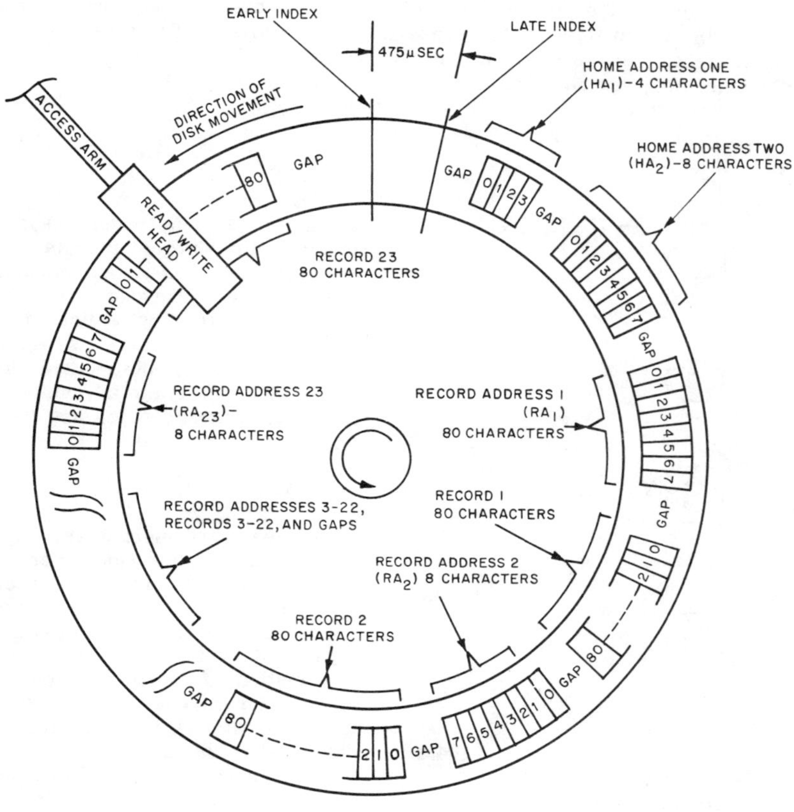

164.43

Figure 6-26.—Circular data track.

affects the data tracks of the entire cylinder that are vertically in line with it. The format track determines the manner in which data will be read from or written on each track of its associated cylinder. The programmer can write or modify the format tracks as desired.

Track capacity is directly related to the configuration of the format tracks. The maximum number of characters that can be written on a data track must include Home Address two (HA_2), Record Addresses (RA), and Gaps.

SYSTEM COMPONENTS

A minimum disk file system consists of a disk file controller (DFC), a file control unit, and a disk storage unit. The disk file controller controls the operation of the file control and disk storage units. Specifically, it provides the following functions necessary for the operation of the disk system:

1. Data assembly and dissembly
2. Signal level conversion
3. Function translation
4. Parity check
5. Parity generation
6. Sense and status response

The file control unit accepts instructions from the disk file controller, decodes them, and transmits the appropriate signals to the disk storage unit. In addition, the file control unit provides control timing, read, write and sense timing, parity and character generation, parity and character checking, format circuits, and data comparison circuitry.

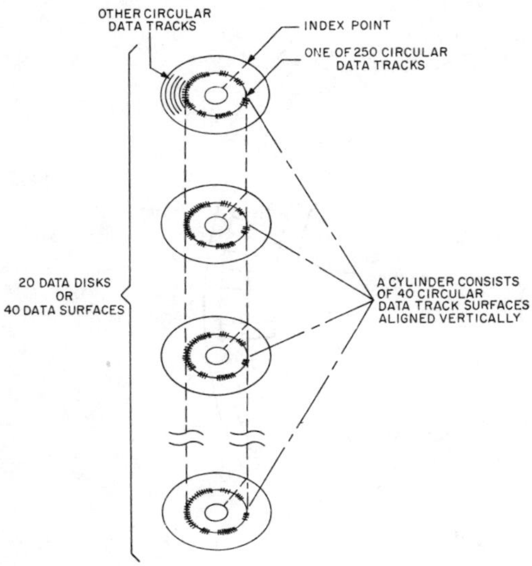

164.44

Figure 6-27.—Description of data storage disk assembly.

The disk storage unit contains magnetic disk modules. The disks in each module are mounted on a common shaft and rotate at a given speed.

MAGNETIC TAPE

Another form of memory is magnetic tape. Magnetic tape is widely used as a storage medium for large amounts of data. It is normally not used as an internal (main) storage medium because of its long access time. This can be readily realized if one considers that needed information is widely (and sometimes randomly) distributed along the tape. Thus, the two main advantages to be gained by using magnetic tapes are its large storage capacity and low cost.

STORAGE TECHNIQUE

A tape drive mechanism (fig. 6-29) is used to control the tape movement. In operation, the tape is unwound from the reel, passed over a read-write (magnetic) head assembly which magnetically writes or extracts data from the tape, and is rewound on the file reel. The distribution of information on tape is similar to that for magnetic drum storage, i.e., the data are stored in magnetic tracks running the length of the tape.

The binary bits of a word are recorded on tape having densities up to many hundred bits

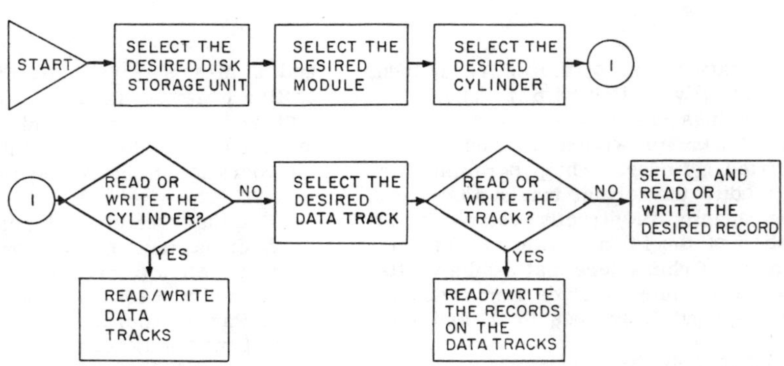

164.45

Figure 6-28.—Flow chart illustrating storage and retrieval of data from disks.

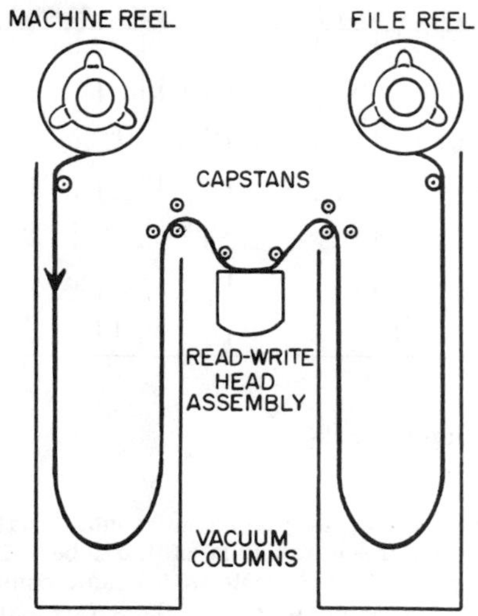

49.162
Figure 6-29.—Basic tape drive mechanism.

per inch. The capacity for a single track of a reel of tape is calculated by first multiplying the tape length by the density of characters per inch. For example, if the tape length is 100 feet (1200 inches) and the recording density is 200 characters per inch, the number of characters that can be recorded 1200 x 200 = 240,000 per track. If the information to be stored is in fixed segments (records) of 100 characters, the record length would be 100 characters divided by the density (200 characters per inch) which equals 0.50 inch. If the gap (space) between record locations is known to be 0.75 inch, this is added to the record length, 0.50, and the sum is 1.25 inches. This figure is divided into the tape length (1200 inches), which produces 960 records. The capacity is then obtained by multiplying the 960 records by the 100-character fixed record to produce 96,000 characters.

Unlike the reading technique used for magnetic cores, data read out of tape does not have to be rewritten. The data on tape are usually eliminated by using an erase magnetic head, which changes all "1" bit to "0". The erase operation is usually performed during the write operation. As the tape is unwound for recording, the tape first passes over the erase head before passing over the read-write head. Thus, old data on the tape are erased before new data are recorded. For a read order, the erase head is disengaged.

TAPE CODE AND ERROR DETECTION

A seven-channel tape code is illustrated in figure 6-30. Some special characters are shown. Because the code is used to represent both alphabet and numerals, it is called a "seven-bit Alphanumeric" code.

The channels or tracks are referred to as C, B, A, 8, 4, 2, and 1. The seven-bit code is popular mainly because it is a wide tape, yet it can be handled easily. Wider tapes would require drive mechanism with greater mechanical abilities. This would create new problems in starting and stopping the mechanisms.

Some tape systems use a single read-write head for each of the seven channels while others use read and write heads separately. As can be seen in figure 6-30, the "C" bit for any column is "1" whenever the total number of "1"s represented in the B, A, 8, 4, 2, and 1 tracks for that column is odd. If any vertical column contains an odd number of "1"s when the "C" bit is included, an error will be indicated.

As each record is written, the number of "1" bits in each of the seven (longitudinal) channels is recorded. At the end of each record, a bit is added to all tracks which contain an odd number of "1" bits. When reading the tape, an odd number of bits in any one of the seven tracks of any record indicates an error. Thus, checks are made across both vertical and horizontal (or longitudinal) dimensions of the tape to ensure accuracy.

Tapes which use a single read-write head cannot detect errors during a continuous recording process. A reading of the tape after recording will reveal the presence of errors, if, in fact, errors exists. Tapes which use separate read and write heads can perform a read operation (for error detection) as the data are being recorded. The data recorded on the tape at the write head are read (or checked) an instant later at the read head. The use of separate read and write heads is therefore faster, since errors are almost immediately detected and may be corrected before

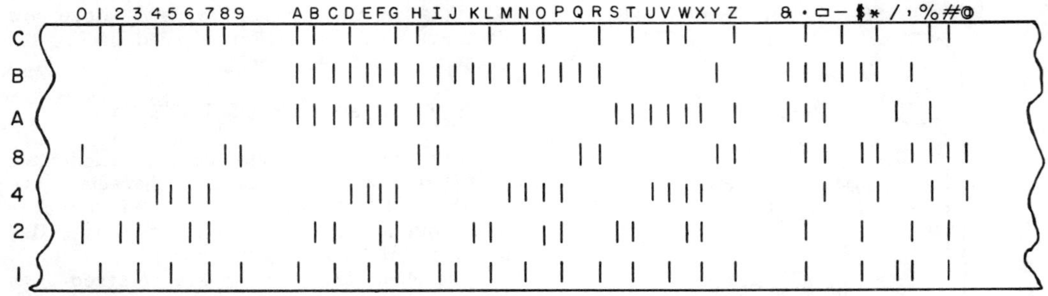

78.25

Figure 6-30.—Seven-bit alphanumeric code.

the total recording process is completed. Similar accuracy or validity checks are made each time the tape is read.

Another common method of using the seven-bit code involves the use of six bits to represent two octal digits, such as 111 011 (73_8), and the seventh bit for parity checking. This method is used for representing numbers only.

ELECTROSTATIC STORAGE

Electrostatic storage, as performed with the aid of cathode-ray type tubes and associated circuitry, can provide a memory with access time of the order of a few microseconds and storage capacities of about 1,000 bits per linear inch.

WILLIAMS TUBE

A representative tube that is employed for this purpose is the Williams tube. The Williams tube is used in a system arrangement similar to the one shown in figure 6-31.

Construction

The overall construction and deflection system of the Williams tube is very similar to that of the familiar television picture tube. However, the tube possesses two additional features. The first is that poor conductor material, instead of the usual fluorescent material, is used to coat the inside of the face of the tube. The second feature is that a metal "signal-pickup" plate is placed in contact with the outside of the glass face of the tube. Consequently, a CAPACITOR is formed, consisting of the inside coating, the glass face, and the signal-pickup plate.

This capacitor is charged and discharged by the electron beam within the tube. Let us first consider how the charging operation is accomplished. If the electron beam is greatly accelerated by a high potential at the accelerating anode of the tube, electrons in the interior coating are "knocked" loose by the impact of the beam electrons. This phenomenon is known as secondary emission. The interior coating acquires a positive charge as the liberated electrons are drawn away to a nearby, positively charged anode. Since this coating consists of a poor conductor material, the positive charge remains within the very small area of beam impact.

Writing

By gating the electron beam on and off (by means of the control grid) as it is swept across the face of the tube, it is possible to store charges that represent the value of the voltage at different instants of time. This procedure produces "writing." If the gating voltage that is applied to the control grid is a serially applied binary word, the word will be stored in the form of charged areas across the face of the tube. These areas represent charges on many individual tiny capacitors that share one common electrode which is the signal-pickup plate.

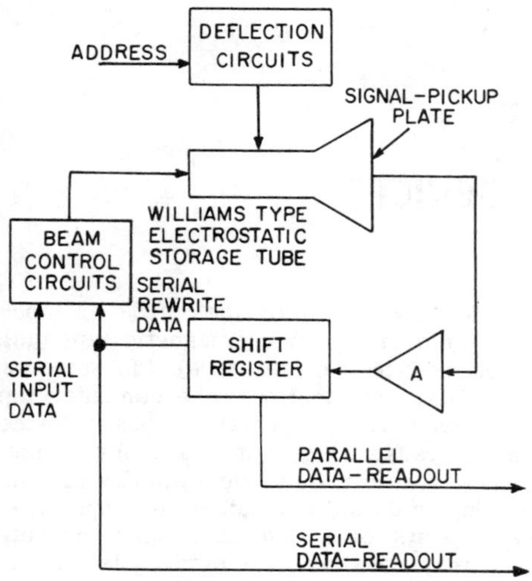

124.69

Figure 6-31.—Block diagram of electrostatic storage using a Williams tube.

Reading

Reading (capacitor discharging) is accomplished by using an electron beam sweep voltage which is not gated on and off (as was true in the writing process). The discharge path of each one of the individual capacitors (charged areas) is through the electron beam.

Note that there is a relationship between time, which is provided by the beam sweep, and the physical location of the individual capacitors.

As the beam sweeps across the tube face, the flow of each pulse of discharge current through the signal-pickup plate indicates the presence of a stored charge within a given area.

The series of pulses thus produced is usually applied to a shift register. The shift register shifts at a repetition rate that is controlled by the tube sweep voltage. Consequently, if NO PULSE appears at the instant corresponding to a bit-position in the original stored binary word, a binary zero is shifted into the register. After all of the pulses have been collected, the original binary word (as it had been stored in the tube) is now present in the shift register, and is ready for any subsequent parallel or serial readout and use. Readout from the register involves a nondestructive sampling of the voltage levels contained in the register. Thus, readout of a given bit of data can be repeated as many times as necessary.

Readout of data from the Williams tube is destructive and the stored charge is "destroyed" during the readout process. This data can be restored by writing it back into the tube. This is accomplished by feeding the contents of the shift register through the beam-control circuits to the control grid of the Williams tube in order to repeat the writing operation.

Computer words are written across the screen at a density up to 1000 bits per inch. Selection of a given location on the face of the tube for either reading or writing requires accurate deflection of the electron beam. The location of each word is therefore identified by an "address" in terms of its X and Y coordinates. This information which is digital, is converted into an analog voltage to permit the beam to be directed to any spot on the screen.

COMPARISON OF ELECTROSTATIC AND MAGNETIC CORE STORAGE SYSTEMS

When comparing electrostatic and magnetic storage systems, the time required to select a given address (access time) is slightly greater using the electrostatic storage method than for magnetic core memories due to the increase in time necessary to produce a voltage of the accuracy required to locate the desired data. Further, once data is stored in cores, it is seldom (if ever) necessary under normal operating conditions to re-record the data lost as a result of leakage. The retentivity of the core stores the data indefinitely. Using the Williams tube (electrostatic storage), data stored must be periodically re-recorded to compensate for leakages in the glass dielectric between the insulation material coated on the tube face and the metal pickup plate outside of the tube.

Chapter 7

INPUT/OUTPUT DEVICES

Input and output devices provide the computer with the facilities necessary for communicating with the users. Input devices such as consoles, card readers, and typewriters supply the computer with data and instructions, while output devices provide the means for changing the data processed by the computer into a form specified by or intelligible to the users. The selection of input/output devices depend on the specific use for which a computer is intended. In the following discussions, the applications, types, and characteristics of input/output devices are presented.

Different types of computers are used for different purposes. The three major areas of application are: business, the solution of scientific problems, and the automatic control of weapons systems. The types of input/output devices used with each application will differ in many respects. In fact, some input/output devices are designed specifically for use with one of these applications and therefore will not be useful with other applications. This chapter restricts its coverage to commonly used devices, leaving treatment of specific devices to other texts.

GENERAL REQUIREMENTS FOR INPUT/OUTPUT DFVICES

Generally, input/output devices must meet two basic requirements. First, the devices must be able to modify all data so that it is acceptable to the computer during the input phase of the operation and must be able to present data in usable form during the output phase. Second, the devices must operate quickly and efficiently in conjunction with the computer.

Conventional input devices read coded data into computers or other devices from punched cards or punched paper tape (using holes punched in various positions of the cards or tape to represent data), or from magnetic tape (using magnetized areas on the tape). In some special military applications, the computer input is received from special purpose devices, such as radar sets, gun platforms, missile guidance systems, or tactical display consoles. In scientific digital computers, the input device may consists of a keyboard, while the output device may consists of a plotting board or an electric typewriter.

Data may be presented at the output in printed form (English or numerals), in plotted form (such as maps and graphs), on punched cards, paper tapes, magnetic tapes, or oscilloscopic displays. Outputs in still other forms are available for special applications.

Nearly all input/output devices suffer the same disadvantages—slowness of response. Most computers can process millions of bits of data per second. Input/output devices, particularly those which require some mechanical operation, are hard-pressed to manipulate several thousand bits per second. There is, of course, a wide disparity in data exchange rates between the various devices, but the computer is faster even when the fastest of these devices are considered.

Various procedures are being used in order to more profitably utilize computer time. One such procedure, designed to minimize computer idling time, is to program I/0 cycles to run concurrently with computation. Another is to use a number of I/0 channels and provide multiplexed inputs to the computer from several I/0 devices. (Multiplexing, as used here, refers to the ability of the computer to sample the data on a number of input channels while maintaining the intelligence of the data from each channel. The rate of the multiplexing action is high enough to permit the operator of each I/0 device to retain immediate access with the computer.)

Common methods for improving computer usage in so far as can be accomplished by the I/O equipments themselves include the use of off-line devices (i.e., devices not under the direct control of the computer), use of electronic switches to multiplex several equipments on one channel, and the use of buffer storage registers in the I/O equipment. Buffer storage is treated later in this chapter.

ON-LINE EQUIPMENT

On-line equipments generally operate at high processing speeds and are connected directly to a computer. Usually, on-line equipments are used when large amounts of data are being processed and when very little computation is required. It is now feasible to use slower equipments such as typewriters, printers, and keyboards to supplement the high-speed on-line equipment. Of course, the selection of a particular device or combination of devices must be determined by the intended use of the computing system.

OFF-LINE EQUIPMENT

The equipment that prepares data (and, in some instances processes data) external to the computer is classified as off-line equipment. Some devices used for on-line purposes can be used off-line, which results in a more flexible system. Some equipment is used off-line exclusively. Sorters and card punchers (which prepare data) and tabulators (which process the data) are in this off-line category. The typewriters and other units mentioned earlier are used for off-line applications, but are classified as auxiliary equipment.

BUFFER STORAGE

Buffers serve as intermediate storage devices to facilitate transfer of data between two mediums whose operating speeds are difficult, or impossible, to synchronize. It is frequently necessary to read data from cards, paper tapes, keyboards, etc., into the main (primary) computer memory. In most cases, the speed at which input devices can supply data to storage cannot be increased sufficiently to match the ability of the computer to read-in the data at electronic speeds. The same incompatibility is encountered when reading data from memory to output devices. A buffer device is therefore designed to read-in or write-out data at speeds which are compatible with both the input/output devices and the main computer memory.

Several types of buffers are in use. The simplest type is an arrangement of flip-flop registers into which data can be slowly accumulated but can be released or read-out at electronic speeds. By design, data can be read-into and out-of the registers in either serial or parallel form. The buffer storage must be capable of reading data slowly from the input device, and, at a later time, writing this data at electronic speeds into the main memory. It must also be capable of reading-in data at electronic speeds from the main memory and writing this data slowly at the output device.

RECORDING MEDIA

Most all input and output systems use recording media. The most popular forms of recording media have been the printed pages, punched cards, punched paper tape, and magnetic tape. The more important considerations that determine the choice of recording media are:

1. Compatibility between input devices and computer.
2. Form and quality required of the displayed data.
3. Ease of handling and accessibility of data.
4. Permanence, erasability, and durability of record medium.
5. Volume of bulk storage capacity, density, and costs associated with storage of data.
6. Size, weight, and power consumption of recording equipment.
7. Speed of reading and recording, and reliability of data and of the recording equipment.
8. Installation, operation, and recording costs.

PUNCHED CARDS

There are two primary punched card formats in use at present. The first of these, developed by Univac, is shown in figure 7-1. In this system 90 columns of 6 bits are used. Forty-five columns across the top and the other forty-five

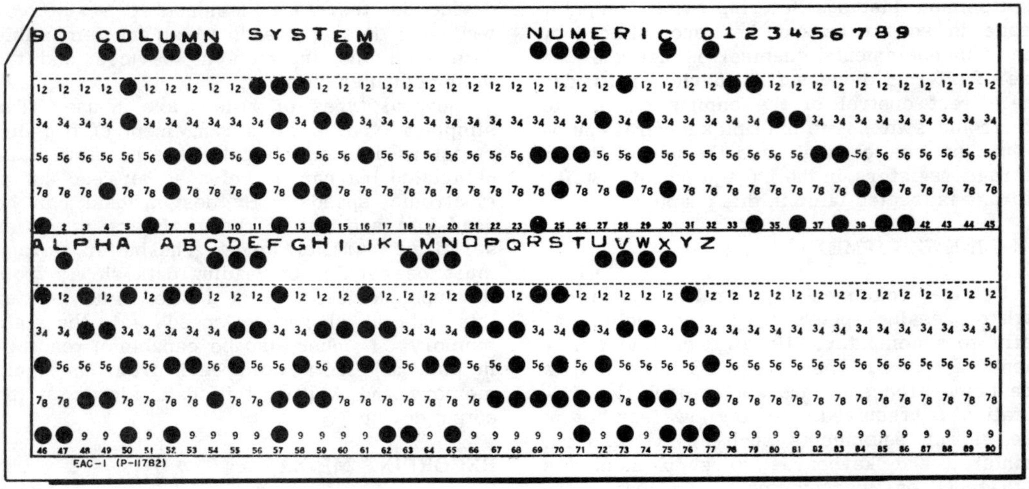

164.46

Figure 7-1.—Univac 90 column punched card.

across the bottom. The codes for the characters may be determined by referencing in figure 7-1. The card dimensions are 3 1/4" x 7 3/8" x .0065". The 90 column card is finding only limited use in present-day applications.

The other major punched card is the IBM card; it dimensions are the same as the Univac card, but its format is different. The IBM card uses 80 columns of 12 bits (fig. 7-2), the rows 1 through 9 are referred to as numeric punch rows, rows 11 and 12 are zone punches, and the zero row is considered to be both zone and numeric. Reference to figure 7-2 demonstrates the usual alpha numeric code used. It is extremely important to realize that data formats are arbitrary and may be modified as conditions necessitate, as long as the computer program is compatible. As an example, assume it is desired to store 36 bit computer words on the card, these may be readily stored using three columns per word (a total of 26 words per card), or they may be stored horizontally, two words per row, for a total of 24 words per card. In addition various portions of the cards may be coded to identify them as members of a set, and upper corners may be clipped to assist in keeping them properly aligned.

CARD HANDLING EQUIPMENT

As might be expected, card handling equipment varies from manufacturer to manufacturer. Certain general characteristics, however, remain true for the equipments in each category. These general characteristics are given primary consideration in this chapter.

Card Punches

Card punches are actuated by a manual keyboard, or in some cases by the computer. The keyboard buttons, when operated, open and close groups of switches which control solenoid-operated punches (fig. 7-3). Once the holes have been punched in one column, the card punch automatically advances the card so that the next column is located under the punching station punches.

A representative card punch is shown in figure 7-4. Card punches, dependent upon punch design, will handle from 100 to 250 cards per minute and have a check read station to verify the data punched. Each has a buffer register (not shown) to receive data from the computer. The computer will place the data it wishes to send on the data lines and set a signal on another line to notify the

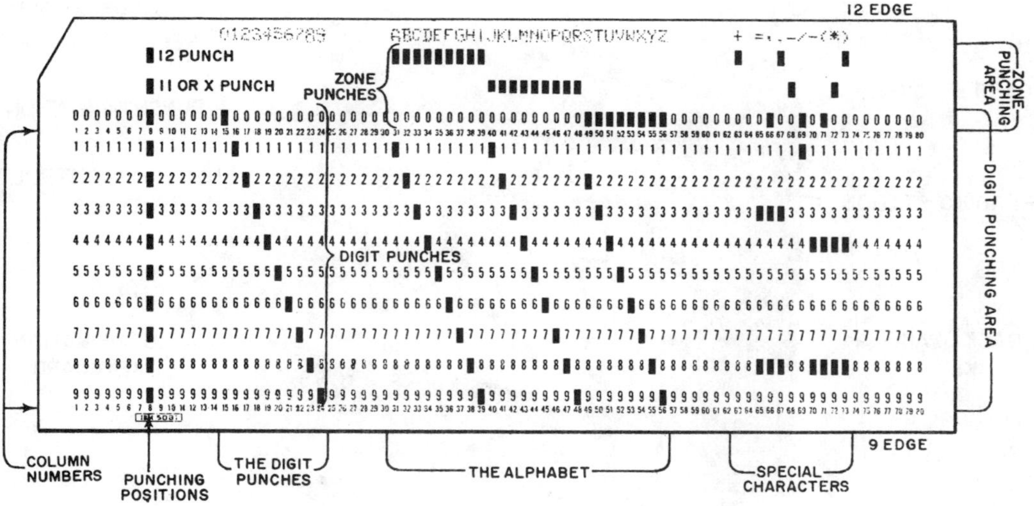

49.220X

Figure 7-2.—IBM 80 column punched card.

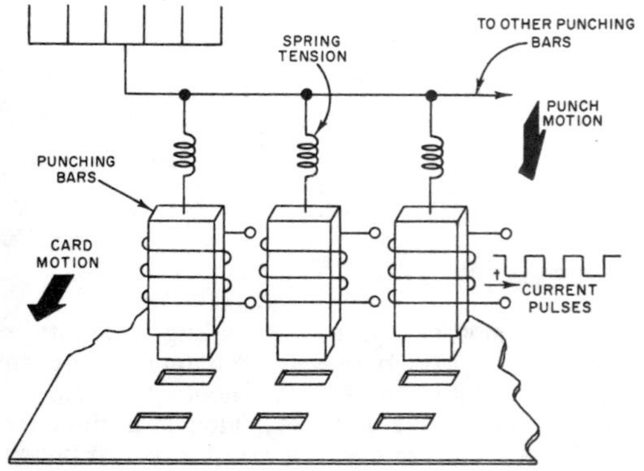

124.75

Figure 7-3.—Card punching mechanism.

punch unit. The punch unit samples the data from the computer and sets a signal line informing the computer of its action. In addition some form of interrupt communication will be used to keep the computer informed of the functional status of the punch, i.e., op/inop, card jam, punching error, number of cards to be rewritten, etc.

With some machines, skipping, duplicating, and shifting can be performed automatically by the program unit of the card punch, thus obviating the necessity for including these functions in the computer program. Each of these operations is controlled by a coded program card. The program card (which has been previously punched) is wrapped around a drum (fig. 7-5) which is a part of the program unit of the card punch. A fixed reading station reads each column of the program card as the drum is rotated. Punched holes in certain zones and digits in the program card cause certain columns or number of columns to be skipped on the card being punched. The program card also causes automatic duplication of material that has already been punched in the same column of the preceding card. Note that the use of a program card in this manner reduces the manual effort required during repetitive card punching.

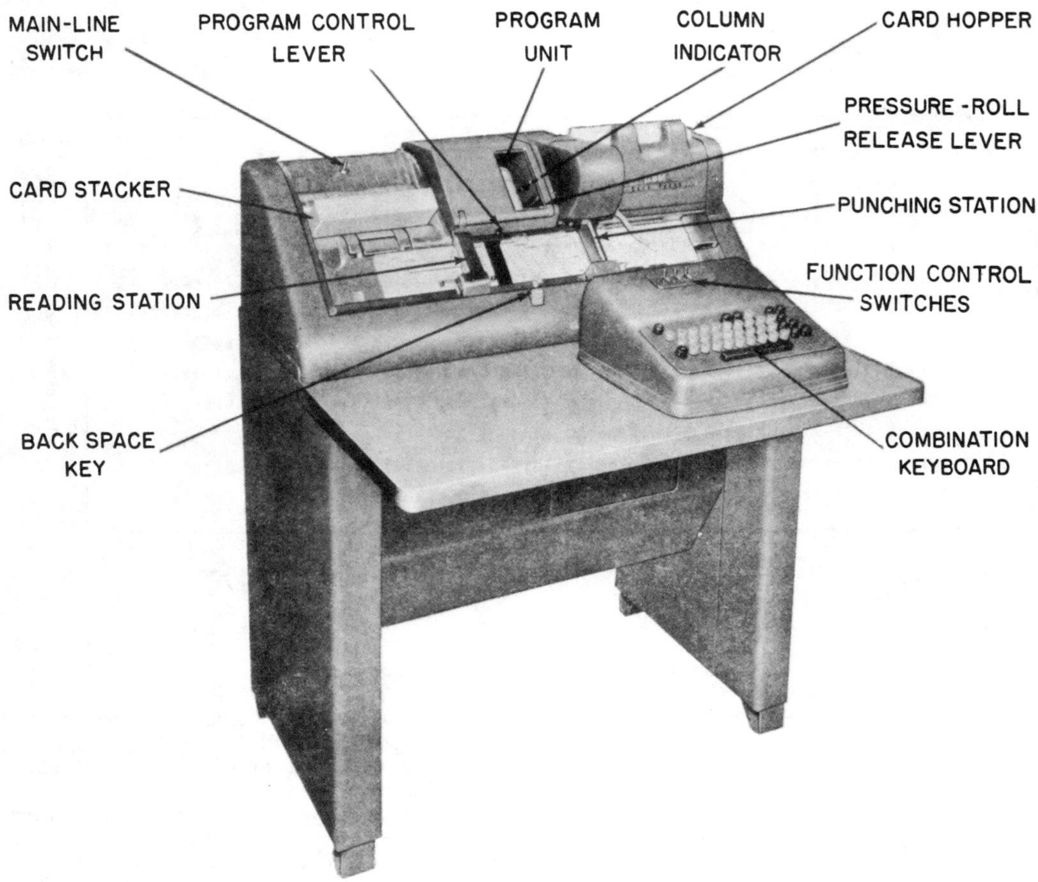

49.5X

Figure 7-4.—Type 26 card punch.

Card Readers

Card readers are used to translate the holes in a punched card back into the signals that represent characters. A card reader is sometimes used as a computer input device, although it is more frequently used to operate an electric typewriter or a printer in order to translate card data back into written form. Card readers are also used in conjunction with conversion devices which convert and transfer card data onto some other medium. Methods of reading data stored on cards into a computer are explained later.

One method of card reading consists of passing a card between a contact roller and spring-mounted electrical contacting fingers or brushes. If a hole is punched in the card, the brushes make contact with the roller underneath, as shown in figure 7-6. The cards move past a column of brushes (often called a reading station). A circuit is completed (closed) each time a brush is permitted to pass through the hole and make contact with the roller. Thus, the circuit closes when a hole is present, and opens when no hole is present. Card equipment devices use this open-close indication to actuate other control

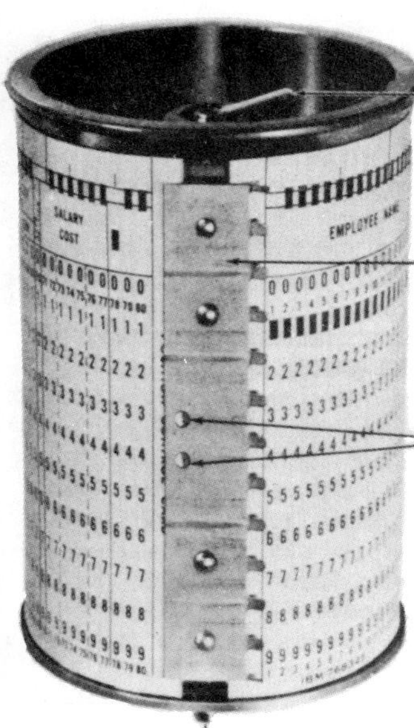

49.6X

Figure 7-5.—Program drum.

and data-processing circuitry. There are as many brushes as there are code areas in a single column on the card being read.

Card readers are available which handle in excess of '1000 cards per minute. These generally use photoelectric read systems, the basic arrangement of which is similar to that shown in figure 7-7. The electromechanical or brush read system (fig. 7-6) is frequently used at the check read station on a card punch.

Card readers for on-line operation will usually have a buffer storage register to permit packing the data read from the card and sending it to the computer in a full word length (unit). (This process is discussed later in this chapter.) Communications with the computer are on a data ready basis. (The information is packed and placed in the output registers of the I/0 device after which a status line is "set." The computer reads the data and places a signal on another line indicating that it has received the information and the reader can continue.) There may be provisions for the reader to send functional status reports to the computer such as operative/inoperative signals, card jam, etc. This is generally accomplished by placing a specific code in the output register and setting an interrupt line. This action informs the computer regarding the status of the I/0 device.

Card Verifiers

Card verifying is a means of checking the accuracy of original card punching. A second operator depresses the keys of the verifier while reading from the same source document the original punch operator used. Instead of punch dies, the verifier contains a sensing mechanism consisting of 12 pins, which pass through the holes punched in the card. If the pins will not pass through the card an error is signalled.

The error causes the error light to light, and gives the verifier an opportunity to recheck the data just entered. If an error, in fact, exists, a notch is cut in the appropriate column. If the card checks correctly, a notch is cut in the right end of the card.

Card Sorters

A typical card sorter is seen in figure 7-8. Card sorters can handle from 500 to 2000 cards per minute (the sorters with the faster rates use photoelectric read systems and vacuum card transports).

Card sorters read portions of each card that is passed through them, (and in some cases compare certain data on the card with data programmed into the sorter) and then route the cards to separate bins or pockets in accordance with the nature of the data contained on the card. For example, if it is desired to determine the relative seniority of a group of servicemen, punched cards containing extracts of each man's service record can be fed to a card sorter. The sorter can be programmed to read those columns on the card that indicate years of service. The sorter transports the cards indicating 30 years of service into the first bin, 25 years of service into the second bin, etc.

The card sorting process described in figure 7-9 uses both mechanical and electromechanical principles to perform card sorting. A column selector (not shown) is used to select

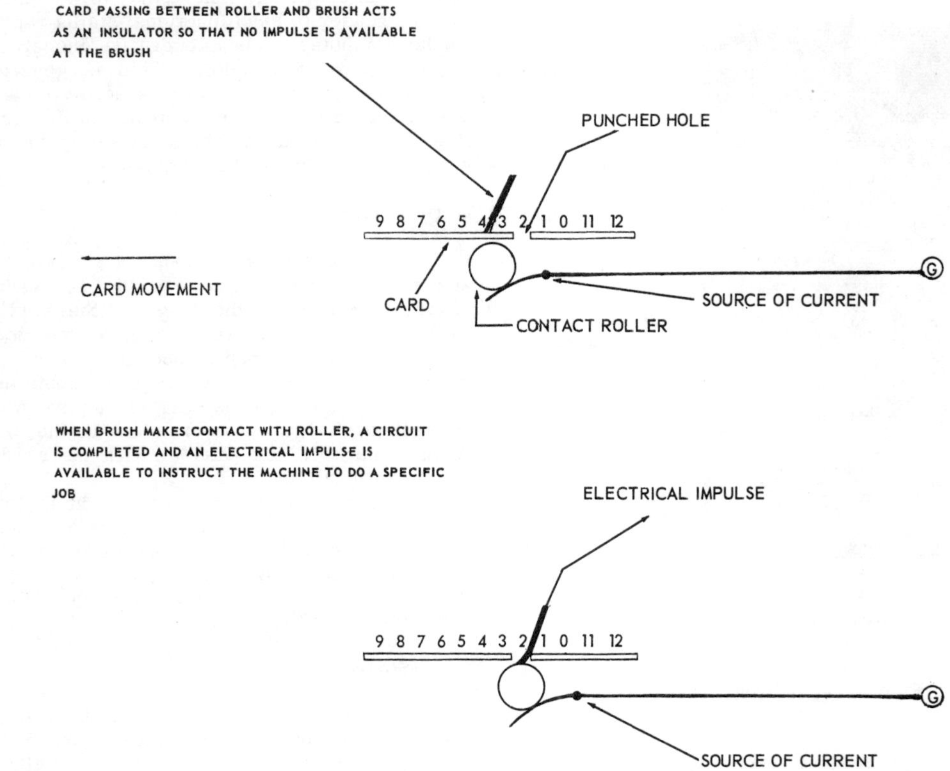

49.2X

Figure 7-6.—Brush reading punch in row 2.

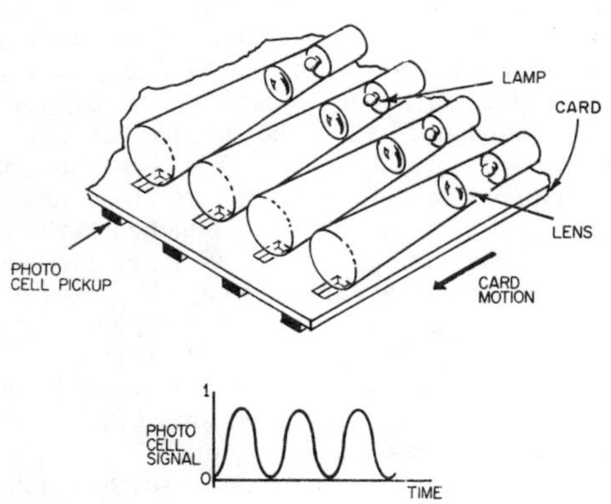

124.77

Figure 7-7.—Photoelectric card reading.

the column to be read. To understand its operation, assume that it is desired to sort all cards which contain a punch (hole) in the 4's row.

In figure 7-9A, a card (shown as a shaded line in which the punch in the 4's row is represented as an unshaded area) is advanced beneath a reading brush by a driven roller. The reading process begins at the 9's row (the bottom row of the card) and ends at the 12's row (the top row). While the card is still passing under the reading brush, the leading edge (the bottom) of that card is passing beneath the ends of chute blades. Each of the numbered chute blades terminate in an associated bin (not shown). The ends of the chute blades are supported by a moveable armature plate.

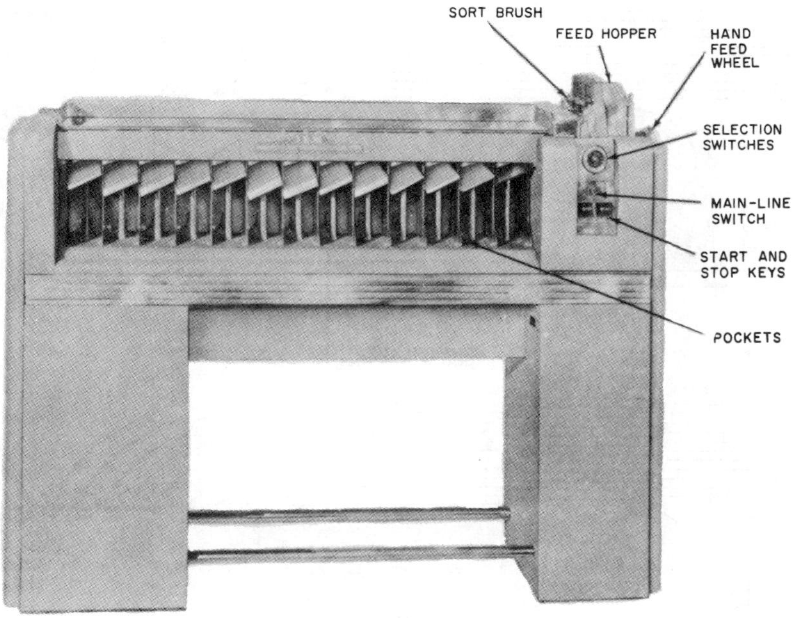

49.9X

Figure 7-8.—Type 82 card sorter.

Figure 7-9B, illustrates how the sorter selects the right chute blade (and therefore the proper bin) for the card. The tips of the chute blades are spaced so that the read brush (also called the "sort brush") drops through the 4-punch in the card immediately after the leading edge of the card passes under the tip of chute blade number 5. The opening in the card permits the brush to make contact with a conductive material beneath the card, thereby closing an electric cirucuit.

The closing of this circuit causes two electromagnets to be energized. This action exerts sufficient force against a spring tension (which normally holds the armature plate as shown in figure 7-9A) to cause the plate (fig. 7-9B) to move downward. This permits all chute blades beyond the forward end of the card to drop, thus permitting the card to pass into the proper bin.

Collators

The collator (fig 7-10) is a card device which will merge two sets of cards without disturbing their original sequence, and, in addition, will select cards to be kept out of the merged sequence. Two hoppers and feed units (fig 7-11), along with four or five pockets for stacking cards are provided.

The two feed units in the collator are called the PRIMARY FEED and the SECONDARY FEED. Cards placed in the primary feed hopper are referred to as primary cards, and those placed in the secondary feed hopper are called secondary cards. Cards are placed in the hoppers face down, with the 9 edge toward the throat.

Most collating operations require that two numbers be compared. For example, when checking sequence, the number coded on one card must be compared with the number on the preceding card to see if the cards are in the proper order. Also, when merging, the number coded on a card in one feed unit must be compared with the number on a card in the other feed unit to see which card is to be fed first.

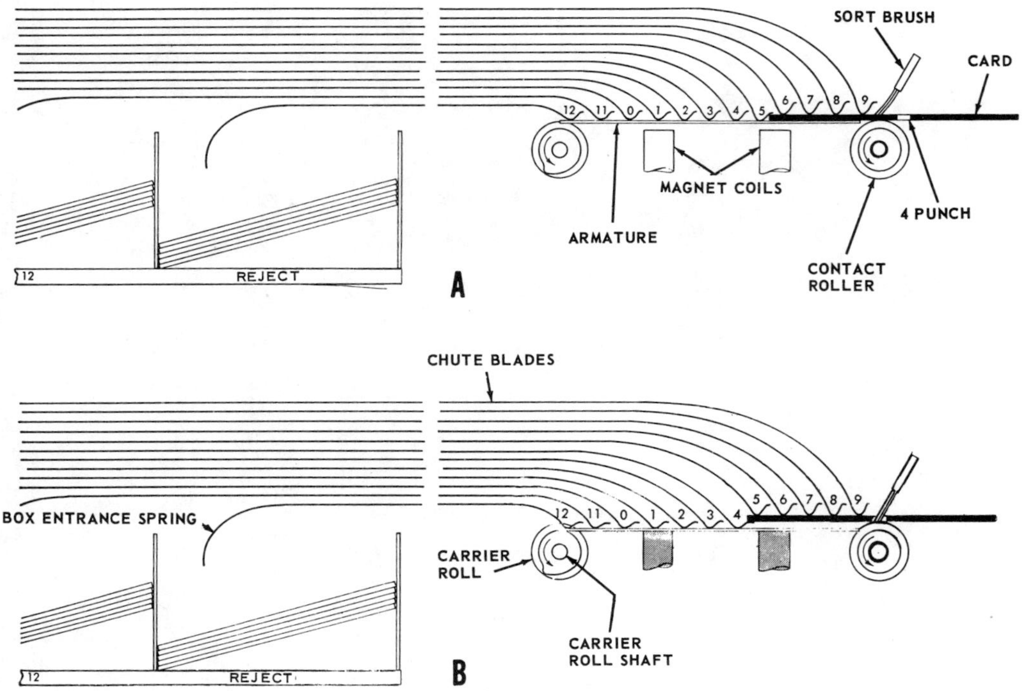

49.12X

Figure 7-9.—Card sorting machine—IBM type 82.

When one card is compared with another, one of three possible conditions may exist with regard to the number coded on the card; it may be lower, equal to, or higher than the number on the other card. Card feeding and selection can be controlled by control panel wiring (not shown) when either of these conditions occurs.

Note from the illustration (fig 7-11) that the primary cards pass two sets of brushes, while the secondary cards pass only one set. The readings from the two sets of brushes in the primary feed unit can be compared with each other, or with the readings from the secondary brushes. Since the secondary feed unit contains only one set of brushes, readings from the secondary brushes can normally be used only for comparing with readings from the primary brushes.

METHODS OF USING CARD READERS WITH BUFFER STORAGE

The following is a discussion of a representative method of using a card reader with buffer storage.

Some card readers are designed for "on-line" operation with a computer. Further, the computer may be capable of selecting any one of several card readers as the input or output device.

The diagram and flow chart in figure 7-12 are used to illustrate one method of reading data from a card reader into the computer memory. Four readers are shown in figure 7-12A.

The request for read-in of data is generally in the form of a programmed instruction. When the instruction is issued, the control unit produces an input request signal on any one of the

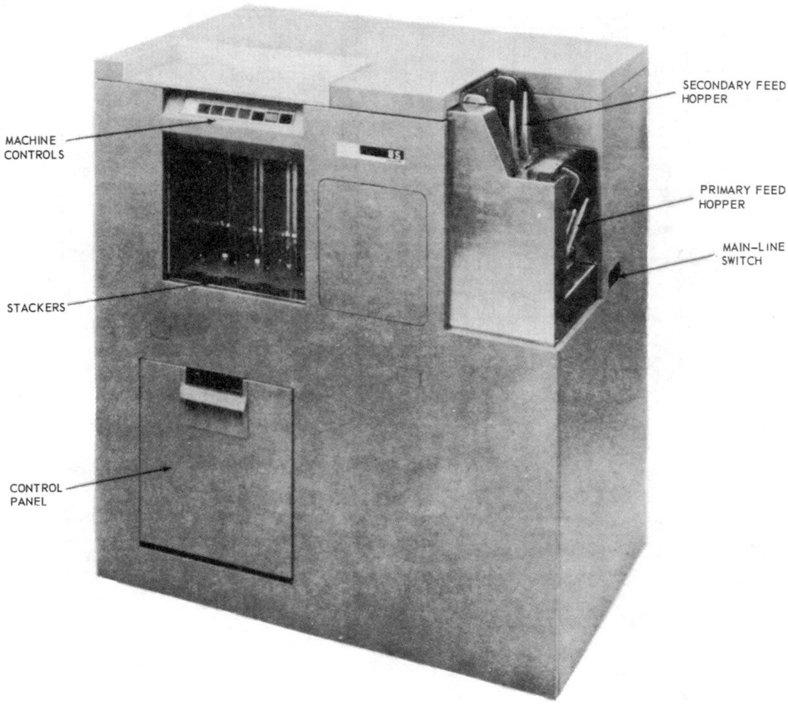

Figure 7-10.—Type 85 collator. 49.53X

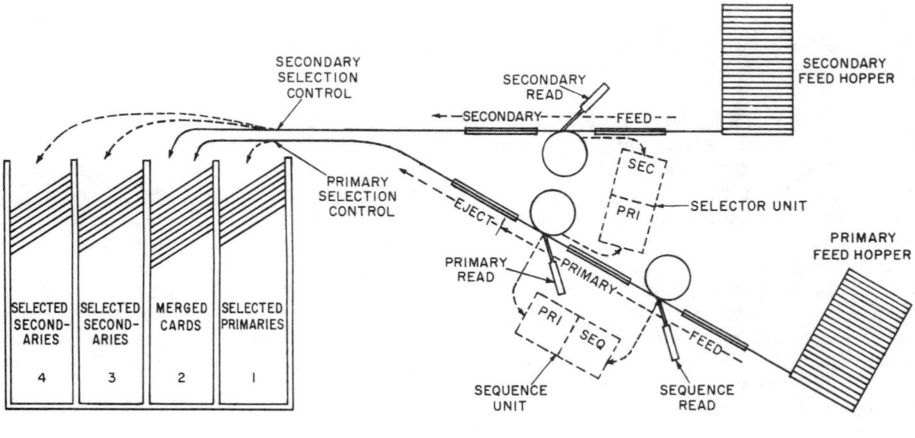

Figure 7-11.—Card feed schematic diagram. 49.55X

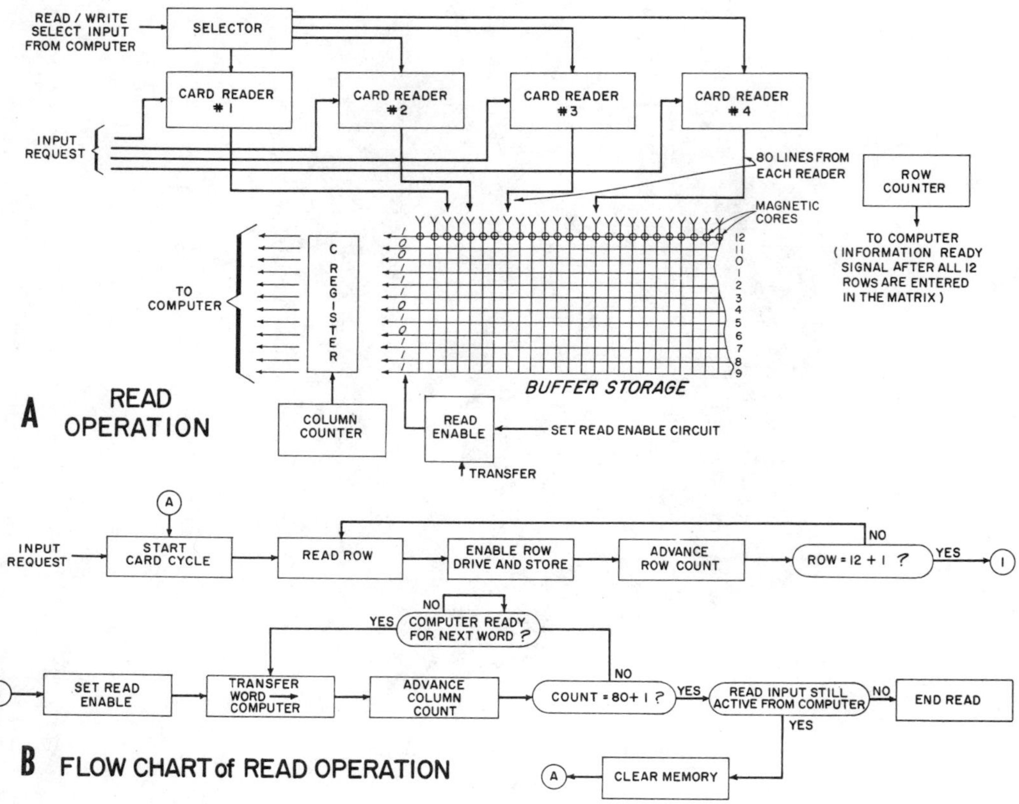

124.82

Figure 7-12.—Card reading operation using buffer storage.

four input request lines as determined by the instruction. The same instruction (or in some cases a subsequent instruction) will select the desired function, either read or write. (A card reader is capable of performing both functions.)

Some readers read the data directly into the computer. This method is slow and does not afford best use of computer time. A more desirable arrangement and the one treated here, uses a buffer storage. The card reader passes its input over 80 transfer lines to the storage medium. (Only one of these lines from each reader is shown.) Cores are used as the storage medium in this discussion because of their simplicity.

The storage matrix contains 960 cores (only top row shown in figure 7-12), each of which can be in either the 0 or 1 state to represent any combination of holes and no holes contained on the card being read. The data are read-in (in parallel form) longitudinally across the matrix so that all 1's in the 9's row of the card are entered first. All 1's in the 8's row are entered next followed by those in rows 7, 6, 5, 4, 3, 2, 1, and 0, in that order. The 1's in the 11's and 12's row are entered (in that order) after the 0's row.

A row counter counts each row as it is entered into the matrix. After entering the last row (the 12's row) the row counter produces an output which indicates that the information is ready for transfer to the computer. If the computer is available to accept the data, a read enable signal will be developed in the computer and transmitted to the card reader to set the read enable circuits. Subsequent instructions will permit the data to be transferred (column by column) into the computer as described later.

The C register provides temporary storage of data en route to the computer. The column counter initiates the "read next card" signal after all 80 columns have been transferred to the computer at high speed. Note that the data are read into the core matrix at the speed of the input device and into the computer at electronic speeds, limited only by the ability of the computer memory to accept and store the data. Thus, the core matrix provides "buffer storage" between the card reader and the main computer memory.

The flow chart (fig. 7-12B) shows how the read-in process is executed. Upon receiving the "input request" signal from the computer, the order to "start card cycle" is issued (A). The "Read-Row" instruction causes the 9's row to be positioned at the reading station, and read. After the holes and no-holes, or 1's and 0's in the 9's row are read, the "enable row drive and store" instruction causes the drive lines in the matrix (which correspond with holes in the card) to be activated, and their selected cores are switched to the 1 state. All other cores remain in the zero state. (The memory matrix is cleared before the read-in of each card.)

The order "advance row count" places the 8's row in the position for read-in. Because the 8's row is the next row to be read, the answer to the question "is row=12+1?" is "no" and a signal is produced to "read-row" (row 8 in this case). The process continues, storing the data from the card row by row into the matrix, until all of the card data is transferred to the matrix. The 12's row is the last to be read-in.

After reading row 12, the answer to the question "is row=12+1?" will be "yes." This action causes a command to be issued which sets the read enable circuits in preparation for the read-out of the data from the memory matrix. (Points ① and ① are connected.) A command line from the computer (explained under control unit in chapter 4) carries the signal to cause the read-out of one vertical word column of data (12 bits) each time this signal appears on the line. The column counter is advanced by 1 each time a 12-bit column is transferred.

If a "no" answer is produced from the "count=80+1 circuit," and the computer is not ready to accept the next word, a method is provided for storing the word to be transferred until the computer memory is able to accept the word for storage.

After the transfer of all 80 columns, a subsequent order to "advance column count" will produce a "yes" output from the interrogation "count=80+1?" This permits an examination of conditions to determine if the "Read input is still active from the computer." Stated differently, "is the computer still demanding the read-in of data?" A "yes" answer causes the memory matrix to be cleared and the entire operation to be repeated during the read-in of the next card (points (A) and (A) are connected). A "no" answer initiates "end read," and all card reader operations are discontinued.

To further understand buffer storage as it applies in the interest of expeditious use of computer time, consider the overall operation and use of the computer with and without the aid of buffer storage and a buffer controlled sequence.

In the flow chart of figure 7-13, the instruction issued to cause read-in designates an address at which the read-in must begin (first word address, fwa) and the address of the last word (Lwa). For a read-in instruction, these addresses refer to the location at which the first word and last word are to be stored in the main computer memory. For a read-out instruction, fwa and Lwa would encompass the total data to be read-out. The data are read into or out of memory in sequential order from the "fwa" to the "Lwa."

A subsequent instruction causes the computer to select the "input device," which in this case is presumed to be a card reader. Next, the status of the selected device is determined. If this device is not available or other conditions are not satisfactory (such as "power switch not on"), a "no" output will result from the "ready" interrogation. In some cases, a light, alarm, or other means of alerting the operator to correct the situation is initiated. If the "ready" interrogation produces a "yes" answer ((1) and (1) are tied together), the command is

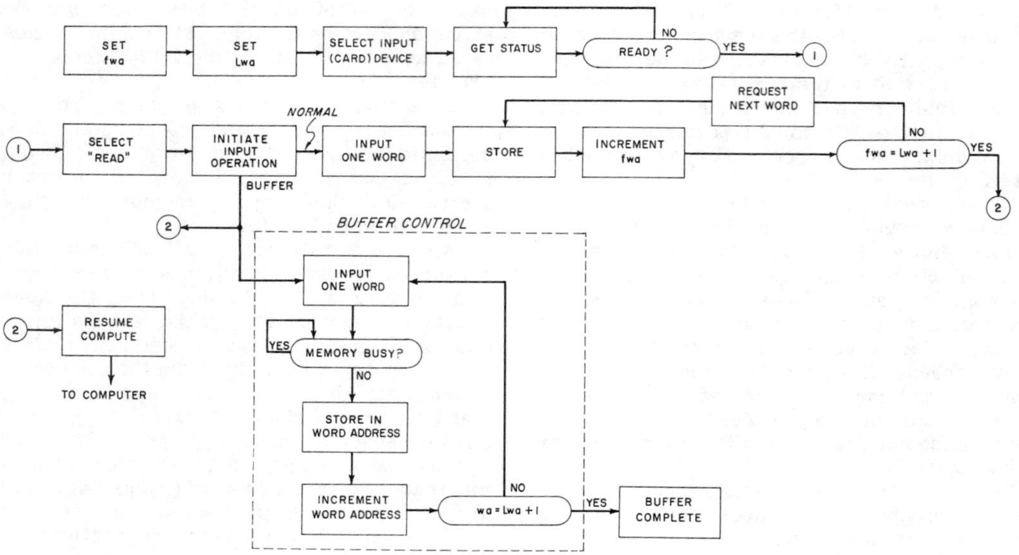

124.83

Figure 7-13.—Flow chart of normal and buffer read-in of card data.

issued to select "read." This action selects the "read function," meaning that data is to be read into the computer rather than written-out.

After all such preparations (as described) are completed, the "initiate input operation" is issued, and the card reading process begins. If buffer storage is not used (the method described here as NORMAL) the computer will issue the order "input one word." This is followed by a store instruction which places the word in the fwa in storage. The computer now causes a counter to increment fwa or count 1, and to examine the new address number to determine if the new word is the same as the last word address plus 1. If the answer is "no" the next word is requested. This process repeats itself until the output from the interrogation "fwa = Lwa+1?" is "yes."

Because the numbers (2) and (2) represent the same point, a "yes" answer from the interrogation "fwa = Lwa+1" causes the command to be issued to permit the computer to resume operations under the influence of the stored program. Note that the computer is not available to perform any operations except read-in during the time that the read-in is in progress.

Now consider the action using the buffer method. All conditions and operations are the same as described earlier up to and including the "initiate input" operation. The fwa and Lwa are stored in a register in the buffer control section so that the buffer operation will stop when the action is completed.

As soon as the "initiate input operation" command is issued a buffer control unit begins to operate and the main computer is released to perform other operations (arithmetic, control, etc.). Buffer control operates independently of the main computer.

After buffer control has caused the read-in of the first word, an interrogation is performed to determine if memory is busy. (It is possible that memory, and all associated drive line and registers, are busy in the performance of some other operation.) If the answer to this interrogation is "yes" no attempt is made by buffer control to enter the data into the main computer storage until memory is available to accept and store the data.

After storing the data, a counter increments the word address (wa), and the new address is compared with the previously stored code which represents Lwa+1 to determine if the last word has already been stored. If the answer is "no," the process repreats until a "yes" output is produced. This "yes" output indicates that the buffer operation is completed. Note in this case that the computer is not directly involved in the buffer operation.

The terms "buffer" and "buffer storage" are used to describe almost any operation which takes place in a computer with the aid of any form of intermediate storage. However, the term "buffer storage" is most frequently used to denote the type of operation just explained. The word "buffer" generally refers to a device or arrangement of devices or registers which perform temporary storage of data as they are being transferred in the computation process.

KEYBOARD INPUTS

Various types of keyboards have been either adopted or designed for on-line computer use. Since they are operated by humans, they are characterized by an extremely low data rate. The use is therefore generally limited (in on-line input applications) to insertion of irregularly occuring parameters and commands. For large amounts of data, they are used either off-line to prepare a tape, or multiplexed.

TELETYPE

Teletype equipment uses a seven bit serial code (table 7-1). Five bits identify the character, the other two denote the beginning and end of the character. The serial code lends itself well to transmission over lines. Thus, teletype equipments are frequently used as remote I/0 devices. An adapter control unit is installed in the teletype unit at a computer site to convert each teletype character into parallel format and supply various signals relating to the status of the equipment. Such a machine is shown in figure 7-14. When the code (tab. 7-1) is converted to parallel format, the start and stop characters are dropped and only the five bits identifying the character (shown in octal code at the far right in the table) are transmitted. Maximum data rate for the teletype machine is 100 five character words per minute. The teletype is capable of input from the keyboard or an auxiliary paper tape reader. The tape reader supplied will accept either five or seven level tape code. For output, the machine will type the data received and also punch a paper tape.

FLEXOWRITER

The flexowriter is another device similar to the teletype, figure 7-15. Unlike the teletype, the flexowriter communicates using a six bit parallel code. It is normally used as an off-line device for paper tape preparation and correction. The flexowriter also communicates at 100 words per minute and has provisions for either on-line or off-line preparation of tape while typing. On-line usage requires an adaptor unit for computer communication. The flexowriter code is shown in table 7-2.

Figure 7-16 illustrates the appearance of the seven level tape. Using either teletype or flexowriter code, each frame represents one character of either five or six bits. Since it is possible to write two octal characters per frame on a seven level tape, a program can be stored in this form referred to as, a bioctal format. The utility level is used, if desired, to provide a check on the accuracy of each frame. This level can be punched to cause each frame to have either an even or odd number of bits. When used, this utility level bit is called the parity bit.

MISCELLANEOUS KEYBOARDS

Various special I/0 keyboard devices are used. Generally they are used to communicate with a running program. They may be used only as input devices (equipped to provide some indication that the data has been accepted or rejected), or they may have some provision for readout of data from the computer. The keyboard and character keys may vary from device to device.

PAPER-TAPE UNITS

Punched paper tapes (fig. 7-17) are often used with military and commercial data-processing systems. The advantage of this form of data recording is that most business machines can easily be modified or designed to

Table 7-1.—Teletype Code

TELETYPE CODE

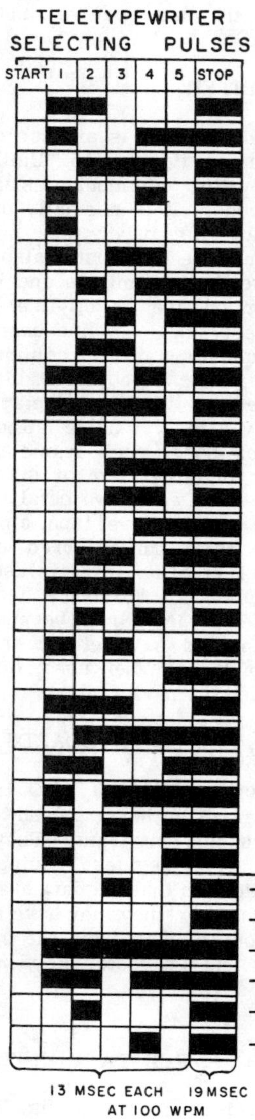

LETTERS	FIGURES	OCTAL
A	–	30
B	?	23
C	:	16
D	$	22
E	3	20
F	!	26
G	&	13
H		05
I	8	14
J	'	32
K	(	36
L	)	11
M	.	07
N	,	06
O	9	03
P	Ø	15
Q	1	35
R	4	12
S	BELL(🔔*)	24
T	5	01
U	7	34
V	;	17
W	2	31
X	/	27
Y	6	25
Z	"	21
SPACE	■*	04
BLANK	≀*	00
LETTERS	↓*	37
FIGURES	↑*	33
LINE FEED	■*	10†
CARRIAGE RETURN	<*	02†

MACHINE FUNCTIONS (SPACE through CARRIAGE RETURN)

164.73

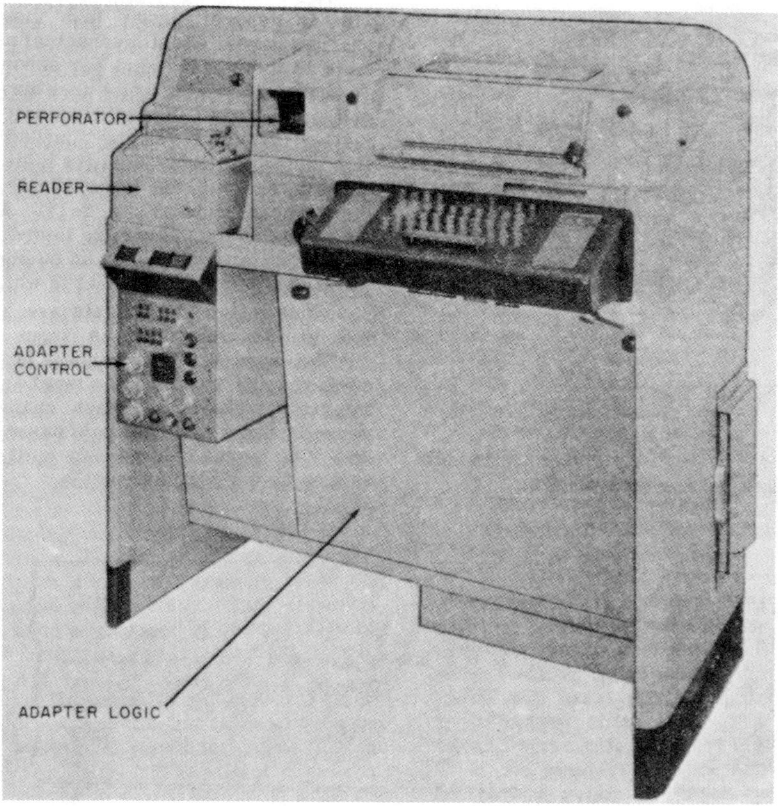

31.29

Figure 7-14. —Teletypewriter set AN/UGC-6, with adapter.

punch paper-tape records of their operations. These paper tapes are punched in a modified teletype code that can be transmitted over wire or radio teletype lines.

Many large installations use paper-tape units as preliminary data-processing devices at the point of transaction. All pertinent data are sent by teletype to a central data-processing installation. The paper tape data can be converted and read onto magnetic tape (or some other suitable medium), then fed into a large computer.

Paper tapes are available in several widths (7/8", 1", 1-1/8", etc.) and in 100-foot, 350-foot, and 700-foot rolls. A sprocket channel (a line of small circular holes that are punched on the tape at the time data are recorded), appears longitudinally along the length of the tape, as shown in figure 7-17. These holes are engaged by sprockets that drive the tape past punching and reading stations. Reels are used to store the tape.

PAPER TAPE WRITING AND READING

The writing and reading techniques used with paper tapes are almost identical to those used with punched cards. The holes that are punched in the paper tape however, are round rather than rectangular in shape.

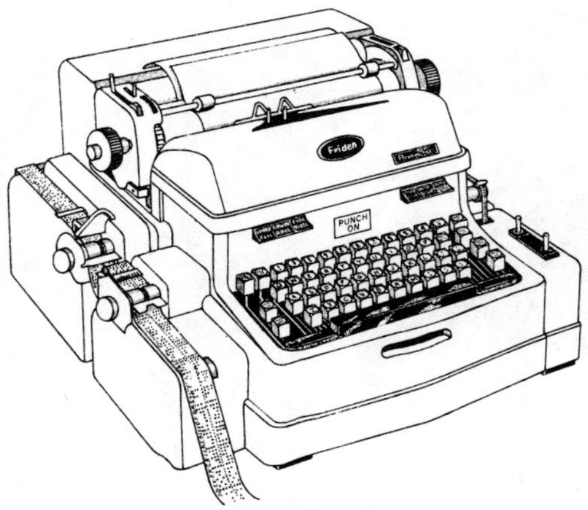

164. 47

Figure 7-15. —Flexowriter.

The speeds used with paper-tape equipment are, in general, lower than those used with punched cards. Most mechanical punches punch from 10 to 60 characters per second.

A type of reader which uses the photoelectric principle (rather than mechanical) provides the fastest means of reading punched tapes. With this method, a light-sensitive material is placed beneath each of the longitudinal channels and the sprocket channel (fig. 7-17). A light placed above the tape and over the light-sensitive material (not shown) causes an output signal to be produced from each channel in which a hole has been punched. The signals are amplified and fed to the computer as input information.

The sprocket hole outputs (which occur at each reading point on the tape) signal the read interval. Therefore, each channel output is sensed when a sprocket hole passes the station. The tape moves continuously until it is ordered to stop by a STOP instruction.

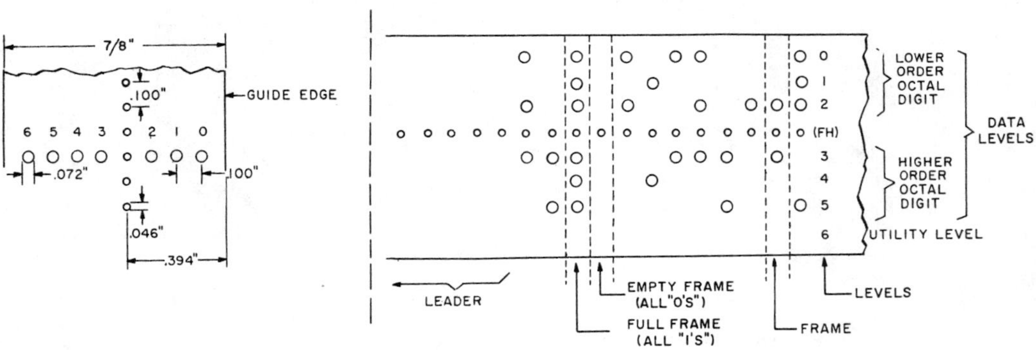

164.48

Figure 7-16.—Seven level tape.

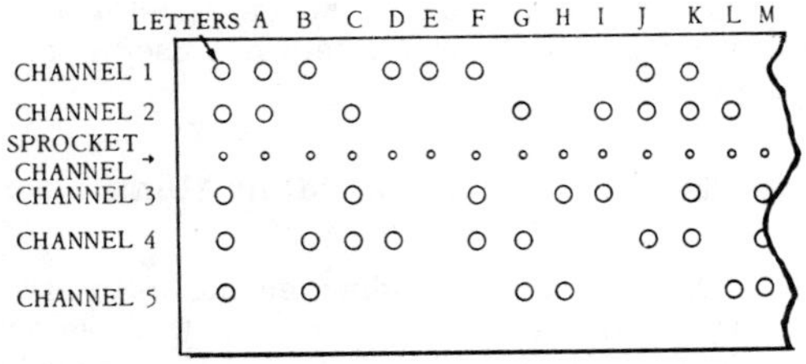

124.84

Figure 7-17.—Five-channel paper tape code.

Photoelectric type readers can feed up to 1000 characters per second into the computer. This speed is comparable with that of the fastest card reader available.

PAPER TAPE CODES

The paper-tape codes that are used with data-processing systems are the five-, six-, seven-, and eight-channel codes. One widely used code (and the only one shown here) is the five-channel, modified, teletype code (fig. 7-17).

Table 7-2. --Flexowriter Code

UC	LC	OCTAL CODE
A	a	30
B	b	23
C	c	16
D	d	22
E	e	20
F	f	26
G	g	13
H	h	05
I	i	14
J	j	32
K	k	36
L	l	11
M	m	07
N	n	06
O	o	03
P	p	15
Q	q	35
R	r	12
S	s	24
T	t	01
U	u	34
V	v	17
W	w	31
X	x	27
Y	y	25
Z	z	21

<table>
<tr><th>UC</th><th>LC</th><th>OCTAL CODE</th></tr>
<tr><td>1</td><td>1</td><td>52</td></tr>
<tr><td>2</td><td>2</td><td>74</td></tr>
<tr><td>3</td><td>3</td><td>70</td></tr>
<tr><td>4</td><td>4</td><td>64</td></tr>
<tr><td>5</td><td>5</td><td>62</td></tr>
<tr><td>6</td><td>6</td><td>66</td></tr>
<tr><td>7</td><td>7</td><td>72</td></tr>
<tr><td>8</td><td>8</td><td>60</td></tr>
<tr><td>9</td><td>9</td><td>33</td></tr>
<tr><td>0</td><td>0</td><td>37</td></tr>
<tr><td colspan="3">SIGNS AND PUNCTUATION</td></tr>
<tr><td>)</td><td>.</td><td>42</td></tr>
<tr><td>(</td><td>,</td><td>46</td></tr>
<tr><td>—</td><td>|</td><td>50</td></tr>
<tr><td>•</td><td>=</td><td>44</td></tr>
<tr><td>/</td><td>+</td><td>54</td></tr>
<tr><td>-</td><td>_</td><td>56</td></tr>
</table>

MOVEMENT	OCTAL CODE
Space	04
Tape feed	00
Shift up	47
Shift down	57
Back Space	61
Stop code	43
Carriage Ret.	45
Tab	51
Color shift	02
Code delete	77

The section of tape shown illustrates how letters are represented on the tape. Figures are similarly represented, although the keyboard symbol for "figures" must be punched before figures can be recorded. The symbol for "letters" must be depressed at the keyboard before letters can be recorded. Thus, the "letters" character represented on the left of the section of tape shown indicates that all subsequent characters represent letters. Table 7-3 shows all letters and figures represented by this code.

HIGH-SPEED PRINTING

In many military computer applications, such as fire control systems, the computer output is used to train weapons or other devices. In many

Table 7-3.—Five-Channel Data Processing Code and Tape

5-CHANNEL DATA PROCESSING CODE*

(MODIFIED TELETYPE CODE)

Character	Punched Channels	Character	Punched Channels	Character	Punched Channels
A	1,2	U	1,2,3	CARRIAGE RETURN	4
B	1,4,5	V	2,3,4,5		
C	2,3,4	W	1,2,5	ADVANCE PAPER	2
D	1,4	X	1,3,4,5		
E	1	Y	1,3,5		
F	1,3,4	Z	-----		
G	2,4,5	1	1,2,3,5		
H	3,5	2	1,2,5		
I	2,3	3	1		
J	1,2,4	4	2,4		
K	1,2,3,4	5	5		
L	2,5	6	1,3,5		
M	3,4,5	7	1,2,3		
N	3,4	8	2,3		
O	4,5	9	4,5		
P	2,3,5	0	2,3,5		
Q	----	FIGURES	1,2,4,5		
R	2,4	LETTERS	1,2,3,4,5		
S	1,3	SPACE	3		
T	5				

*NOTE Letters are preceded by the symbol for "Letters," and numbers are preceded by the symbol for "Figures."

other applications, the end result is printed data. Punched cards, punched paper tape, and magnetic tape are satisfactory for providing data in forms intelligible to computers, but numbers and words are most easily interpreted by human beings. Therefore, printing units are required to translate internal computer data into words and numbers that a human operator can understand.

MECHANICAL PRINTERS

Any type of page printing equipment that uses a mechanical motion of a hammer or type bar to transfer characters to paper is a mechanical printer. Some widely used examples of mechanical printers are discussed presently.

The operating principles of a mechanical typewriter (figure 7-18A) are easily understood. Downward force on a key actuates a mechanical linkage. This moves an arm that holds a single character. The type strikes an inked ribbon and presses it in contact with a sheet of paper that is held against a roller. The pressure that is placed on the ribbon by the piece of type causes the raised outline of the type to be printed on the paper.

The electric typewriter (fig. 7-18B) uses a rotating roller to drive the type arm linkage. Pressing a typewriter key causes a particular linkage to be pressed against the rotating roller. With this arrangement a character can be printed in a shorter time than is possible with mechanical typewriters.

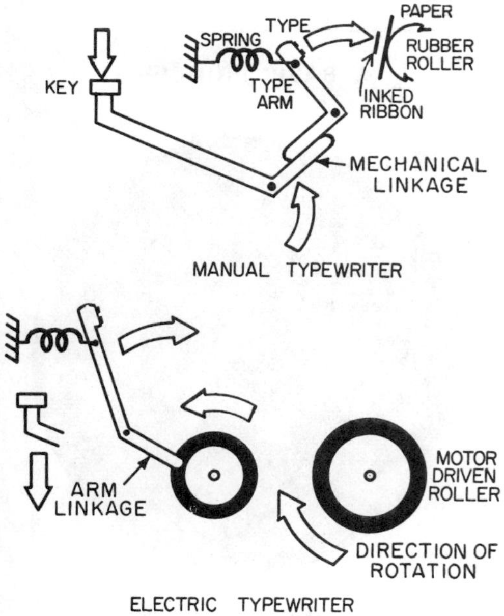

124.85

Figure 7-18.—Comparison of manual and electric typewriter principles.

LINE-A-TIME PRINTERS

As the name implies, the line-a-time printer is a machine that prints an entire line at one time. In general, these machines can print a page faster than a typewriter because the operation of printing each character on a line is performed simultaneously rather than separately.

There are two major types of line-a-time printers: type bar printers and type wheel printers.

Type Bar Printers

A computer-operated electric typewriter can print at speeds of approximately 10 letters or numbers (referred to as printed characters or digits) per second. Even though this results in printing 600 characters per minute, as compared with the 300 characters per minute that are produced by the average human typist, the electric typewriter is not fast enough for all operations.

The bar printer (fig. 7-19) is a variation of the typewriter. The type characters protrude from the edge of a bar. A character is printed by a hammer which strikes the paper and presses it against an inked ribbon and the type bar.

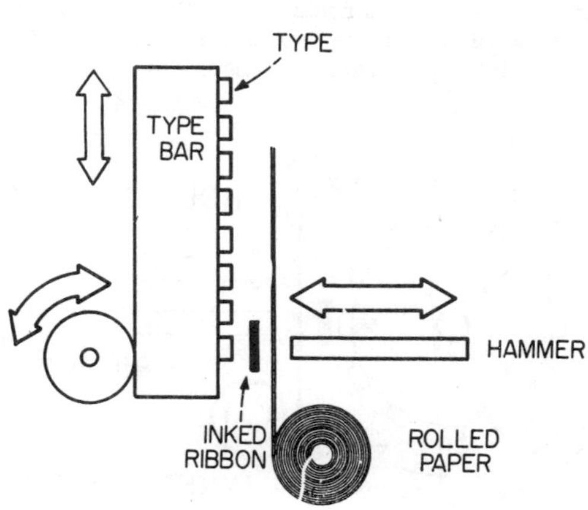

124.86

Figure 7-19.-Bar printer.

The type characters are mounted so that one appears above the other. A particular character is selected for printing by raising and lowering the type bar so that the desired character is lined up with the hammer.

Groups, or "gangs," of type bars are used to make up a multibar printer. The number of type bars that are used depends upon the number of characters that must be printed simultaneously. The bars are geared so that they are similar to toothed racks. The digitally operated pinions (not shown) that move the racks are driven by two stepping-switch mechanisms (one for each direction of motion).

Let us assume, for example, that the letter S is printed by stepping the type bar ten times. An S in computer code must be converted into ten stepping pulses which advance the type bar ten times. The printing hammer is then actuated and the letter is printed. After printing, the type bar is returned to a suitable rest position, or it is permitted to remain at the S position until the next stepping pulses are applied. These new stepping pulses are automatically corrected to allow for the fact that the bar is presently at the S position.

Type Wheel Printer

Another type of printer has the character type on the edge of a wheel (fig. 7-20). As many wheels as desired are arranged in parallel. The type wheels are continuously rotated. The striking of the hammers against the paper and ribbon is synchronized with the wheel rotation so that certain characters are selected for printing. This arrangement decreases the time required to position characters under the hammers, and provides higher printing speeds than the gang printer.

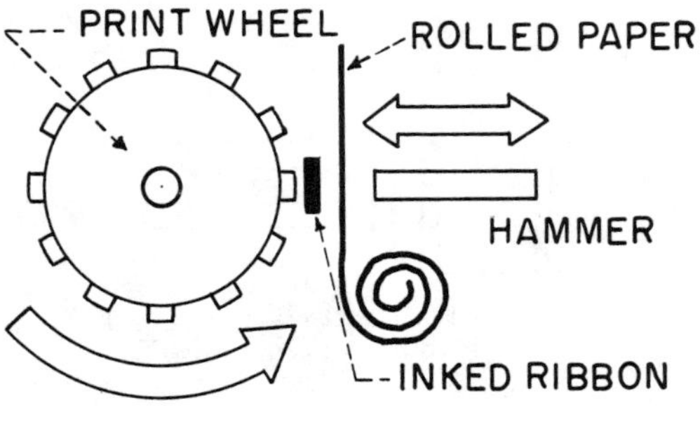

124.87
Figure 7-20.—The type wheel printer.

PHOTOGRAPHIC PRINTING

Photographic printing is accomplished by photographing the display produced by any one of several types of electronic character-writing tubes. The basic principle is illustrated in figure 7-21A. The negatives produced using this process can be used to make photographic prints or for offset printing.

The electronic character-writing tube and its associated circuitry (not shown) receive

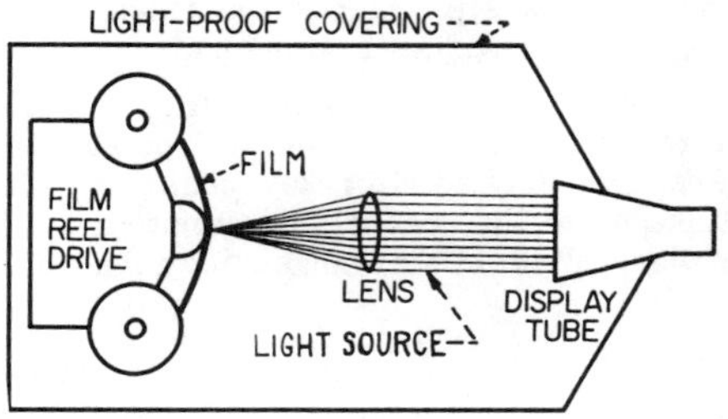

A BASIC PRINCIPLE

B MATRIX (GRID)

124.88
Figure 7-21.—Photographic printing.

binary signals that represent alphanumeric characters. Translating circuits operate a cathode-ray (display) tube that is designed to display the alphanumeric characters in English letters and Arabic numbers.

The simplest display tubes use a form of grid or matrix (fig. 7-21B) which, in effect, is an electronic stencil. The electron beam is aimed at a specific character in the metallic grid plate. The holes in the grid are in the shape of the characters to be printed. When the beam is deflected to the desired character the electron beam that passes through the hole has the shape of the character. A second deflection positions the character-shaped beam to its proper position on a flourescent screen. This process is continually repeated, so that the screen displays a series of characters which are photographed.

Other photographic systems use waveshaping circuits which generate voltages to approximate the component lines of each character, so that a simple cathode-ray tube can be used to display characters.

Both of the cathode-ray tube arrangements that have been discussed require elaborate beam-gating and deflection systems. However, they possess the advantages of being extremely fast and of requiring no mechanical moving parts.

The camera is usually contained in a light-proof box that surrounds the face of the tube. An optical system is used for recording the tube display on film. The film is reel-fed, and is stepped to the next frame each time that the tube message changes. A shutter is not required, since the cathode-ray tube blanking pulses perform the same function. The film-drive mechanism is the only mechanical device in this entire system.

The wire punch printer uses a different approach for forming characters. A matrix of stiff wires is used either to print letters or to punch holes (fig. 7-22). By using the proper combination of wires, it is possible to punch any character or letter. The wires of each matrix are bundled together and are run to a cylindrical code tube that has holes machined into its surface. The wires are fanned out along the longitudinal axis of the tube, with each wire resting against the surface of the cylinder. When a particular character is to be printed, the tube is rotated and moved along its axis so that the correct combination of individual wires is backed by metal, and the

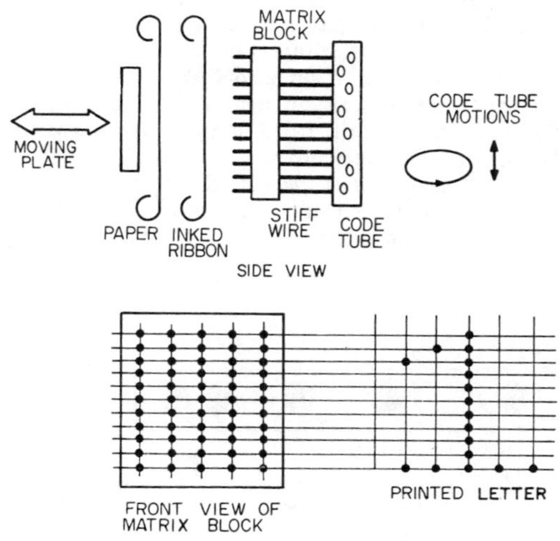

124.89

Figure 7-22.—Wire punch printer.

other wires are located over holes. At the printing end of the wire bundle, a moving plate pushes paper into contact with the matrix of wire ends. Those wires that are backed by metal will exert sufficient force on the paper to print the character. The remaining, unbacked wires will not exert this force.

If the plate is smooth, and an inked ribbon or carbon paper is placed between the wires and the paper, the backed wires will press against the ribbon and will print the appropriate character as a group of black dots. The wires are spring loaded (not shown on the diagram) so that they will return to their original positions when the plate pressure is removed.

ERROR DETECTION AND CORRECTION

When you consider that a digital computer is a machine that receives information, delivers information, and continually transfers information from one integral part to another the problem of information loss or errors is a serious one. Even if you manage to eliminate human errors, there are many other possible sources of error. The information that is stored in the computer simply consists of a series of lights, relays, transistors, diodes, or cores that are activated in a certain pattern. If one component fails, the pattern changes, and the information becomes distorted.

You can use a series of lights (fig. 7-23) on the computer as an example. The number 0110 represents 6. If the lamp in the 4's place fails, the number changes to 0010, which is 2. This is a loss of two-thirds of the number's original value. Thus, the failure of a single component can produce a relatively large loss of information.

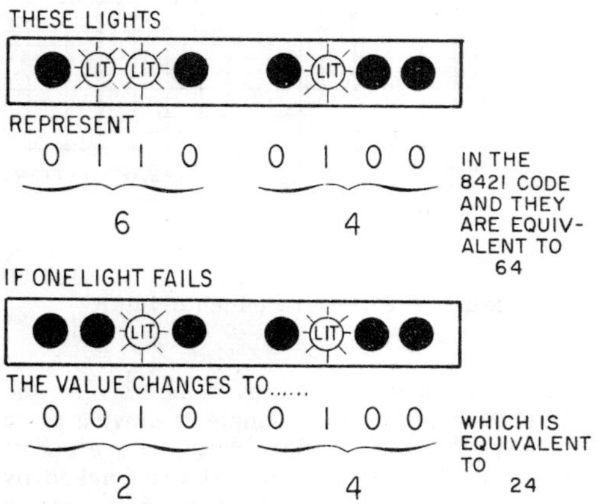

164.49

Figure 7-23.—Example of error by component failure.

ERROR DETECTION METHODS

Unlike the radio receiver, the computer generally exhibits no natural symptoms, such as hum, distortion, or erratic volume to warn the operator that something has gone wrong. Instead, the computer simply provides the wrong answer. Furthermore, component failure is not the only way by which information can be made erroneous or be lost. There is some distortion each time a pulse passes from one circuit to another. Added to this is the distortion caused by the inductive effects from nearby circuits. Thus, it should be understood that a pulse can sometimes become so distorted that it may produce an error.

One method of detecting errors, which may be called a redundancy method, involves running the problem through the computer twice and noting whether the solutions are identical. However, a computer's major function is to save time, and this type of check doubles the amount of time that is required to solve a problem. In addition, this check is useless if a component has failed; for the faulty component will probably distort both solutions in exactly the same manner.

A better solution is to provide two sets of identical circuitry, as shown in figure 7-24. When this is done, the same problem is run simultaneously through both circuits. This is called parallel operation. Unless both circuits commit exactly the same error, obtaining identical solutions indicates that the answer is correct. (You may recall that the exclusive-OR circuit produces an output only when its two inputs are different.)

When using this method, the inputs should always be the same. A signal at the output of any of the exclusive-OR circuits indicates that the two parallel major section outputs are not identical, and that one of them is in error. A signal at B, for example, means that either section B1 or section B2 is in error.

Again, the cost factor must be considered. While parallel operation is an excellent technical concept, and its use requires no extra time, it does double the circuitry costs. Thus, a different solution must be found. The following is a discussion of various codes and coding techniques which find wide usage in error-detecting applications.

COMMONLY USED CODES

It is important to understand the principles of coding, so that memorization of the codes is not necessary. In fact, it is sometimes impossible. There are so many different computer codes that no one individual knows all of them. A small portion of such codes is shown below. They are named by their four lowest integral weights.

5, 3, 1, 1	6, 3, 1, 1
4, 3, 2, 1	5, 3, 2, 1
4, 2, 2, 1	2, 4, 2, 1
8, 4, 2, 1	6, 4, 2, 1

Another fact of which one should be made aware is that two different computers seldom use exactly the same code. If one begins to

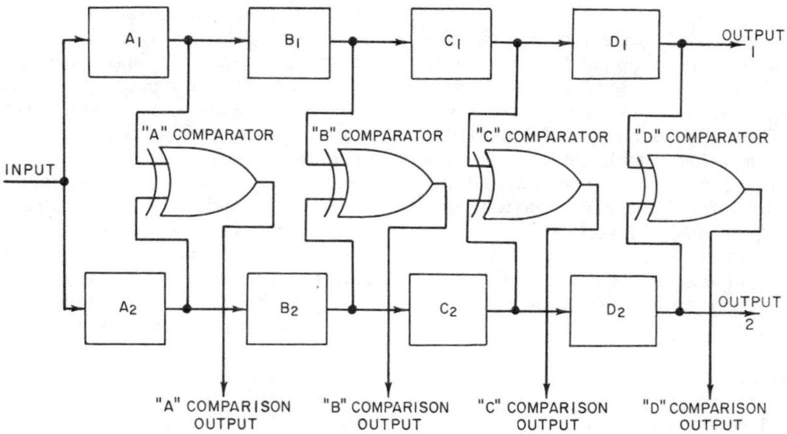

164.50

Figure 7-24.—Exclusive-OR circuits used as comparator in error detection process.

work with a specific computer, one will become so familiar with it and with its coding that memorization will be automatic.

Computer codes can be divided into three categories:

1. Regularly weighted codes
2. Arbitrarily weighted codes
3. Nonweighted codes

Regularly Weighted Codes

When considering regularly weighted codes, each number position has a weighting value, just as the decimal number system, and its weighting values are regular. For example, 9_{10} and 5_{10} are formed in the 7, 4, 2, 1 code as shown in figure 7-25. The weighting values form a simple arithmetic series which begins with 1 and increases regularly, plus one unit, plus two units, plus three units, plus four units, etc.

The important point to remember about regularly weighted codes is that the weights are determined by some rule. If one knows the rule, i.e., how the various weights are derived, he can find the weighting value for any desired position.

	WEIGHTS				
DECIMAL	7	4	2	1	
9_{10} =	1	0	1	0	$= 1 \times 7 + 0 \times 4 + 1 \times 2 + 0 \times 1 = 9_{10}$
5_{10} =	0	1	0	1	$= 0 \times 7 + 1 \times 4 + 0 \times 2 + 1 \times 1 = 5_{10}$

124.60

Figure 7-25.—Formation of 9_{10} and 5_{10} in the 7, 4, 2, 1 code.

Arbitrarily Weighted Codes

Arbitrarily weighted codes also use weighting values, but have no rules for forming them. Consider the 4, 2, 2, 1 code in which the first four weighting values from left to right are 4, 2, 2, 1. There is no rule, or formula, for generating these values, and one cannot know what the weighting value of the fifth digit from the right might be. However, one will find that the 4, 2, 2, 1 code, as well as many other arbitrarily weighted codes, can be a very practical one, and that it makes no difference what the fifth digit weight might be, because it is never used.

Nonweighted Codes

Nonweighted codes have no weighting values at all. Each coded group is defined so as to represent some quantity. The Roman numeral system is such a nonweighted code.

Pure Binary Coding

Although the decimal code is quite appropriate for use in the small mechanical office calculator, it is impractical for use in the electronic digital computer. One important reason for this limitation, which has been mentioned before, is that electronic digital computers use binary components such as magnetic cores, flip-flops, and diodes, that function best with pure binary numbers.

The simplicity of binary calculation means fewer and simpler instructions are required to program the computer. This, in turn, means less hardware and lower cost. For these reasons straight binary coding, as it is called, provides a definite design advantage.

Every design advantage is usually accompanied by some limitations. The major disadvantage is that one must first convert the problem into binary code, and then he must convert the binary solution back into decimal numbers. Obviously, while binary calculation is convenient for the machine's internal operations, the machine's input and output must be able to "talk" man's language.

In order to do this, two translation units are required. These include a decimal-to-binary converter immediately after the input, and a binary-to-decimal converter just before the output. This arrangement is shown in figure 7-26. These converters must be able to convert any number from one system into the other. Because they must handle an infinite number of possibilities, these converters are complex, expensive, and difficult to maintain. Despite these disadvantages, however, the balance remains in favor of the pure binary code, and computers are built in accordance with this system.

BINARY-CODED DECIMALS— (A COMPROMISE)

Our decimal number language is different from the one used by a large electronic computer. Although we understand decimal numbers best, all digital computers, (except the simplest mechanical calculators), function best

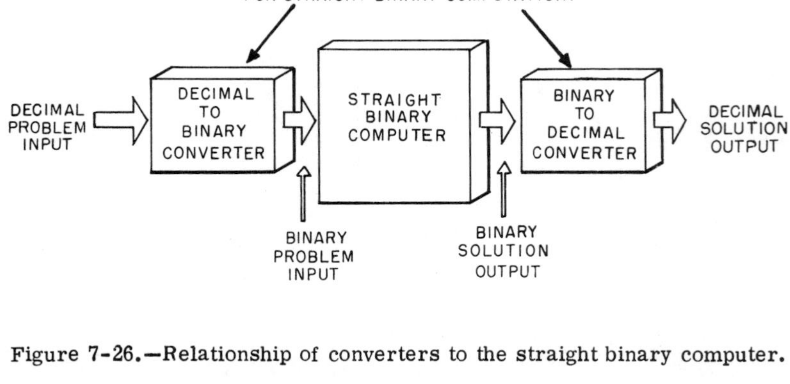

124.7

Figure 7-26.—Relationship of converters to the straight binary computer.

by using the pure binary number system. In order to bridge the two systems, it was necessary to sacrifice some of the computer's simplicity by adding complex encoding and decoding circuits.

At the present time no complete solution has been developed for this problem. Even the best modern computer employs a system that is a compromise. Thus, one of the better modern computers uses a combination of both the binary and decimal codes, and the outstanding features of its operation will be described in the paragraphs that follow.

Recall that each decimal digit can be represented by a binary number, as shown in figure 7-27. Each of the binary numbers that is shown in the figure is called a "binary-coded decimal digit" or "coded digit." One can see that without using any other binary numbers, it is possible to represent any desired quantity by means of these coded digits. For example, in order to represent 736, we simply write the coded digit for each decimal, then we place the digit in the same order as the decimals thus: 011100110110.

DECIMAL DIGIT	BINARY-CODED DECIMAL DIGIT
0	0 0 0 0
1	0 0 0 1
2	0 0 1 0
3	0 0 1 1
4	0 1 0 0
5	0 1 0 1
6	0 1 1 0
7	0 1 1 1
8	1 0 0 0
9	1 0 0 1

124.8

Figure 7-27.—Binary-coded decimal digits.

Binary coded decimal digits need not be spaced because we know that each one is composed of four binary digits. For easier reading, however, a space usually will be placed between each coded digit, thus: 0111 0011 0110. Note that this number is not pure binary; it is, instead, a binary-coded decimal number, as shown in figure 7-28.

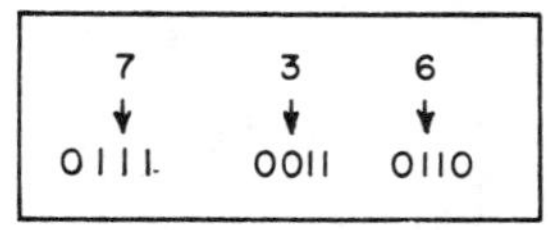

124.9

Figure 7-28.—Binary-coded decimal digits for 736_{10}

This notation possesses important advantages for computer applications. Any decimal number can be expressed in the binary-coded decimal system, but only ten different conversions are necessary—one for each decimal. Therefore, the machine is designed to compute with each coded decimal as its basic unit, not with each binary digit. Thus, although the computer never operated with anything but binary numbers, it remains, from one point of view, a decimal calculator.

Binary-coded decimals are not a complete solution because they are longer than pure binary numbers. For example, the number 0111 0011 0110 (12 bits) can be written in pure binary code as 1011100000 (10 bits). Thus, more components are needed to represent the extra digits of binary-coded decimals. Calculating circuits must also be made more complex, in order to process each coded-digit as a unit.

There is a net gain, however. The increase in calculating circuit complexity is more than balanced by the vastly simplified encoding and decoding circuits.

THE BIQUINARY CODE

The biquinary code (fig. 7-29) is a binary-coded decimal system that uses seven-bit words instead of four-bit words. The code derives

DECIMAL DIGIT	BIQUINARY CODE "BI" 50	"QUINARY" 43210	8421 CODE 8 4 2 1
0	01	00001	0000
1	01	0001C	0001
2	01	00100	0010
3	01	01000	0011
4	01	10000	0100
5	10	00001	0101
6	10	00010	0110
7	10	00100	0111
8	10	01000	1000
9	10	10000	1001

BIQUINARY-CODED DIGITS CAN REPRESENT ANY DECIMAL NUMBER

3	0	6
0101000	0100001	1000010

124.10

Figure 7-29.—Comparing the biquinary and and 8, 4, 2, 1 codes.

its name from the fact that it can be conveniently divided into two parts: the "bi"-part, which consists of the first two bits at the left, and the "quinary" -part, which makes up the other five digits. With this code, the decimal number 306 is written as:

0101000 0100001 1000010

As compared to the 8, 4, 2, 1 code, the major disadvantage of the biquinary code is obvious. It requires more bits per word, and is therefore more expensive. On the other hand, with this code, it is easy to detect an error. Note that every single biquinary digit representation has exactly two 1's in it; no more, no less.

Let us assume, for example, that a computer contains the biquinary number 2, using a positive pulse to represent 1, and no pulse to represent 0, as shown in figure 7-30. Let us assume further that during the process of passing this coded pulse train from one circuit to another, a pulse is dropped (lower section of fig. 7-30).

We can easily determine that an error has occurred, even if we do not know the exact value of each biquinary number. The error will be detected when we fail to find two 1's in the pulse train. This method of looking for pairs is called a parity check.

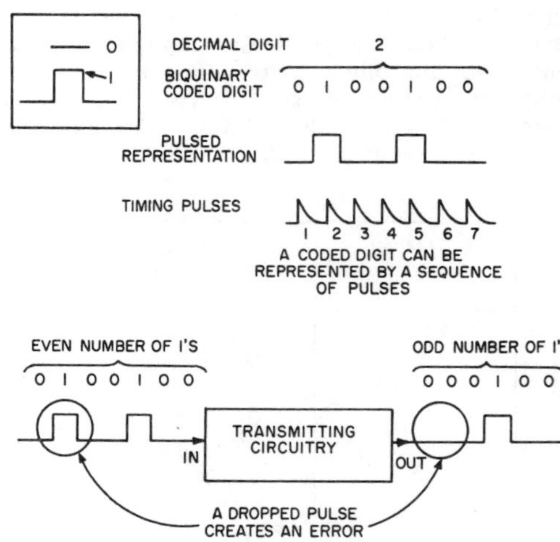

124.11

Figure 7-30.—Biquinary code used for parity.

ERROR DETECTING CODES

The biquinary code is only one of a class of codes called two-out-of-seven codes, all of which have the same error-detecting property. The quibinary code, for example, uses a different notation to produce the same effect. Its seven weighting values are:

8, 6, 4, 2, 0, 1, 0

and its decimal equivalents are given in figure 7-31.

Another group of codes, called two-out-of-five codes, possess error-detecting qualities,

DECIMAL DIGIT	QUI WEIGHTS	BINARY WEIGHTS
	86420	10
0	00001	01
1	00001	10
2	00010	01
3	00010	10
4	00100	01
5	00100	10
6	01000	01
7	01000	10
8	10000	01
9	10000	10

124.12
Figure 7-31.—The quibinary code.

DECIMAL DIGIT	WEIGHTS 7 4 2 1 0 (PARITY CHECK COLUMN)
0	00000
1	00011
2	00101
3	00110
4	01001
5	01010
6	01100
7	10001
8	10010
9	10100

124.13
Figure 7-32.—Two-out-of-five code.

but are less expensive. As their name implies, two-out-of-five codes require only five bits instead of seven bits to represent a decimal digit.

A two-out-of-five code can be generated very simply from the 7, 4, 2, 1 code (fig. 7-32). Like the biquinary code, this code never has more than two 1's in any single word. Now add a fifth bit to each four-bit word in the 7, 4, 2, 1 code in such a manner that the total number of 1's per word is always an even number. In other words, if there is one 1 in a coded digit, 0010 for example, then another 1 is added to it, making it 00101. On the other hand, if there are two 1's in the word, such as 0110, then a zero is added to produce 01100, thus retaining the quality of evenness.

Note that each word has exactly two 1's in it, except for the zero, which has none. Although this complete lack of the 1 bit does no harm to the code's error-detecting properties, it can cause trouble in certain instances. If 1 is represented by a pulse, and 0 is represented by no pulse, there is no method of telling whether 00000 means zero or whether it means a complete absence of information (fig. 7-33).

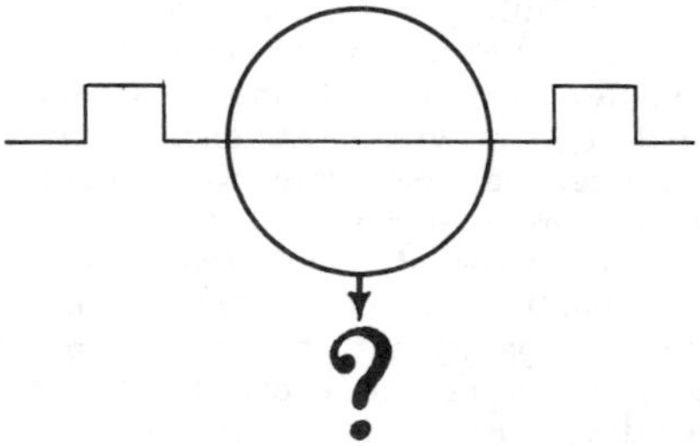

124.14
Figure 7-33.—Is it 00000.....or simply a pause between pulses?

Although this dilemna can be resolved by means of the computer's timer (a count of five time-units with no pulses is defined as representing zero), it is safer to have 1's in every word. Besides, it is not difficult to find a 7, 4, 2, 1 code word that has not been used. For example, the decimal number eleven (7 + 4) in the 7, 4, 2, 1 code is the word 1100. Since we do not need this "spare," we can use it to represent zero. If we add a 0, to its right, we have 11000, which satisfies the two-out-of-five requirements perfectly (see fig. 7-34).

DECIMAL DIGIT	WEIGHTS 7 4 2 1 0
0	1 1 0 0 0 ← AN IMPROVEMENT
1	0 0 0 1 1
2	0 0 1 0 1
3	0 0 1 1 0
4	0 1 0 0 1
5	0 1 0 1 0
6	0 1 1 0 0
7	1 0 0 0 1
8	1 0 0 1 0
9	1 0 1 0 0

124.15

Figure 7-34.—Revised two-out-of-five code.

We are obviously willing to pay for reliability with an extra bit per word, although these extra bits possess no code values. If these extra bits represent no number, how does the computer calculate with them? One answer is that if it is provided with enough circuitry, the computer can calculate with almost any number system. However, this is not a very economical method of calculation. The method more frequently used is to remove the redundant bit (or parity bit, as it is sometimes called) just before the coded number enters a calculating circuit, and to replace the redundant bit as soon as the coded number leaves the circuit. This method requires fewer extra circuits.

For further economy, the parity bit can be removed before a word is stored, and it can be added on as soon as the word leaves storage. One important fact about the error-detecting codes so far discussed is that they have been misnamed. The term "error-detecting" is not completely accurate. Consider, for example, a situation in which the word 01001 enters a faulty component, and leaves it with two errors, such as 00101. The parity check circuitry will allow the erroneous 7, 4, 2, 1-coded word to pass, for it has an even number of 1's. Obviously, the "error-detecting" codes should be called "single-error detecting" codes for that is the full limit of their capability.

Before continuing, note that there is nothing in the parity check principle that states that the number of 1's in each word must be even. It is just as easy to detect an odd number of 1's in a group of bits. Sometimes, in fact, there is a definite advantage in selecting the check-bit to form an odd number of 1's. Recall that the binary-coded zero, 00000, might be mistaken for the complete absence of information. An odd parity check eliminates this problem, since with this check every word must contain at least a single 1. Thus, zero becomes 00001. For this reason, the odd parity check code is used more frequently than the even parity code.

ERROR-PREVENTING CODES

We have already considered error-detecting codes, and one should understand that these codes are useful only after the error has been committed. Sometimes, however, it is important to detect an error, or at least to minimize the error, before it occurs. This is where error-preventing codes can be used.

Gray Code

An analog-to-digital converter (discussed in a later chapter) frequently uses error-preventing codes. Basically, an analog-to-digital converter is a device that changes a number from analog to digital form. If the analog value is a mechanical movement, the quantity can be expressed in terms of a specific angle of shaft rotation or by the longitudinal movement of a rack and pinion. An error-preventing code frequently used with an analog-to-digital converter is the Gray code. This Gray code is a cyclic code which changes only by one bit when going from one number to the one immediately following. Operational errors are reduced if only one digit at a time changes as the numerical value increases.

Let us examine the Gray code in figure 7-35. If we cover the leftmost digit in the first and last rows under the reflected binary code, we will observe that the bits that represent 0 are identical with the bits that represent 15. Thus, all but the leftmost digit of 0000 and 1000 "reflect" each other. Similarly, the number that represents 1 is reflected by the number that represents 14, etc.

DECIMAL DIGIT	REFLECTED BINARY CODE
0	0 0 0 0
1	0 0 0 1
2	0 0 1 1
3	0 0 1 0
4	0 1 1 0
5	0 1 1 1
6	0 1 0 1
7	0 1 0 0
8	1 1 0 0
9	1 1 0 1
10	1 1 1 1
11	1 1 1 0
12	1 0 1 0
13	1 0 1 1
14	1 0 0 1
15	1 0 0 0

124.16

Figure 7-35.—The Gray code.

A simple method of constructing the Gray code is to employ the following steps:

1. Write the number 00, and the number 01 below it.

   00
   01

2. Now "reflect" the least significant digits of these two numbers, thus

   0
   1
   ― reflection line
   1
   0

3. Place 0's to the left of the top half of the numbers and 1's to the left of the bottom half.

   00
   01
   11
   10

4. Again, "reflect" these numbers, thus

   00
   01
   11
   10
   ―― reflection line
   10
   11
   01
   00

5. Once more, place 0's to the left of the top half of the numbers and 1's to the left of the bottom half.

   000
   001
   011
   010
   ――― reflection line
   110
   111
   101
   100

6. Reflect, and again add 0's to the left of the top half of the numbers and 1's to the left of the bottom half. Remember to add these extra 0's to the left.

   0000
   0001
   0011
   0010
   0110
   0111
   0101
   0100
   ―――― reflection line
   1100
   1101
   1111
   1110
   1010
   1011
   1001
   1000

Of course, we could continue this process of adding and reflecting, thus making this code as large as we desire.

The reflected binary code that has been constructed, is called the Gray code. It is only one of a number of reflected binary codes. These codes, in turn, belong to a large group of cyclic codes.

THE "TWO-DIMENSIONAL" CHECK

By extending the five-bit parity check, discussed earlier, we can covert it into an error-correcting code. Consider the decimal number 52,407. In the 8 4 2 1 0 odd-parity check code (in which each word must have an odd number of 1's) this decimal number would be written as follows:

5	2	4	0	7
01011	00100	01000	00001	01110

Note that the code is 8 4 2 1 0 for each of the binary-coded numbers, and not just 8 4 2 1. The extra 0 is added simply to show that the last bit is there only for error detection (or correction), and has no numerical value. Another common practice is to call such a code the 8 4 2 1 R code, where "R" stands for redundant. For convenience, let us arrange the coded digits in a column, as shown in figure 7-36. Each word can be regarded as a horizontal row of bits. Now, just as redundancy bits have been added to make each horizontal row contain an odd number of 1's, redundancy bits can also be added vertically to make each column contain an odd number of 1's, as shown in figure 7-37.

It is not difficult to construct digital circuits that can effectively "line up" such a series of coded digits, and check for parity (in this instance, oddness) in every row and in every column. Assume, for example, that there was an error in the binary-coded digit 4, and that it read 01100 instead of 01000. There would then be an even number of 1's in the horizontal row that represents 4, so that it would be known which word contained the error. Furthermore, the vertical 2's column would have an even number of 1's in it. Thus, we would immediately know that the erroneous bit was located at the point where the even row and even column crossed just as we can locate a point if we know its x and y coordinates.

	8 4 2 1	R
5	0 1 0 1	1
2	0 0 1 0	0
4	0 1 0 0	0
0	0 0 0 0	1
7	0 1 1 1	0

HORIZONTAL (WORD) CHECK-BITS

Figure 7-36.—Horizontal checks. 164.51

	8 4 2 1	R
5	0 1 0 1	1
2	0 0 1 0	0
4	0 1 0 0	0
0	0 0 0 0	1
7	0 1 1 1	0
R	1 0 1 1	

VERTICAL (COLUMN) CHECK-BITS

Figure 7-37.—Vertical checks. 164.52

DOUBLE-ERROR DETECTION

This two-dimensional parity check possesses the advantage that it can indicate the presence of two errors, although it cannot reveal which word contains the error. For example, assume that 01011, the representation for 5, has gained a 1 in the eight bit and has dropped a 1 in the one bit, becoming 11001. Although every horizontal row would still have an odd number of 1's, two of the four columns would have an even number of 1's. Again this indicates that something is wrong, although it is not known exactly where the error is located.

If any error now occurs in the bottom row of redundancy bits, it is immediately detected by a bottom-row parity check. An error in the vertical column of redundancy bits can also be detected, although not so readily. Let us assume that a parity check reveals an error in one of the rows. If this error is in the information-carrying part of the word (that is, in the 8 4 2 or 1 column), then a vertical parity check will also show an error in one of the columns. If all four information-carrying columns show no error, however, the error must lie in the redundancy column.

Finally, an error among the redundancy bits themselves can be detected by adding only one more bit to the bottom row. It is selected to produce an odd total number of 1's in this row and, in this case, is a 0 as shown in figure 7-38. It has been placed to the left of the row to emphasize the fact that it has absolutely nothing to do with the right-hand column of redundancy bits.

A disadvantage of the two-dimensional check for error correction is that a single word cannot be tested for errors. Only a set of words can be tested at the same time. On the other hand, it should be noted that such "wholesale" testing is inexpensive when compared with other methods. If five words are checked at one time, for example, only two redundancy bits per word are required; that is, ten redundancy bits (five vertical plus five horizontal) are sufficient to handle five words. If more words are checked in one column, the number of redundancy bits per word is even less. Thus, for checking a ten-word column, only one and a half bits per word are needed: ten vertical and five horizontal.

		8	4	2	1	R
5		0	1	0	1	1
2		0	0	1	0	0
4		0	1	0	0	0
0		0	0	0	0	1
7		0	1	1	1	0
	0	1	0	1	1	

EXTRA BIT
TO CHECK
BOTTOM ROW

164.53

Figure 7-38.—Extra bit error detection.

WORD-BY-WORD ERROR CORRECTION

The word-by-word error correcting code is also based on the parity check principle.

Even parity checks are used for the code, and a "check failure" will indicate that the number of 1's in a group is found to be odd, and not even. In the error-detecting parity check, one redundancy bit was assigned to each word. For error correction, however, more redundancy bits are required, and each one is assigned to only some of the bits in a word.

Let us consider the 8 4 2 1 code, for example. We will assign one redundancy bit, R_1, only to that part of the word under the 4 2 and 1 weights. That is, select R_1 so that the number of bits in the 4 2 and 1 columns, plus the R_1 bit, equals an even number of bits. "Failure in R_1" means that the total number of 1's in these four bits have been found to be odd. Figure 7-39 shows how the code looks with only the R_1 bit attached.

	8	4	2	1	R_1	R_2	R_3
0	0	0	0	0	0		
1	0	0	0	1	1		
2	0	0	1	0	1		
3	0	0	1	1	0	(R2 , R3	
4	0	1	0	0	1	LEFT OUT	
5	0	1	0	1	0	FOR CLARITY)	
6	0	1	1	0	0		
7	0	1	1	1	1		
8	1	0	0	0	0		
9	1	0	0	1	1		

164.54

Figure 7-39.—Word-by-word error correction—R_1 bit added to 8, 4, 2, 1 code.

	8	4	2	1	R_1	R_2	R_3	
0	0	0	0	0		0		
1	0	0	0	1		1		
2	0	0	1	0		1		
3	0	0	1	1		0		(R_1, R_3
4	0	1	0	0		0		LEFT OUT
5	0	1	0	1		1		FOR CLARITY)
6	0	1	1	0		1		
7	0	1	1	1		0		
8	1	0	0	0		1		
9	1	0	0	1		0		

164.55

Figure 7-40.—Word-by-word error correction—R_2 bit added to 8, 4, 2, 1 code.

	8	4	2	1	R_1	R_2	R_3	
0	0	0	0	0			0	
1	0	0	0	1			1	
2	0	0	1	0			0	
3	0	0	1	1			1	(R_1, R_2
4	0	1	0	0			1	LEFT OUT
5	0	1	0	1			0	FOR CLARITY
6	0	1	1	0			1	
7	0	1	1	1			0	
8	1	0	0	0			1	
9	1	0	0	1			0	

164.56

Figure 7-41.—Word-by-word error correction—R_3 bit added to 8, 4, 2, 1 code.

Similarly, we will select a second redundancy bit, R_2, for the bits in the 8 2 and 1 columns. With the R_2 bit attached, the binary coded digits look as shown in figure 7-40. For simplicity, the R_1 bit is not included.

Finally, we will select R_3, a third redundancy bit, to cover the bits on the 8 4 and 1 columns, so that the number of 1's in this group is always even, as shown in figure 7-41.

If the three redundancy bits are placed together with the four information-carrying bits, a seven-bit error-correcting code is derived, as shown in figure 7-42.

It is relatively simple to isolate an erroneous bit with the aid of the 8 4 2 1 R_1 R_2 R_3 code, as it may be called. If both the R_1 and R_2 checks fail, the bit that is common to both of them, but is not common to R_3, must be incorrect. An R_1 failure means that either the 4 2 or 1 bit is incorrect. An R_2 failure means that either the 8, 2, or 1 bit is incorrect. However, the R_3 check has not failed, which means that the 8 4 and 1 bit have no errors, leaving the 2 bit as the only one that could have failed.

A failure in R_2 and R_3 means that the error is in the 8 bit. All three checks will fail if the error is in the 1 bit.

This code is error correcting in another sense. Not only can it locate a fault in any of the information-carrying bits (that is, bits in the 8 4 2 or 1 position), but erratic redundancy bits can be found. Thus, if only one check fails consistently, then the check bit itself is incorrect.

	8	4	2	1	R_1	R_2	R_3
0	0	0	0	0	0	0	0
1	0	0	0	1	1	1	1
2	0	0	1	0	1	1	0
3	0	0	1	1	0	0	1
4	0	1	0	0	1	0	1
5	0	1	0	1	0	1	0
6	0	1	1	0	0	1	1
7	0	1	1	1	1	0	0
8	1	0	0	0	0	1	1
9	1	0	0	1	1	0	0

164.57

Figure 7-42.—Seven-bit error-correcting code.

Chapter 8

PROGRAMMING (PART I)

Programming is, simply, the process of planning the solution to a problem. Thus, by writing:

1. Take the reciprocal of the resistance of all resistors (expressed in ohms).
2. Sum the values obtained in step 1.
3. Take the reciprocal of the sum derived in step 2,

a generalized program for the solution of total resistance in a parallel resistance circuit has been written.

To progress from this example to preparing a program for a computer is not difficult; however, one basic characteristic of a computer must be kept in mind. The computer is a moron; it can follow only certain basic commands and these must be correctly expressed. Thus, the foregoing program to be usable in a computer would have to be elaborated on to locate data, transfer it, explicitly define the operations to be performed, store partial answers, and, finally, to store the solution. In addition, the computer must be told how to obtain the parameters of the problem and, finally, how to give the programmer its solution.

In a program of elementary character, as the one shown this would involve breaking the steps down to the point where each step could be executed by giving the machine one instruction. Then each instruction must be written in a language intelligible to the machine. These machine instructions, or instruction words, were described briefly in chapter 4, and will be covered in greater detail in chapter 9.

Consideration of the previous paragraphs indicates that programming a fairly complex problem will involve writing a large number of instructions and keeping track of a great number of data and instruction cells. This gives the programmer an opportunity to do something humans are particularly adept at, make an error.

To reduce the amount of time required for writing a complex program and the opportunity to err, an aid called the compiler has been developed. The compiler is, itself, a program which takes certain orders and then writes the instruction words to execute the orders. Compilers are built at various levels, or degrees of complexity. The simplest form of compiler takes one mnemonic phrase and writes one machine instruction, i.e.,

RSH. A9

would cause the compiler to write an instruction which would shift the contents of the A register right 11_8 places. Note the advantages: 1) no opportunity to use the wrong function code; and 2) no necessity to convert the shift count to octal.

Compilers with a higher degree of complexity may write a greater number of instructions from a similar phrase, i.e.,

$$SQR\ (X+6) \rightarrow X+7$$

In this example the compiler would write all instructions necessary to move the contents of cell X+6 to some location, extract the square root, and store the result in location X+7. Furthermore, the compiler would keep track of all memory cells, whether being used for data or instructions. Compilers will be discussed at greater lengths in chapter 10.

PARTS OF A PROGRAM

Programs vary from a length of several hundred instructions to those containing thousands of instructions. Ultimately, the program begins to occupy a significant portion of the computer memory, perhaps even an excessive portion. One method of overcoming this problem is to segment the program, i.e., place a portion of it in auxiliary storage, and read it into main memory only when it is required. This is particularly convenient with seldom used segments. Another step which is taken is to ensure that the program is as concise as possible.

SUBROUTINES

An important method of developing this conciseness is through the use of subroutines. Obviously as a program grows larger certain functions are repeated. If the instructions required to perform these functions are grouped they may be referenced by a relatively few instructions in the main program, thus obviating writing the instructions in the main program each time the function is performed.

Dependent upon the function being performed, a subroutine may contain other subroutines and also be part of a larger subroutine.

EXECUTIVE ROUTINES

The instructions which control access to the various subroutines are referred to as the executive routine or the main program. Dependent upon the complexity of the program, there may be sub-executive routines within the executive routines.

Housekeeping is a term frequently used with subroutines. A programmer may not be sure of the contents of the various addressable registers upon entry into a subroutine, and thus will not know if there are contents which must not be lost. Under these circumstances the programmer will take steps to preserve the contents of these registers upon entry into the subroutine, and to restore them prior to exit. This process is termed housekeeping.

JUMP AND RETURN JUMP

A special type instruction may be in the computer's repertoire to assist subroutine programming. This is the return jump instruction. Execution of the return jump causes the address of the next instruction in the main program to be stored (generally in the first cell of the subroutine) and then causes the instruction in the second cell to be executed. After completing the subroutine, it is then possible to return to the executive routine by executing a straight jump to the address contained in the entry cell. (A jump instruction specifies the address of the instruction to be executed next.)

PROGRAM CONSTRUCTION

The process of writing a program can be broken down into six basic steps.

1. Statement—Form a clear, comprehensive statement of the problem. At first thought, it may seem a trifle facetious to say that stating the problem is, in effect, one step in solving it. However, consider the following statements: 1) Solve to find the parallel resistance of a circuit; 2) Solve to find the total resistance of circuit containing as many as ten parallel resistors varying between 10Ω and 1000Ω.; all values to be correct to 3 decimal places. Now, it is obvious that the second statement is much more meaningful and will contribute more to laying out the problem for solution.

2. Analysis—Analysis consists of laying out the problem in a form susceptible of arithmetical, and/or logical computation, determining what logical decisions must be made, and what scaling is required. (Scaling is discussed as a separate topic later in this chapter.) Depending upon the programmer and the problem, outside assistance may be required. This step is occasionally referred to as "making a model." For the problem under consideration, the first step is to determine the proper method for calculating parallel resistance. This equation is readily available either from the programmer's own experience or a basic text. Then considering the equation and the statement of the problem the following equation can be written:

$$R_t = \frac{1}{\frac{1}{R_1} + \frac{1}{R_2} \cdots \frac{1}{R_{10}}}$$

where $R_1 - R_{10} = 10.000_{10}\Omega$ to $1000.000_{10}\Omega$ and $R_t = 1.000_{10} - 1000.000_{10}$.

The next step is to note that a programmed test must be made to discover how many branch values must be determined. Finally, the programmer must determine how many binary places must be retained to give the required base 10 accuracy. A good analysis of the problem leads directly to the next step in construction.

3. Flow diagram—A flow diagram, or chart, is an elaboration of step two in which special

symbols are used to denote the various operations to be performed and the sequence in which they fall. Later in this chapter a flow chart will be developed for the problem just analyzed.

4. Encoding—Encoding is the process of converting the operations listed in the flow chart into the language the computer will use, either the instruction words or compiler statements.

5. Debugging—Debugging is the process of locating errors in the program. Various techniques are available for this purpose. A program may be written to include some aids itself or a separate debugging program may be run to test the operation of a malfunctioning program. Additionally for a very simple program, a trial solution may be done on paper and computed results compared with those actually obtained at each step. Debugging will be further discussed in chapter 12.

6. Documentation—It is not sufficient to merely write a program which runs properly. Changes may be necessary later or it may be desirable to use the program or subroutines from it within another program. In order to accomplish any of these tasks readily it is necessary to include the following information in the documentation:

a. Title of Program
b. Statement of the Problem
c. Programmer's name
d. Date
e. Memory Area Used and/or Number of Cells Used
f. Registers used
g. I/O devices required
h. Flow diagrams
i. Hard copy (the machine coded instructions)

INDEXING

Various operations are included under the title indexing. These are: 1) counting the number of times an operation is performed; 2) the process of modifying the operand portion of an instruction word prior to its execution without modifying it as contained in memory; and 3) tagging data in a file in memory. The first two processes are of particular interest at this time.

To facilitate indexing, certain addressable registers are built into the computer. These index registers and their associated circuitry are usually able to increment and/or decrement themselves as the result of a comparison of their contents and some other value; also dependent upon the outcome of this comparison a program branch decision will be made.

For example, a computer might well have in its repertoire of instructions an instruction which would do the following upon execution: 1) test the contents of a specific index register for equality to zero; 2) if not equal to zero, decrement the contents by one and execute the next instruction; and 3) if equal to zero, execute the instruction whose address is contained in the operand portion of the instruction. This, of course, is just one example and a great many variations are possible.

In addition to the foregoing, additional circuits are built which permit adding the contents of a specific index register to the operand portion of an instruction word after it is brought from memory and prior to its execution.

These index instructions are powerful programming tools; particularly in the next area discussed.

LOOPS

A loop is a group of instructions intended to perform an iterative function. Therefore, the loop must perform the following tasks; 1) initialize, 2) compute, 3) modify, and 4) terminate.

PARTS OF A LOOP

Initializing the loop consists of setting the various parameters which will determine the number of times the loop will be repeated and what modifications are to be made.

Computing refers to the instructions which perform the desired function of the loop.

Modifying is not necessarily a part of a loop. When it is, it refers to the changes made to any of the instructions in the loop or any of the parameters.

Terminating a loop consists of leaving the group of instructions and continuing with some other part of the program. The termination may be due to exhausting the index (loop count) or compliance with some test applied during execution of the loop. There may be any number of terminations or exits to a loop.

SAMPLE LOOP

The following problem is posed to more thoroughly demonstrate the process of setting up a loop. It is desired to take two sets of paired numbers, sum each pair and place the sum in a new location. If any sum equals zero, the loop is terminated. There will be 10_8 numbers in each set. Set one will be in memory cells M→M+7; set two in cells M+10 →M+17; the sums will be stored in cells M+20→M+27.

Initialize—It is desired to go through the loop 10_8 times unless an unusual condition develops. Therefore, if the loop is indexed at the beginning, a count of 10_8 is used; if it is indexed at the end, a count of 7 will be used since the loop has already been traversed once. (Note: Using a wrong count is a very common error when programming and can cause serious confusion.) This loop will be indexed at the end, so a count of 7 will be entered in index register number 1.

Index register number 2 will hold an address modifier and will be cleared prior to entering the loop.

Compute—This portion covers the addition of the pairs and storage of the sums; the zero test is performed and the loop goes directly to termination if the sum is zero.

Modifying—Index register 1 will be decremented by one each time the loop is completed. Index register 2 will be incremented by one after each pass.

Termination—The termination is reached if a zero sum is found and causes a move to a different part of the program. The termination is also reached when the index is zero. A phrase occasionally used when describing terminations of loops and subroutines is "normal exit." This refers to the usual or expected exit if there is more than one exit.

Listing the steps in the order they would be performed gives the following:

STEP	OPERATION
1	Set index register 1 = 7
2	Clear index register 2
3	(M + IR#2)* → accumulator
4	(accum) + (M + 10 + IR#2) → accum
5	(accum) = 0; Yes → term; No → step 6
6	(accum) → M + 20 + IR#2
7	(IR#2) + 1 → IR#2
10	IR#1 = 0; Yes → step 11; No → step 12
11	leave loop, continue program
12	(IR#1) - 1 → IR#1
13	go to step 3

*(M + IR#2) is read: The contents of the memory cell whose address is M plus the value in index register 2. Thus, if M = 1004 and (IR#2 = 4) the contents of address 1010 are read.

REPEAT INSTRUCTIONS

Another method is usually available to execute the functions of a simple loop; this is a repeat instruction. Execution of the repeat instruction causes the next instruction to be repeated the number of times specified in the repeat instruction operand. Provision is generally made to permit modifications to the repeated instruction after each execution, and for some repeated instructions a test may be executed after each repetition and the repeat mode may be aborted (exit from the loop prior to exhausting the repeat count). The repeat instruction will be discussed to greater length in chapter 9.

SCALING

Scaling was mentioned briefly as a part of the analysis of the problem. However, dependent upon the method of programming it may be an item of continuing concern throughout the construction of the program, and is therefore discussed as a separate topic. There are three different methods of scaling used: fixed point, floating point, and double precision. The selection of the system used will be based upon the range in magnitude of the numbers handled, the number of significant digits required in the solution, and the word size of the computer.

FIXED POINT

In the situation where all numbers can be located in a register with the desired degree of accuracy, the fixed point system is used.

In the fixed point system the radix is abritrarily located and all numbers aligned accordingly.

Assume that a 30 bit word length is available, the most significant bit is the sign bit, and the radix point is located between 2^{14} and 2^{15}. Then the absolute value of the smallest number which can be entered is $00000.00001_{(8)}$ and the absolute value of the largest is $37777.77777_{(8)}$.

Any number which exceeded these limits would have to be multiplied by some power of two and the programmer must keep track of the operation. If for example, it became necessary to add $527641.00342_{(8)}$ and $00153.43200_{(8)}$ the numbers 05276.41003 and 00001.53432 would be used and the programmer would have to note somewhere that the numbers had been scaled down, and the solution must be scaled back up. When numbers of widely varying magnitude are encountered the fixed point system is no longer usable and the floating point system is used.

FLOATING POINT

All numbers in floating point arithmetic are expressed as a fraction multiplied by some power of two.

Thus:	1010011	=	.1010011	x	2^{7}
	.000101	=	.101	x	2^{-3}
	-111011	=	-.111011	x	2^{6}
	-.0001101	=	-.1101	x	2^{-3}

and each data word would be broken into sign bits, fractional part (the mantissa), and exponential part (the characteristic). All rules of exponents must be observed when handling the numbers.

In some situations neither of the systems described is by itself sufficient. For example, it is possible that a calculation must be carried to 10 or 15 significant decimal places. Because it takes an average of 3.23 binary digits to write a decimal digit, it is easy to see that a computer word length may be readily exceeded.

DOUBLE PRECISION

Double precision arithmetic is the method used to overcome this problem. Double precision indicates the use of two computer words to store a single data entry; however, in actual practice it is entirely possible that more than two words will be used. Thus, using a combination of floating point and double precision permits handling data of widely varying magnitudes and as many significant places as necessary.

It is apparent that a large amount of programming is required to use these systems. Fortunately, however, the programming has already been done, and unless required as an exercise, a programmer only has to go to the library to find a program for his needs. The various compilers have the required routines in them for performing these functions also. These will be discussed further in chapter 10.

INPUT/OUTPUT PROGRAMMING

I/O programming is the process of communicating with the computer. It involves not only the transfer of data, but also commands, which control the operation of the peripheral equipment. Although computers differ in the manner in which they handle the problem, certain factors are common to all.

First of all, the computer will have several I/O channels and/or provisions for multiplexing equipments on a channel. The reason is, of course, the relative slowness of the peripheral equipment. Thus an I/O instruction will have a portion used to identify the channel or equipment.

The computer's I/O section will probably be independent of the rest of the computer once initiated; this permits I/O operations and computations to occur simultaneously. This is particularly convenient when a large number of cells are to be filled or transmitted. (NOTE: Transmission of one cell's data is referred to as a single cell buffer; transmission of the data in more than one cell with a single command is called a block buffer.) It may be desirable to alert the main program when a block buffer is completed; if so, the I/O instruction must be capable of performing the function. Additionally, since the peripheral equipment is relatively slow the necessity may occur to hold up the main program while the buffer is completed. Instructions will probably be available to test for an I/O channel active as part of this requirement. Different computers use different methods of defining the buffer limits (either a single cell or block). A common method is to reference an address in the I/O word. Then stored at the referenced address is a word which defines the buffer limits.

Two additional I/O instructions are used to control the operation of the peripheral equipment. The execution of the first of these, the external function (EXF) instruction, sets a command line and causes data to be placed on the lines to the equipment. The control section of the peripheral equipments detects the command signal, translates the data, and causes the equipment to execute the function. (Examples of these functions for a magtape unit might be rewind, write forward, read reverse, etc.) Dependent upon the system used, the EXF code may occur in the operand portion of the EXF instruction, or in a separate data word. If the code is in a separate data word, the operand portion of the EXF word contains the address of the cell containing the code.

It is usually desirable for the peripheral equipment to keep the computer informed of its status. It would be absurd to give the magtape unit a rewind command when it is at the beginning of tape and then wait for it to rewind, or to give a write command when the unit is not enabled and then wait for it. Therefore, peripheral equipment is designed to keep the computer informed. This is done by placing a signal on a command line and a code on the data lines. When detected by the computer, the signal causes the computer to leave the main program and go to a special address (a separate address is usually associated with each channel). Thus, this signal is usually referred to as an interrupt since it interrupts the main program. The interrupt will occur in response to any of the following situations: 1) EXF word sent and equipment able/unable to comply; 2) a function ordered by the computer has been completed; or 3) there is a change in the operational status of the equipment.

Since the computer jumps from the main program, steps must be taken to preserve the next program address; this is done by programmer action and with the aid of the return jump instruction.

It may not always be desirable to honor an interrupt. Consider the case where although I/O equipment is connected on all channels, it is not all used by a particular program. (Particularly true when time sharing a computer.) Then an inadvertent interrupt could disrupt the program. This problem is handled in different ways in different computers, but the process is referred to as interrupt lockout. As a result, the computer does not respond to the interrupts on any unused channel.

The second I/O instruction applicable to this equipment command structure is employed when an interrupt is honored. This instruction is used to store the interrupt code in the computer and is required because the interrupt is out of sync with the timing employed for an input buffer instruction.

Another concept involved in I/O programming is that of packing and unpacking words. In view of the fact that many I/O devices use less bits in each data transfer than are contained in a computer word, for economical storage within the computer, a number of characters may be placed in a single cell. These cells must then be packed or unpacked as the data are transmitted. This is elaborated on in the next chapter.

FLOW CHARTING

A flow diagram, or chart, serves a multitude of very important functions. As has been already noted, it is a map of how the programmer intends to solve a problem. The chart illustrates the logical steps required, the decisions to be reached, and the paths to be followed as a result of the decisions. Properly annotated it calls the programmer's attention to memory cell allocation, input/output requirements, data accuracy considerations, and register usage.

When writing complex programs, a flow chart can be used to "section" the program and assign the various sections to different programmers. This procedure also calls attention to parts of the program which might be found in other programs or as a program.

The flow diagram is of vital importance when making such future program changes as may be required, and in debugging a malfunctioning program.

LEVELS OF FLOW CHARTING

Flow diagrams may be constructed at various levels, or degrees of complexity. A high level flow chart is a very general overview, while a low level flow chart may reach a one-to-one correspondence between symbols and instructions. There will usually be several flow charts for a given program area. These may be compared to the prints found in a maintenance manual, i.e., the block diagram to show the relationship of major units (high level), functional block diagrams showing the major circuits in a unit (intermediate level), or the schematics of the circuits (low level). Flow charts should always be available at a level low enough to implement all the uses previously discussed. Additional time spent flow charting will inevitably be returned when encoding and debugging; and the more complex the program, the more true the fact.

SYMBOLS

At the present writing, the American Standards Institute has adopted the following symbols for flow diagram use. The reader is warned that this standardization is not, at present, industry wide. Familiarity with these symbols will, however, facilitate the use of flow charts employing different symbols. NOTE: This same situation exists in regard to the standardization of logic symbols.

1. INPUT / OUTPUT

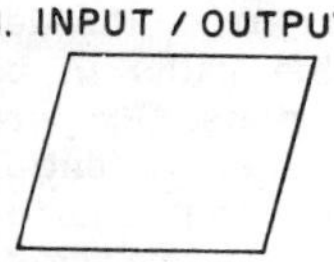

This symbol represents the basic functions of entering data into the computer, or of "outputting" the data. This symbol would customarily be used for either a high level diagram or a chart where various devices are used simultaneously, since unique symbols are available for I/O processors.

2. PUNCHED TAPE

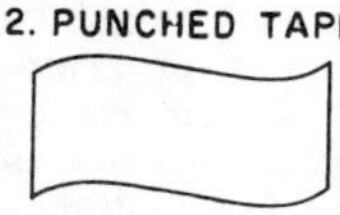

This symbol represents an I/O function using metallic or paper punched tape. It can represent the reading in of data from punched tape via a paper tape reader, or of dumping data by punching a tape.

3. ON LINE STORAGE

The on line storage symbol indicates the use of a mass storage unit such as a disk-file or drum. The symbol may indicate the storage and/or retrieval of data. The data is directly accessible to the computer.

4. MAGNETIC TAPE

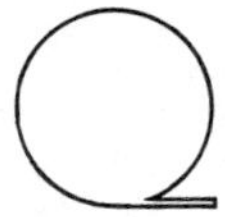

This symbol indicates the use of magnetic tape as the I/O medium.

5. DOCUMENT

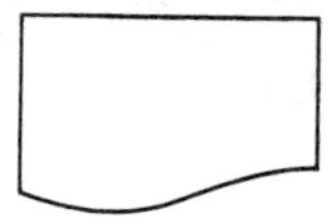

The document symbol denotes the use of a line or page printer as an output device.

6. DISPLAY OUTPUT

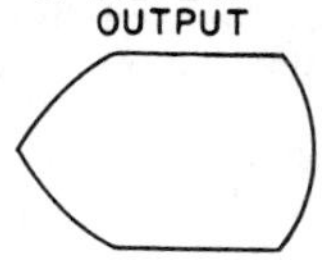

This symbol represents the video display of computer data.

7. PUNCHED CARD

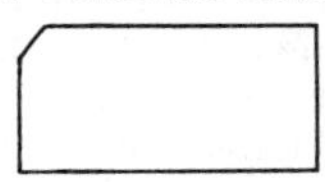

Whenever the input and/or output data will be on a punched card this symbol is used.

8. OFF LINE STORAGE

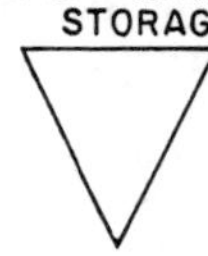

The use of this symbol indicates reference to data storage not directly accessible by the computer.

9. MANUAL INPUT

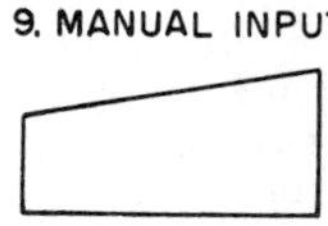

The manual input symbol represents the use of a keyboard device, such as teletype, to enter data into the computer.

10. MANUAL OPERATION

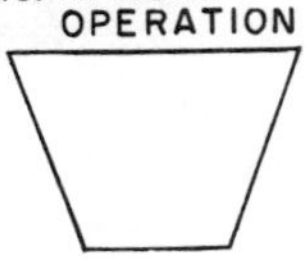

This symbol is used to denote data handling not involving the computer, or throwing a switch on the computer, etc.

11. PROCESSING

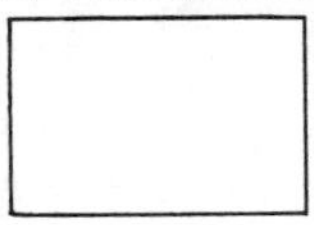

The processing symbol is used for several functions. It may, at the lowest level, represent one instruction, at a higher level it will represent all of the instruction necessary to perform a given task, and the highest level represent an entire program. In addition, when set aside from the main flow and connected to it by a dotted line, the symbol is used to contain amplifying remarks. It is then referred to as an annotation symbol.

12. DECISION

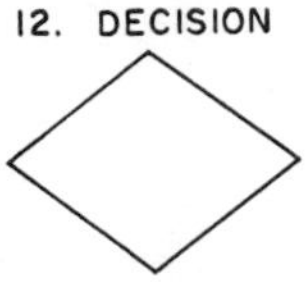

The decision symbol marks the branch point in a program. Therefore, there are two possible exits from the symbol.

13. TERMINAL

The terminal marks the beginning and all of the possible terminations to the program.

14. COMMUNICATION LINK

This symbol indicates the transferral of data between various locations. Phone lines and radio networks are common examples of such links.

15. FLOW DIRECTION

The various symbols are connected by lines; convention dictates that the flow will normally be from top to bottom and from left to right. When the conventions are followed, it is not necessary to use arrowheads unless desired, all deviations should be clearly indicated.

16. CONNECTOR

The connector symbol is used to identify common points in the flow paths when connecting lines cannot be drawn, or would be confusing. Usually, breaks in the main flow are annotated with letters and other common points with numbers.

CONSTRUCTING A FLOW DIAGRAM

At this point the problem previously considered will be diagramed. Certain embellishments will be added to more fully illustrate the preparation and uses of a flow diagram. Therefore, the problem is restated.

It is desired to determine the resistance of various circuits each containing as many as ten resistors in parallel. All values will be accurate to three decimal places, and the resistors values will range from 10.000 to 1000.000.

The values for all circuits will be entered at one time from a paper tape punched in teletype code. The resistances will be in decimal.

It is further stated that the program may be used as a subroutine if desired. When used as a subroutine the value found for R_t will be stored and an exit made from the subroutine. If not used as a subroutine the R_t will be typed on a teletype and the R_t for the next circuit, if any, computed. This process will continue until all circuits have been computed and typed.

Additionally, it is assumed that if the program is used as a subroutine, the programmer does not know the contents of the various registers.

Careful study of figure 8-1 should bring to light several interesting facts. The most

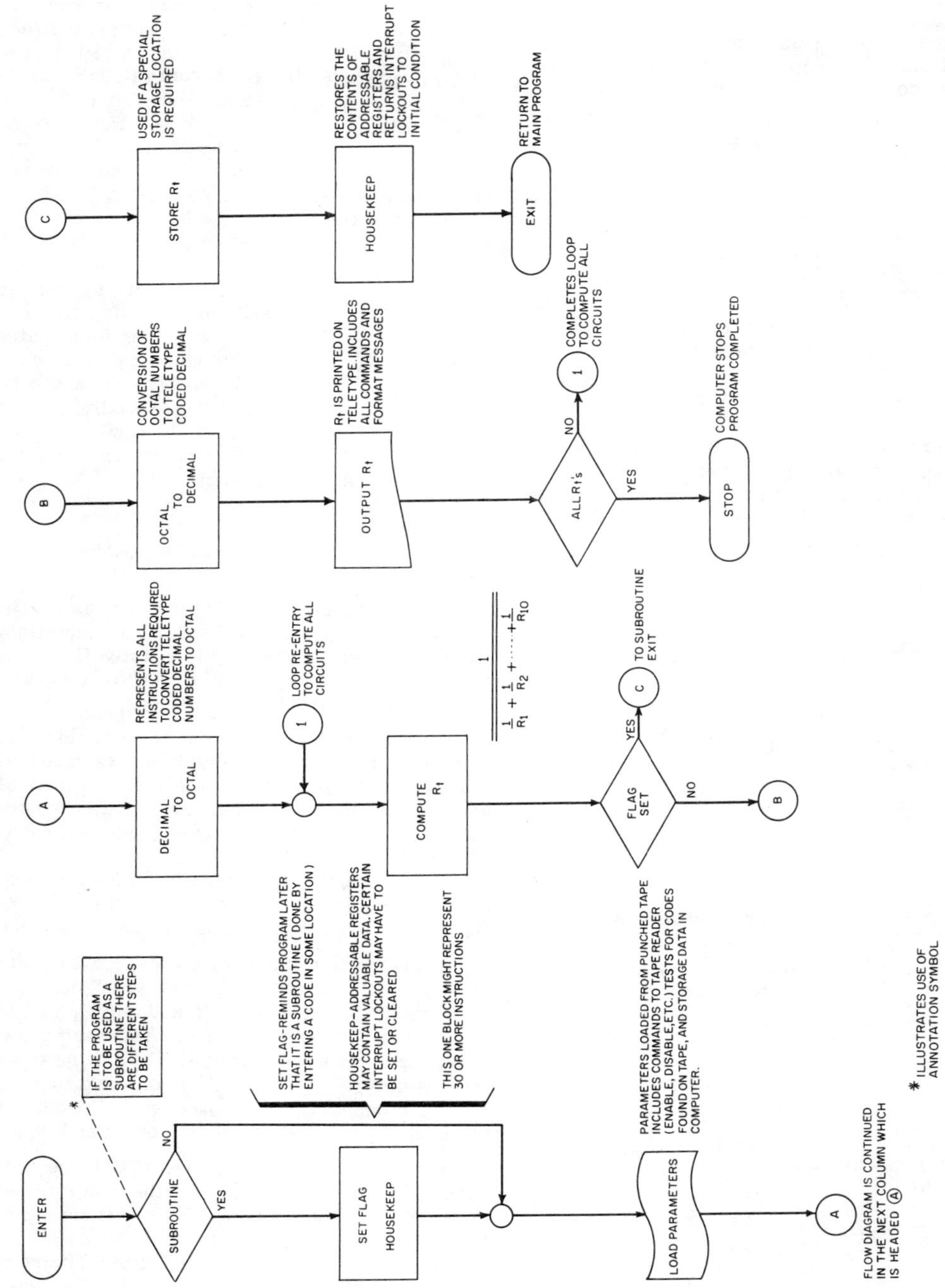

164.58

Figure 8-1.—Parallel resistance computation flow diagram.

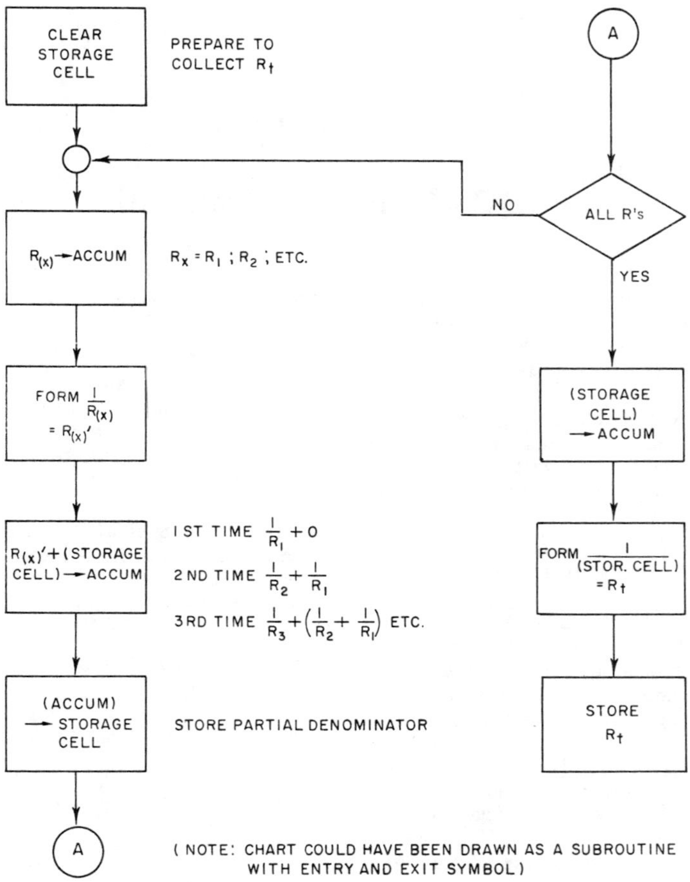

164.59

Figure 8-2.—Compute R_t.

important observation to be made is that the actual computation will comprise a relatively small portion of the instructions. The total number of instructions could be reduced, particularly by doing the octal/decimal conversions outside the computer and by making the parameter entries into the maintenance panel and reading the solution from it. These steps would, however, largely negate the advantages of the computer. The important conclusion to be drawn from these facts is that unless a relatively simple operation must be repeated a large number of times, there is no reason to program it.

After studying the following two chapters, the reader who returns to this flow diagram will observe that there are many other ways in which this program could have been charted. As an example, the load parameters and decimal to octal conversion might well be combined into one routine. As a matter of fact, if a given problem was assigned to ten programmers it is highly probable that no two programs would agree.

As a further illustration of flow diagraming, the compute R_t routine is reduced, without further discussion, to a low level in figure 8-2.

Chapter 9

PROGRAMMING (PART II)

The basic concepts of programming are introduced in chapter 8. These concepts were expanded upon until it was possible at the end of the chapter to construct and interpret a flow diagram.

This chapter will treat the process of converting a flow chart into machine language instructions. Chapter 10 will describe the process of converting to a special language (the compiler).

THE COMPUTER

To convert a problem directly into instructions requires a fairly comprehensive knowledge of the computer characteristics, and of the instruction word format. The following portion of this chapter will provide this knowledge, and is based upon the characteristics of a computer widely used throughout the Navy at the present time. It is to be understood that computers exist with greatly differing characteristics; however, careful study of this chapter will greatly facilitate the transition from one computer to another.

CHARACTERISTICS

The TPJ-7 (a hypothetical computer discussed here for training purposes only) is a single address, sequential instruction machine. This means, of course, that only one address may be referenced in an instruction word, and if no special condition arises the TPJ-7 will take the contents of the next higher order memory cell and execute them. Thus, the programmer must ensure a segregation of instruction words and data words in the memory.

Four I/O channels are available and it will not be necessary to consider their priority of access. Once initiated a buffer operation will be independent of the main computer sequences. Each channel is capable of handling 30 bit, parallel words in either the input or output mode; all channels can be activated at one time.

The TPJ-7's basic memory consists of 4096, 30 bit words in core storage. Some of these are special purpose cells and should not be used for other program instructions or data. Table 9-1 lists the cells and their special purposes.

Table 9-1. —Special Purpose Memory Cells

ADDRESSES	PURPOSE
00000	Fault
00001 - 00020	Bootstrap
00021 - 00024	Input Buffer
00025 - 00030	Input Buffer with Interrupt
00031 - 00034	Output Buffer
00035 - 00040	Output Buffer with Interrupt
00041 - 00044	External Interrupt

The function of these cells will be discussed to greater length later in the chapter.

The TPJ-7 has six addressable registers. Two of them, the A and Q, are in the arithmetic section. They are 30 bit registers, although for some purposes they will be treated as a single 60 bit register. When so used, the Q register will contain the lower 30 bits.

The other four registers are the B, or index registers. These registers B^1 through B^4 are capable of being incremented or decremented automatically through use of the index instructions. In addition, the B^4 register contains the index count of a repeated instruction. (This characteristic of the TPJ-7 requires that the programmer be aware of the B^4 contents since executing a repeat instruction will destroy them.)

Certain other characteristics of the TPJ-7 which are important from the programmer's viewpoint are:

1. All registers "entered" with data are cleared first; thus, entering a 15 bit word into a 30 bit register first clears the register and then enters the data into the lower 15 bits, leaving the upper 15 bits clear.
2. Entering the 30 bit word into a 15 bit register enters only the lower 15 bits of a word.
3. Memory cells may be referenced either in toto or by 15 bit halves. (When referencing either half of a memory cell the data transfer is the same as for the 15 bit registers.)
4. The contents of a register or cell are not affected by reading data out.

THE INSTRUCTION WORD

The 30 bit instruction word of the TPJ-7 is broken into five functional parts. Each part is comprised of one or more octal digits. The five parts and their location within the word are:

XX	X	X	X	XXXXX
F	S	L	B	O

F denotes the portion of the word which describes the basic operation the machine will perform. F is generally referred to as the function code. Although codes 00-77 could appear in this position, the TPJ-7 uses only codes 20 through 60 (fig. 9-1). Attempting to execute a word not containing one of these codes will cause the TPJ-7 to fault. When the machine faults, its normal sequence of operation is broken, and the machine unconditionally takes the instruction contained at address 00000 for execution. This function serves as a programm debugging aid and is covered in greater detail after the instructions are discussed.

The S digit determines for what conditions the normal sequence of instructions will be broken. Its interpretation varies dependent upon the instruction being executed. For several instructions it is used to reference a B register. These variations will be pointed out as the individual instructions are discussed. The interpretations for the S designator for normal, compare, jump, subroutine jump, and repeat instructions are tabulated for easy reference in figure 9-1.

The L designator (fig. 9-1) locates the operand for execution. The operand may be located in memory, the A register, or the lower half of the instruction word. If located in memory, the operand may be in either the upper or lower half or the entire memory cell. When using a 15 bit operand, provision is made to treat its sign properly. Thus, if the number 77632 is located in M_L and is to be added to the A register (which can be assumed to contain zero) the A register will contain either 00000 77632, or 77777 77632 after execution, dependent upon the value of L used in the instruction. Using a value for L of 6 (fig. 9-1) therefore, permits treating 77632 as -145.

The B designator for values of 1 through 4 causes the contents of the referenced B register to be added to the lower half of the instruction word prior to execution. For other values of B no modification takes place. The adder performing this addition uses R-1 arithmetic as does the adder in the arithmetic section.

The lower five digits form the operand (O) designator. Dependent upon the value of L, this may be the address of the operand or the operand itself; also dependent upon B, it may or may not be modified.

THE REPERTOIRE OF INSTRUCTIONS

The repertoire of instructions which follows lists the various function codes, discusses the results of their execution, and gives examples of the various effects of the other designators. A tabulation of the codes for programming use is found in figure 9-1.

20 Right Shift A

The contents of the A register are shifted right by the number of places specified by O. The shift is open ended (i.e., the bits shifted out are lost) and the sign of the contents is not lost. The highest shift count used is 35_8 and at that time the contents of A are either a positive or negative zero.

For example, assume A initially equals 77777 15234 in each step below: If we execute 20 000 00006, then A equals

77777 77152

If we execute 20 000 00011, then A equals

77777 77715

F DESIGNATOR

INSTRUCTIONS			
20	RIGHT SHIFT A	40	MULTIPLY
21	RIGHT SHIFT Q	41	DIVIDE
22	RIGHT SHIFT AQ	42	COMPARE
23	LEFT SHIFT A	43	COMPARE LOGICAL PRODUCT
24	LEFT SHIFT Q	44	JUMP
25	LEFT SHIFT AQ	45	SUBROUTINE JUMP
26	ENTER A	46	INPUT JUMP
27	ENTER Q	47	OUTPUT JUMP
30	ENTER B	50	STORE CHANNEL
31	STORE A	51	B JUMP $B^s \neq \emptyset$ $B^s - 1$ & Jp
32	STORE Q	52	B SKIP $B^s \neq 0$ $B^s + 1$ & Skip
33	STORE B	53	REPEAT
34	ADD TO A	54	INPUT
35	ADD TO Q	55	INPUT WITH INTERRUPT
36	SUBTRACT FROM A	56	OUTPUT
37	SUBTRACT FROM Q	57	OUTPUT WITH INTERRUPT
		60	EXTERNAL FUNCTION

S DESIGNATOR
(See individual instructions for test performed.)

NORMAL		COMPARE	
0	NO SKIP	0	NO SKIP
1	SKIP (Unconditional)	1	SKIP (Unconditional)
2	SKIP if A = 0	2	SKIP if $0 \leq A$
3	SKIP if A ≠ 0	3	SKIP if $0 > A$
4	SKIP if Q = 0/Overflow	4	SKIP if $Q \leq 0$
5	SKIP if Q ≠ 0/No Overflow	5	SKIP if $0 > Q$
6	SKIP if A/Q Pos (Read A or Q)	6	SKIP if $A > 0 \geq Q$
7	SKIP if A/Q Neg	7	SKIP if $0 > [A-Q] \geq 0$

JUMP AND SUBROUTINE JUMP		REPEAT	
0	NO JUMP	0	NO MODIFICATION
1	UNCONDITIONAL JUMP	1	0 + 1
2	JUMP AND STOP	2	0 − 1
3	JUMP, AND IF KEY STOP	3	0 + B
4	IF KEY JUMP	4	0 − B
5	A POS JUMP	5	0 + B + 1
6	Q POS JUMP	6	0 − B − 1
7	A = ∅ JUMP	7	NOT USED

L DESIGNATOR

NORMAL INSTRUCTIONS	
0	0 (Lower 15 Bits)
1	MEMORY LOWER (M_L)
2	MEMORY UPPER (M_U)
3	MEMORY
4	A REGISTER
5	0 WITH SIGN EXTENSION (X_0)
6	M_L WITH SIGN EXTENSION (XM_L)
7	M_U WITH SIGN EXTENSION (XM_U)

164.60

Figure 9-1.—Designators.

If we execute 20 000 00156, then A equals

77777 77777

If B^1 = 00002, 20 001 00000, after right shifting, A equals

77777 63247

and, 20 001 00001, after right shifting, A equals

77777 71523

Note: The operand is added to B^1 before execution.

21 Right Shift Q

The same as right shift A except that the contents of Q are shifted.

22 Right Shift AQ

A and Q are treated as a single 60 bit register. This instruction is the same as right shift A, except that a shift count $\geq 73_8$ sets AQ to a positive or negative zero.

23 Left Shift A

The contents of A are shifted left by the number of places specified by the operand. The register may be thought of as circular for this function (i.e., the digit in 2^{29} goes to 2^0). If the shift count is $\geq 35_8$ there is no execution.

24 Left Shift Q

Same as for left shift A.

25 Left Shift AQ

Same as for left shift A, except that when the shift count is $\geq 73_8$ there is no execution.

26 Enter A

The contents of the location indicated by L are placed in A. Using an S of 4 or 5 (fig. 9-1), is the same as using an S of zero. Using L = 4 (fig. 9-1), causes A→A. (The contents of A are unchanged.) Thus, instruction

26 0 3 0 01000

enters A with the contents of memory cell 1000; no skip. A

26 6 3 1 01000

instruction enters A with the contents of memory cell 1000 + (B^1); if A is positive, the next instruction is skipped.

27 Enter Q

This instruction is the same as the 26 instruction, except S = 2 or 3 is the same as S = 0.

30 Enter B

For this instruction S = 1 - 4 is used to designate the B register to be entered, leaving B available to select a modification of 0 if desired. Thus, for instruction

30 2 3 0 01000,

the lower 15 bits of address 1000 are entered into B^2. A

30 2 0 1 00000

instruction will enter the contents of B^1 into B^2. Again, a

30 3 0 3 00001

instruction will increment the contents of B^3 at each execution.

31 Store A

The contents of A are placed in a location as determined by L. (Only L = 1 - 4 should be used.) Using L = 4 causes A'→A, i.e., the contents of A are complemented. Use of incorrect values of L results in no execution. S values referencing Q have no effect. Instruction

31 0 2 0 01000

stores the lower 15 bits of A in the upper half of memory cell 1000.

32 Store Q

The same as for the 31 instruction. Skip tests (see S designator, fig. 9-1) now only affect the Q register. A

32 2 4 0 00000

instruction stores Q in the A register. A is not tested, therefore, no skip.

33 Store B

The contents of the B registers designated by S are stored in the location determined by L. Use of S = 0 causes the storage location to be cleared. (S = 5, 6, 7 are the same as S = 0 for this instruction.)

34 Add to A

The operand as located by L is added to the contents of A. For a

34 6 6 1 01000

instruction, the contents of the lower half of memory cell 1000 + (B^1) with sign extension are added to the contents of the A register. If the addition causes A to become positive, skip the next instruction.

35 Add to Q

The same as for the 34 instruction. Thus, for a

35 2 3 0 01000

instruction, the contents of cell 1000 are added to Q. The skip test is not performed.

36 Subtract from A

The operand is subtracted from the contents of A.

37 Subtract from Q

The operand is subtracted from the contents of Q.

40 Multiply

The contents of Q are multiplied by the operand. The product appears in AQ; sign is handled (extended) automatically. Since, regardless of the length of the product, the contents of A are affected they should be preserved if necessary prior to executing this instruction, and L = 4 should not be used. An S of 2 or 3 would normally be used to test for a double-length product. For a

40 2 3 0 01000

instruction, the contents of Q are multiplied by the contents of cell 1000. If significant digits of the product form in A the next instruction is executed. If significant digits are not formed in A, it will contain either +0 or -0, dependent upon the sign of the product, and the next instruction is skipped.

41 Divide

The dividend is located in AQ prior to execution (the most significant digits in A), and L locates the divisor. The quotient is formed in Q and the remainder, if any, in A. Sign is handled automatically. Since the dividend may be as large as 59 bits and the divisor is no greater than 29 bits, it is obvious that a quotient greater than 29 bits might be formed if the programmer is not careful. There is, however, no place to form a quotient of this magnitude since Q can accommodate only 30 bits. Therefore, S = 4 and 5 are assigned special functions for the divide instruction. An S of 4 will cause the next instruction to be skipped if the quotient would exceed 29 bits (overflow condition), and an S of 5 causes a skip, if the quotient is of the proper magnitude, no overflow. Thus, the programmer can by appropriate action determine overflow conditions and take corrective action. If it is certain that no overflow will occur, an S of 2 or 3 may be used to test for the presence of a remainder. (This is particularly convenient if it is desired to round off the quotient.) Since the dividend is entered into AQ prior to execution an L of 4 would not be used in this instruction.

42 Compare

The operand is either compared with a value contained in the A or Q register or it is evaluated to determine if it is within or without a range of values as determined by A and Q. The value of the S designator determines the compare action and satisfying the condition results in a skip. The S values are tabulated in figure 9-1. The TPJ-7 automatically handles sign for this instruction. When using an S = 6 or 7, note that A will contain the largest number for the range to be tested and Q the smallest.

43 Compare Logical Product

This instruction permits comparing a selected portion of the operand with a value in the A register. Significant in this process is the fact that when taking the logical product certain portions of Q are masked, and a 1 is produced in the result only when the bits in the same location in the mask and operand are ones.

Prior to executing this instruction, the value to be tested for is entered into the A register, and the bits used for this value are set to ones in Q. Then, executing the 43 instruction causes the logical product of 0 and Q to be compared with A (only an S of 2 or 3 is used with this instruction). For purposes of explanation, assume that a block of data exists in cells 01000—01777 and that the type of data is identified by a code entered in the upper three octal digits of the cell. Then, let the various codes be entered in memory cells 02000—02177 (codes 000-177) with cell 02066 containing the explicit code (066) to be tested for at this time. Cell 02200 will contain the bits to be set in Q (77700 00000). Then the following simple loop will permit testing to find the cells which contain data identified by code 066. Let the instruction cells begin at 03000. Then:

03000 27 0 3 0 02200
[77700 00000] goes to Q
03001 26 0 3 0 02066
[06600 00000] goes to A

03002 Repeat the next instruction 1000_8 times increasing the 0 (operand) of the next instruction by 1 after each execution. NOTE: This is the 53 instruction and this routine will be used to demonstrate its use when the 53 instruction is covered.

03003 43 2 3 0 01000 takes the logical product of cells 01000-01777 and Q (this logical product is the code associated with each cell) and compares it with (A). If the code is found (A = 0) the repeat mode is aborted and the next instruction skipped.

(Note: An exit routine is entered each time a data cell containing the code is found. This routine will have as part of its function a method of reentry to the loop to permit testing the rest of the cells.)

44 Jump

The jump instruction permits leaving one portion of the program and going to another. Whether the jump is made or not is determined by certain values contained in the registers, whether certain keys (front panel switches, not shown) have been set and arbitrarily. In addition, provision is made to stop the program, either unconditionally or as the result of a key setting. The various options are selected by the value used for the S designator. These values are tabulated in figure 9-1 (jump and subroutine codes). The operand for these instructions is the address of the next instruction. Thus:

44 1 0 0 02000,

the instruction at address 02000, is executed next without regard to prevailing conditions.

44 3 1 0 02000,

the instruction at the address contained in M_L (02000), is executed next, but only if key 3 (a front panel control, not shown) is set. If key 3 is not set, no jump occurs and the next instruction is executed.

45 Subroutine Jump

The subroutine jump provides for leaving the main program and reentry after execution of the subroutine. The S designator specifies the conditions. Consider the following:

05000 45 1 0 0 02000

Execution of this instruction at address 05000 will cause the computer to place 05001 in M_L (02000) and jump to the instruction at 02001 for execution. Thus, the subroutine has been entered and the next sequential main program address preserved for reentry. The last instruction of the subroutine could well be

44 1 1 0 02000.

(Jump to the instruction addressed by M_L 02000 which is 05001.) Thus, the reentry to the main routine is executed.

46 Input Jump

This instruction causes the computer to test the channel as specified by the S designator (fig. 9-1). The channels are designated using an S of 0 - 3. Thus, when S = 0, channel 1 is designated. If the channel is active (i.e., an input action already initiated has not been completed) the program jumps to the address specified by L. For example,

46 2 0 0 02000.

(If channel 3 still has an active input buffer, jump to the instruction at address 02000.)

47 Output Jump

This instruction serves the same purpose as the 46 instruction, except that the specified channel is tested for an output active buffer.

50 Store Channel

This instruction is used in a subroutine which is entered as a result of an interrupt generated by the peripheral equipment. For purposes of explanation, assume that the computer is executing an instruction at address 02000 when an interrupt occurs on channel 2. The computer unconditionally goes to address 00042 (table 9-1) to select its next instruction. This cell will contain a 45 instruction. Thus:

00042 45 0 0 0 05000

(jump to instruction at 05001, store 02001 in 05000 lower);

05001 50 0 3 0 05XXX

(store data in specified cell and clear interrupt);

05002 – 050XX } Perform such test as may be desired on interrupt code

050XX + 1 44 1 1 0 05000

(Return to main program.)

It is possible that the programmer does not desire to honor an interrupt on channel 2. In this case, 00042 would contain

44 0 0 0 00000

(jump, don't jump).

After executing this instruction, the computer returns to the main program and no further interrupts are honored on this channel until steps are taken to clear it.

51 B Jump

This instruction tests the B register referenced by S. If the contents do not equal zero, one is subtracted from them and a jump to the instruction located by L occurs. When B^s = Ø the next sequential instruction is executed.

52 B Skip

When executing this instruction the contents of the B register designated by S are compared to the operand located by L. If they are not equal, the contents of B^s are incremented by 1 and the next instruction is skipped. When equality occurs B^s is cleared and the next sequential instruction is executed.

53 Repeat

The execution of this instruction causes the next sequential instruction to be executed the number of times indicated by the operand of the 53 instruction. This instruction by selection of an appropriate value of S, can cause modifications to the 0 of the repeated instruction (see repeat code in fig. 9-1).

Now, referring to the routine developed for originally demonstrating the 43 instruction (compare logical product), consider the following:

03000	27 0 3 0	02200
03001	26 0 3 0	02066
03002	53 1 0 0	01000
03003	43 2 3 0	01000

NOTE: The instruction contained in 03002 will cause the instruction at 03003 to be repeated 1000_8 times, or until the skip condition tested for in 03003 is met. It also causes the operand of the instruction contained in 03003 to be incremented by one after each execution.

For repeat instructions using an S of from 3 to 6, the B designator specifies the B register whose contents are to be used in modifying the operand of the repeated instruction.

Thus:

53 5 0 1 00003
32 0 3 0 01000.

If B^1 = 010, these instruction will cause the contents of Q to be stored in cells 01010, 01011, 01012.

NOTE: The modification by the contents of the B register occurs only once; and that prior to the first execution.

54 Input

The input instruction initiates all actions to cause data to be entered into the computer. In the input instruction S designates the channel to be activated, L the location of the address of a word which defines the buffer limits, and B may be used to modify the address if desired. Thus:

54 0 3 0 01000

causes activation of an input buffer on channel 1. Data will be entered into cells specified by the addresses contained in cell 01000; the first cell into which data is entered will be specified by M_L (01000), the last by M_U (01000). If M_U = M_L then one cell of data will be entered. At no time will the contents of 01000 be altered by executing the 54 instruction. Since the data contained in 01000 is also entered into the appropriate Input Buffer cell when executing the 54 instruction, the I/O section of the TPJ-7 then uses the Input Buffer cell for keeping track of the input data cell.

The word at address 01000 which defines the buffer limits is referred to as the buffer control word (BCW). As an example, assume it is desired to load one word of data into the TPJ-7 at address 02000. Then cell 01000 would contain 02000 02000. If 01000 contained 02004 02000 a block of five words would be entered into the indicated addresses.

55 Input with Interrupt

The only difference in the 54 and 55 instruction is that completion of the buffer initiated by the 55 Instruction causes the generation of an internal interrupt. When this is detected the main program is left and the next instruction is found in a special cell (00025 - 00030) dependent upon the channel activated. Thus, provision is made for initiating a buffer, permitting the computer to continue any other action desired, and then take note of any special actions required due to completion of the buffer.

56 Output

The actions of the output instruction parallel those of the input, with the exception that for the 56 instruction, data will be outputted from the cell(s) specified by the BCW; the data being outputted from the address specified by the lower half of the BCW first.

57 Output with Interrupt

Serves the same purpose when outputting data as does the 55 instruction when inputting data.

60 External Function

The external function instruction causes the issuing of a command to a peripheral equipment on a channel specified by S (table 9-1). The L of the 60 instruction locates the operand, which is the address of a cell containing the appropriate code for the desired command.

Thus:

60 1 3 0 01000

tells the computer to place the contents of cell 01000 in the output register and set the external function line.

BOOTSTRAP PROGRAM

As noted in table 9-1, cells 00001 thru 00020 are reserved for the bootstrap program. The instructions contained in this program are wired into the machine. The program consist of 20_8 instructions. These instructions will be discussed presently. Initiation of this program is under control of a front panel switch (not shown) on the TPJ-7. When the bootstrap is activated it will load 100_8 instructions into cells 00100 - 00177 from a bioctally coded paper tape. (Bioctal coding is treated in chapter 7.) The program then jumps to tne first instruction in the new program and stops. This new program contains a more elaborate load program which also contains certain error check functions.

The following stipulations are made before considering the bootstrap instructions.

1. The leader of the tape may consist of as many zero frames as desired; and

2. The paper tape reader is on channel 3. Although descriptive detail is supplied with the bootstrap program the reader should make every effort to decode the program without reference to the expository information.

00001	30 000 00006	Clear B^2 (will be used to test instruction word count).
00002	60 230 00017	Enable paper tape reader (PTR) channel 3. Ext. Function word found at 00017.
00003	27 000 00000	Clear Q (prepare to load first bioctal coded frame as part of the process to construct or pack a word).
00004	30 100 00004	Set frame index count in B^1 to pack 5 bioctal frames in Q. NOTE: Despite the instructions position this is an end of loop index (see instruction at 00012).
00005	54 230 00020	Input 1 frame into cell 00076. NOTE: BCW at 00020 = 00076 00076.
00006	46 200 00006	Until one frame has been loaded, this ties up the computer. When the input on channel 3 is no longer active, the jump is not executed.
00007	24 000 00006	LSH Q 6 binary places. (Prepare to pack word.)
00010	35 530 00076	Add to Q; if $Q \neq 0$, skip the next instruction. The frame just loaded is added to Q. Once the leader is exhausted, the skip condition will no longer occur.
00011	44 100 00005	A zero frame was entered. Jump to address of operand and initiate another buffer.
00012	51 100 00005	$B^1 \neq 0$ then $B^1 - 1$ and jump. The first time this instruction is executed the first frame (two octal digits) of the first instruction word is in Q.
00013	32 032 00100	Store Q in address ($00100 + B^2$). Instruction word has been packed and is now stored in cell 00100 (for the first word).
00014	52 200 00100	$B^2 = 100$ skip; $B^2 \neq 100$ then $B^2 + 1$ and execute next instruction. This tests the word count and sets the index for storing the remaining words.
00015	44 100 00003	Jump to instruction at 00003. A word has been stored, but all have not been loaded.
00016	44 200 00100	Jump to address 00100 and stop. The new program is loaded. Jump to its first instruction and stop.
00017	00 000 00020	External function code; Enable Reader
00020	00 076 00076	BCW data frame will be loaded into address 00076 by I/O section.

FAULT CONDITION

As was previously noted attempting to execute an illegal function code causes the TPJ-7 to unconditionally execute the instruction contained in address 00000 next. It would naturally be of inestimable help to be able to determine in what cell the error occurs.

Consider the following example. The TPJ-7 attempts to execute the instruction at address 01000 which is

15 0 5 0 01500

(Note that an F of 15 is not valid.) Thus, jumping to address 00000, the program is as follows:

```
00000  45 000 02000  Address 01001 is
                     stored at 02000 lower.
02001  26 010 02000  01001→A
02002  36 000 00001  A = 01000
02003  30 041 00000  (A)→B¹
02004  26 001 00000  (01000)→A
02005  44 201 00000,
```

and the computer stops at the fault address with the erroneous instruction in A and the fault address in B^1.

Chapter 10

PROGRAMMING (PART II)

When discussing operational programs, we are usually talking in terms of programs containing hundreds or thousands of operational machine instructions per program; all of which must be stored either in the computer memory or in an auxiliary memory device in a logical sequence which is readily accessible. Designated memory cells or areas in computer memory must be set aside for the storage of operational parameters for the program, and permanent or temporary storage of machine computations. As can be seen from above, it would be time consuming and difficult, if not nearly impossible to accomplish, if the programmer had to write a program using machine language and absolute addressing techniques.

COMPILERS

To aid the programmer and facilitate the generation of these large programs, devices called compiling systems (or compilers) have been developed. Compilers are nothing more than programs fed into the computer to aid in the preparation of other programs, that is, from information coded in alphanumeric or mnemonic codes, a compiler will produce an operational program complete with memory allocations suitable for use with a computer. In addition, these compiling systems can be designed to produce printed indications of errors in the input format, and a means of correcting these errors and making other program modifications. Also, they can be devised to produce program listings and program diagnostic routines for debugging of the program once it is in operation.

There have been many different compilers developed, such as CS-1, COBOL, and FORTRAN, which differ mainly in the way they are oriented. CS-1 is NTDS oriented (although it can be used for many other types of programming), COBOL is business oriented, and FORTRAN is oriented for formula solving. A discussion of the CS-1 compiler is included here as being representative. Lighter treatments of COBOL and FORTRAN are treated at the end of the chapter.

The CS-1 compiler uses English words or a mnemonic code for its input (source) language, that is, the programmer states the problem using relative addressing techniques. The CS-1 compiler will convert this information into an object or operational program, which when fed into the computer along with the necessary parameters will solve the problem. Figure 10-1 illustrates the relationship.

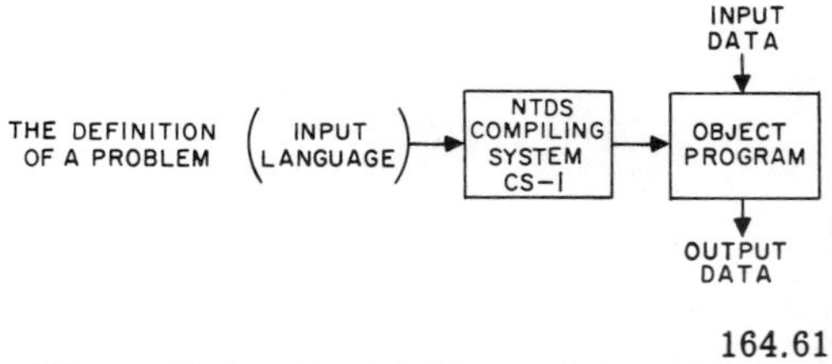

164.61

Figure 10-1.—CS-1 Solution of a Problem.

INPUT LANGUAGE (OPERATIONS)

The CS-1 input language consists of a large repertoire of operations which either state certain facts about entities in the input language, or perform a well defined logical action. A list of these operations, which are the basic unit of language, defines a problem. These operations have the following basic configuration:

L S N

[label] → [statement] → [notes] ⅄

L—the label is a name that uniquely identifies the operation. A tag is a reference to the label of one operation in the statement of another.

S—the statement defines the operation and is always required.

N—descriptive notes may follow the statement: they are for the user's convenience and in no way alter the meaning of the operation.

→—the straight arrow is a major separator which limits the statement.

↘—the curved arrow designates the end of each operation and signals the start of the next one. It must precede the first operation of a program.

In general the statement involves two sections: the operator (W) and a list of operands (V) as follows:

W—the operator specifies the general characteristics of the operation.

V—the operands further define the operation. The number and the configuration of the operands depend upon the operator used.

•—the point separator separates the operator from the operand section and separates other operands from one another.

Example:

W V_0 V_1 V_n
→ [operator] • [operand] • [operand] • • • [operand] →

Any list of operation serving as CS-1 input must begin with a header operation. A header consists of (1) a program name as the label in position L, (2) a header-type W, which specifies basic information about the operations which follow the header, and (3) two identifying operands, V0 and V1. The basic header format is:

L W V0 V1
↘ [program name] → [header-type] • [programmer's name] • [date] ↘

CLASSES OF OPERATIONS

Operations are divided into three classes:

1. Computer - oriented operations,
2. Problem - oriented operations, and
3. Compiler - control operations.

1. Computer - oriented operations express in mnemonic form, either a machine instruction or groups of machine instructions which perform a simple function, or input/output control on the standard external equipment. These operations generally refer to memory locations by their addresses (a label or a tag), to machine registers by name (A, Q, B3), and to date by the 30 bit word concept. A thorough knowledge of the computer is necessary to use these operations.

2. Problem-oriented operations express information and rules of processing in the terms of flow chart language. These terms refer to data by mnemonic names instead of addresses, express computations by algebraic equations, and state the control program sequencing by a powerful English-like shorthand. Both classes of operations can exist in one program and can be intermixed at will. Some operations could be either computer oriented or problem oriented.

3. Compiler—control operations specify information to the compiler executive routine. This information states on what series of computers the object program is to be run, what external equipment is available for the compiler as extra storage, and what process it is to perform, such as compiling, editing, etc.

DECLARATIVE AND ACTION OPERATIONS

Operations are also divided into two categories: Declarative and Action.

a. Declarative operations state certain facts about entities in the input language of which they are part. Some of them are computer oriented, others are problem oriented. They (1) adapt the program to a specified memory configuration and input/output capabilities of the computer, (2) define data and areas as to their format and use, and (3) identify different segments of input to the compiler. No machine instructions result directly from declarative operations.

b. Action operations have operational or dynamic meaning and state rules of processing which give rise to actual machine instructions.

COMPILING PROCESS

The process of transforming the input language (relative addressed mnemonic code) to the object program (absolute addresses and machine instructions) is called "compiling."

It is a series of language translation, conversions, and allocations under control of the compiler routines.

The source (input) language loads into CS-1 via paper tape, magnetic tape, etc. This working language is called L_0. Through a series of translations to intermediate language levels (L_1, L_2, and L_3) the object program is produced. This working language is called L_4. A description of each of these languages follows:

L_0—is the original input language consisting of CS-1 operations and is used by the programmer in writing routines and preparing them for compiler input.

L_1—is a slightly modified L_0 in which the operation items are stored (in a special 6-bit code) within compiler tables. Certain input translations and error detection steps have been performed; operations remain in mnemonic form, however, and their basic characteristics are similar to L_0. The conversion of L_0 operations to L_1 operations is a one-to-one relationship.

L_2—consists of information tables and a list of operation items which are very similar to machine instructions. The designators (such as f, j, k, and b) are in absolute octal code, but the addresses are symbolic. The program is not yet committed to any given memory area.

L_3—is the language of the object program stored in table form within the compiler. All addresses have been assigned a permanent (absolute) address.

L_4—is the object program on paper tape or magnetic tape, which can be loaded directly into the Unit Computer and executed. Examples of L_0 and L_4 instructions are shown in figure 10-2.

Figure 10-3 is a block diagram of the CS-1. Illustrated are the 39 various tables used by CS-1 and the basic data flow for conversion, translation allocation, and error detection.

The L_0 input is converted and stored in Table 1, the L_1 program level. At this level the L_0 has been slightly modified and the operation items are stored in a special 6-bit code within this table. Any library function will be read in from magnetic tape at this time by the CS-1 librarian and are merged into table 1. In the process of going from L_1 to L_2 a translation takes place, and using the information tables operation items are transformed into the f, j, k, and b designators in octal form. At this time, however, the addresses are still in the mnemonic form. The allocation process which assigns absolute addresses to all symbolic labels and tags takes place as instructions leave the L_2 table. A separate tape or card deck input assigns values to pertinent label/tags of the L_0 program and stores them in the allocation table for later use. As the absolute addresses are allocated the language of the object program is stored in the L_3 table. The outputs of the compiler are available in a wide selection of output formats. Editing data are available at language levels L_1, L_2, and/or L_3. The programmer may request any one or combination of these. Assembled object programs L_4 are obtainable in flex code, in absolute bioctal, or relative bioctal format. The programmer must request these by number before compilation begins.

During the process of compiling, the CS-1 has an elaborate error detection scheme. A printout of error is made by the on-line flexowriter or TTY immediately upon detection. The programmer can make corrections to operation items at the L_1 language level. An error is corrected by replacing a bad card with one that has been punched correctly. A routine known as the L_1 Corrector will make the necessary alterations in L_1 table storage. The programmer then uses the resulting corrected L_0 tape for subsequent compilation.

COMPUTER - ORIENTED OPERATIONS

Computer-oriented operations as previously stated define a problem in a language that closely resembles machine concepts and terminology. A thorough knowledge of the computer is necessary to use these operations. A discussion of computer-oriented operations (as being representative of the three different classes of operations) follows.

MONO-OPERATIONS

Operations which mnemonically express machine instructions are mono-operations. CS-1 translates each mono-operation in the source language (L_0) to one machine instruction in the object language (L_4); i.e., the translation is one-to-one.

Mono-operations have a definite format.

$$\underset{\rightarrow[\text{Operator}]}{W} \bullet \underset{[\text{allied operand}]}{V_0} \bullet \underset{[\text{y-operand}]}{V_1} \bullet \underset{[\text{j-operand}]}{V_2}$$

L_0 LEVEL INSTRUCTIONS	L_4 LEVEL INSTRUCTIONS			
JP. PKGS2	00140	61000	00272	ENTER
U-TAGSWTH*MSWTH	00141	00315	00313	TLADDR
	BLOAD			
ENTRY	00142	61000	00000	BLOAD
RJP. RDFRS	00143	65000	00171	
STR. Q. W(BLOAD1). SKIP	00144	14130	00145	
	00145	00000	00000	BLOAD1
CL. W(TWXFT)	00146	16030	00261	
ENT. B4. U(BLOAD1)	00147	12420	00145	
RJP. RDFR5	00150	65000	00171	BLOAD2
ENT. A. U(BLOAD). ANOT	00151	11520	00142	
JP. BLOAD3	00152	61000	00155	
RJP. CKREAD	11053	65000	02431	
ENT. Q. W(B4)	00154	10034	00000	
STR. Q. W(B4)	00155	14034	00000	BLOAD3
RJP. CKSUMCK	00156	65000	00207	
RJP. SMP	00157	65000	00214	BLOAD4
BSK. B4. L(BLOAD1)	00160	71410	00145	
JP. BLOAD2	00161	61000	00150	
RJP. RDFR5	00162	65000	00171	
RPL. Y-Q. W(TWXFT)	00163	35030	00261	
RJP. RDFR5	00164	65000	00171	
RPL. Y-Q. W(TWXFT)	00165	35030	00261	
ENT. A. U(BLOAD). AZERO	00166	11420	00142	
CL. W(TWXFT)	00167	16030	00261	
EXIT	00170	61010	00142	

164.62

Figure 10-2.—L_0 to L_4 conversion.

W—gives a mono code, which defines a class of machine instructions such as enter, store, and replace.

V_0—gives added information, which further defines a machine instruction, thus, is called the allied operand. The allied operand may specify a register or a simple logical or arithmetic expression. In some operations it is absent.

V_1—specifies either (1) a numberic value, (2) the address of a memory location, or (3) a register (A, Q, Bn). The y-operand is a Read-class operand. V_1 is absent in some operations.

V_2—specifies a j-operand which is primarily used for jump or skip determination or for repeat status interpretation. The action caused by these may be conditional or unconditional as directed by the operand used. Seven j-operands are applicable to the majority of mono-operations. These are called normal j-operands. Certain operations require the usage of unique j-operands, called special j-operands and are applicable to jump, return jump, divide, repeat, add Q, subtract Q, and all non-mask compares.

Mono code operators, combining with allied operands, in most cases are capable of generating all the irredundant instructions of the unit computer's repertoire. Additional operations, such as, "do-nothing" operation, NO-OP, and "complement a register," CP, produce single instructions which achieve such actions which are not apparent in the names of computer function codes.

All of the mono-codes appear as the bold type on the computer repetoire cards. Therefore, it is only necessary to go into a few examples to show the relationships between W, V_0, V_1, V_2, etc.

ENT•Q•X77776: QNEG generates the machine instruction

1 0   3 0 0   7 7 7 7 6

(Enter Q with operand and jump if Q is negative.)

NO-OP generates the machine instruction

1 2   0 0 0   0 0 0 0 0

(This is a NO-operation instruction which delays the main program while an I/O instruction is being executed.)

POLY-OPERATIONS

Operations which mnemonically express functions that may give rise to more than one machine instruction are poly-operations. CS-1 translates poly-operations in the source language L_0 to many machine instructions in the object language L_4; i.e., the translation is one-to-many.

Quite frequently, groups of contiguous instructions occur in a program and always perform the same specific job or function. For example, any time a programmer wanted a flexowriter type-out of the contents of a register or group of memory cells, the housekeeping necessary to set up the computer to output to the flexowriter is redundant. With this particular routine as an integral function of CS-1, with the label TYPEC, all he must do is to write ⟶ TYPEC • [information to be typed] ⟶ and the compiler will include this routine in the object program. Many of the poly-operations have been included in CS-1 and will be discussed in the following paragraphs.

It is permissible during the coding of a routine to intermix mono- and poly-operations in any order desired. However, the programmer must not attempt to skip a poly-operation with the j-operand of a mono-operation as poly operation usually results in the generation of more than one instruction in the assembled

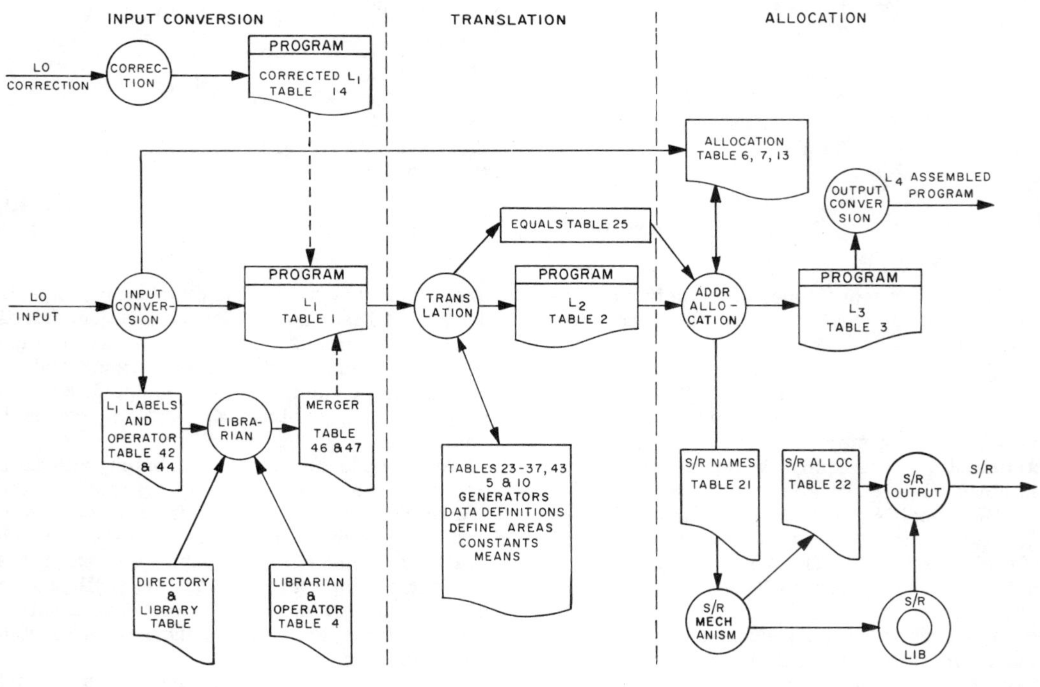

164.63

Figure 10-3.—Block diagram of CS-1.

object program, and the j-operand will cause only a skip of the first of these instructions when the program is operating and not the whole poly-operation as desired. The compiler-generated computer instructions appear in the object program in the order specified by the CS-1 coding.

ENTRY Operation

The ENTRY operation establishes a standard means of starting all subroutines. It produces either a normal entry with no jump conditions or a jump capability with Key Stop options. This operation is the first one in each subroutine, and because of this it must have a label which gives the subroutine a name.

L		W		V_0
[subroutine name]	→	ENTRY	•	[stop condition]

Although each ENTRY operation generates only one instruction, the variations which the instruction can assume make it a poly-operation.

EXIT Operation

The EXIT operation provides a means of exiting normally from a subroutine. It generates a jump back to the ENTRY operation of the subroutine and thence to the main routine. The EXIT operation is used at a place in the subroutine where an exit from it is desired. Therefore, any number of exits can be permitted. The label is optional.

L		W		V_0
[optional label]	→	EXIT	•	[jump condition]

RESERVE Operation

The RESERVE operation sets aside a block of memory locations in the running (object) program. It does so by adding the number expressed by the V_0 operand to the current allocation address and storing the next generated instruction at the incremented address. Thus, the reservation of space begins at the location following that of the previously generated instruction and includes the V_0 number of continuous locations. The compiler does not clear these locations; it merely bypasses them during allocation.

	W		V_0
→	[RESERVE]	•	[number of words]

Some of the special reasons for reserving such an area include:

(a) Setting aside a specific area for the storage of parameters.

(b) Leaving an area open for working storage.

(c) Reserving space at the end of the program for expansion purposes.

(d) Subsequent insertion of other program instructions.

CLEAR Operation

The CLEAR operation clears (fills with 0's) a number of words of an area of core memory.

	W		V_0		V_1
→	CLEAR	•	[number of words]	•	[starting address]

PUT Operation

The PUT operation places a single word or half-word in a designated storage address.

			V_0		V_1
→	PUT	•	[the word]	•	[destination address]

MOVE Operation

The MOVE operation moves masses of data from one area to another. The computer moves the words of information sequentially through the Q register and may use B for indexing. It does not reinstate the original contents to either the B or Q register. The programmer must save and restore such information if he wishes to retain it.

	W		V_0		V_1		V_2
→	MOVE	•	[number of words]	•	[from address]	•	[to address]

INCREMENT Operation

The INCREMENT operation provides a means to either increase or decrease the number contained in a B register by a fixed amount.

W V_0 V_1
→ INCREMENT • [B register] • [increment]

Upper-TAG Operation

The U-TAG is the primary method for inserting the absolute address of any previously allocated label in either the upper half or lower half of a memory cell.

W V_0 V_1
→ U-TAG • [upper tag name] • [lower tag name constant, or zero]

DISABLE Operation

The DISABLE operation disables any of a number of pieces of external equipment.

W V_0
→ DISABLE • [name of equipment]

This operation calls for subroutines from the compiler library which perform the disabling functions and generate return jumps to the subroutines. DISABLE operations subsequent to the first do not call for subroutines. They generate the return jump(s).

The V_0 operand may assume any one or combination of the following: (1) PUNCH, (2) PRINTER, (3) READER, (4) FLEX, (5) DRUM, or (6) TWX.

ENABLE Operation

The ENABLE operation enables one or more pieces of external equipment. The permissible V_0 operands include: 1) PRINTER, (2) FLEX IN, (3) FLEX OUT, (4) DRUM IN, (5) DRUM OUT, (6) READER, (7) PUNCH, and (8) TWX. This operation calls for subroutines from the compiler library which perform the enabling functions, and generate return jumps to these subroutines.

COMMENT Operation

The COMMENT operation permits the programmer to place a message within the input program to provide added information for edited records of the problem definition. This operation is declarative and it has no dynamic meaning to the input language.

W V_0
→ COMMENT • [message]

PRINT Operation

The PRINT operation provides the programmer with a method of activating the print-out of information on the high-speed printer. The operation initiates a subroutine PRINTB, which causes the contents of a 24 bit word core buffer area (in excess - 3 code) with base address, β, to be transferred to the high-speed printer as a 120 bit character line of print. The PRINTB subroutine is capable of transferring the contents of the buffer area either directly to the high-speed printer (on-line), or to a paper tape unit for subsequent off-line printing. The programmer must enable the printer by using the ENABLE operation once before using the PRINT operation.

W V_0 V_1
→ PRINT • [base address of print buffer] • [jump condition]

TYPEC Operation

The TYPEC or TYPEC, TWXX operation causes the contents (in octal) of A, Q, and B register, or any storage location to be typed by the on-line flexowriter or TTY. In addition to specifying that the numerical information in any of the above registers be typed, the programmer may issue special commands to the flexowriter or TTY to cause a carriage return, space, or tabulator stop. The compiled object program uses the TYPEC subroutine to produce the typeout. In general, this poly-operation generates a return jump to the TYPEC subroutine, followed by an operation statement for each operand, directing the computer either to type the information as specified or to perform the command given.

W	V_0
→ TYPEC •	[information to be typed] →
→ TYPEC, TWXX •	[information to be typed] →

TYPET Operation

The TYPET or TYPET, TWXX operation generates a section of object language program which, when run on the computer, causes the flexowriter or TTY to type the message given by the $-V_0$-operand of the TYPET operation. During the running of the object program, the TYPET subroutine is referenced to produce the typewriter printout.

W	V_0
→ TYPET •	[text and flexowriter commands] →
→ TYPET, TWXX •	[text and TTY commands] →

PUNCHC Operation

The PUNCHC or PUNCHC, TWXX operation causes the content (in octal) of A, Q, and B register or any memory location to be punched by the high-speed punch. In addition, the programmer may include commands to the flexowriter or TTY for space, carriage return or tabulator stop. The compiler object program uses the PUNCHC subroutine to produce the output. In general, this poly-operation generates a return jump to the PUNCHC subroutine, followed by an operation statement for each operand, directing the computer either to punch the information to be punched or the commands to be performed.

W	V_0
→ PUNCHC •	[parameters for information and/or flexowriter commands] →
→ PUNCHC, TWXX •	[parameters for information and/or TTY commands] →

PUNCHT Operation

The PUNCHT or PUNCHT, TWXX operation causes the high-speed punch to punch the text(s) which the programmer has written in the $-V_0$-operand position of the operation for either the flexowriter or TTY. During the running of the object program, the PUNCHT subroutine is referenced to produce the punched tape output.

W	V_0
PUNCHT •	[text and/or flexowriter commands] →
PUNCHT, TWXX •	[text and/or TTY commands] →

TYPE-DECimal Operation

The TYPE-DEC operation causes the contents (in decimal) of A, Q, any B register, or any storage location to be typed by the online flexowriter or TTY.

W	V_0
→ TYPE-DEC •	[information to be typed] →
→ TYPEDEC, TWXX •	[information to be typed] →

PUNCH-DEC Operation

The PUNCH-DEC operation causes the contents (in decimal) of A, Q, any B register or any storage to be punched by the high-speed punch for type-out on the flexowriter or TTY.

W	V_0
→ PUNCH-DEC •	[parameters for information and/or flexowriter commands] →
→ PUNCHDEC, TWXX •	[parameters for information and/or TTY commands] →

DECLARATIVE OPERATIONS

Operations which state information to the compiler and result in no machine instructions are declarative operations. These declarative operations adapt the program to a specific memory configuration and to input/output capabilities of the computer, define data and areas, and identify different segments of input. The programmer frequently wishes to supply to the computer certain information for use in the compiling process which does not generate an instruction. The information may be involved in subsequent operations in constructing a machine-code instruction, or it may be substituted for already existing data or information, and thereby extending the scope and power of the operation. Declarative operations give information about relationships, such as, equality between data and/or symbolic names, make assertions, and define a procedure. Declarative operations state facts and provide information which the compiler either utilizes, or stores and later incorporates into program instructions it generates.

In all cases, the programmer must state the declarative operation at some place ahead of the action operation which is to use it. These operations can intermingle with action operations anywhere in the program provided they comply with the above priority restriction.

EQUALS Operation

The EQUALS operation establishes an equivalence between one expression, L, whose allocation value is unknown and another expression, V_0, for which the allocation value is known. This provides the programmer with a versatile allocation aid whereby he can transfer an allocation value from one label or tag to another label or tag. Since this operator is concerned solely with allocation, a compiler function, it generates no instructions in the internal program.

$$\underset{\text{[unknown tag]}}{L} \rightarrow \underset{\text{EQUALS}}{W} \bullet \underset{\left[\begin{array}{l}\text{known value (label, tag,}\\ \text{or a constant)}\end{array}\right]}{V_0} \rightarrow$$

MEANS Operation

The MEANS operation replaces a tentative label with the input/output information expressed in mnemonics. For certain computer applications, it permits programs to be written with complete flexibility concerning the assignment of I/O channels to external equipment.

COBOL

As was previously stated, the major difference between the various compiling systems in use is the way they are oriented (that is, the major difference is the input language or code in which the programmer states his problem). The end results are still the same; a series of machine coded instructions which tell the computer what to do. Thus, COBOL, being business oriented, the input language used is a modified form of business English. The programmer will therefore state his problem in this modified business English and will include in his statement all of the necessary instructions and information for the computer to recognize and solve the problem.

Included in the processor or compiling program is a reference library (a series of tables of data and subroutines), which will enable it to translate the programmer's code into an operational program (in machine code) with the operational instructions listed in order of execution and the data listed in tables.

As an example, assume it is necessary to find the amount of interest which will accumulate on a certain account. The COBOL language will allow you to state the problem as follows:

MULTIPLY PRINCIPLE TIMES RATE.

In order for the processor (compiler program) to interpret this statement it will require that certain information be written into this program. This information must be included in a special part of the program called the "data division." For example, the words "principle" and "rate" must be listed along with any facts about these words or data, such as, size and percentage and how they are to be expressed (used) and so on.

The processor will need certain other information to help it translate the statement. This information (tables of special words, subroutines, and etc.) is included as part of the processor itself.

The exact procedure used in processing the statement will vary from machine to machine, but the processor will examine each word in the statement individually. That is, the processor will take the word "multiply" and consult a special list of words which have clearly defined meanings in COBOL language. This list is part of the processor and if the word "multiply" is included in this list, then the processor will interpret this to mean that a series of machine instructions (one or more), necessary to perform the multiplication, must be included in the operational or object program.

Next, it will examine the word "principle". Since it has certain information about this word, it will know where and how this information is to be stored in the computer and will generate the necessary instructions in the operational program to enable the operational program to locate and use this information.

While examining the next word "times," the processor will consult its special word list and find that "times" is a word that directs it to the value or rate it is to multiply by to find the interest. It then examines the word "rate" and knowing certain information about this word, it will store this information in computer memory and generate in the operational program the necessary instructions to locate and use this information.

Finally, when the processor looks at the period at the end of the statement, it knows that it has completed its translation of the statement and will start processing the next statement, or if there are no more statements it will cease operation.

FORTRAN

The language used in the FORTRAN system is quite similar to that used in the COBOL system. For example, the statement:

MULTIPLY PRINCIPLE TIMES RATE

as used in the COBOL system could be stated as follows in the FORTRAN system:

Interest = Principle x Rate

The FORTRAN system is used primarily for formula translation (problem solving) in the scientific field.

Chapter 11

ANALOG-DIGITAL AND DIGITAL-ANALOG CONVERSIONS

There are three general types of computers, as pointed out in chapter 1 of this course. These are: (1) digital, (2) analog, and (3) hybrid. The selection of a particular type of computer to perform a certain type of operation is dependent upon several factors.

One factor involved in this selection is the method and source of input information. For example, data received from a radar set, an airspeed probe, or a shaft position are readily accepted and worked upon by an analog computer, since this type of data is analog in nature. Conversely, the type of data obtained from a ballistic table, a census tabulation, or a logistics manual are most readily accepted and worked upon by a digital computer, since this type of data is digital in nature.

Digital computers are generally more versatile than analog computers. Analog computers are designed to solve a specific problem. In practice then, it would be necessary to have as many types of analog computers as there are analogous problems to be solved. A digital computer can solve a variety of different problems; the only requirements being that the problem be stated in a language that the computer understands and that the computer be supplied with sufficient data to solve the problem. The limitations of analog computers and the cited advantages of digital computers, particularly in their ability to process large quantities of data, gives rise to the use of analog-digital converters.

ANALOG-TO-DIGITAL CONVERSION

An analog-to-digital converter is defined as a device that receives an analog input and supplies a digital output. A converter of this type is capable of accepting instantaneous values of a constantly changing variable and expressing these values in incremental form. The converter may or may not perform some computation in addition to its primary function of data conversion.

The process of analog-to-digital conversions is not uncommon. Our minds make hundreds of analog-digital conversions each day. For example, if you ask a young child what time it is, he will probably look at a clock and tell you that the long hand is near the six and the short hand is between the four and the five. The child is performing the function of data transmission, not data conversion. He is accepting the instantaneous value of the constantly moving hands of the clock, but he is transmitting the information in analog, not digital, form. The data which the child transmitted is converted into numerical values, in this case, four thirty. You, the inquirer, are therefore performing the analog-to-digital conversion, the child is not.

Care must be taken to avoid confusing truly digital read-outs with others that merely appear to be digital. The needle of a voltmeter or the pointer on an automobile speedometer provides analog data by indicating the instantaneous value of volts or miles per hour in a constantly changing manner. It is only by reading these meters and assigning numerical values that a truly digital read-out is obtained. Just as in the example of the clock, the human observer is serving as the analog-to-digital converter. Similarly, the type of data that is obtained from a micrometer scale or from the mercury column of a thermometer is analog in nature, until converted by the reader. The accuracy of each of these devices is, in large measure, a function of the ability of the reader to convert the information accurately from analog to digital form.

On the other hand, mechanical counters such as those commonly used to count the number of people entering a building provide a true digital read-out. No great amount of skill is required for reading such a device because its accuracy does not depend on the reader, but upon its design. If each click of the counter corresponds to a count of one, no amount of skill on the part of the reader will increase its inherent precision.

MECHANICAL TECHNIQUES FOR ANALOG TO DIGITAL CONVERSION

Probably the simplest method of converting analog information, such as shaft rotation, into digital form is the obvious method of connecting the shaft through a gear drive to a decade counter. This process is sometimes called shaft rotation digitation, since each rotation of the shaft is explained in digital form. One common application of the gear drive and counter method of conversion is used by the mileage counter (odometer) of an automobile.

In addition to providing a digital read-out from analog data, the odometer also performs some simple analog computing. The basic information is the rotation of a shaft. A gear train multiplies this by the correct constant to produce miles per revolution. The data are still in analog form. After multiplication, the data are summed by the counter and displayed in digital form to represent the total miles traveled. The original input is analog, the computing is performed by means of analog techniques, but the read-out is digital.

This technique is also used in various other applications. Many airborne and ship-based analog computers used in bombing, navigation, or fire control applications, use this form of read-out both for output indications and for an indication of input information that has been cranked in manually. Although this technique is simple and widely used, it is of rather limited value. It can be used for read-out or read-in purposes only. Since the digital output must be visually observed on the counter wheels, it cannot be used to feed another computer except through a human operator. In fact, this technique is not suitable for automatic operation.

Shaft-Position Digitation By Geared Counter

Shaft position digitation is defined as the process of converting and expressing the instantaneous position of a shaft in digital form. The simplest method of shaft-position digitation is similar to the technique that has been described in connection with shaft-rotation digitation. In the shaft rotation method, where the total revolutions or a function of total revolutions is to be read-out, a decade-type counter is used in order to obtain relatively high readings. For position indication, only a relatively small number of positions are required. It is therefore possible to use only one counter wheel which contains as many digits as may be desired, each digit representing a definite rotary position of the shaft.

If the number of positions is very large, a decade type counter would be helpful. The use of seven counter wheels could theoretically produce extremely fine readings, with a resolution as fine as one second of arc. Two of the wheels, for example the two right-hand wheels on an odometer type counter could be used to produce the readings from 00 to 60 seconds; the next two to the left could read from 00 to 60 minutes; and the last three from 000 to 360 degrees.

Unfortunately, the similarities between this technique and the preceding one also reveal the limitations involved, since this method also provides only a read-out or read-in capability.

Shaft-Position Digitation by Mechanical Switching

A device that is more useful than the previous devices in at least one respect can be devised by replacing the counter with a mechanical switching arrangement. Either cam-operated sensitive switches or a multiposition rotary switch can be used. With this method, the output is electrical, although the device is basically mechanical. If each switch or tap feeds separate lines, the various output signals will correspond to each separate shaft position. The signals could be used either as an input to some type of computing device, or to feed numbered output lamps.

A disadvantage of this device is the physical limitation associated with the number of positions that can be read out. Each additional position requires the addition of another sensitive switch, or the use of a larger rotary switch, plus another lamp. Although such a device might be practical for applications such as calling out sixteen main points of a compass, any greater number of points would require the use of either an additional coding device or an entirely different technique.

Shaft-Position Digitation by Coding Disks

Until now, none of the devices discussed provides any type of numerical code, although most devices designed to receive digital inputs from a converter require the use of some special code. The most frequently used types of codes for these applications generally involve some form of binary coding.

If lamp read-out is desired, the binary system will reduce the number of lamps required. For example, the binary-coded decimal (BCD) system of counting reduces the number of lamps required for reading out the numbers between 0 and 9 from ten lamps to four lamps (since 1 lamp is required in each of 4 columns, to be capable of representing any decimal number from 0 to 9 in the binary system).

When you recall that this ratio increases by powers of 2, the tremendous advantage of the binary system becomes readily apparent. Twenty-two lamps can, in this manner, represent over a million-and-a-half numbers. The lamps can be replaced by tubes, transistors, relays, diode networks, etc., to yield over 1.5 million bits of information in the form of electrical signals.

The coded disk (fig. 11-1) is a device used for adapting a binary code for shaft position digitation. If it is assumed that the shaded areas represent conductors, the light areas represent insulators, and the small rectangles represent brushes, the operation of the device can be described as follows.

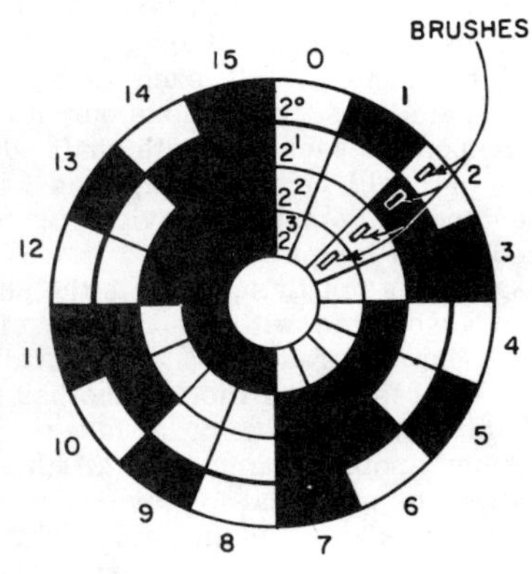

124.99
Figure 11-1.—The binary coded disk.

The disk is attached to the associated shaft so that as the disk rotates in a counterclockwise direction under the brushes, an ON ("1") signal is generated each time a brush contacts a dark area, and an OFF ("0") signal is generated each time a brush contacts a light (unshaded) area. The circles which produce values of 2^0, 2^1, 2^2, and 2^3 are as shown at the "0" position (segment) of the wheel. Thus, the outermost circle produces the least significant digit (LSD) in the code, followed by increasing orders to the most significant digit (MSD) produced by the innermost circle.

The binary number represented by each segment of the disk is read by interpreting the shaded and light areas in the segment containing the brushes reading from the innermost to the outermost circle. Read a "0" for each light area and a "1" for each dark area. The areas in segment 1 are read 0001, representing the number 1 in the decimal system. The areas in segment 12 are read 1100, (BCD) representing the number 12 in the decimal system. The brushes are shown in a position which reads 0010_2, or 2_{10}.

Because only four zones are used (2^0, 2^1, 2^2 and 2^3), the resolution of the disk is 1 part in 16, (counting zero as 1 part). If a circle which contains 32 alternating ON and OFF areas (each of which is approximately half the size of the present outer circle) were added, a resolution of 1 part in 32 could be obtained. The resolution can thus be increased by a factor of two for each additional circle that is added.

A circuit can be completed through the disk by connecting each conducting segment to a conductor on the rear of the disk, which would serve as a slipring.

Another form of coding disk (not shown) uses the photoelectric principle of reading out digital information. The disk consists of opaque and transparent segments. A light source is placed on one side of the disk, and an arrangement of photocells is placed on the other side. An aperture through which the light must pass in order to reach the disk replaces the brushes as discussed in the previous example of coding disk.

Ambiguity With Natural Binary Code

The major difficulty with the coded disk described above is illustrated by considering the

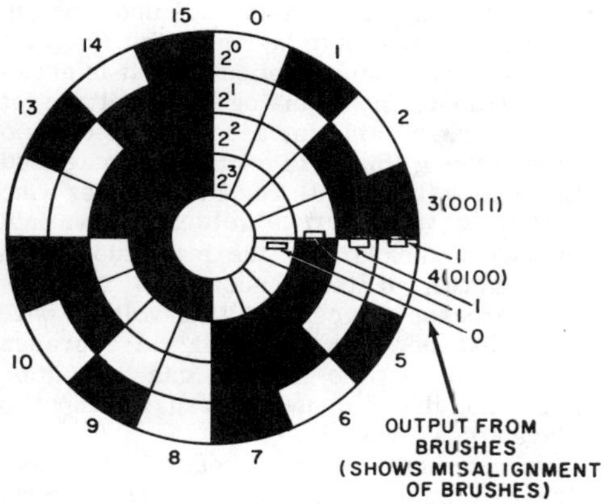

124.100
Figure 11-2.—Coded disk showing erroneous output due to misalignment of brushes.

disk to be in a position where the output number is changing from 0011 to 0100 (fig. 11-2).

Because the brushes used for read-out from the disk cannot be perfectly aligned, it is probable that all bits will not change simultaneously. If the shaft stops at a position where the 2^2 brush is in the conductive (shaded) area and the 2^1 and 2^0 brushes are not completely in the insulated (unshaded) areas, the output will be 0111. This represents an appreciable error. If, on the other hand, the 2^2 brush is not in the shaded area and the 2^1 and 2^0 brushes are in the unshaded areas, the output will read 0000. This again represents a large error. The possibility of large error is most severe when more than one bit changes value simultaneously. Table 11-1, in which the sequentially changing bits are underlined, reveals how frequently this condition arises. Starting with the 0000 in the natural binary code or binary coded decimal, alternate numbers require a change in more than one bit. Thus, the possibility or error is great and this code is not satisfactory for use in shaft position digitation.

The most popular code used to circumvent this problem is the "Gray" code (fig. 11-3) sometimes called the "unit distance" code. The Gray code representation of numbers from zero to fifteen is shown. Note that only one bit changes value from one position to

Table 11-1. —Natural Binary Code Showing Sequentially Changing Bits Underlined

Decimal	Natural Binary Code
0	0000
1	0001
2	0010
3	0011
4	0100
5	0101
6	0110
7	0111
8	1000

the next higher or lower position. In this way, the magnitude of the error introduced by imperfect alignment of the read-out brushes or by reading out data from a brush (or brushes) which spans a shaded and unshaded section cannot exceed 1. Thus, a 4 may be read for a 5, or a 7 may be read for an 8. Larger errors cannot be made.

Most computers are not designed to perform computations using Gray code. When this code is used in the analog to digital conversion process, it is necessary to convert the data from Gray code to binary coded decimal—

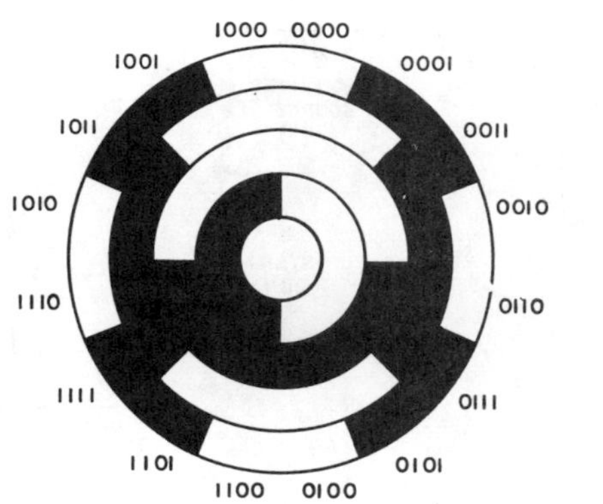

124.101
Figure 11-3.—Coded disk (Gray code).

a form more suitable for computer use. Decoding matrices of the type discussed in chapter 5 of this text may be used for this purpose.

ELECTRICAL TECHNIQUES

The important differences in the electrical and mechanical techniques for analog-to-digital conversion are now noted. They both convert or "encode" analog inputs into digital outputs. Both types usually make use of a zero value setting as a reference point.

The mechanical encoder (explained earlier) generally uses some technique for the ON and OFF switching of a number of electrical contacts on a coded drum (not discussed) or disk, thereby generating coded digital outputs. The digital read-out is sometimes accomplished by causing the mechanical switch to advance a counter.

The analog input to an analog-digital (AD) converter which uses the electrical technique for encoding must first be converted to a voltage. This conversion is achieved by using some type of transducer (a device which converts energy from one form to another, as from mechanical energy to electrical energy). Some common types of transducers are microphones, loudspeakers, phonograph pickup heads, and synchro systems which use a transmitter as the input device and a control transformer as the output device. The type of transducer used for a specific application depends upon the type of analog information to be converted.

In many computer applications it is necessary to transform an analog input voltage into a form more suitable for decoding. A common method of doing this is to express the magnitude of the analog input with respect to time. Once a period to time versus voltage is available to provide a measure of the magnitude of the analog signal, it then becomes a relatively simple process to convert this voltage-with-respect-to-time data into a digital representation. A given time interval can be summed and fed into the computer as a digital input, or displayed on a counter.

Two commonly used methods of performing analog-to-digital conversion by electrical means are explained below. They differ mainly in the method used to determine the magnitude of the analog input. The first method (called the comparison method) uses a locally generated sawtooth (ramp) voltage as a reference voltage with which the analog voltage is compared. The second method determines the magnitude of the analog input by means of a coding tube.

Comparison Method

The block diagram of figure 11-4 is used to illustrate the comparison method of determining the magnitude of the analog input.

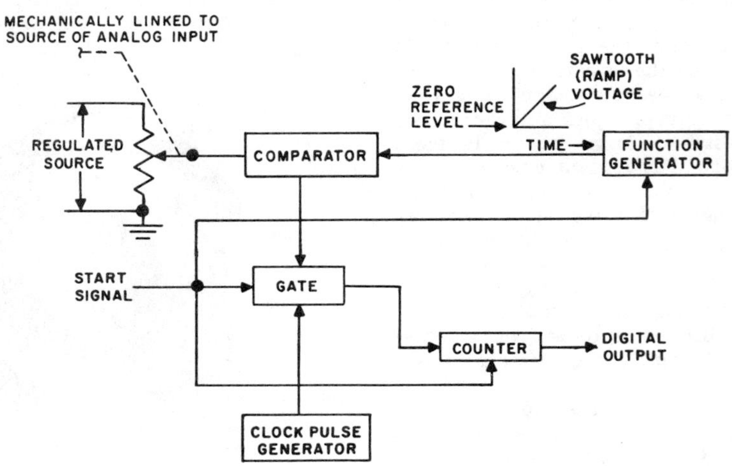

124.102

Figure 11-4.—Determining the magnitude of an analog input using the comparison method.

Generally the arm of the potentiometer is mechanically linked to the device which produces the analog signal, i.e., the float in a tank, the temperature gauge, the pressure gauge, or the servomechanism. Used in this way, the potentiometer and the regulated source voltage serve as a transducer to convert the mechanical input into an electrical output.

Because each position of the potentiometer arm produces a different value of voltage between its arm and ground, each position is unique in its content.

Thus, each position is considered as a specific address called the "analog address." It should be noted that in theory a total possible number of addresses greater than any pre-assigned number can be obtained from the arm of the potentiometer. Thus, no attempt is made to assign specific address numbers to the various positions of the potentiometer arm when it is used in this manner.

A specific address number can be assigned to each position of the potentiometer arm if the movement of the arm across the "pot" is made in a specified number of steps rather than by continuous movement. This, of course, is accomplished only by sacrificing accuracy. If specific steps are used the accuracy of the input data increases as the number of evenly spaced taps or steps across the "pot" increases.

Two inputs are applied to the comparator in figure 11-4. These are: (1) the analog input from the potentiometer, and (2) a linear sawtooth voltage from the function generator. The function generator output is initiated each time a start signal is applied. The start signal also enables the gate circuit.

As long as the analog and function generator inputs to the comparator differ in magnitude, the clock pulse generator will be permitted to transmit pulses at a constant repetition rate through the gate into the digital counting circuits in the counter. When the two inputs to the comparator become equal (as a result of the linearly rising sawtooth) the comparator will generate a stop signal which disables the gate circuit and ends the comparison time interval. The disabled gate circuit blocks the flow of pulses from the clock pulse generator to the counter.

The number of pulses accumulated in the counter during the comparison time interval is proportional to the amplitude of the analog input voltage. The counter indication is the desired digital representation.

Sawtooth generators of the "Bootstrap" type produce output voltages with sufficient linearity to be used as the basic circuit of the function generator. However, linearity is not the only consideration. The slope of the sawtooth voltage must also be controlled since the counter sums the fixed frequency pulses throughout the time interval required for the sawtooth voltage to equal the voltage of the analog sample. Hence, even if the sawtooth were perfectly linear, any variation in its slope would cause the total number of pulses accumulated in a given period to vary accordingly.

The clock pulse generator is a stable pulse oscillator. It may be a form of stabilized multivibrator. The counter may be an arrangement of flip-flops of the type discussed in chapter 4.

Coding Tube Method

The coding tube method uses a specially designed cathode-ray tube (fig. 11-5). The special features of the tube are in the form of a grid, which contains rows of coded slots, and a special sensing element.

The coding tube method of performing analog-to-digital conversion consists of the following operations. The voltage that is to be converted is connected (after amplification) to the vertical deflection plates. A linear sawtooth sweep voltage is connected to the horizontal deflection plates. The connections to the vertical

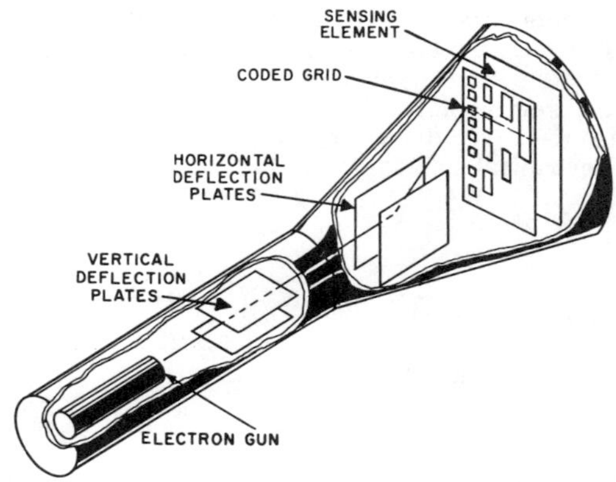

20.320

Figure 11-5.—The cathode-ray coding tube.

and horizontal deflection plates are not shown. The stream of electrons, which is emitted, focused, and accelerated by the electron gun, is positioned vertically on the grid so that it strikes a particular line of slots that correspond to the amplitude of the voltage to be converted.

The linear sawtooth voltage on the horizontal deflection plates causes the beam to be scanned across the line of slots. This action causes a coded image to be developed on the sensing element, which serves as the digital read-out device.

High speed is the main advantage of the coding tube method of conversion. The disadvantages are that its accuracy is limited by the linearity of the scanning beam, and by the beam diameter or spot size. The greater the spot size the less reliable is the result.

DIGITAL-TO-ANALOG CONVERSION

Digital-to-analog conversion, like analog-to-digital conversion, can be accomplished by both mechanical and electrical methods. The purpose of mechanical digital-to-analog conversions is to convert digital information into a mechanical movement or shaft position. Some of the basic principles involved in both methods are explained in the following paragraphs.

MECHANICAL TECHNIQUES

Mechanical digital-to-analog conversion is almost always based upon feedback and comparison principles. A representative example of this action is illustrated in figure 11-6. The digital input is fed into a comparator which produces an input to a servoamplifier and servomotor combination. The servomotor is used to drive any of the many types of mechanical analog-to-digital converters. The digital output of the converter is fed back to the comparator, which operates as the error-detection circuit. As long as the digital output does not equal the input, an error signal will persist. This signal, in turn, causes the servomotor to continue to rotate until the error is reduced to zero.

The shaft or other mechanically driven device at the output of the analog-to-digital converter moves through a certain angle which is the analog representation of the digital input. If a transducer arrangement which uses a potentiometer for read-out purposes is connected to the output shaft, an electrical signal will be produced which represents the same analog quantity.

One form of the comparator which will perform the desired error detection function is illustrated in figure 11-7. Using this arrangement, the difference between the digital or binary input and the present actual instantaneous position of the servo shaft is constantly being converted into an analog signal which is applied to the servoamplifier. The flip-flop (FF) registers store their respective inputs. The subtracting circuit computes the difference and interprets this difference as the existing error. When the analog shaft position corresponds to the digital input (as indicated by a zero difference in the subtracting circuit), the signal to the servoamplifier will be zero and no further shaft rotation will occur.

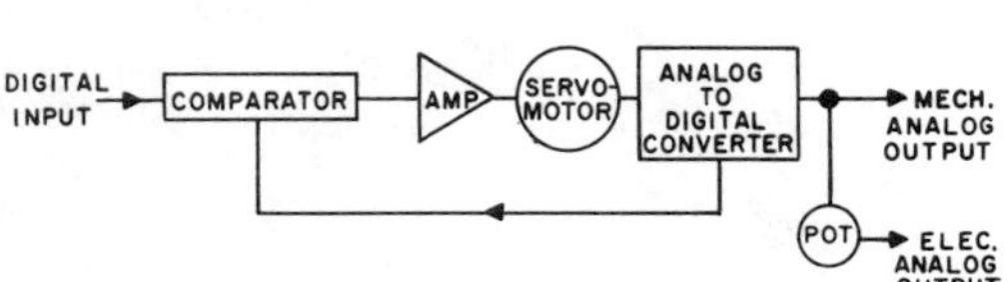

124.104

Figure 11-6.—Block diagram of a mechanical digital-to-analog (DA) converter.

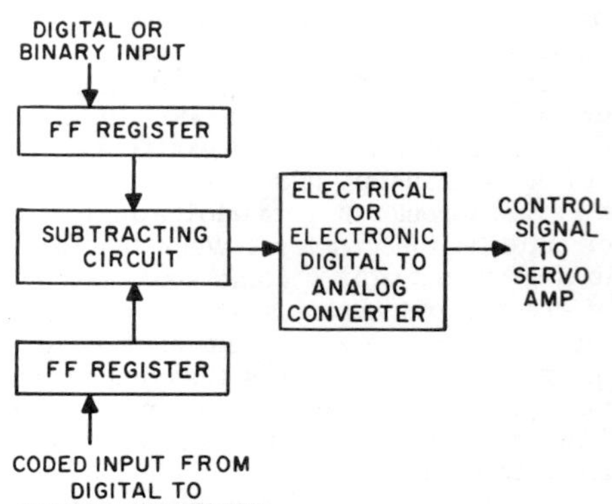

124.105

Figure 11-7.—Representative comparator, block diagram.

ELECTRICAL TECHNIQUES

Many electrical digital-to-analog converters operate on the principle of voltage division using selective relays and a series-parallel network of precision resistors. One of the simplest circuit arrangements based on this principle is shown in figure 11-8.

The binary (digital) input is fed into the bank of flip-flops. The 1 bits in the word stored in the flip-flops cause their respective relays to energize, which results in the closing of the associated contacts. Each of the resistors R_1 through R_4 are precision resistors, i.e., they have very low tolerances. Assuming that each of the parallel branches conducts a given current value when its associated circuit switch is closed, it follows that the value of current through R_L is a function of the number of branches which are placed in the conducting state. If high accuracy is to be maintained, R_L must be kept small in comparison with resistors R_1, R_2, R_3, and R_4, even when these resistors are all connected in parallel. Because R_L is necessarily of low value, the output voltage (E_o across R_L) is low compared to the value of the input voltage (usually of the order of one volt). When higher output voltage levels or higher power outputs are required, the output voltage, E_0, can be amplified. (See Basic Electronics, NP 10087-revised.)

A similar method of performing digital-to-analog conversion involves the use of a series arrangement of resistors connected in a feed-back loop of an operational amplifier circuit. In order to understand this method it is first necessary to discuss the basic

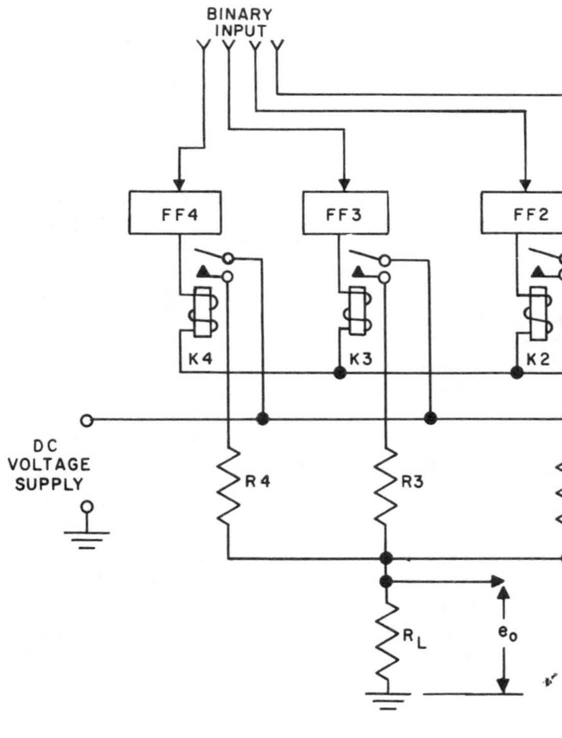

124.106
Figure 11-8.—Digital-to-analog conversion using selective relays and voltage dividers.

principles of the operational amplifier, and also the principle of negative feedback amplifiers as they are used in operational amplifiers.

NEGATIVE FEEDBACK AMPLIFIER

A schematic diagram of an amplifier which uses an electron tube and degenerative (negative) feedback is shown in figure 11-9. The characteristics of this amplifier are largely determined by the amount and type of feedback developed across R_f as will be shown presently.

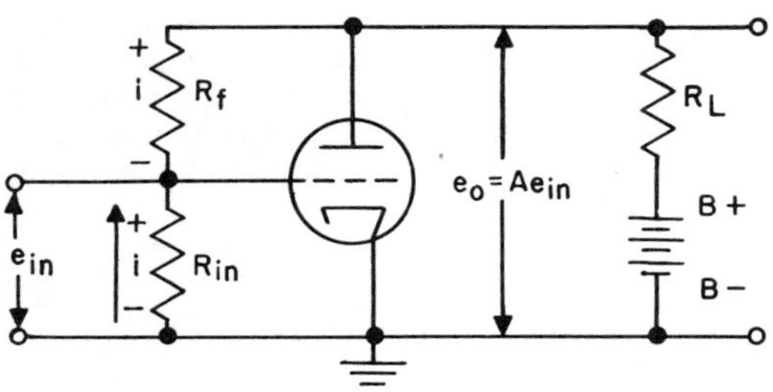

124.107

Figure 11-9.—Schematic diagram of a negative feedback amplifier using an electron tube.

In conventional amplifiers, any attempt to calculate the amount of amplifier voltage gain along a given parameter is complicated by changes in input and output impedances, polarity and amount of feedback, increases or decreases in frequency, and several other factors. The voltage gain in a negative feedback amplifier is determined by the ratio of the feedback resistance (R_f) to the grid resistance (R_g or R_{in}).

In the schematic diagram of figure 11-9, it is shown that the e_{in} represents the input signal voltage which, in this case, is developed across R_{in} between grid and cathode of the tube. Simultaneously, an amplified voltage, which appears between grid and plate of the tube, is developed from plate to ground (across R_L and the B supply in one path, and across R_f and R_{in} in the other). Because of the inherent 180° triode phase shift between grid and plate, the feedback voltage developed across R_{in} is 180° out of phase with the input signal voltage e_{in}. The opposing voltages across this resistor produce the degenerative feedback.

That the gain A of the amplifier is equal to R_f/R_{in} can be shown as follows:

(1) $iR_{in} - iR_f = -AiR_{in}$

(2) $\not{i}R_{in} - \not{i}R_f = -A\not{i}R_{in}$

(3) $\dfrac{R_{in} - R_f}{R_{in}} = -A$

(4) $1 - \dfrac{R_f}{R_{in}} = -A$

Since $\dfrac{R_f}{R_{in}}$ is much larger than 1, the 1 is disregarded, and

(5) $\dfrac{R_f}{R_{in}} = A$

where A = stage gain

and $e_g = iR_{in}$

The stage gain of the transistorized degenerative amplifier in figure 11-10 is calculated in the same way. The series connection of R_{in} with respect to the emitter-base junction and the input signal source permits the emitter-base current to vary only slightly when relatively large signal voltage changes occur at the input. Likewise, the effect of feedback

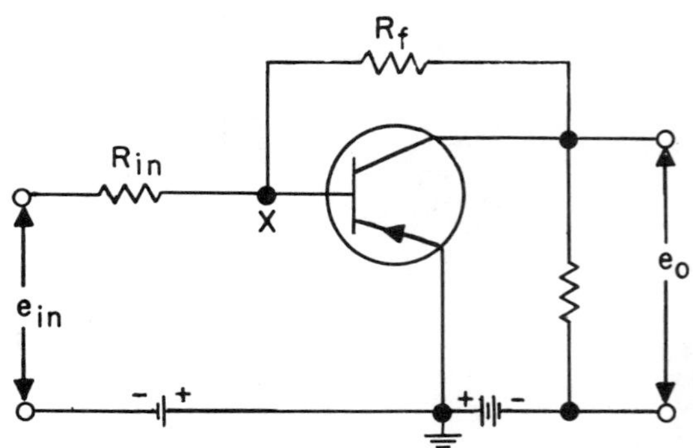

124.108

Figure 11-10.—Schematic diagram of a negative feedback amplifier using a PNP transistor.

current changes through R_{in} (which is very large compared to the forward emitter-base resistance) produces a large controlling effect on the amplifier output.

Also note that the large ohmic value of R_{in} with respect to the emitter-base junction permits point X to maintain only a slight voltage value (negative) to ground.

Feedback and emitter-base currents flowing at point X are relatively high. These factors make point X a point of low impedance, i.e.,

$$Z_x = \frac{e_x}{i_x} \quad \begin{matrix}\text{(low)} \\ \text{(high)}\end{matrix}$$

Because of the large value of R_{in} with respect to the emitter-base resistance, the input current does not change appreciably over wide variations of the input signal amplitude. Thus the input source (as seen from point X) is, in effect, a constant current source. The input impedance is essentially the value of R_{in} and point X is very near ground potential. The circuit will not produce a useful output if point X is maintained at zero volts, since this would mean that the amplifier input is zero. Rather, point X must be maintained at a slight voltage value to ground to permit accurate amplification. The type amplifier just described is frequently used in computers to multiply the DC input by a constant (A), the stage gain.

OPERATIONAL AMPLIFIERS

An operational amplifier is a very high gain direct-coupled feedback amplifier. It may consist of several stages, which, combined, produce output signals several million times the amplitude of the input.

An operational amplifier circuit is arranged so that the input signal is applied with respect to ground and the output signal is taken from a point on the final amplifier which is at zero volts DC with respect to ground. The zero DC level at the output is established by connecting the final amplifier stage across two power sources (fig. 11-11) whose outputs are of opposite polarity to ground. The output terminal is connected to that point on the amplifier which is at the zero volt DC ground potential. It follows that AC output signals alternate above and below the ground reference level.

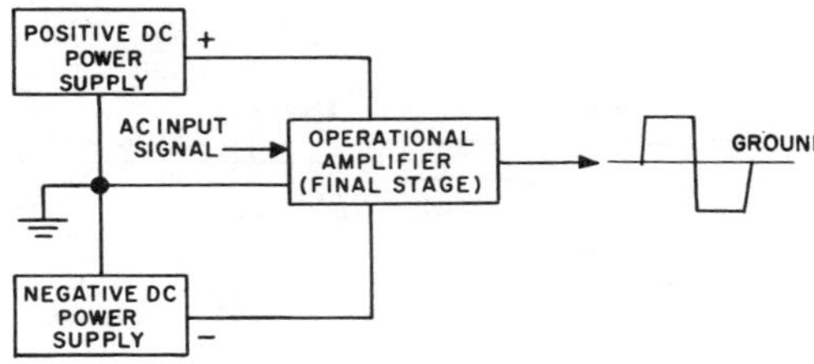

124.109

Figure 11-11.—Basic block diagram of operational amplifier showing method used to obtain DC ground at output.

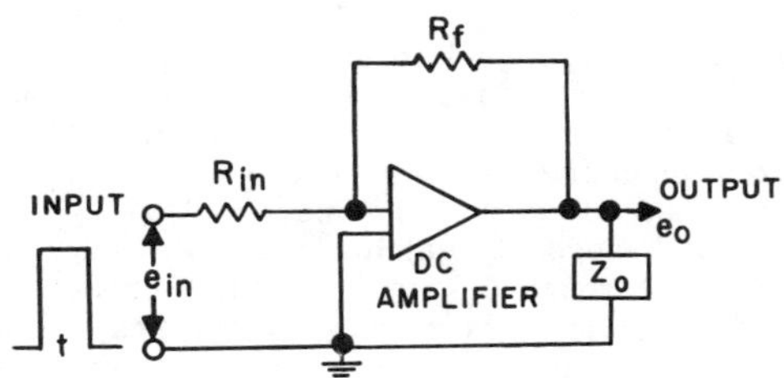

124.110

Figure 11-12.—Operational amplifier using resistive feedback circuit.

An operational amplifier circuit (fig. 11-12) functions as follows. Assume that an input signal, e_{in} (which tends to increase the DC amplifier output current), is applied across the input terminals. The current output from the circuit flows through R_f and the output impedance (Z_o) in parallel. Because R_f is (in general usage) several hundred times the size of R_{in}, and because the current through R_{in} is smaller than the current through R_f, it follows that the voltage across R_f will be many times the voltage across R_{in}. This ratio is a measure of the amplification.

Since the voltage across R_{in} is the input voltage (minus the negligible drop across the emitter-base junction), the ratio of R_f/R_{in} represents the stage gain (A).

An operational amplifier can be used as a Miller sweep generator, or an integrator by replacing the feedback resistor R_f with a capacitor, C, as shown in figure 11-13. Switch, S, is added so that the integrating process can

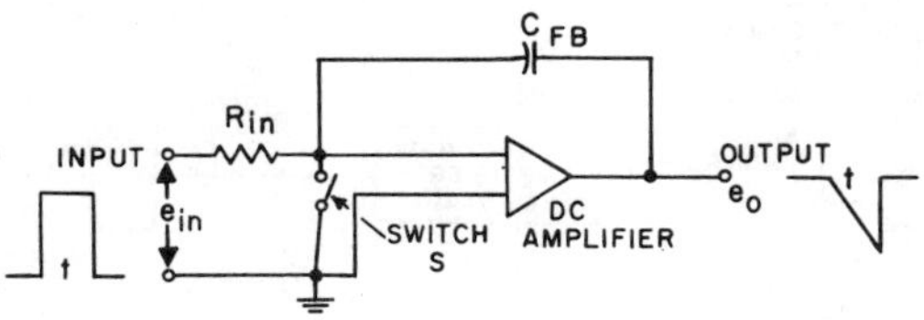

124.111
Figure 11-13.—Operational amplifier using capacitive feedback circuit.

be started and stopped at a desired rate. In practice, switch, S, is replaced by an electronic switching device such as an electron tube or a transistor. The voltage amplifier is a high-gain high-impedance circuit.

The degenerative feedback current through capacitor, C, prevents the amplifier input voltage from changing instantaneously with e_{in}. The combined effects of the input voltage and the negative feedback maintain a constant charging current through C, which, in turn, produces a linear voltage change across this capacitor. The output voltage is proportioned to the integrated input voltage. The slope of the output waveform is dependent upon the times constant R_{in} C_{FB}. Where R_{in} = 1 megohm and C_{FB} = 1 microfarad the time constant is 1 and the scope is linear.

DIGITAL-TO-ANALOG CONVERSION USING THE SERIES RESISTOR METHOD

The circuit in figure 11-14 contains a series array of resistors (R_1 through R_4, of selected sizes) in the feedback loop of an operational amplifier. Each resistor is bypassed by a pair of relay contacts which represent zero (or OFF) in the closed position and one (or ON) in the open position. When all of the contacts are closed there is zero resistance in the feedback path, and the amplifier will not produce a voltage gain. When a 1 binary input is applied across any or all of the relay solenoids, the associated contacts open (as shown) causing series resistances to be added to the feedback loop. The amount of increase in the amplifier gain is in direct proportion to the amount of resistance placed in the feedback loop by the opening of the relay contacts. The voltage, e_o, therefore represents the analog value of a digital input.

THE DIGILOG CIRCUIT

A digilog circuit (sometimes called a decoder) is used to convert digital signals to analog voltages. In effect, it is a translator. It translates the language of digital devices, ("1's" and "0's") into the language of analog devices. These analog voltages are then used to position needles on meters, oscilloscopic sweeps, and/or dots on cathode ray tubes, turn motor shafts, drive analog circuits, etc.

The digilog is composed of a bank of transistor switches and a resistive network known as a "ladder-adder". Figure 11-15 shows a block diagram of one transistor switch and the ladder-adder network. In an actual circuit where several digital inputs are received, a transistor switch is needed for each binary input digit. The transistor switches are opened and closed by the digital signal, allowing either a voltage or ground to be presented to the ladder-adder resistive network. The output of the ladder-adder is the required analog voltage.

DIGILOG TRANSISTOR SWITCH

The purpose of the transistor switche is to supply a voltage to the ladder-adder as determined by the binary value of the digit which controls each switch. There are, of course, many transistor circuit configurations which may be used to accomplish the switching. Generally, the digilog switching circuit will be similar to that shown in figure 11-16. The circuit of figure 11-16 uses a positive reference voltage V_{Ref}, as indicated at the emitter of Q1.

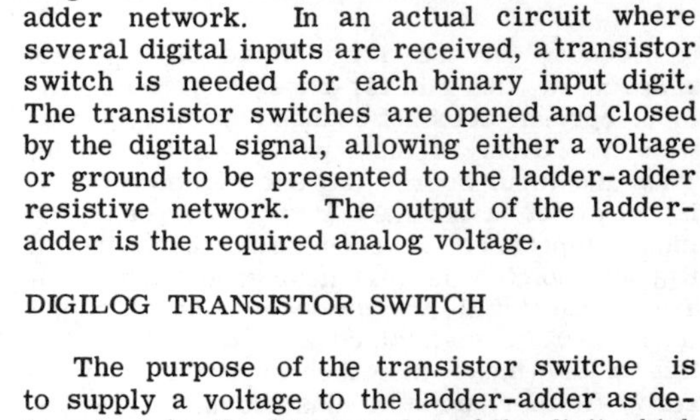

124.112
Figure 11-14.—Digital-to-analog conversion using operational amplifier and a series array of feedback resistor.

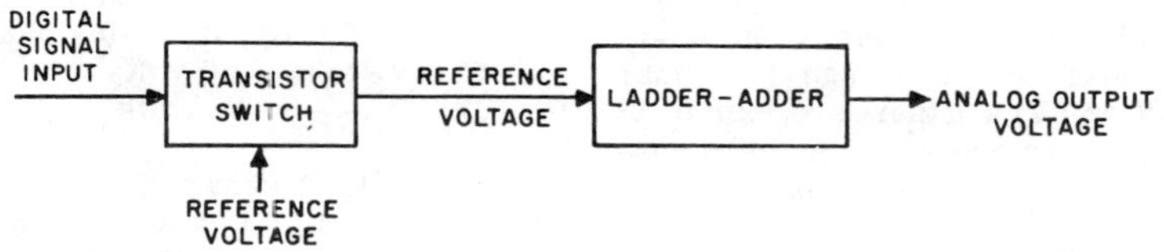

124.113

Figure 11-15.—Block diagram of digilog action.

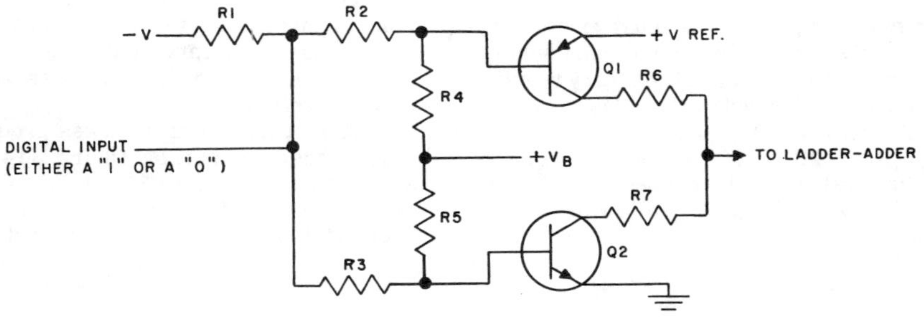

124.114

Figure 11-16.—Digilog transistor switch.

By replacing Q1 with an NPN transistor and Q2 with a PNP transistor and properly biasing the transistors, a negative reference voltage can be switched into the ladder-adder.

As stated earlier, a transistor switch is needed for each binary input digit. For example: A four-digit word requires four transistor switches and a ten-digit word requires ten transistor switches. In figure 11-16 it is assumed that the true or "1" state is represented by a -V at the input and that the false or "0" input state is represented as 0V. With a true (-V) at the digital input terminal, Q1 conducts heavily and Q2 is cut off. Hence, the $+V_{Ref}$ is supplied to the ladder-adder via the low conducting resistance of Q1 in series with R6. When the input is false (0V), Q1 is cut off and Q2 conducts, applying ground to the ladder-adder via the low conducting resistance of Q2 in series with R7.

THE LADDER-ADDER RESISTIVE NETWORK

For purposes of explanation, four transistor switches and a ladder-adder network are illustrated in figure 11-17.

It is important to remember that in a practical application, the digilog can have as many transistor switches as desired and the associated

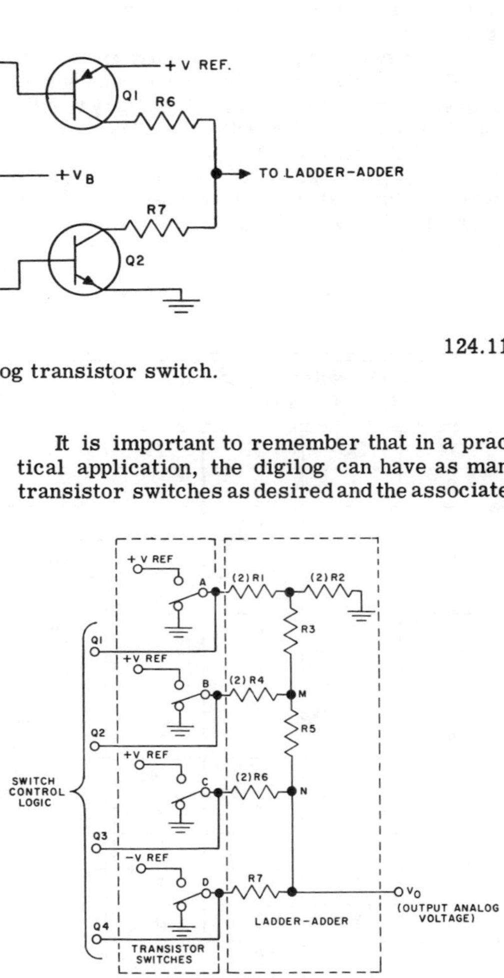

124.115

Figure 11-17.—A four-digit digilog.

ladder-adder network. A four-switch digilog has sixteen possible voltage levels as an output. This is so because the input can be either true or false (-V or 0V) and there are four input switches. Hence, there are 2^4, or sixteen, possible input and output combinations. A ten-switch digilog has 2^{10} or 1024 possible output voltage levels. The greater the number of switches in the digilog, the smaller the incremental difference in the output voltage levels, as will be shown later. For simplification, the transistor switches have been replaced by toggle switches.

Certain basic requirements must be met with regard to relative resistance values and supply voltages in order to produce satisfactory results from the ladder-adder network. These are as follows: Resistors R3 = R5 = R7 and R1 = R2 = R4 = R6 = 2R3. A + V_{Ref} and -V_{Ref} of equal absolute value must be used. To aid in understanding the digilog, the following values are assigned:

A. R3, R5, R7 = 5 K ohms
B. R1, R2, R4, R6 = 10 k ohms
C. +V_{REF} = + 10 volts
D. -V_{REF} = -10 volts

Table 11-2 shows the possible input conditions to the digilog switches, the corresponding position of each switch (either ground or a reference voltage), and the analog output voltage. A positive reference voltage is utilized at switches A, B, and C, and a negative reference voltage for switch D, so that the output voltage, (V_0) can swing from a maximum positive voltage value through zero volts to a maximum negative voltage. In practice though, the digilog can be constructed to vary between any two voltage levels desired.

A few of the output voltages produced at the ladder-adder output of figure 11-17 will be calculated using figure 11-18A, B, C, D, and E. When points A, B, and C are grounded and D is connected to the - 10 volts reference, the

Table 11-2. —Input and Output Levels for Four Digit Digilog

Possible Switch Controlling Input Conditions				Switch Position Due To Input Conditions				Analog Output Voltage
Q4	Q3	Q2	Q1	D	C	B	A	V_0 (volts)
0	0	0	0	gnd	gnd	gnd	gnd	0
0	0	0	1	gnd	gnd	gnd	+10v	+0. 625
0	0	1	0	gnd	gnd	+10v	gnd	+1. 250
0	0.	1	1	gnd	gnd	+10v	+10v	+1. 875
0	1	0	0	gnd	+10v	gnd	gnd	+2. 500
0	1	0	1	gnd	+10v	gnd	+10v	+3. 125
0	1	1	0	gnd	+10v	+10v	gnd	+3. 750
0	1	1	1	gnd	+10v	+10v	+10v	+4. 375
1	0	0	0	-10v	gnd	gnd	gnd	-5. 000
1	0	0	1	-10v	gnd	gnd	+10v	-4. 375
1	0	1	0	-10v	gnd	+10v	gnd	-3. 750
1	0	1	1	-10v	gnd	+10v	+10v	-3. 125
1	1	0	0	-10v	+10v	gnd	gnd	-2. 500
1	1	0	1	-10v	+10v	gnd	+10v	-1. 875
1	1	1	0	-10v	+10v	+10v	gnd	-1. 250
1	1	1	1	-10v	+10v	+10v	+10v	-0. 625

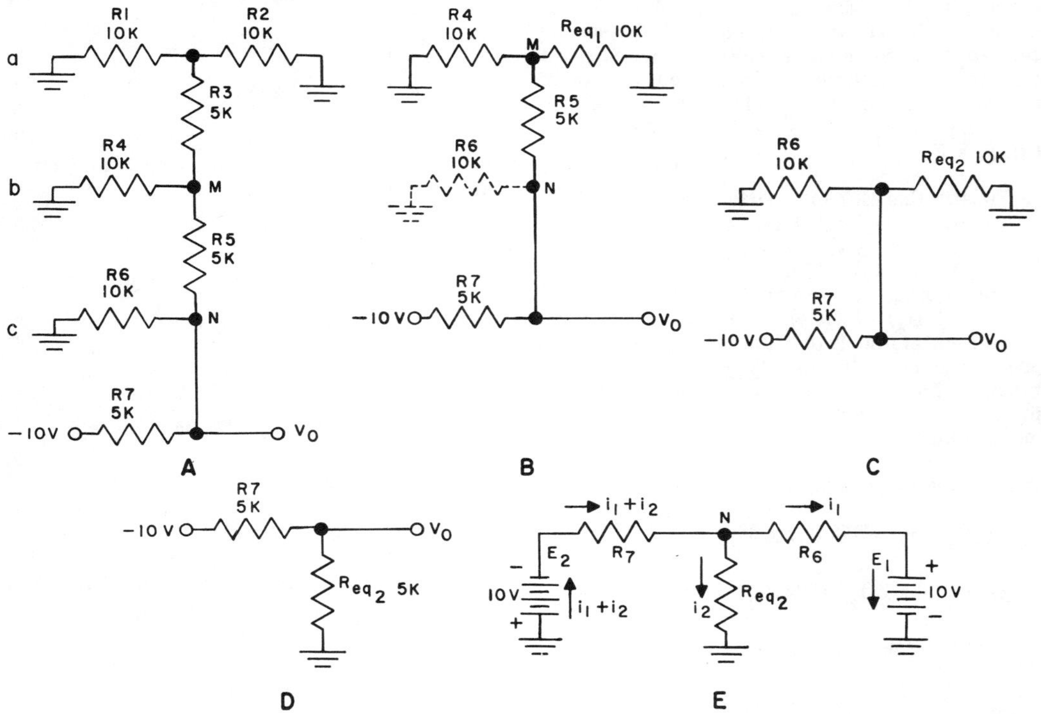

124.116

Figure 11-18.—Analysis of ladder-adder circuit.

circuit equivalent is as illustrated in figure 11-18A. Note that resistors R1 and R2, are in parallel to ground. Hence, R1 and R2 combine into a single 5K resistance in series with R3 (5K) to ground. The resistance from point M to ground is now 5K as illustrated in the equivalent circuit of figure 11-18B.

$R_{eq1} = (R3 + \frac{R1 \times R2}{R1 + R2})$ is in parallel with R4 to ground and the combination is in series with R5. Disregarding R_6, these three resistors (R4, R5, and R_{eq1}) combine to form a new equivalent resistance to ground from point N (fig. 11-18B) which is 10K. This results in $R_{eq2} = (R5 + \frac{R4 \times R_{eq1}}{R4 + R_{eq1}})$ as shown in figure 11-18C.

Resistor R6 and R_{eq2} constitute a parallel combination which results in R_{eq3} (fig. 11-18D) from point N to ground of 5K. This represents the final equivalent of the circuit in figure 11-17 with points A, B, and C grounded and point D connected to a -10v supply. In figure 11-18D, V_0 is -5V which is the maximum negative voltage obtainable from the digilog in figure 11-17.

Now consider another condition which can exist in the circuit of figure 11-17. Leaving point D connected to the -10V reference and points A and B connected to ground, the V_0 will be calculated when point C is connected to the + 10V reference.

From the previous discussion the equivalent circuit will be as shown in figure 11-18E (batteries added for continuity). The output voltage is calculated using simultaneous equations. The current through R6 is arbitrarily referred to as i_1, the current through R_{eq2} is called i_2, and the current through R7 is $i_1 + i_2$ by Kirchhoff's law; the sum of the voltage drops around a closed circuit is equal to the source voltage. (The source voltage applied in a circuit is sometimes the combined voltage of two or more supplies.) Thus (1) $E_{R7} + E_{R6} = E_1 + E_2$ (2) $E_{R7} + E_{Req2} = E_2$ and (3) $E_{R6} - E_{Req2} = E_1$.

Substituting IXR in equation (1)

$$5K(i_1 + i_2) + 10K(i_1) = 20$$

Substituting IXR in equation (2)

$$5K(i_1 + i_2) + 10K(i_2) = 10$$

Substituting IXR in equation (3)

$$10K(i_1) - 10K(i_2) = 10$$

(Note that the two voltage supplies tend to produce currents through R_{eq2} in opposite directions. Thus the voltage developed across R_{eq2} is the resultant voltage established by the opposing supplies.)

Simplifying the equations

$$5K(i_1 + i_2) + 10K(i_1) = 20$$

$$5K(i_1) + 5K(i_2) + 10K(i_1) = 20$$

$$15K(i_1) + 5K(i_2) = 20 \qquad \text{(a)}$$

$$5K(i_1 + i_2) + 10K(i_2) = 10$$

$$5K(i_1) + 5K(i_2) + 10K(i_2) = 10$$

$$5K(i_1) + 15K(i_2) = 10 \qquad \text{(b)}$$

Using equations (a) and (b); (where equation (b) is multiplied by 3), subtract 3(b) from (a) as follows:

$$15K(i_1) + 5K(i_2) = 20 \qquad \text{(a)}$$

$$15K(i_1) + 45K(i_2) = 30 \qquad 3\text{(b)}$$

$$-40K(i_2) = -10$$

$$i_2 = \frac{-10}{-40K}$$

$$i_2 = .00025 \text{ ampere}$$

Solving for current (i_1)

$$15K(i_1) + 5K(1/4 \text{ ma}) = 20\text{v}$$

$$15K(i_1) = 20\text{v} - 1.25\text{v}$$

$$i_1 = \frac{18.75\text{v}}{15K}$$

$$i_1 = .00125 \text{ ampere}$$

Using Ohm's law and substituting in equation (2)

$$E_{R7} + E_{Req2} = E_2$$

$$5K(i_1 + i_2) + 10K(i_2) = 10\text{v}$$

$$5 \times 10^3 (.00125 + .00025) + 10 \times 10^3 (.00025) = 10\text{v}$$

$$5 \times 10^3 (.00150) + 10 \times 10^3 (.00025) = 10\text{v}$$

$$5 \times 10^3 (150 \times 10^{-5}) + 10 \times 10^3 (25 \times 10^{-5}) = 10 \text{ v}$$

$$750\text{v} \times 10^{-2} + 250\text{v} \times 10^{-2} = 10\text{v}$$

$$7.5\text{v} + 2.5\text{v} = 10\text{v}$$

$$7.5\text{v} - 10\text{v} = -2.5\text{v}$$

Thus, $E_{Req2} = 2.5V$ when point D (fig. 11-17) is connected to the -10V reference, points A and B are grounded, and point C is connected to the +10V reference.

Leaving point D (fig. 11-17) connected to the -10V reference, C to the +10V reference, and A to ground, the V_0 will be -1.25V when point B is connected to the +10V reference (calculation not shown). With all points (A, B, C, and D) connected to reference voltages, the V_0 is -.625V which is the minimum negative voltage output available. If all inputs to the ladder-adder are at ground, V_0 is zero volts. Minimum positive voltage output is obtained when point A is connected to the +10V reference and points B, C, and D are grounded. Maximum positive output voltage is obtained when points A, B, and C are connected to the +10V reference, and point D is grounded.

Chapter 12

DIAGNOSTIC MAINTENANCE ROUTINES

As discussed in chapter 8, a routine or program is a series of instructions which control the operations of a computer. Each instruction is used to cause some action which is part of the overall task that the computer must perform. Therefore, an instruction may be considered to be the basic building block of a computer program.

Computers can be given an overall check by means of maintenance programs. A maintenance program provides a thorough and rapid method for you to detect failure in a special portion of a computer. This type of overall maintenance check is very flexible and efficient. The programs use the same type tape, memory, computing, and drum circuits as operational programs.

MAINTENANCE PROGRAMS

Maintenance programs are divided into three main classes: reliability, diagnostic, and utility programs.

RELIABILITY PROGRAMS

Reliability programs are used in both preventive and corrective maintenance tests to detect circuit failures rapidly and to discover failures that may occur only under particular operating conditions. Examples of troubles that are not evident at all times are failures that appear at specific repetition rates or for certain combinations of bits. In order to detect such failures, it is necessary to use reliability programs which check logical operation, paths of information flow, timing, ability of the computer to perform all functions, executions of instructions, etc.

Reliability programs check either the logical functioning of an entire computer section or the logical functioning of individual circuit groups in a section. Whichever method i used, it is assumed that associated circuit which are not directly checked by the progran are in satisfactory operation condition. Thus these programs can be considered to fall intc two categories, first order and second order. First-order reliability programs check the operation of assemblies or circuit groups, such as registers and counters. Second-order programs are designed to check basic circuits and components. In most cases, first-order programs are merely a combination of several second-order programs.

A reliability program provides a good-or-bad indication regarding the ability of the tested computer section or circuit to perform its operating functions. For example, consider a reliability program that checks the switching time for relays within a specific section of a computer. As long as the switching time of the relays is within normal limits, the reliability program will indicate satisfactory operation. When the switching time is excessive however, there is an indication that maintenance is required. If the program runs successfully, there are no failures within the checked area. In the event of a failure indication, the failure may be in the area being checked or in another area that has been assumed free of trouble. Diagnostic maintenance programs should then be used to locate the source of trouble.

DIAGNOSTIC PROGRAMS

To be efficient, maintenance programs for diagnostic applications must enable you to narrow the area of a failure down to the smallest possible number of circuits. This can be accomplished by employing increasing-area, decreasing-area, overlapping-area, and large-area checks. The most effective method will depend on the particular type of computer being tested.

Increasing-Area Check

A maintenance program using the increasing-area check initially tests a small number of circuits. If a check indicates that all tested circuits are operating properly, successive checks are run in which progressively greater numbers of circuits are added. By this method, circuits which are found to be operating correctly are used to check other circuits. This process is continued until all circuits that can be checked by a maintenance program have been tested.

Decreasing-Area Check

When this method is used to find a trouble, a large number of circuits are initially checked by the maintenance program. If trouble is detected in a large area, additional checks are made of successively smaller portions of the equipment until the stages affected by the failure are not included in the test area. You should then be able to determine which stages are defective. If the check of a large area reveals no error, the remaining large areas of the equipment are checked until the trouble is detected. In many cases, trouble can be located more rapidly by this procedure than by the increasing-area method.

Overlapping-Area Check

Another efficient method of locating trouble to within a small section of the equipment is the overlapping-area check. The routines of this type of maintenance program overlap each other. Thus, a failure can be located at the overlapping portions of routines which indicate the presence of trouble.

Large-Area Check

You may not be able to program an effective maintenance test for a small section of a computer. In such cases, a maintenance program can be used only to determine the general area in which the malfunction occurs. When the general area is located, conventional troubleshooting will be necessary to find the circuit in which a failure has occurred.

UTILITY PROGRAMS

Utility programs are used as aids for both operation and maintenance programming procedures. This type of program is used to print out information from magnetic cores, magnetic drums, or other storage devices within the computer memory section. It is also used to transfer maintenance programs from punched cards or magnetic tape into the computer memory section. Utility tracing programs provide a printed record of the contents of various computer registers to enable you to follow maintenance program operations.

USE OF MAINTENANCE PROGRAMS IN TROUBLESHOOTING

The use of maintenance programs as a means of locating malfunctions must be considered from the system-and computer-levels. The system, of course, includes the computer and peripheral devices, and may sometimes include more than one computer. Because of the wide variety of equipments used to form a data processing system, it is not possible to give specific details concerning system troubleshooting and maintenance. The same is true at the computer level. Thus, the following discussion treats the use of maintenance programs as may be common to broadest usage.

SYSTEM-LEVEL TESTS

The system-level diagnostic test is a comprehensive program which checks the peformance of the system equipments against design specifications. This program has the following design goals:

1. To subject each piece of equipment in the system to comprehensive diagnostic maintenance routines. These routines are designed to test the utmost in performance from each device in the entire system.

2. To subject the entire equipment complex to sustained system-level operation under the direction of a control computer. This system-level type operation:

   a. simulates normal system operation;

   b. makes full use of central control facility (if used); and,

   c. provides for the overall direction and monitoring of the individual equipment tests.

3. To provide for random operation of the entire equipment complex. This is accomplished by:

a. using a random number to influence selection of tests;

b. developing random configurations of computers and equipments; and,

c. permitting random and asynchronous timing relationships between tests running simultaneously.

4. To provide a built-in System-Level Bootstrap program which elevates the system from an inactive status to full operation capacity. Besides allowing for automatic operation of the system diagnostic test, the bootstrap should demonstrate the ability of the system control to recover in case of loss of the program in a system computer.

To Achieve These Objectives:

1. The design specifications and functional characteristics of each piece of peripheral equipment must be analyzed and comprehensive diagnostic maintenance routines written to verify that the system will perform to these specifications. These routines are usually developed by the programmers and field engineers employed by the manufacturer. Generally, routines allow the equipment tested to be on any input/output channel and, if more than a single unit is connected to a channel, the routines check all units.

Detailed programs should be available to check the control, arithmetic, and storage sections of each of the system computers. These programs must be capable of determining whether the separate computers in the systems are performing to all specifications and are capable of complete system-level operation.

2. The entire equipment complex must be analyzed as a system and then a general system operational plan, called the master control program, should be devised. This master control program simulates normal system operation while it submits computers and separate devices to comprehensive maintenance routines. A bootstrap reads in peripheral equipment parameter cards, locates the master tape, and reads in the master control program. Under direction of the master control program the control computer schedules, directs, and summarizes computer task assignments. These task assignments are generated in a random fashion on the basis of computer, channel, and available equipment. The master control program also provides a complete system monitoring service, and serves as the interface (matching point) between the operator and the system.

COMPUTER-LEVEL TESTS

The computer-level program consists of a sequence of operations that will indicate whether or not each section of the computer is operating correctly. It will generally localize a particular malfunction to a large subsection, such as the control, memory, arithmetic, or input/output units. The diagnostic programs are designed to localize trouble within a smaller element, perhaps down to the level of a particular stage or module. There will usually be separate diagnostic programs for each section of the computer.

It is essential for you to understand that maintenance routines are programs in the fullest sense of the word. They consist of an ordered sequence of instructions to the machine. They involve only the normal operations and components that the machine would use to solve any problem. They are inserted into the machine in exactly the same manner as any other program. They operate by checking the complete capabilities of the machine. Actually, maintenance programs exert somewhat more stringent requirements on the computer than most problem solving programs, since they have been designed to give the machine a thorough "workout".

The basic purpose of test and diagnostic programs is to execute certain operations and compare the result with precalculated "correct" answers. The program automatically executes calculations and comparisons. The machine is programmed to stop when the results of any calculation do not agree with the precalculated result.

A program step counter is usually used to indicate the step in the program at which the machine stops. Assume that you know which circuits are used to perform each step of the program, the instruction in the program step counter (indicating where the program stopped) is an indication to you concerning the region in which the circuits are not functioning properly.

The computing-comparison process is programmed by setting the correct answer into a register, programming a problem that should produce the correct answer, subtracting one of the two answer registers from the other, and then sensing the results. The machine must also be programmed to proceed to the next step if the results are zero, and to stop if they are not.

Comparison testing can be used to check data transfer operations, arithmetic operations, and input/output operations.

Maintaining Optimum Equipment Performance

Digital computer performance is affected by many factors. The operation of each circuit, section, and input/output device is so interrelated that overall system tests are the only way to determine if the computer is operating properly. Unlike a radar system, for example, which can operate at reduced efficiency, a digital computer is a yes-no device. The computer is either operating properly or it is malfunctioning. Optimum performance of a digital computer is the only level of performance from which accurate results can be achieved.

The complexity of the digital computer makes it necessary to test every circuit. A single malfunction or the simultaneous malfunctioning of a few sections of the computer cause tremendous time losses and may be very difficult to localize. Consequently, extensive testing is necessary to localize malfunctioning areas and to maintain optimum equipment performance.

MARGINAL CHECKING

Marginal checking is a preventive-maintenance technique that is used for Navy and commercial computer equipment to detect the decrease in reliability of circuit parts due to aging. Aging circuit parts almost invariably change in value, current-handling capabilities, or voltage limitations. Generally, the changes brought about by aging are gradual, and you will not notice any variation in the normal operation of the equipment. For maximum equipment reliability, parts that are beginning to deteriorate must be detected and replaced before a failure occurs.

Marginal checking is usually controlled by the operator or a maintenance program. The program directs the computer to perform the normal computer operations of addition, subtraction, etc., while the program or operator vary certain circuit parameters about their normal values. In this way, the computer is made to perform normal functions under adverse operating conditions.

To accomplish marginal checking, certain operating conditions are changed from their normal values. Since circuit part values normally change with age, the variations that can be introduced before a failure occurs become less as the parts age. The amount of variation from the normal value, that can be introduced before equipment failure occurs is called the margin of reliability of the circuit or group of circuits being tested. If the margin is regularly checked and its gradual decrease noted, as shown in figure 12-1, the time of circuit failure can be anticipated. Three methods of changing operating conditions for marginal checking are as follows:

1. Variation of DC supply voltages.
2. Variation of circuit values.
3. Variation of master clock output.

DC SUPPLY VOLTAGE VARIATION

The most versatile method of marginal checking is by variation (excursion) of the DC supply voltage for one or more circuits. Causing an excursion of a circuit' sDC supply voltage will simulate the changes that normally result from the aging of circuit parts. Gradually increasing the excursion of the supply voltage to a circuit will eventually result in a circuit failure, regardless of the circuit's age. Figure 12-2 shows the relationship between circuit reliability and the excursion voltage required to cause a circuit failure. The magnitude of the voltage excursion necessary to cause a failure is called the margin of the voltage on the circuit. This margin becomes smaller as the circuit ages.

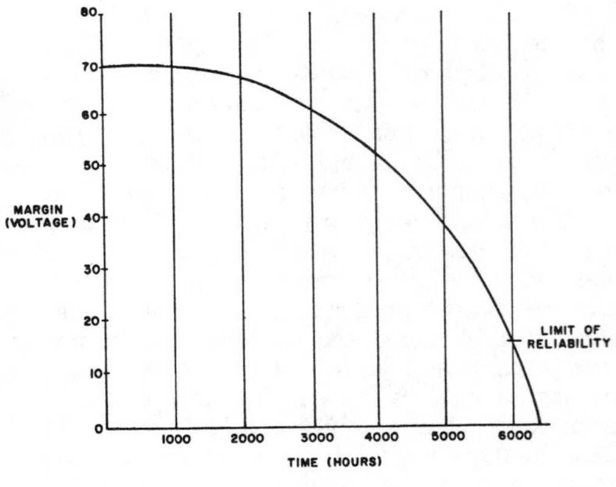

124.230
Figure 12-1.—Typical circuit part, life curve.

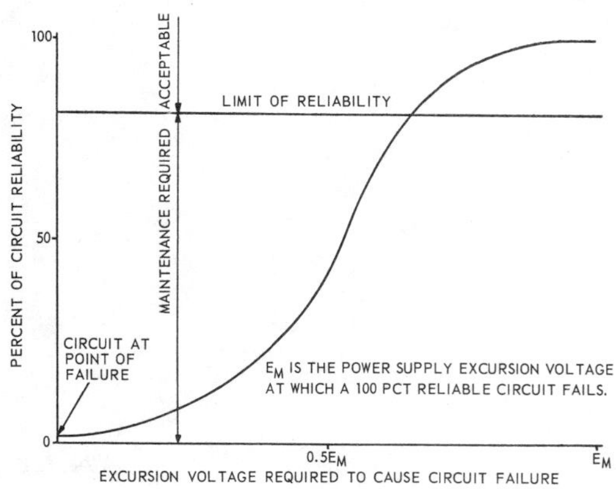

124.231

Figure 12-2.—Circuit reliability versus excursion voltage required to cause circuit failure.

When the circuit fails at the normal operation voltage, the margin is zero.

As long as the possibility of circuit failure is low the circuit is considered satisfactory. For the example shown in figure 12-2, the circuit reliability of 80 percent is acceptable. When the voltage excursion necessary to cause a circuit failure decreases so that the circuit reliability is below the 80-percent value, maintenance must be performed to replace parts or an entire plug-in assembly. The level at which the circuit reliability is acceptable must be determined for each circuit or circuit group that is tested by marginal-checking methods.

A life curve for a circuit can be drawn as shown in figure 12-1; you can then estimate the time for a circuit to age to the point where failure is expected. Maintenance will be performed on the equipment when the marginal check indicates that a failure will probably occur before the next marginal check is due. Such a life curve is useful for maintenance application when the margin limit is approached gradually during each successive testing period.

Certain circuits will not have useful life curves because they age gradually but fail suddenly. These circuits may operate for long periods with practically no change in margin, and then the margin drops sharply in a short period of time. Since no appreciable decrease in margin takes place before the circuit fails, it is difficult to determine when a faulty part should be replaced, and marginal checks are not effective. The circuits for which useful life curves cannot be established, however, represent only a small percentage of general computer circuits. Most circuits have life curves that enable you to determine the time at which a circuit part must be replaced to prevent failure during computer operating time.

CIRCUIT PART VALUE VARIATION

Failure of circuit parts can be anticipated by periodically simulating the aging of the parts. Aging can be simulated by changing resistor, capacitor, or inductor values of a circuit and noting the effects of such changes. This can be done when adjustable electrical parts are included in the circuits to be tested. By periodically measuring the amount of change necessary to cause circuit failure, and by determining how much normal component aging will produce such a change, it is possible to establish the time at which a part must be replaced to prevent circuit failure before the next scheduled test.

MARGINAL CHECKING OF FLIP-FLOP COUNTER

Figure 12-3 represents a circuit that can be selected by a maintenance program for marginal checking. The operation of this circuit is such that successive pulses place a "1" in FF1, transfer it to FF2, and then clear both flip-flop stages.

During the marginal checking operation, an excursion is applied to the supply voltage line of FF1. Assume that at some voltage value the computer senses that a "1" was not transferred to FF2. The excursion is stopped and the margin noted. To determine which stage has failed, you might first make voltage and resistance checks of the circuit parts of FF1. If this check indicates the FF1 is functioning correctly, it is possible that the output pulse from gate AG1 is so small that a slight change in the supply voltage applied to FF1 causes the circuit to fail. It is also possible that gate AG2 has aged to the point where any decrease in the signal output level of FF1 will result in failure of the pulse to be transferred to FF2.

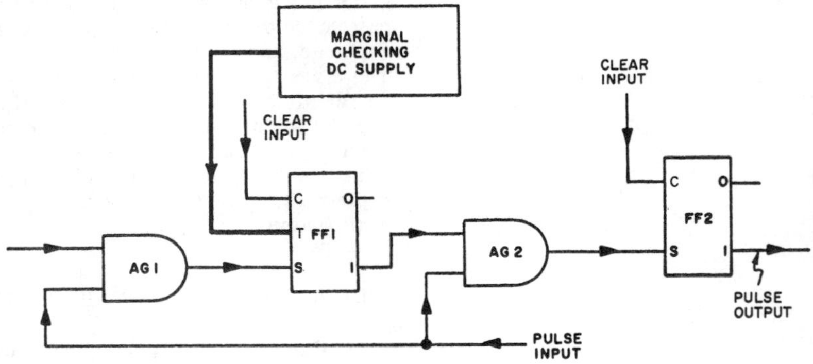

124.232

Figure 12-3.—Typical circuit selected for marginal checking, logic diagram.

MARGINAL CHECKING UNITS

Marginal checking units for variable supply voltage applications include a voltage-regulator unit, relays to connect the test voltage to circuits, and control circuits necessary to initiate marginal checking. When high currents must be furnished by the regulator, an amplidyne may be used to provide a variable DC supply voltage. This device provides a well-regulated output voltage that can be accurately controlled over a wide positive-to-negative range.

A simplified block diagram of marginal checking units is shown in figure 12-4. The relays, which are controlled by maintenance programs, can connect any one of three circuit groups to the marginal-checking voltage regulator. Circuit group A represents circuits that cannot be effectively tested by this method; therefore, it is not connected to a relay in the marginal checking circuit.

DEBUGGING A PROGRAM

After a coded program has been written out completely and the manuscript reviewed carefully, the program must be put on some input medium for loading into the computer. Once the program has been stored in the computer in binary form, either directly from the input medium or by means of some translation, the computer is ready to execute the program. If the program is lengthy, it is likely the coded program, as stored, has errors. Three common types of errors are:

1. Tape preparation errors made in the program for input.

2. Coding errors, such as listing incorrect or incomplete addresses, transposition of digits in the operand address or operation codes, and transcription errors.

3. Logical errors: incomplete or erroneous method used to obtain the solutions.

Debugging is the term applied to the process of locating errors in a program and correcting them. Debugging a program usually involves a series of trial runs of the program on the computer. Each time the program fails to run properly, the failure must be analyzed, and the error corrected. Frequently one can immediately discover the error, correct it manually from the console, and proceed with trial runs. At other times the detection of errors is more difficult and requires a thoughtful reconsideration of the program, keeping in mind any clues which may have been provided as to the origin of the error during the run.

The methods that can be used to debug a program vary depending on the nature of the programs, the service routines available, the availability of computer time, and personal preference of the individual for one procedure over another. The following discussion suggests possible patterns to follow in debugging.

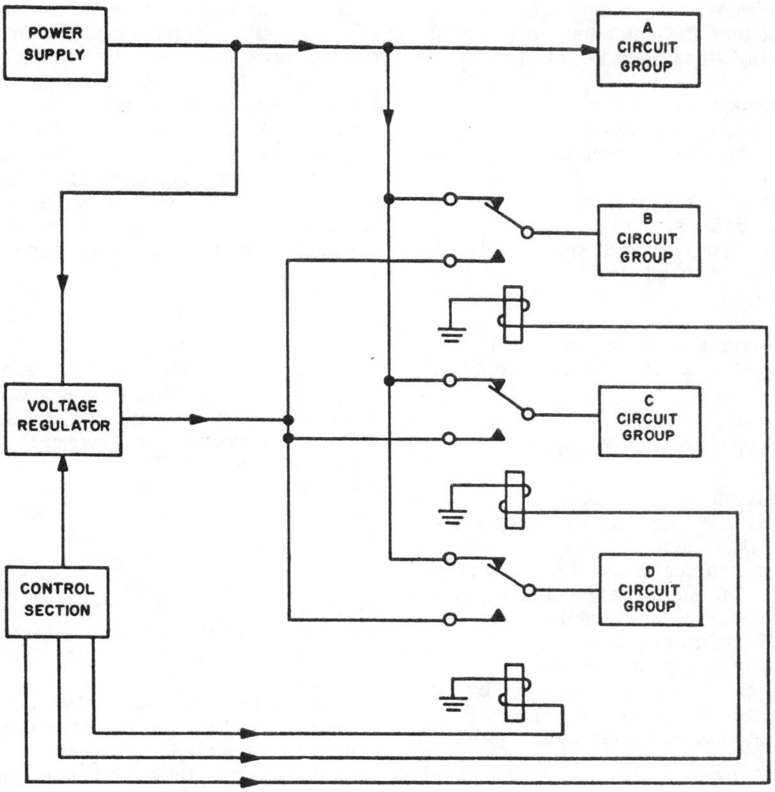

124.233

Figure 12-4.—Marginal checking units, simplified block diagram.

PAPER TAPE PREPARATION ERRORS

Paper tape errors can be minimized by systematic checking of all input tapes before their information is read into the computer. The usual method used to prepare input tapes is as follows:

Step 1. Use the typewriter or teletype equipment to punch tape from the coder's manuscript.

Step 2. Discard the resulting typed manuscript from the typewriter.

Step 3. Prepare a new typed manuscript from the punched paper tape.

Step 4. Compare the typed manuscript with the coder's manuscript to detect errors in punching.

Step 5. Correct all detected punching errors, and prepare a new tape.

Step 6. Obtain from the corrected punched tape a new manuscript which should be retained by the coder to use while debugging.

MANUAL DEBUGGING

Manual debugging is the process used to locate errors in a program by controlling the operations of the program from the console and visually checking these operations as they occur and indicate on the control panel. Although manual debugging does not make for efficient use of computer time, it can, if done correctly, reduce the overall time required to debug a program because of the versatility afforded to the programmer. In preparing a finished program that can be inserted into the computer in machine code, the following steps must be taken:

Step 1. Analyze the entire problem.

Step 2. Construct the flow diagram which shows the general computational steps to be taken.

Step 3. Create the program written in terms of computer instructions.

Step 4. If the program in Step 3 is coded in octal, the program is ready for execution after being put on the paper tape and loaded into the computer.

Step 5. Perform the debugging of the program by means of trial runs on the computer.

PREVENTIVE MAINTENANCE

Preventive maintenance for computer equipment is basically the same as for other electrical equipment; it consists of inspection, cleaning, preservation, lubrication, and performance checks. However, a unique feature of computer preventive maintenance is that you can use reliability programs to quickly determine whether a computer is operating properly. In some computers marginal checks can be controlled by the reliability program, or performed manually to detect deterioration of computer parts before a failure occurs.

Because of the extensive amount of wiring in large computers, you should carefully inspect wiring and cabling. Check the wires for loose or broken lacing, and frayed insulation. Check the cables and connectors for improper placement that might subject them to strains or kinks. Inspect the connectors and wires for burned or charred parts, dirt, cracks, and breaks.

RELAYS AND SWITCHES

Inspect relays to see that they are securely mounted, that the contacts are not pitted, that the springs have sufficient tension, that the armature does not stick, and that there are no signs of overheating and corrosion. You can check the action of the armature by operating the relay manually. Relay contacts can be examined with the aid of a flashlight and a mirror. Avoid bending the springs, and do not open sealed relays.

Inspect switches for loose mountings and connections. Examine the contacts for dirt, pitting, and corrosion. Test the action of the switches and see that they operate without binding. In gang and wafer switches, see that the movable blade makes good contact with the stationary member. Make sure that the stationary contact leaves spread as the movable blade slides into them. Some switches have contacts that are impossible to reach without damaging the switch assembly. Check these switches for defective mechanical action and looseness of mountings and connections.

Cleaning

Clean the exteriors of relays and switches carefully. If the connections are dirty, clean them with trichloroethylene. If it is necessary to remove covers from relays or switches, make sure that no dirt, lint, or other undesirable material is present that might get into the contacts. You can remove dust and lint from a switch or relay with a soft-bristled brush.

There are various types of contacts in the relays used in a computer. For cleaning purposes they are divided into hard-surfaced contacts, made of palladium or platinum and soft-surfaced contacts, which are either silver or silverplated.

Clear hard-surfaced relay contacts, when necessary, by using a flat blade in a burnishing tool. Clean the blade by wiping it with a lintfree cloth moistened with trichloroethylene, and then move the blade two or three times between the relay contacts to brighten them. Open contacts can be pressed gently together with the fingers or an orange stick to apply pressure against the blade of the burnisher. Closed contacts will usually apply enough pressure against the blade of the burnisher. Therefore, you can open the relay armature manually, insert the blade of the burnishing tool between the contacts to be cleaned, release the relay armature, and burnish.

NOTE: Avoid excessive burnishing. When too much of the contact metal is removed, the contact movement is altered and readjustment is necessary. Separate contacts carefully, when necessary, and use care never to bend the springs.

If burnishing does not correct the contact trouble, deposit a few drops of trichloroethylene, with a toothpick, on the contacts. Before the solvent has had a chance to dry, add a few more drops to flush away dirt loosened by the first application. Allow the solvent to dry on the contacts, and then burnish the contacts as described above to remove any remaining residue. Always burnish the contacts after cleaning with trichloroethylene.

Clean solid-silver contacts by inserting a strip of hard-surfaced bond paper between the contacts and press them lightly together. Repeat with fresh strips of paper until the contact surfaces are clean. If this does not adequately clean the contacts, apply trichloroethylene as described above, and again polish them with a paper strip.

Silver-plated relay contacts are ordinarily not cleaned. However, if such maintenance is necessary, they are cleaned in the same manner as for solid-silver contacts. Extreme care must be taken not to wear away the thin silver plate.

NOTE: Never use newspaper or any soft paper, emery cloth, or highly abrasive material such as coarse sandpaper to clean relay or switch contacts.

MAGNETIC DRUM UNITS

To eliminate noise which may be generated by the rotating drum, you must periodically inspect the static grounding brush that is mounted at the end of the drum assembly. If the brush wears to less than half its original length, you should replace it. After a brush has been replaced, check to make sure that there is low resistance between the end plate of the rotor and the drum unit. This check will assure you that the brush is seated properly in the holder and is making good electrical contact.

The drum rotor, drive motor, bolt, and pulleys are all subject to mechanical wear during normal operation; therefore, they must be regularly inspected and maintained. Check the drum drive motor pulley for tightness. An indication of a loose pulley is an accumulation of belt rubber on the pulley and pulley guard. If the pulley is allowed to remain loose, the belt will be chafed and its life shortened.

TAPE DRIVE UNITS

Many digital computers include tape handling equipment. This equipment must be cleaned, lubricated, and periodically checked to ensure proper operation. Daily maintenance includes cleaning the head assembly at the beginning of each day's operation and running a short reliability maintenance program, if the computer has this feature.

Weekly maintenance may include the cleaning of items such as the friction drive clutch and the air filters. You should check the machine's forward and reverse transfer time, the high-speed rewind, creeping of the tape reel, and the tape break circuitry. You may also be able to check the ability of the equipment to reproduce test pulses, to measure the tape speed, and to measure the moving coil and erase coil currents. A more comprehensive reliability maintenance program than is used for the daily check can then be run to determine whether error-free operation can be achieved for a period of 15 minutes.

MAGNETIC TAPE

Dust and dirt can reduce the intensity of the reading and recording pulses by increasing the gap between the tape and the head. Therefore, you should take care of tape in the following manner:

1. Keep tape in a dustproof container whenever it is not in use on a tape unit.
2. While the tape is on the machine, keep the container closed and store it where it is not exposed to dust or dirt.
3. Store tapes in some type of cabinet that is elevated from the floor and away from sources of paper or card dust. This should minimize the transfer of dust from the outside of the containers to the tape reel during loading and unloading operations.
4. Do not use the top of tape units as a working area. Placing materials on top of the units may expose the tape to heat and dust from the blowers in the unit.
5. When identifying tape reels, use a material that can be removed without leaving a residue. Adhesive stickers, that can be easily applied and removed, are satisfactory. Never alter a label identification by means of an eraser, since particles from the eraser may come in contact with the tape.
6. Inspect tape containers periodically and remove any dust by washing with a regular household detergent.
7. When necessary to clean tape, gently wipe it with a clean, lint-free cloth moistened with an approved cleaning fluid, such as trichloroethylene.

Recorded information normally comes very close to the edge of a tape. Therefore, for proper operation, the edges of the tape must be free from nicks and kinks. To accomplish this, observe the following precautions:

1. When you remove a tape reel from a recorder, handle the reel near the hub whenever possible. If there is resistance in removing the reel, press it from the rear with your hands as near to the hub as possible. Under no circumstances should the reel be racked by grasping the outer edge.
2. Avoid throwing or dropping reels, and do not make contact with the exposed edge of the tape. Dropping a reel can easily damage both the reel and the tape. The use of a reel and tape after the reel has been dropped is usually unsatisfactory. Therefore, never throw or mishandle reels, even while they are in their containers.
3. When mounting reels on the recorder, push them firmly against the stop on the mounting hub to ensure good alignment.
4. When placing the tape on the takeup reel, carefully align the tape to prevent damaging the edge on the first few turns.
5. If a tape break occurs, wind the resulting pieces onto two smaller reels. Splicing is not recommended unless it is necessary to make a temporary splice to recover information.

Magnetic tape is sensitive to changes in humidity and temperature. Recommendations for tape storage are as follows:

1. If possible, store the tape in the computer room where it is to be used. Location of tape storage near the tape drives reduces both handling and variations in atmospheric conditions.
2. The storage area should be kept at a temperature of 65°F to 80°F and a relative humidity of 40 to 60 percent.
3. If the tape must be removed from the computer room, you can hermetically seal it in a plastic bag to reduce the effect of temperature and humidity changes on the tape's physical dimensions. If the tape is not hermetically sealed before it is reused it should be allowed to remain in the computer room for a length of time equal to the time it was out of the computer room. If the tape is out of the computer room for a period longer than 24 hours, it should be conditioned to the computer room for 24 hours before being reused.
4. For long-term storage, enclose the reel and container in a hermetically sealed plastic bag. Store in an area of constant temperature. Either cold or hot temperature can harm tape.

APPENDIX I

TRAINING FILM LIST

Certain training films that are directly related to the information presented in this training course are listed below under appropriate chapter numbers and titles. Unless otherwise specified, all films listed are black and white with sound, and are unclassified. For a description of these and other training films that may be of interest, see the United States Navy Film Catalog, NavWeps 10-1-777.

Chapter 1

INTRODUCTION TO DATA PROCESSING

MN8969A Digital Computer Techniques--Introduction. (20 min--1962)

MN8891 Introduction to Automatic Data Processing. (31 min--1958)

Chapter 2

NUMBER SYSTEMS

MN8969B Digital Computer Techniques—Computer Logic Part I. Binary Numbers. (20 min—Color—1962)

MN8969C Digital Computer Techniques—Computer Logic Part II. Logic Symbology. (15 min—Color—1962)

Chapter 3

BOOLEAN ALGEBRA

MN8969B Digital Computer Techniques—Computer Logic Part I. Binary Numbers. (20 min—Color—1962)

MN8969C Digital Computer Techniques—Computer Logic Part II. Logic Symbology. (15 min—Color—1962)

Chapter 4

CONTROL UNIT

MN8969D Digital Computer Techniques—Computer Units. (24 min—Color—1962)

MN8969E Digital Computer Techniques—Logic Element Circuits. (16 min—Color—1962)

Chapter 5

ARITHMETIC UNIT

MN8969D Digital Computer Techniques—Computer Units. (24 min—Color—1962)

MN8969E Digital Computer Techniques—Logic Element Circuits. (16 min—Color—1962)

Chapter 6

MEMORY AND STORAGE DEVICES

MN8969D Digital Computer Techniques—Computer Units. (24 min—Color—1962)

MA9820A Magnetic Cores—Part I—Properties. (29 min—1962)

MA9820B Magnetic Cores—Part II—Basic Circuits. (30 min—1962)

Chapter 7

INPUT/OUTPUT DEVICES

MN8969D Digital Computer Techniques—Computer Units. (24 min—Color—1962)

Chapter 8

PROGRAMMING (PART I)

MN8969F Digital Computer Techniques—Programming. (14 min—Color—1962)

Chapter 9

PROGRAMMING (PART II)

MN8969F Digital Computer Techniques—Programming. (14 min—Color—1962)

Chapter 10

PROGRAMMING (PART III)

MN8969F Digital Computer Techniques—Programming. (14 min—Color—1962)

Chapter 11

ANALOG-DIGITAL AND DIGITAL-ANALOG CONVERSIONS

MN8969A Digital Computer Techniques—Introduction. (20 min—Color—1962)

MN8891 Introduction to Automatic Data Processing. (31 min—1958)

APPENDIX II

GLOSSARY

ABORT—The condition in the computer that results in the skipping of the next sequential instruction.

ACCESS TIME—The time it takes a computer to locate data or an instruction word in its storage section and transfer it to its arithmetic unit where the required computations are performed. The time it takes to transfer information which has been operated on from the arithmetic unit to the location in storage where the information is to be stored. Synonymous with read time.

ACKNOWLEDGE—Indication of the status of data on the input/output lines. Abbreviated as ACK.

ACCUMULATOR—The register and associated equipment in the arithmetic unit of the computer in which arithmetical and logical operations are performed.

ADDRESS—A coded number that specifically designates a computer register or other internal storage location. Information is referenced by its address. Portions of computer control are responsible for directing information to or from an addressed location.

ADDRESSABLE—Capable of being referenced by an instruction.

ADDRESS, DIRECT—An address which indicates the location where the referenced operand is to be found or stored with no reference to an index register or B-box. Synonymous with (first level address).

ADDRESS, EFFECTIVE—(1) A modified address. (2) The address actually considered to be used in a particular execution of a computer instruction.

ADDRESS INDEXED—An address that is to be modified or has been modified by an index register or similar device. Synonymous with (variable address).

ADDRESS, ONE-PLUS-ONE—An instruction system having the property that each complete instruction includes an operation and two addresses, one for the location of a register in the storage containing the item to be operated upon, and one for the location containing the next instruction.

ADDRESS, RELATIVE—(1) An address to which the base address must be added in order to find the machine address. (2) An address used for convenience when constructing a program but not the actual address in the final program.

ADP—Automatic Data Processing.

ALGEBRA, BOOLEAN—A process of reasoning, or a deductive system of theorems using a symbolic logic, and dealing with classes, propositions, or on-off circuit elements. It employs symbols to represent operators such as AND, OR, NOT, etc., to permit mathematical calculation. Named after George Boole, famous English mathematician (1815-1864).

ALPHANUMERIC—A contraction of alphabetic-numeric.

ANALOG—The representation of numerical quantities by means of physical variables; e.g., translation, rotation, voltage, or resistance. Contrasted with (digital).

ANALOG COMPUTER—See (computer, analog).

ANALYST—A person skilled in the definition of and the development of techniques for the solving of a problem; especially those techniques for solutions on a computer.

AND—Same as (operator, and).

AND CIRCUIT—Same as (gate, and).

AND GATE—See (gate, and).

AND OPERATOR—See (operator, and).

ARITHMETIC—A section within the computer where reasonable processes such as addition, subtraction, multiplication, and division are performed, and operands and results are stored temporarily.

ARITHMETIC, FIXED POINT—(1) A method of calculation in which operations take place in invariant manner, and in which the computer does not consider the location of the radix point. This is illustrated by desk calculators or slide rules, with which the operator must keep track of the decimal point. Similarly with many automatic computers, in which the location of the radix point is the programmer's responsibility. Contrasted with (arithmetic, floating point). (2) A type of arithmetic in which the operands and results of all arithmetic operations must be properly scaled so as to have a magnitude between certain fixed values.

ARITHMETIC, FLOATING POINT—A method of calculation which automatically accounts for the location of the radix point. This is usually accomplished by handling the number as a signed mantissa times the radix raised to an integral exponent; e.g., the decimal number +88.3 might be written as $+.883 \times 10^2$; the binary number -.0011 as $-.11 \times 2^{-2}$. Synonymous with (floating decimal arithmetic) and contrasted with (arithmetic, fixed point).

ASSEMBLER—A computer program which operates on symbolic input data to produce from such data machine instructions by carrying out such functions as: translation of symbolic operation codes into computer operating instructions; assigning locations in storage for successive instructions; or computation of absolute addresses from symbolic addresses. An assembler generally translates input symbolic codes into machine instructions item for item, and produces as output the same number of instructions or constants which were defined in the input symbolic codes. Synonymous with (assembly routine); (assembly program) and related to (compiler).

ASYNCHRONOUS—Pertaining to a lack of time coincidence in a set of repeated events where this term is applied to a computer to indicate that the execution of one operation is dependent on a signal that the previous operation is completed.

AUTOMATION—(1) The implementation of processes by automatic means; (2) the theory, art, or technique of making a process more automatic; (3) the investigation, design, development, and application of methods of rendering processes automatic, self-moving, or self-controlling.

BASE—Same as (radix).

BINARY—A characteristic, property, or condition in which there are but two possible alternatives; e.g., the binary number system using 2 as its base and using only the digits zero (0) and one (1).

BINARY NUMBER SYSTEM—A number system with two symbols ("0" and "1") that has two as its base just as the decimal system uses ten symbols ("0, 1, ..., 9") and a base of ten. See also (positional notation and radix).

BIONICS—The application of knowledge gained from the analysis of living systems to the creation of hardware that will perform functions in a manner analogous to the more sophisticated functions of the living system.

BI-STABLE—The capability of assuming either of two stable states, hence, of storing one bit of information.

BIT—A binary digit, zero or one, represented in the computer by the condition (set or clear) of a stage.

BIT RATE—See (rate, bit).

BOOKKEEPING OPERATION—A computer operation which does not directly contribute to the result; i.e., arithmetical, logical, and transfer operations used in modifying the address section of other instructions, in counting cycles and in rearranging data. Synonymous with (red tape operation).

BOOLEAN ALGEBRA—See (algebra, boolean).

BOOTSTRAP—A technique for loading the first few instructions of a routine into storage; then using these instructions to bring in the rest of the routine. This usually involves either the entering of a few instructions manually or the use of a special key on the console.

BORROW—A borrow in subtraction is the additional subtraction of a one from the next partial difference and is initiated when a digit of the minuend is zero and the corresponding digit of the subtrahend is one. In a binary system of modules $2^k - 1$, where k is the number of stages in a register, the borrow produced from the leftmost digit $2^k - 1$ of the minuend is called the end-around borrow. A final correction is made by applying the end-around borrow to the partial difference of the rightmost digits.

BRANCH POINT—A point in a program or instruction where a decision is made on the basis of arithmetic results. The result of the decision indicates whether the main program is to be continued or branched to a different program. See also (jump).

B-REGISTER—(1) Same as (index register).

BUFFER—Mode of operation that involves inter-register or inter-equipment data transfer, usually connects an input or output device with the main or high-speed storage.

BYTE—(1) A generic term to indicate a measurable portion of consecutive binary digits; e.g., an 8-bit or 6-bit byte. (2) A group of binary digits usually operated upon as a unit.

CAPACITY—The upper and lower limits of the numbers that may be processed in a computer register.

CAPACITY, STORAGE—The number of elementary pieces of data that can be contained in a storage device. Frequently defined in terms of characters in a particular code or words of a fixed size that can be so contained. Synonymous with (memory capacity).

CELL—The storage for one unit of information, usually one character or one word.

CHANNEL—(1) A path along which information, particularly a series of digits or characters, may flow. (2) A path for electrical communication. (3) A band of frequencies used for communication.

CHARACTER—(1) One symbol of a set of elementary symbols such as those corresponding to the keys on a typewriter. The symbols usually include the decimal digits 0 through 9, the letters A through Z, punctuation marks, operation symbols, and any other single symbols which a computer may read, store, or write. (2) The electrical, magnetic, or mechanical profile used to represent a character in a computer, and its various storage and peripheral devices. A character may be represented by a group of other elementary marks, such as bits or pulses.

CLEAR (VERB)—To restore a storage or memory device to the zero state.

CLOCK—(1) A master timing device used to provide the basic sequencing pulses for the operation of a synchronous computer; (2) a register which automatically records the progress of real time, or perhaps some approximation to it, records the number of operations performed, and whose contents are available to a computer program.

CLOCK RATE—See (rate, clock).

COBOL—Common Business Oriented Language.

CODE—(1) A system of symbols for meaningful communication. (2) A system of symbols for representing data or instructions in a computer or a tabulating machine. (3) To translate the program for the solution of a problem on a given computer into a sequence of machine language or psuedo instructions and addresses acceptable to that computer. (4) A machine language program.

CODED PROGRAM—A procedure for solving a problem by means of a digital computer. The program may vary in detail from a mere outline of the procedure to an explicit list of instructions coded in machine language. See also (program).

COINCIDENCE GATE—A circuit with the ability to produce an output which is dependent upon a specified type of or the coincident nature of the input; e.g., an AND gate has an output pulse when there are pulses in time coincidence at all inputs; an OR gate has an output when any one or any combination of input pulses occur in time coincidence. Any gate may contain a number of inhibits, in which there is no output under any condition of input if there is time coincidence of an inhibit or except signal.

COLLATOR—A device used to collate or merge sets or decks of cards or other units into a sequence.

COLUMN—In positional notation, a position corresponding to a given power of the radix. A digit located in any particular column is a coefficient of a corresponding power of the radix.

COMMAND—One of a set of signals or groups of signals resulting from an instruction. Commands initiate the individual steps of the instruction. See also (instruction).

COMPARATOR—(1) A device for comparing two different transcriptions of the same information to verify the accuracy of transcription, storage, arithmetic operation or other processes, in which a signal is given dependent upon some relation between two items, i.e., one item is larger than, smaller than, or equal to the other. (2) A form of verifier.

COMPILE—To produce a machine language routine from a routine written in source language by selecting appropriate subroutines from a subroutine library, as directed by the instructions or other symbols of the original routine, supplying the linkage which combines the subroutines into a workable routine and translating the subroutines and linkage into machine language. The compiled routine is then ready to be loaded into storage and run; i.e., the compiler does not usually run the routine it produces.

COMPILER—A computer program more powerful than an assembler. In addition to its translating function which is generally the same process as that used in an assembler it is able to replace certain items of input with series of instructions, usually called subroutines. Thus, where an assembler translates item for item, and produces as output the same number of instructions or constants which were put into it, a compiler will do more than this. The program which results from compiling is a translated and expanded version of the original. Synonymous with (compiling routine) and related to (assembler).

COMPLEMENT—(1) A quantity expressed to the base N, which is derived from a given quantity by a particular rule; frequently used to represent the negative of the given quantity. (2) A complement on N, obtained by subtracting each digit of the given quantity from N-1, adding unity to the least significant digit, and performing all resultant carrys; e.g., the two's complement of binary 11010 is 00110; the tens complement of decimal 456 is 544. (3) A complement on N-1, obtained by subtracting each digit of the given quantity from N-1; e.g., the one's complement of binary 11010 is 00101; the nines complement of decimal 456 is 543.

COMPUTER—A device capable of accepting information, applying prescribed processes to the information, and supplying the results of these processes. It usually consists of input and output devices, storage, arithmetic, and logical units, and a control unit.

COMPUTER, ANALOG—A computer which represents variables by physical analogies. Thus, any computer which solves problems by translating physical conditions such as flow, temperature, pressure, angular position, or voltage into related mechanical or electrical quantities and uses mechanical or electrical equivalent circuits as an analog for the physical phenomenon being investigated. In general it is a computer which uses an analog for each variable and produces analogs as output. Thus, an analog computer measures continuously whereas a digital computer counts discretely.

COMPUTER ASYNCHRONOUS—A computer in which the performance of each operation starts as a result of a signal either that the previous operation has been completed, or that the parts of the computer required for the next operation are now available. Contrasted with (computer synchronous).

COMPUTER, DIGITAL—A computer which processes information represented by combinations of discrete or discontinuous data as compared with an analog computer for continuous data. More specifically, it is a device for performing sequences of arithmetic and logical operations, not only on data but its own program. Still more specifically, it is a stored program digital computer capable of performing sequences of internally stored instructions, as opposed to calculators, such as card programmed calculators on which the sequence is impressed manually.

COMPUTER, FIXED PROGRAM—A computer in which the sequence of instructions are permanently stored or wired in, and perform automatically and are not subject to change either by the computer or the programmer, except by rewiring or changing the storage input. Synonymous with (special purpose computer).

COMPUTER, GENERAL PURPOSE—A computer designed to solve a large variety of problems; e.g., a stored program computer which may be adapted to any of a very large class of applications.

COMPUTER, SYNCHRONOUS—A computer in which all operations and events are controlled by equally spaced pulses from a clock. Contrasted with (computer, asynchronous).

COMPUTER, WIRED PROGRAM—A computer in which the instructions that specify the operations to be performed are specified by the placement and interconnection of wires. The wires are usually held by a removable control panel, allowing flexibility of operation, but the term is also applied to permanently wired machines which are then called fixed program computers.

CONDITIONAL TRANSFER—See (transfer, conditional).

CONTROL—The computer circuits that affect the carrying out of instructions in the proper sequence, the interpretation of each instruction, and the application of the proper commands to other sections and circuits in accordance with the interpretation.

CONTROL WORD—See (word, control).

CONVERTER—A device which converts the representation of information, or which permits the changing of the method for data processing from one form to another; e.g., a unit which accepts information from punch cards and records the information on magnetic tape, and possibly including editing facilities.

COUNTER—A device capable of increasing or decreasing its own contents upon receipt of separate input signals.

CORE MATRIX—An array of cores, each of which represents the same column for each storage register in the magnetic core storage system.

CORE STORAGE—A type of storage system in which the magnetic core is the basic memory element.

CPU—Central Processing Unit.

CRYOGENICS—The field of technology in which devices utilizing properties assumed by metals at absolute zero are used. At these temperatures large current changes can be obtained by relatively small magnetic field changes.

CYBERNETICS—The field of technology involved in the comparative study of the control and intracommunication of information handling machines and nervous systems of animals and man in order to understand and improve communication.

DATA—A general term used to denote any or all facts, numbers, letters, and symbols, or facts that refer to or describe an object, idea, condition, situation, or other factors. It connotes basic elements of information which can be processed or produced by a computer. Sometimes data is considered to be expressible only in numerical form, but information is not so limited. Related to (information).

DATA, RAW—Data which has not been processed. Such data may or may not be in machine-sensible form.

DEBUG—To isolate and remove all malfunctions from the computer, or all mistakes from a routine or program.

DECIMAL, BINARY CODED—Describing a decimal notation in which the individual decimal digits are represented by a pattern of ones and zeros; e.g., in the 8-4-2-1 coded decimal notation, the number twelve is represented as 0001 0010 for 1 and 2, respectively, whereas in pure or straight binary notation is represented as 1100. Related to (binary).

DECODER—(1) A device which determines the meaning of a set of signals and initiates a computer operation based thereon. (2) A matrix of switching elements which selects one or more output channels according to the combination of input signals present. Contrasted with (encoder).

DECREMENT—The quantity by which a variable is decreased.

DENSITY CHARACTER—The number of characters that can be stored per unit of length.

DIAGNOSTIC ROUTINE—See (routine, diagnostic).

DIAGRAM, FLOW—Same as (flow chart).

DIAGRAM, VENN—A diagram in which each point represents an individual. Sets are represented by closed regions including all members of the set and excluding all nonmembers. The diagram is used to facilitate determination whether several sets include or exclude the same individuals.

DIGIT—One of a set of characters used as coefficients or powers of the radix in the positional notation of numbers.

DIGITAL COMPUTER—See (computer, digital).

DISK, MAGNETIC—A storage device on which information is recorded on the magnetizable surface of a rotating disk. A magnetic disk storage system is an array of such devices, with associated reading and writing heads which are mounted on movable arms. Related to (storage, disk).

DRUM, MAGNETIC—A cylinder having a surface coating of magnetic material, which stores binary information by the orientation of magnetic dipoles near or on its surface. Since the drum is rotated at a uniform rate, the information stored is available periodically as a given portion of the surface moves past one or more flux detecting devices called heads located near the surface of the drum.

DUMP—Transfer of information from one piece of equipment to another (normally from computer to external equipment such as paper tape, high-speed printer, etc.).

DYNAMIC STORAGE—The storage of data on a device or in a manner that permits the data to move or vary with time, and thus the data is not always available instantly for recovery; e.g., acoustic delay line, magnetic drum, or circulating or recirculating of information in a medium. Synonymous with (dynamic memory).

EDP—Electronic Data Processing.

EFFECTIVE ADDRESS—See (address, effective).

ELECTROSTATIC STORAGE—(1) The storage of data on a dielectric surface such as the screen of a cathode ray tube, in the form of the presence or absence of spots bearing electrostatic charges, that can persist for a short time after the electrostatic charging force is removed. (2) A storage device so used.

ENABLE—The application of a pulse that prepares a circuit for some subsequent action.

ENCODER—A device capable of translating from one method of expression to another method of expression, e.g., translating a message, "add the contents of A to the contents of B," into a series of binary digits. Contrasted with (decoder).

EOF—End of File.

ERASE—To replace all the binary digits in a storage device by binary zeros.

EXCLUSIVE OR OPERATOR—A logical operator which has the property that, if P and Q are two statements, then the statement P*Q, where the * is the Exclusive OR operator, is true if either P or Q, but not both are true, and false if P and Q are both false or both true.

EXECUTION TIME—The portion of an instruction cycle during which the actual work is performed or operation executed; i.e., the time required to decode and perform an instruction. Synonymous with (time, instruction (2)).

FAULT—(1) The condition resulting from the execution of an improper instruction, (2) a malfunction.

FILE—An organized collection of information directed toward some purpose. The records in a file may or may not be sequenced according to a key contained in each record.

FIXED POINT ARITHMETIC—See (arithmetic, fixed point).

FIXED PROGRAM COMPUTER—See (computer, fixed program).

FIXED WORD LENGTH—Having the property that a machine word always contains the same number of characters or digits.

FLIP-FLOP—(1) A bi-stable device; i.e., a device capable of assuming two stable states. (2) A bi-stable device which may assume a given stable state depending upon the pulse of history of one or more input points and having one or more output points. The device is capable of storing a bit of information. (3) A control device for opening or closing gates; i.e., a toggle. Synonymous with (Eccles-Jordan circuit) and (Eccles-Jordan trigger).

FLOATING POINT ARITHMETIC—See (arithmetic, floating point).

FLOW CHART—A graphic representation of the major steps of work in process. The illustrative symbols may represent documents, machines, or actions taken during the process. The area of concentration is on where or who does what rather than how it is to be done. Synonymous with (process chart) and (flow diagram).

FLOW DIAGRAM—Same as (flow chart).

FORMAT—The predetermined arrangement of characters, fields, lines, page numbers, and punctuation marks, usually on a single sheet or in a file. This refers to input, output, and files.

FORTRAN—A programming language designed for problems which can be expressed in algebraic notation, allowing for exponentiation and up to three subscripts. The FORTRAN compiler is a routine for a given machine which accepts a program written in FORTRAN source language and produces a machine language routine object program. FORTRAN II added considerably to the power of the original language by giving it the ability to define and use almost unlimited hierarchies of subroutines, all sharing a common storage region, if desired. Later improvements have added the ability to use Boolean expressions, and some capabilities for inserting symbolic machine language sequences within a source program.

FUNCTION CODE—The portion of the instruction word that specifies to the control section the particular instruction which is to be performed.

GATE, AND—A signal circuit with two or more input wires in which the output wire gives a signal, if and only if, all input wires receive coincident signals. Synonymous with (and circuit) and clarified by (conjunction).

GATE, OR—An electrical gate or mechanical device which implements the logical OR operator. An output signal occurs whenever there is one or more inputs on a multi-channel input. An OR gate performs the function of the logical "inclusive OR Operator." Synonymous with (OR circuit) and clarified by (disjunction).

GENERAL PURPOSE COMPUTER—See (computer, general purpose).

GRAY CODE—A binary code in which sequential numbers are represented by expressions which are the same except in one place, and in that place differ by one unit.

HALF-ADDER—A circuit having two output points, S and C, representing sum and carry, and two input points A and B, representing addend and augend, such that the output is related to the input according to the following table:

INPUT		OUTPUT	
A	B	S	C
0	0	0	0
0	1	1	0
1	0	1	0
1	1	0	1

A and B are arbitrary input pulses, and S and C are sum without carry and carry, respectively. Two half-adders properly connected, may be used for performing binary addition and form a full serial adder.

HALF-SUBTRACT—The bit-by-bit subtraction of two binary numbers with no regard for borrows. Abbreviated as HS. The complement of the half-subtract is "half-subtract not," abbreviated as $\overline{HS}$.

INCLUSIVE, OR OPERATOR—A logical operator which has the property that P or Q is true if P or Q or both is true; when the term OR is used alone, as in OR-gate, the Inclusive-OR is usually implied.

INDEX REGISTER—A register which contains a quantity which may be used to modify addresses. Synonymous with (B-register), and (B-box).

INSTRUCTION WORD—Designators specifying a particular function. The designators are listed below as they appear from highest to lowest order significance in the instruction word of a representative computer:

f = Function Code
j = Branch Condition
k = Operand Interpretation
b = Address Modification
y = Operand Address

INPUT/OUTPUT—A section providing the means of communication between the computer and external equipment or other computers. Input and output operations involve units of external equipment, certain registers in the computer, and portions of the computer control section. Abbreviated I/O.

INTERFACE—A common boundary between automatic data processing systems or parts of a single system.

INTERRUPT—(1) Internal: indicates the termination of an input or output buffer; (2) External: signal on the data lines that requires computer attention.

I/O—The abbreviation for input/output. Synonymous with (input-output).

JUMP—An instruction that specifies the location of the next instruction and directs the computer. A jump is used to alter the normal sequence control of the computer. Under certain conditions, a jump may be contingent upon manual intervention.

JUMP, CONDITIONAL—An instruction which, if a specified condition or set of conditions is satisfied, is interpreted as an unconditional transfer. If the condition is not satisfied, the instruction causes the computer to proceed in its normal sequence of control. A conditional transfer also includes the testing of the condition. Synonymous with (conditional jump) and (conditional branch).

JUMP, UNCONDITIONAL—An instruction which switches the sequence of control to some specified location. Synonymous with (unconditional branch); (unconditional jump) and (unconditional transfer of control).

KEY—(1) A group of characters which identifies or is part of a record or item, thus, any entry in a record or item can be used as a key for collating or sorting purposes. (2) A marked lever manually operated for copying a character; e.g., a typewriter, paper tape perforator, card punch, manual keyboard, digitizer or manual word generator. (3) A lever or switch on a computer console for the purpose of manually altering computer action.

LIBRARY—(1) A collection of information available to a computer, usually on magnetic tapes; (2) a file of magnetic tapes.

LOAD—To enter information into either the computer or a storage location.

LOGIC—(1) The science dealing with the criteria or formal principles of reasoning and thought. (2) The systematic scheme which defines the interactions of signals in the design of an automatic data processing system. (3) The basic principles and application of truth tables and interconnection between logical elements required for arithmetic computation in an automatic data processing system. Related to (symbolic logic).

LOGICAL SUM—The bit-by-bit addition of two binary numbers with no regard for carries. Abbreviated as LS. The complement of the logical sum is "logical sum not," abbreviated as $\overline{\text{LS}}$.

LOOP—(1) Self-contained series of instructions in which the last instruction can modify and repeat itself until a terminal condition is reached. The productive instructions in the loop generally manipulate the operands, while bookkeeping instructions modify the productive instructions, and keep count of the number of repetitions. A loop may contain any number of conditions for termination. The equivalent of a loop can be achieved by the technique of straight line coding, whereby the repetition of productive and bookkeeping operations is accomplished by explicitly writing the instruction for each repetition.

MALFUNCTION—Nonoperation of the computer due to component failure.

MARGIN—A measure of the tolerance of a circuit; the range between an established operating point and the point at which the circuit first starts to fail.

MASK—A machine word that specifies which parts of another machine word are to be operated upon, thus, the criterion for an external command. Synonymous with (extractor).

MASKING—(1) The process of extracting a nonword group or a field of characters from a word or a string of words, (2) the process of setting internal program controls to prevent transfers which otherwise would occur upon setting of internal machine latches.

MASTER CLOCK—The primary source of timing signals.

MEMORY—Same as (storage).

MNEMONIC—Pertaining to the assisting, or intending to assist, human memory; thus, a mnemonic term, usually an abbreviation, that is easy to remember; e.g., mpy for multiply and acc for accumulator.

MODE—(1) A computer system of data representation; e.g., the binary mode. (2) A selected mode of computer operation.

MODEL, MATHEMATICAL—The general characterization of a process, object, or concept, in terms of mathematics, which enables the relatively simple manipulation of variables to be accomplished in order to determine how the process, object, or concept would behave in different situations.

MODIFY—(1) To alter a portion of an instruction so its interpretation and execution will be other than normal. The modification may permanently change the instruction or leave it unchanged and affect only the current execution. The most frequent modification is that of the effective address through use of index registers. (2) To alter a subroutine according to a defined parameter.

MODULUS—The number of permissible numbers used in a process or system. For example, if only the integers from -15 to +15 inclusive are considered, 31 is the modulus of this set of numbers.

MOST SIGNIFICANT DIGIT—The first digit from the left, different from zero.

NON DESTRUCTIVE READ—See (read, non destructive).

NONVOLATILE STORAGE—Storage media that retains information during the absence of power. These media include magnetic tapes, drums, and magnetic cores.

NOTATION—(1) The act, process, or method of representing facts or quantities by a system or set of marks, signs, figures, or characters. (2) A system of such symbols or abbreviations used to express technical facts or quantities; as mathematical notation. (3) An annotation; note.

OBJECT LANGUAGE—A language which is the output of an automatic coding routine. Usually object language and machine language are the same; however, a series of steps in an automatic coding system may involve the object language of one step serving as a source language for the next step and so forth.

OCTAL NUMBER—Numbers in a system using eight symbols, 0, 1, ..., 6, 7, with eight as its base.

OFF-LINE—Descriptive of a system and of the peripheral equipment or devices in a system in which the operation of peripheral equipment is not under the control of the central processing unit.

ON-LINE—Descriptive of a system and of the peripheral equipment or devices in a system in which the operation of such equipment is under control of the central processing unit, and in which information reflecting current activity is introduced into the data processing system as soon as it occurs. Thus, directly in-line with the main flow of transaction processing.

OPEN-ENDED—The quality by which the addition of new terms, subject headings, or classifications does not disturb the pre-existing system.

OPERAND—A quantity entering or arising in an instruction. An operand may be an argument, a result, a parameter, or an indication of the location of the next instruction, as opposed to the operation code or symbol itself. It may even be the address portion of an instruction.

OPERATION CODE—The part of a computer instruction word which specifies, in coded form, the operation to be performed.

OPERATOR, AND—(1) A logical operator which has the property that if P is a statement and Q is a statement, the P AND Q is true if both statements are true, false if either is false or both are false. Truth is normally expressed by the value 1, falsity by 0. The AND operator is often represented by a centered dot (P· Q), by no sign (PQ), by an inverted "u" or logical product symbol (PnQ), or by the letter "x" or multiplication symbol (PxQ). Note that the letters AND are capitalized to differentiate between the logical operator AND and the word and in common usage. (2) The logical operation which makes use of the AND operator or logical product. Synonymous with (and; logical multiply) and clarified by (conjunction).

OPERATOR, OR—A logical operator which has the property such that if P or Q are two statements, then the statement P OR Q is true or false varies according to the following table of possible combinations:

P	Q	P or Q
False	True	True
True	False	True
True	True	True
False	False	False

OR GATE—See (gate, or).

OR OPERATOR—See (operator, or).

OVERFLOW—The condition which arises when the result of an arithmetic operation exceeds the capacity of the storage space alloted in a digital computer.

PACK—To include several short items of information into one machine item or word by utilizing different sets of digits to specify each brief item.

PADDING—A technique used to fill out a block of information with dummy records.

PARALLEL TRANSMISSION—The system of information transfer in which the characters of a word are transmitted simultaneously over separate lines.

PARAMETER—(1) A quantity in a subroutine, whose value specifies or partly specifies the process to be performed. It may be given different values when the subroutine is used in different main routines or in different parts of one main routine, but which usually remains unchanged throughout any one such use. Related to (parameter, program). (2) A quantity used in a generator to specify machine configuration, designate subroutines to be included, or otherwise to describe the desired routine to be generated. (3) A constant or a variable in mathematics, which remains constant during some calculation. (4) A definable characteristic of an item, device, or system.

PARITY BIT—A check bit that indicates whether the total number of binary "1" digits in a character or word (exclusing the parity bit) is odd or even. If a "1" parity bit indicates an odd number of "1" digits, then a "0" bit indicates an even number of them. If the total number of "1" bits, including the parity bit, is always even, the system is called an even parity system. In an odd parity system, the total number of "1" bits, including the parity bit, is always odd.

PARTIAL CARRY—A system of executing the carry process in which the carries that arise as a result of a carry are not allowed to be transmitted to the next higher stage.

PERIPHERAL EQUIPMENT—The auxiliary machines which may be placed under the control of the central computer. Examples of this are card readers, card punches, magnetic tape feeds and high-speed printers. Peripheral equipment may be used on-line or off-line depending upon computer design, job requirements, and economics.

PING-PONG—The programming technique of using two magnetic tape units for multiple reel files and switching automatically between the two units until the complete file is processed.

PLOTTER—A visual display or board in which a dependent variable is graphed by an automatically controlled pen or pencil as a function of one or more variables.

POSITIONAL NOTATION—A method for expressing a quantity, using two or more figures, wherein the successive right to left figures are to be interpreted as coefficients of ascending integer powers of the radix.

PRECISION, DOUBLE—The retention of twice as many digits of a quantity as the computer normally handles; e.g., if a computer, whose basic word consists of 10 decimal digits is called upon to handle 20 decimal digit quantities, then double precision arithmetic must be resorted to.

PROBLEM ORIENTED LANGUAGE—(1) A language designed for convenience of program specification in a general problem area rather than for easy conversion to machine instruction code. The components of such a language may bear little resemblance to machine instructions. (2) A machine independent language where one needs only to state the problem, not the how of solution. Related to (generators, program) and contrasted with (language, procedure oriented).

PROGRAM—(1) The complete plan for the solution of a problem, more specifically the complete sequence of machine instructions and routines necessary to solve a problem. (2) To plan the procedures for solving a problem. This may involve among other things the analysis of the problem, preparation of a flow diagram, preparing details, testing, and developing subroutines, allocation of storage locations, specification of input and output formats, and the incorporation of a computer run into a complete data processing system. Related to (routine).

PROGRAM, OBJECT—The program which is the output of an automatic coding system. Often the object program is a machine language program ready for execution, but it may well be in an intermediate language. Synonymous with (target program); (object routine) and contrasted with (program source).

PROGRAM, SOURCE—A computer program written in a language designed for ease of expression of a class of problems or procedures, by humans; e.g., symbolic or algebraic. A generator, assembler translator or compiler routine is used to perform the mechanics of translating the source program into an object program in machine language.

PROGRAMMER—A person who prepares problem solving procedures and flow charts and who may also write and debug routines.

PROGRAMMING, AUTOMATIC—The method or technique whereby the computer itself is used to transform or translate programming from a language or form that is easy for a human being to produce into a language that is efficient for the computer to carry out. Examples of automatic programming are compiling, assembling, and interpretive routines.

PROGRAMMING, INTERPRETIVE—The writing of programs in a pseudo machine language, which is precisely converted by the computer into actual machine language instructions before being performed by the computer.

PROGRAMMING, RANDOM ACCESS—Programming without regard to the time required for access to the storage positions called for in the program. Contrasted with (programming, minimum access).

RADIX—The quantity of characters for use in each of the digital positions of a numbering system. In the more common numbering systems the characters are some or all of the Arabic numerals as follows:

System Name	Characters	Radix
BINARY	(0,1)	2
OCTAL	(0, 1, 2, 3, 4, 5, 6, 7)	8
DECIMAL	(0,1,2,3,4,5,6,7,8,9)	10

Unless otherwise indicated, the radix of any number is assumed to be 10. For positive identification of a radix 10 number, the radix is written in parentheses as a subscript to the expressed number; i.e., $126_{(10)}$. The radix of any nondecimal number is expressed in similar fashion; e.g., $11_{(2)}$ and $5_{(8)}$. Synonymous with (base); (base number) and (radix number).

RADIX MINUS 1 COMPLEMENT—Same as (complement (3)).

RATE, BIT—The rate at which binary digits, or pulses representing them pass a given point on a communications line or channel.

RATE, CLOCK—The time rate at which pulses are emitted from the clock. The clock rate determines the rate at which logical or arithmetic gating is performed with a synchronous computer.

RATE, SAMPLING—The rate at which measurements of physical quantities are made; e.g., if it is desired to calculate the velocity of a missile and its position is measured each millisecond, then the sampling rate is 1,000 measurements per second.

RAW DATA—See (data, raw).

READ-IN—To sense information contained in some source and transmit this information to an internal storage.

READ, NON DESTRUCTIVE—A reading of the information in a register without changing that information.

READ-OUT—To sense information contained in some internal storage and transmit this information to a storage external to the computer.

READ TIME—Same as (access time).

REAL TIME—Computer operation with regard to a related process so that the computer results are available to conduct or guide the process.

RECORD—(1) A group of related facts or fields of information treated as a unit, thus a listing of information, usually in printed or printable form; (2) to put data into a storage device.

REGISTER—A hardware device used to store a certain amount of bits or characters. A register is usually constructed of elements such as transistors and usually contains approximately one word of information. Common programming usage demands that a register have the ability to operate upon information and not merely store information; hardware usage does not make the distinction.

REGISTER, B—See (index register).

REGISTER, STORAGE—A register in the storage of the computer, in contrast with a register in one of the other units of the computer.

RELATIVE ADDRESS—See (address, relative).

RELIABILITY—(1) A measure of the ability to function without failure; (2) the amount of credence placed in a result.

REPERTOIRE OF INSTRUCTIONS—(1) The set of instructions which a computing or data processing system is capable of performing, (2) the set of instructions which an automatic coding system assembles.

RETURN—The mechanism providing for a return in the usual sense. In particular a set of instructions at the end of a subroutine which permit control to return to the proper point in the main routine.

ROUTINE—A set of coded instructions arranged in proper sequence to direct the computer to perform a desired operation or sequence of operations. A subdivision of a program consisting of two or more instructions that are functionally related; therefore, a program.

ROUTINE, DIAGNOSTIC—A routine used to locate malfunction in a computer, or to aid in locating mistakes in a computer program. Thus, in general any routine specifically designed to aid in debugging or trouble shooting. Synonymous with (malfunction routine).

ROUTINE, EXECUTIVE—A routine which controls loading and relocation of routines and in some cases makes use of instructions which are unknown to the general programmer. Effectively, an executive routine is part of the machine itself.

ROUTINE, SERVICE—A broad class of routines which are standardized at a particular installation for the purpose of assisting in maintenance and operation of the computer as well as the preparation of programs as opposed to routines for the actual solution of production problems. This class includes monitoring or supervisory routines, assemblers, compilers, diagnostics for computer malfunctions, simulation of peripheral equipment, general diagnostics and input data. The distinguishing quality of service routines is that they are generally standardized so as to meet the servicing needs at a particular installation, independent of any specific production type routine requiring such services.

SAMPLING RATE—See (rate, sampling).

SCALE—A range of values frequently dictated by the computer word-length or routine at hand.

SEMICONDUCTOR—A solid with an electrical conductivity that lies between the high conductivity of metals and the low conductivity of insulators. Semiconductor circuit elements include crystal diodes and transistors.

SENSE—(1) To examine, particularly relative to a criterion; (2) to determine the present arrangement of some element of hardware, especially a manually-set switch; (3) to read punched holes or other marks.

SENSITIVITY—The degree of response of an instrument or control unit to a change in the incoming signal.

SERIAL—(1) The handling of one after the other in a single facility, such as transfer or store in a digit-by-digit time sequence, or to process a sequence of instructions one at a time, i.e., sequentially. (2) The time sequence transmission of storage, or logical operations on the parts of a word with the same facilities for successive parts.

SERIAL-PARALLEL—(1) A combination of serial and parallel; e.g., serial by character, parallel by bits comprising the character. (2) Descriptive of a device which converts a serial input into a parallel output.

SERVOMECHANISM—A device to monitor an operation as it proceeds, and make necessary adjustments to keep the operation under control.

SET—(1) To place a storage device in a prescribed state. (2) To place a binary cell in the one state. (3) A collection of elements having some feature in common or which bear a certain relation to one another; e.g., all even numbers, geometrical figures, terms in a series, a group of irrational numbers, all positive even integers less than 100 may be a set or a sub-set.

SHIFT—To move the characters of a unit of information columnwise right or left. For a number, this is equivalent of multiplying or dividing by a power of the base of notation.

SHIFT, ARITHMETIC—To multiply or divide a quantity by a power of the number base; e.g., if binary 1101, which represents decimal 13, is arithmetically shifted twice to the left, the result is 110100, which represents 52, which is also obtained by multiplying 13 by 2 twice; on the other hand, if the decimal 13 were to be shifted to the left twice, the result would be the same as multiplying by 10 twice, or 1300.

SHIFT REGISTER—A register in which the characters may be shifted one or more positions to the right or left.

SIGN DIGIT—A binary digit used as a sign.

SKIP INSTRUCTION—An instruction having no effect other than directing the processor to proceed to another instruction designated in the storage portion.

SKIP, TAPE—A machine instruction to space forward and erase a portion of tape when a defect on the tape surface causes a write error to persist.

SOFTWARE—The totality of programs and routines used to extend the capabilities of computers, such as compilers, assemblers, narrators, routines, and subroutines. Contrasted with (hardware).

SOLID STATE—The electronic components that convey or control electrons within solid materials.

SORTER—A machine which puts items of information into a particular order; e.g., it will determine whether A is greater than, equal to, or less than B and sort or order accordingly.

STORAGE—(1) The term preferred to memory. (2) Pertaining to a device in which data can be stored and from which it can be obtained at a later time. The means of storing data may be chemical, electrical, or mechanical. (3) A device consisting of electronic, electrostatic, electrical, hardware, or other elements into which data may be entered, and from which data may be obtained as desired.

STORAGE, AUXILIARY—A storage device in addition to the main storage of a computer; e.g., magnetic tape, disk, or magnetic drum. Auxiliary storage usually holds much larger amounts of information than the main storage, and the information is accessible less rapidly.

STORAGE, BUFFER—(1) A synchronizing element between two different forms of storage, usually between internal and external. (2) An input device in which information is assembled from external or secondary storage and stored ready for transfer to internal storage. (3) An output device into which information is copied from internal storage. Computation continues while transfers between buffer storage and internal storage or vice versa take place. (4) Any device which stores information temporarily during data transfers.

STORAGE CAPACITY—See (capacity, storage).

STORAGE DISK—The storage of data on the surface of magnetic disks.

STORAGE, EXTERNAL—(1) The storage of data on a device which is not an integral part of a computer, but in a form prescribed for use by the computer. (2) A facility or device, not an integral part of a computer, on which data usable by a computer is stored such as, off-line magnetic tape units or punch card devices.

STORAGE, INTERNAL—(1) The storage of data on a device which is an integral part of a computer. (2) The storage facilities forming an integral physical part of the computer and directly controlled by the computer. In such facilities all data are automatically accessible to the computer; e.g., magnetic core and magnetic tape on-line.

STORAGE, MAGNETIC—A device or devices which utilize the magnetic properties of materials to store information.

STORAGE, MAGNETIC CORE—A storage device in which binary data is represented by the direction of magnetization in each unit of an array of magnetic material, usually in the shape of toroidal rings, but also in other forms such as thin film. Synonymous with (core storage).

STORAGE, MAGNETIC DRUM—The storage of data on the surface of magnetic drums.

STORAGE, MAGNETIC TAPE—A storage device in which data is stored in the form of magnetic spots on metal or coated plastic tape. Binary data are stored as small magnetized spots arranged in column form across the width of the tape. A read-write head is usually associated with each row of magnetized spots so that one column can be read or written at a time as the tape traverses the head.

STORAGE, MAIN—Usually internal, and the fastest storage device of a computer. The one from which instructions are executed. Contrasted with (storage, auxiliary).

STORAGE, NON VOLATILE—A storage medium which retains information in the absence of power and which may be made available upon restoration of power; e.g., magnetic tapes, cores, drums, and disks. Contrasted with (storage, volatile).

STORAGE, PROGRAM—A portion of the internal storage reserved for the storage of programs, routines, and subroutines. In many systems protection devices are used to prevent inadvertent alteration of the contents of the program storage.

STORAGE, RANDOM ACCESS—A storage technique in which the time required to obtain information is independent of the location of the information most recently obtained. This strict definition must be qualified by the observation that we usually mean relatively random.

STORAGE REGISTER—See (register, storage).

STORAGE, SECONDARY—The storage facilities not an integral part of the computer but directly connected to and controlled by the computer; e.g., magnetic drum and magnetic tapes.

STORAGE, SEQUENTIAL ACCESS—A storage technique in which the items of information stored become available only in a one after the other sequence, whether or not all the information or only some of it is desired; e.g., magnetic tape storage.

STORAGE, SERIAL—A storage technique in which time is one of the factors used to locate any given bit, character, word, or group of words appearing one after the other in time sequence, and in which access time includes a variable latency or waiting time of from zero to many word times. A storage is said to be serial by word when the individual bits comprising a word appear serially in time; or a storage is serial by character when the characters representing coded decimal or other non-binary numbers appear serially in time; e.g., magnetic drums are usually serial by word but may be serial by bit, or parallel by bit, or serial by character and parallel by bit.

STORAGE, VOLATILE—A storage medium in which information cannot be retained without continuous power dissipation. Contrasted with (storage, non volatile).

STORAGE, WILLIAMS TUBE—A cathode ray tube used as an electrostatic storage device and of the type designed by F. C. Williams, University of Manchester, England. Synonymous with (Williams tube storage).

STORE—(1) To transfer an element of information to a device from which the unaltered information can be obtained at a later time, (2) to retain data in a device from which it can be obtained at a later time.

SUBPROGRAM—A part of a larger program which can be converted into machine language independently.

SUBROUTINE—(1) The set of instructions necessary to direct the computer to carry out a well defined mathematical or logical operation. (2) A subunit of a routine. A subroutine is often written in relative or symbolic coding even when the routine to which it belongs is not. (3) A portion of a routine that causes a computer to carry out a well-defined mathematical or logical operation. (4) A routine which is arranged so that control may be transferred to it from a master routine and so that, at the conclusion of the subroutine, control reverts to the master routine. Such a subroutine is usually called a closed subroutine. (5) A single routine may simultaneously be both a subroutine with respect to another routine and a master routine with respect to a third. Usually control is transferred to a single subroutine from more than one place in the master routine and the reason for using the subroutine is to avoid having to repeat the same sequence of instructions in different places in the master routine.

SUBROUTINE, DYNAMIC—A subroutine which involves parameters, such as decimal point position or item size, from which a relatively coded subroutine is derived. The computer itself is expected to adjust or generate the subroutine according to the parametric values chosen.

SWITCH, TOGGLE—(1) An electronically operated circuit that holds either of two states until changed. (2) A manually operated electric switch, with a small projecting knob or arm that may be placed in either of two positions, "on" or "off," and will remain in that position until changed.

TABLE—A collection of data in a form suitable for ready reference, frequently as stored in sequenced machine locations or written in the form of an array of rows and columns for easy entry and in which an intersection of labeled rows and columns serves to locate a specific piece of data or information.

TABLE, TRUTH—A representation of a switching function, or truth function, in which every possible configuration of argument values 0, 1, or true-false is listed, and beside each is given the associated function value 0-1 or true-false. The number of configurations is 2^N, where N is the number of arguments.

TAPE—A strip of material, which may be punched, coated, or impregnated with magnetic or optically sensitive substances, and used for data input, storage, or output. The data are stored serially in several channels across the tape transversely to the reading or writing motion.

TERNARY—Pertaining to a system of notation utilizing the base of 3.

TEST, DIAGNOSTIC—The running of a machine program or routine for the purpose of discovering a failure or a potential failure of a machine element, and to determine its location or its potential location.

TIME, EXECUTION—See (execution time).

TIME, INSTRUCTION—(1) The portion of an instruction cycle during which the control unit is analyzing the instruction and setting up to perform the indicated operation; (2) same as (execution time).

TIME, REAL—See (real time).

TIME SHARING—The use of a device for two or more purposes during the same overall time interval, accomplished by interspersing component actions in time.

TOGGLE—(1) A flip-flop. (2) Pertaining to a manually operated on-off switch; i.e., a two position switch. (3) Pertaining to flip-flop, see-saw, or bi-stable action.

TRANSFER—(1) The conveyance of control from one mode to another by means of instructions or signals. (2) The conveyance of data from one place to another. (3) An instruction for transfer. (4) To copy, exchange, read, record, store, transmit, transport, or write data. (5) An instruction which provides the ability to break the normal sequential flow of control. Synonymous with (jump), and (control transfer).

TRANSFER, BLOCK—The conveyance of a group of consecutive words from one place to another.

TRANSFER, CONDITIONAL—An instruction which, if a specified condition or set of conditions is satisfied, is interpreted as an unconditional transfer. If the condition is not satisfied, the instruction causes the computer to proceed in its normal sequence of control. A conditional transfer also includes the testing of the condition. Synonymous with (conditional jump) and (conditional branch).

TRANSFER, PARALLEL—A method of data transfer in which the characters of an element of information are transferred simultaneously over a set of paths.

TRANSFER, UNCONDITIONAL—See (jump unconditional).

TRANSFLUXOR—A magnetic core having two or more openings. Control of the magnetic flux in the various legs of the magnetic circuits and the binary magnetic characteristics of the material permits storage.

TRANSIENT—(1) A physical disturbance, intermediate to two steady-state conditions. (2) Pertaining to rapid change. (3) A buildup or breakdown in the intensity of a phenomenon until a steady state condition is reached. The time rate of change of energy is finite and some form of energy storage is usually involved.

TRANSISTOR—An electronic device utilizing semiconductor properties to control the flow of currents.

TRANSLATOR—(1) A program whose input is a sequence of statements in some language and whose output is an equivalent sequence of statements in another language. (2) A translating device.

TRANSMISSION, SERIAL—To move data in sequence, one character at a time as contrasted with parallel transmission.

TRANSPORT, TAPE—The mechanism which moves magnetic or paper tape past sensing and recording heads and usually associated with data processing equipment. Synonymous with (tape transport), (tape drive), and (feed, tape).

TRUTH TABLE—See (table, truth).

ULTRASONICS—The field of science devoted to frequencies of sound above the human audio range; i.e., above 20 kHz.

UNCONDITIONAL JUMP—Same as (jump, unconditional).

UNIT, ARITHMETIC—The portion of the hardware of a computer in which arithmetic and logical operations are performed. The arithmetic unit generally consists of an accumulator, some special registers for the storage of operands, and results supplemented by shifting and sequencing circuitry for implementing multiplication, division, and other desired operations.

UNIT CONTROL—The portion of a computer which directs the sequence of operations, interprets the coded instructions, and initiates the proper commands to the computer circuits preparatory to execution.

UNPACK—To separate various sections of a tape record or computer word, and store them in separate locations. The sections usually correspond to format fields within the record or word.

UPDATE—(1) To put into a master file changes required by current information or transactions, (2) to modify an instruction so that the address numbers it contains are increased by a stated amount each time the instruction is performed.

VARIABLE—(1) A quantity which can assume any of the numbers of some set of numbers, (2) a condition, transaction, or event which changes or may be changed as a result of processing additional data thru the system.

VARIABLE WORD-LENGTH—See (word-length, variable).

VECTOR—A quantity having magnitude and direction, as contrasted with scalar which has quantity only.

VENN DIAGRAM—See (diagram, venn).

VERIFIER—A device on which a record can be compared or tested for identity character-by-character with a retranscription or copy as it is being prepared.

VOCABULARY—A list of operating codes or instructions available to the programmer for writing the program for a given problem for a specific computer.

VOLATILE STORAGE—See (storage, volatile).

WILLIAMS TUBE—See (storage, williams tube).

WORD—An ordered set of characters which occupies one storage location and is treated by the computer circuits as a unit and transferred as such. Ordinarily a word is treated by the control unit as an instruction, and by the arithmetic unit as a quantity. Word lengths may be fixed or variable depending on the particular computer.

WORD, CONTROL—A word, usually the first or last of a record, or first or last word of a block, which carries indicative information for the following words, records, or blocks.

WORD, DATA—A word which may be primarily regarded as part of the information manipulated by a given program. A data word may be used to modify a program instruction, or to be arithmetically combined with other data words.

WORD-LENGTH, FIXED—Same as (fixed word-length).

WORD-LENGTH, VARIABLE—Having the property that a machine word may have a variable number of characters. It may be applied either to a single entry whose information content may be changed from time to time, or to a group of functionally similar entries whose corresponding components are of different lengths.

WRITE—(1) To transfer information, usually from main storage, to an output device; (2) to record data in a register, location, or other storage device or medium.

XEROGRAPHY—A dry copying process involving the photo electric discharge of an electrostatically charged plate. The copy is made by tumbling a resinous powder over the plate, the remaining electrostatic charge discharged and the resin transferred to paper or offset printing master.

ZERO ADDRESS INSTRUCTION—An instruction consisting of an operation which does not require the designation of an address in the usual sense; e.g., the instruction, "shift left 0003," has in its normal address position the amount of the shift desired.

ZONE—(1) A portion of internal storage allocated for a particular function or purpose. (2) The three top positions of 12, 11, and 10 on certain punch cards. In these positions, a second punch can be inserted so that with punches in the remaining positions 1 to 9, alphabetic characters may be represented.

INDEX